'Something has happened in ... programmes are noticing it – ... and simultaneously less and less ... ... say the ... are pure coincidence will find their theories blown apart in page after page of this book. Oliver James has travelled the world and come home to the human heart; showing how our drive for money and success is often not just a nine-to-five habit but a disease of the mind. This is the best kind of psychoanalysis, rigorous with the facts and scrupulous in research, but always open-minded and humane as it draws on the vivid encounters Oliver had on his travels. Never before have I read a book that so precisely captures the way we are all being emotionally snookered by the demands of 21st-century living. Anyone who's decided they want to become famous or powerful, or just stinking rich, should hold that thought and read this book first.'

– Jeremy Vine

'Oliver James is our foremost chronicler of what ails us. This book elegantly, authoritatively and devastatingly delivers his diagnosis, and heroically resists the kind of glib 'cures' offered by so many psycho-babblers. *Affluenza* should be mandatory reading for everyone, but especially those in politics, business and the media who are intent on upping our society's dosage of toxic affluence.'

– Will Self

'Oliver James is excellent at showing why social scientists think that the surge in material affluence can produce the opposite of happiness. What he adds is a sizzling reality check, which takes us into homes, workplaces and streets in seven cities worldwide. For the people we meet there, well-being and unhappiness are not statistical artefacts. They speak in many unsynchronised voices: tangible, engaging, uninventable individuals who feel the undertow of obsession with goods and status on their quest for well-being. They give us eloquent and surprising answers to questions which nobody thought to ask before.

... Offer, Chichele Professor of Economic History, Uni... ...ffluence

To my wife, Clare

Affluenza (ˌæflu'enza)

How to be Successful *and* Stay Sane

Oliver James

Vermilion
LONDON

15 17 19 20 18 16

Published in 2007 by Vermilion, an imprint of Ebury Publishing
A Random House Group Company

The Random House Group Limited Reg. No. 954009

Addresses for companies within the Random House Group
can be found at www.randomhouse.co.uk

A CIP catalogue record for this book
is available from the British Library

The Random House Group Limited supports The Forest Stewardship Council
(FSC®), the leading international forest certification organisation. Our books
carrying the FSC label are printed on FSC® certified paper. FSC is the only
forest certification scheme endorsed by the leading environmental
organisations, including Greenpeace. Our paper procurement policy can be
found at www.randomhouse.co.uk/environment

Printed and bound by CPI Group (UK) Ltd, Croydon, CR0 4YY

ISBN 9780091900113

To buy books by your favourite authors
and register for offers visit www.randomhouse.co.uk

Contents

Are You Infected with Affluenza?

The Affluenza Virus is a set of values which increase our vulnerability to emotional distress. It entails placing a high value on acquiring money and possessions, looking good in the eyes of others and wanting to be famous.

Just as having the HIV virus places you at risk of developing the physical disease of AIDS, infection with the Affluenza Virus increases your susceptibility to the commonest emotional distresses: depression, anxiety, substance abuse and personality disorder (like 'me, me, me' narcissism, febrile moods or confused identity).

Before you read this book, take the two tests on the following pages to find out whether you have the Virus and the associated symptoms of distress.

Have You Contracted the Affluenza Virus?

Do you agree with any of the following statements?
(yes/no)

☑☐ I would like to be a very wealthy person.

☑☐ I would like to have my name known by many people.

☑☐ I would like to successfully hide the signs of ageing.

☑☐ I would like to be admired by many people.

☑☐ I would like to have people comment often about how attractive I look.

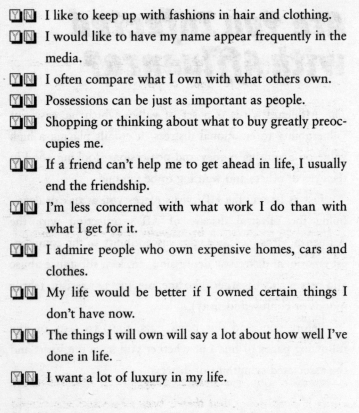

□□ I like to keep up with fashions in hair and clothing.

□□ I would like to have my name appear frequently in the media.

□□ I often compare what I own with what others own.

□□ Possessions can be just as important as people.

□□ Shopping or thinking about what to buy greatly preoccupies me.

□□ If a friend can't help me to get ahead in life, I usually end the friendship.

□□ I'm less concerned with what work I do than with what I get for it.

□□ I admire people who own expensive homes, cars and clothes.

□□ My life would be better if I owned certain things I don't have now.

□□ The things I will own will say a lot about how well I've done in life.

□□ I want a lot of luxury in my life.

Scoring

If you answered 'yes' to any of the questions, then you have, like most people in the English-speaking world, contracted the Virus. The more you answered 'yes', the more infected you are and the greater your likelihood of becoming emotionally distressed.

Now take the test to see how distressed you are.

Do You Suffer From Affluenza Distress?

1. *Recently, have you felt so down that no amount of anything made you feel more chipper?*
❏ Never
❏ Occasionally
❏ Off and on
❏ Quite often
❏ Always

2. *Have you recently felt irrationally worried about things?*
❏ Never
❏ Occasionally
❏ Off and on
❏ Quite often
❏ Always

3. *Recently, have you been so shagged out that it's a real effort to keep going, but there's been no reason you should feel that way?*
❏ Never
❏ Occasionally
❏ Off and on
❏ Quite often
❏ Always

4. *Recently, have you been so jumpy or irritable that feeling relaxed is impossible?*

❑ Never
❑ Occasionally
❑ Off and on
❑ Quite often
❑ Always

5. *Recently, has it seemed to you that there is no light at the end of the tunnel, that the future is bleak?*

❑ Never
❑ Occasionally
❑ Off and on
❑ Quite often
❑ Always

6. *Recently, have you found yourself unable to stay in your chair for more than a few moments at a time?*

❑ Never
❑ Occasionally
❑ Off and on
❑ Quite often
❑ Always

7. *Recently, have you felt pathetic, incompetent or useless?*

❑ Never
❑ Occasionally
❑ Off and on

Prologue

In September of 2003, the proposal for this book was sent to a publisher. What happened next illustrates its main point.

I had high hopes of being offered a substantial advance because my last book had sold a fair few copies. I was living with my wife and twenty-one-month-old daughter in a fairly modest house in Shepherd's Bush, and apart from book-writing, my sources of income were journalism and the occasional television appearance. The wedge for the new book would need to be decent-sized because the gag was to visit seven nations and spend three weeks in each, interviewing citizens about their lives. My wife and daughter would accompany me to New Zealand, Australia, Singapore, Shanghai, Moscow, Copenhagen and New York, and this mind tour was likely to take the best part of a year. I would investigate the extent to which the different nations were afflicted by what I term the 'Affluenza Virus' – the placing of a high value on money, possessions, appearances (physical and social) and fame. Many international studies have shown that people who hold such values are at a greater risk of being emotionally distressed – depressed, anxious, substance abusing and personality-disordered. I would use existing scientific studies of national rates of such problems as my starting point, and then see how Affluenza was panning out locally, around the world. I also pictured myself as an itinerant Marie Curie, returning triumphantly clutching vaccines which immunise us against the Virus, phials of tactics for making the best of the very bad job that the world has become. But to do this I needed money.

Money – to buy a new computer, a better mobile phone, an international datacard for emails, a portable DVD to keep our daughter quiet, and sundry other essential goods and services for the intrepid twenty-first-century investigator of the harm done by being over-preoccupied with money. Although the British Council had very generously agreed to help by providing accommodation and finding the interviewees, it would take a lot of time and cost a good deal in air fares, even though British Airways' business magazine (for which I wrote) was prepared to stump up for some of mine.

When the publisher came back with an offer that was less than half the amount they had paid for my last book, a black and impenetrable cloud descended on our household. My agent expressed incredulity, my wife despaired at losing an extended holiday from our normal suburban bliss, our daughter continued enjoying *Teletubbies*, and I? I did not know what to think. Perhaps the idea was worthless, maybe the proposal had been badly written. But worst of all, could it be that the publisher's valuation had exposed a gulf between a bloated self-estimation and The Market? Surely not. Unbowed, I rewrote the proposal and sent it off again. Oh yes, this time they would see sense. A further derisory bid was returned to sender.

I confess to having suffered a measure of discombobulation. It was true that a bird in the hand can't see the wood for the trees; then again, maybe a poke in the eye with a blunt stick meant the world was my oyster. It did seem a bit rum that I was being offered considerably less than I had received for my (successful) last book. I liked to think that my own sense of worth as a writer of psychology books was not tied to some publisher's grubby estimate of how much they could make from selling them. Nonetheless, despite my pronouncements that one should look within oneself for authenticity and identity, which I frequently intoned to friends, readers of my journalism and indeed anyone who would listen, I was feeling less than chipper.

But you are reading this book, and we did make that journey, so you will know that the story didn't end there. My agent sent the proposal to other publishers, and within a very short time a bidding war ensued, which was won by Vermilion. 'Well, come on then, what was the final amount?' you ask. To which I am tempted to reply, 'None of your business!' But suppose I were to say £300,000 – what then? If you are a merchant banker, you might think, 'Pathetic! Call that money?' If a nurse, 'Nice work if you can get it'; if a Tesco checkout worker, 'Jammy bastard!' But whatever your response, how you are feeling about me at this moment is profoundly affected by how much I have been paid, just as I am ashamed to say that it affected my view of myself – my inner life was governed by how much The Market valued my work. Unless you are most unusual, you cannot help comparing what I get with what you get, and your attitude to me is affected by that, as is mine.

In fact, the figure I have given is fictitious. My point is to underline a very simple and fundamental fact about our lives: we have become absolutely obsessed with measuring ourselves and others through the distorted lens of Affluenza values.

These values are nothing new. They go back at least as far as 10,000 BC, ever since the introduction of private property. They were more or less rife amongst the elites of Mesopotamia, Egypt and Rome, not to mention the courts of European monarchs in subsequent centuries. What has changed fundamentally is that since the 1970s, they have become ubiquitous. The great majority of people in English-speaking nations (Britain, America, Australia, Canada, Singapore) now define their lives through earnings, possessions, appearances and celebrity, and those things are making them miserable because they impede the meeting of our fundamental needs.

Psychologists squabble over what those needs are, but usually agree on four: we need to feel secure, emotionally and materially; we need to feel part of a community, to give and receive from family, neighbours and friends; we need to feel competent, that we're not useless, are effective in chosen tasks; and we need to feel autonomous and authentic, masters of our destinies to some degree and not living behind masks. Virus values screw us up by conflating what we want with what we truly need, Having with Being.

Nearly ten years ago, in my book *Britain on the Couch*, I pointed out that a twenty-five-year-old American is (depending on which studies you believe) between three and ten times more likely to be suffering depression today than in 1950. By the standards of the fifties, a normal American child today has pathological levels of anxiety. In the case of British people, nearly one-quarter suffered from emotional distress (a 'mental illness' like depression, anxiety or psychosis) in the past twelve months and there is strong evidence that a further one-quarter of us are on the verge thereof. There are strong reasons for supposing that there has been a very real increase in distress, not just a greater preparedness amongst younger generations to report it – the misery is not merely the whinging of the affluent 'Worried Well' who have watched too many Woody Allen films. What is more, a considerable body of evidence suggests that much of this increase in angst occurred after the 1970s and in English-speaking nations.

Since the publication of *Britain on the Couch*, many American authors – and more recently, British ones – have followed me into its worrying terrain, nearly all of them concentrating on happiness. I would like to stress that what I have to say is quite different. Typical of our time in history, rather than facing the fact that we are truly in a bad way, emotionally, the facts of our despair, frustration and anger are spun, and in place of analysis of its real cause come endless treatises on how to have positive psychology and be happy. I regard happiness as chimeric and temporary, akin to pleasure, and I tend to agree with the saying 'we were not put on this earth to be happy'. The evidence regarding happiness, rather than emotional distress, is anyway not very sound. My focus is on why we are so fucked up, not with dangling a false promise of the possibility of happiness. In short, my new theory is that the nasty form of political economy that I call Selfish Capitalism caused an epidemic of the Affluenza Virus, accounting for much of the increase in distress since the 1970s.

By Selfish Capitalism I mean four basic things. The first is that the success of businesses is judged almost exclusively by their current share price. The second is a strong drive to privatise public utilities, such as water, gas and electricity, or, in the case of America, to keep them in private hands. The third is that there should be as little regulation of business as possible, with taxation for the rich and very rich so limited that whether to contribute becomes almost a matter of choice. The fourth is the conviction that consumption and market forces can meet human needs of almost every kind. America is the apotheosis of Selfish Capitalism, Denmark the nearest thing to its Unselfish opposite.

Research I have done for this book reveals two fundamental facts about Selfish Capitalism and emotional distress (for reasons I shall explain, throughout the book I use the words 'emotional distress', or just 'distress', when referring to what psychiatrists call mental illness). First, in a developed nation, rates of emotional distress (disturbances such as depression, anxiety and substance abuse) increase in direct proportion to the degree of income inequality (see Appendix 1). Since Selfish Capitalism is the main cause of inequality in developed nations, this strongly suggests that Selfish Capitalism is not a good way to run things, if you care about people's emotional well-being. Second, rates are at least twice as high in English-speaking nations as in mainland Western Europe (see Appendix 2). Since the former are far more

Selfish Capitalist than the latter, this is further reason to avoid it if you do not want to have a screwed-up population. Take this illustration, from my mind tour.

Sam is a thirty-five-year-old New York stockbroker who earns £20 million a year and will inherit about a billion when his dad dies. He lives alone in a five-storey apartment in central Manhattan. He used to be addicted to heroin, now it is sex with teenagers. He is paranoid, pessimistic, lonely, riddled with Affluenza and not a very nice person. By contrast, Chet, the Nigerian-born immigrant taxi driver who gave me a lift the next day, earns a thousand times less, is happily married, not at all paranoid despite frequently being physically attacked by his passengers, full of optimism and a very decent human being. Believe me, if you had to hang out with one of these two, you would choose Chet every time.

The definitive World Health Organization study of rates of emotional distress in fifteen different nations (see Appendix 3) revealed that over one-quarter of Americans had suffered from some form of distress in the previous twelve months, whereas only one-sixth as many indigenous Nigerians had. Despite being the second-wealthiest nation in the world, over forty times richer than Nigeria, America is by some margin the most emotionally distressed of all nations. Selfish Capitalism and Affluenza are not the only reasons for this difference, but they are the major ones.

Of course, it is not my contention that all emotional distress is caused by Affluenza. The kind of care we receive in our early years greatly affects how vulnerable we are to social pressures and adversities later in life. Likewise, being of low social class, young, female, part of an ethnic minority and living in a city rather than the country all greatly increase our susceptibility. On top of that – and the main subject of this book – what nation you are in makes a big difference. Clearly, if your country suffers massive social upheavals or economic disasters, its people are much more likely to experience distress. But my main point is that the extent to which a developed nation is Selfish Capitalist and infected by Affluenza is crucial to the well-being of its inhabitants.

The above list of causes of emotional distress is the reason I have rejected 'mental illness' altogether as a way of characterizing disturbance. Like many before me, I have come to the conclusion that it is grossly inaccurate to depict depression, anxiety, or even schizophrenia and other psychoses, as physical diseases of the body requiring medical treatment. Although it is still possible that in some cases, sometimes, genes may affect our vulnerability to distress, the massive differences that exist between rates in different nations and different groups within nations strongly suggest that genes play a minimal role in the vast majority of cases. Cards on the table, I contend that most emotional distress is best understood as a rational response to sick societies. Change those societies, and we will all be less distressed.

Although much of this book is devoted to interviews with the people I met, scientific evidence of many different kinds is also frequently mentioned. Unfortunately, there is simply not sufficient space to present all that evidence here, alongside the account of my travels and the vaccines. Those readers who thirst for the full scientific evidence for my new theory will need to consult a companion volume to this book, a monograph entitled *Selfish Capitalist Origins of Emotional Distress* planned for publication in 2007. Whenever I make a statement of fact, I do provide a reference to the specialist literature in a note (these appear at the end of the book); clinicians or scientists wanting more will have to await that second volume.

On my travels, in searching for ways to improve the individual's emotional lot I constantly reminded myself of how a lawyer I once met had characterised his life. 'My goal is to keep earning for thirty years, educate the kids, pay for my daughter's wedding and then die.' He was wealthy by most people's standards, an amusing man with a fascinating job living in a time of unimaginable affluence and technological sophistication. But he felt 'like a hamster on a wheel'. He never had enough time for anything, and he never seemed to have enough money. Above all, he was waiting for a promotion which was his due, and this, more than anything, is what scarred his thoughts last thing at night after he turned out the light. In seeking vaccines against the Virus, my question was always 'what does this person need to know in order to live, rather than partly live?' Whilst I would not pretend to have discovered the secret of life, I like to think that that lawyer will gain great benefit from the vaccines described in Part 2 of this book.

Having interviewed about 240 people on my travels, I do not despair. I met many who have overcome considerable obstacles to carve out niches in which they fulfil themselves. In telling their stories, with relevant scientific evidence mixed into the text, it is my earnest intention to provide a real basis for hope.

With your intellectual seatbelts fastened by these preliminary observations, we are now ready to embark on the mind tour. But before we take off there are a few final obligatory messages I need to convey in order for you to enjoy the trip.

In all but one case, I have gone to considerable lengths to conceal the identities of the people whose stories I tell, because anonymity was a guaranteed basis for all the interviews. In some cases, that has entailed making short people tall, married people single and the fair-haired dark-haired.

On several occasions I make reference to my parents, Martin and Lydia James, both RIP, and you need to know a couple of things about them to put these remarks in context. My dad was a doctor who trained as a psychoanalyst. My mum was a psychiatric social worker who also trained as a psychoanalyst before giving up work to care for my three sisters and me.

I set off on 12 January 2004. My wife and daughter accompanied me to New Zealand, Australia and Singapore, at which point they returned to London because my wife had fallen pregnant with our second child, a son, born in January 2005. I continued to Shanghai, Moscow, Copenhagen and New York, in that order, completing my travels (but not, alas, the book) in October 2004.

With these preliminaries out of the way, it only remains for me to wish you a pleasant journey. Your oxygen mask and safety exit are situated in the thought that life is to be enjoyed, not endured.

Oliver James
November 2006

Part One
The Virus

Chapter 1
New York

HIV may have originated in an African monkey, but the hunt for the origins of Affluenza starts in New York.

One evening there, a friend called Tom took me to visit Sam, a rich thirty-five-year-old Wall Street stockbroker. Sam's Manhattan apartment takes up the top five floors of a residential block overlooking the river. A designer has gutted the central area and converted the apartment into a one-bedroom residence on five floors with no interior walls, except for the lavatories. A glass lift takes us up to Sam's office, from where there is a grandstand view of the central atrium, a void at the heart of the home. Heartlessness turned out to be Sam's most conspicuous trait.

'So, what's going on in the world?' asks Tom. 'Nothing much,' says Sam. He has been spending the day sorting out his photographs, which he will pay someone to put into albums. Tom did it for him last time; 'This guy's much better at it than you,' Sam says, without any hint of humour.

I am pretty sure he intended this slightly cruel comment to be distressing.

Sam shows us the house security system, a mini-computer screen that provides live footage of every area. As we flip through the rooms on the screen, Sam sees a movement. 'There's someone there,' he says, pressing the zoom button. We stare for a while, and then the illusion of movement in this heavily protected, empty apartment is exposed when a car's lights passing the window cause a spectral flicker. Sam continues to look at the screen suspiciously, still not completely reassured that there is no intruder. Then he takes us up to the deck on his roof, where we hang out before dinner.

Well over six feet tall and built like a boxer, Sam has already inherited a huge amount of money and will inherit even more when his father dies – perhaps a billion pounds. But he is also highly motivated to make his own, earning about £20 million a year through his investment company, enough to pay for his own private jet and many homes around the world without drawing on his inheritance. He spends little time here, constantly travelling, often to Russia, on whose women he seems very keen. Apparently, in New York it is possible to call up a real model agency and get them to send one over, like a pizza. 'Of course,' he says, 'you give them a "present" at the end of the evening or the next morning, but these girls also are real models.' He had recently met the main scout for Russian models here, and only last night had been introduced to 'an eighteen-year-old who is so perfect that she looks as if she has just hatched from an egg. You know something interesting? I swear that when they are young they really do taste different.' That is just how one

might speak of the upholstery of an expensive car, or some
other possession. His view of women as manipulable
commodities is underlined by his next comment. 'What is so
great about the Russian women is that they only want to get
out of there, a visa or some practical help, that's enough to
make them happy. My girlfriend in London has got a student
visa and lives in my flat there. That's all she wants from me.'
Tom is astonished to hear that Sam has a girlfriend, saying,
'What makes you call her your girlfriend, compared with the
four or five other girls you've always got on the go?' Rather
testily, Sam replies that 'she lives in my flat, she is my girlfriend'; perhaps he is beginning to feel a bit abnormal
compared with his friends and wants a social possession of
this category as a sign that he is not weird.

On our way down to dinner, Tom catches his finger on
some poorly finished panelling next to the lift, which he
points out. 'You'd better be more careful, then,' says Sam,
without a trace of sympathy. Dinner is served by his chef ('I
brought him over from London because he wouldn't have
anything to do there') in lonely baronial splendour at the end
of a twenty-place, white marble table on the floor devoted to
dining. He asks me about my book, and comments: 'I feel
happiness is not something worth thinking about. I know
that depression is a real thing, though I have not suffered it,
but a woman friend of mine did. She committed suicide
recently, although she was happy at the time she did it, so far
as I know.' For someone who says he is not depressed, he has
a remarkably bleak view of the world, railing against various
bogeymen. He loathes the England football team – 'Beckham
is disgusting' – and speaks with disgust ('I really do mean that

word, I find it disgusting') of a newspaper report he read recently when he was in Britain that along a one-mile stretch of country road there are sixty signs. 'They say "Do not cross here", "Speed bumps ahead", "Speed limit" – Brits seem to have no idea any more how to function on their own and expect to be told.' Although Sam finds both Britain and America equally disgusting, he comments that at least 'America, and to a lesser degree Britain, are ahead in forcing self-reliance, more so than the socialist countries in Europe who have not realised that people must understand that they will get no help from the State if they do not earn enough money to pay for their medical care or old age. In the socialist countries everyone is dependent.' Dependence is definitely disgusting; it also happens to be something he appears to be terrified of in his love-life.

Sam is very exercised, to the point of paranoia, by the threat of terrorism. 'It horrifies me that there are ten million Muslims in France. The EU has been taken over by Muslims,' he says. He is well acquainted with 'the world's leading expert on terrorism'. This man had told him that it was a question of when, rather than if, terrorists will explode a nuclear suitcase bomb in New York or London. Asked for more detail, Sam says that all the Russian bombs have been accounted for, so the real danger will come from countries such as North Korea or from Pakistan, a poor nation that has the nuclear wherewithal and needs the dosh. 'For $10 billion someone will sell one, and then it will be curtains for a big city. Apparently it would mean the end of Greater London or the Five Boroughs, with something as flat as a field for the central five square miles of the blast and then people dying of cancer within a radius of twenty-five. I really do believe that is going to happen, which is why I'm having a house built in the Pyrenees mountains, with a bomb shelter.' After a bit more of this he says, perfunctorily, 'Let's change the subject. Are there any decent British girls who have come to Manhattan recently?'

Later, as we wander in search of a taxi, Tom (who is urbane, considerate and thoughtful) explains that Sam was a fanatical drug addict in his youth, taking astonishing quantities of heroin and only able to relax when he had done so. Since cleaning up, 'nothing excites or interests him', says Tom. 'I suppose he gets a mild buzz from sleeping with a new girl or making some money from shares, but most of the time he seems bored.' I said I thought it must be hell being him. If you think how it is to be bored, imagine if nothing could lift you out of that. Sam's problem seems to be that he has no personal relationships with anyone at all. He has no feelings for others – witness the casual dismissal of Tom's pain on catching his finger – and is sealed off. When a conversation or a girl or a place begins to bore him, he wants it changed, immediately. He cannot keep still for long, in any sense, sexually, geographically or indeed physically. He keeps getting up and moving around. When he does settle down he has an impassive face, eyes slightly glazed, seemingly uninterested in what is being said. I would guess that all this activity is because, when he does occasionally come to rest, he runs the risk of being quickly swamped by a mixture of paranoia (imagined intruders, suitcase bombs) and total despair (a world filled with over-dependent people who need a computer to tell them to lock their car).

Sam was unable to analyse the causes of Affluenza, which he found dull ('perhaps too many people have more time and money than they know what to do with' he drawled, languidly), but on the causes of suicide he made one interesting point. I had explained that no-one could explain what marks out those who do it from the hundred thousand who contemplate it, but do not. 'Maybe it's because it's often just a spur-of-the-moment event,' he said. 'My friend who committed suicide seemed fine when I last saw her, and no-one expected what happened. If they suddenly decide to jump off a building, maybe there's nothing else that's different except that they are impulsive.' I had a suspicion that he knew exactly what he was talking about when he said that, that an impulsive urge for self-destruction had seized him more than once. This must be especially scary in his insulated world, with no intimates close enough to know his feelings, anticipate the danger and protect him.

I speculated to Tom that Sam must have suffered cruelty as a child and dreadful emotional deprivation as an infant. Whilst he did not know about the infancy, he confirmed that Sam's world-famous (in business circles) father is a very cruel man. We concluded that, for all his rude imperiousness, we could not help finding Sam's eccentricity intriguing, and that we felt sorry for him because he must be dreadfully lonely. Tom said, 'Occasionally when I read interviews with him in a magazine, I find he has described me as his best friend. That's incredible, if it's true. If I am the person closest to him, then no-one is.'

If an in-depth study of New York stockbrokers is to be believed, Sam is not the only member of that fraternity to be pretty screwed up. Collectively they were cold fish: they showed high levels of depersonalisation (feeling detached from one's surroundings). Almost two-thirds were depressed, plagued by negative thoughts, nearly all agreeing with the statement 'I am critical of myself for my weaknesses and mistakes'. There were also extremely high levels of anxiety and sleeplessness (on average it took them 38 minutes to drop off at night). Interestingly, the more they earned, the more likely they were to have all these problems. On average they spent twelve hours a day at work; daily, they smoked nearly two packs of cigarettes, consuming both alcohol and some form of illegal substance (mostly cocaine) twice a day. For relaxation they chose solitary pursuits: jogging, masturbation and fishing being commoner than dining with friends or sex with others. At least in this latter respect, Sam did not conform to the pattern of his stockbroking peers.

Although he is exceptional in the scale of his wealth, Sam's pathology is unexceptional in New York's financial service industries. A glimpse of life at less affluent levels was provided by Jill, a happily married thirty-eight-year-old personal assistant who has worked for fifteen years in one of the world's leading investment banks. She earns around £40,000 a year (depending on bonuses) and claims to be the only person she knows in her industry who is pretty satisfied with their lot, apart from one other woman who does the same lowly job in another bank. Jill went to secretarial school rather than university. She cooks for her husband every night, and believes that 'this is what I'm going to be doing for the rest of my life, and if it works out well with my retirement plan, I'm happy with that'. This is in marked contrast to the average banker's career path and well-being, at least as outlined by Jill.

It starts with working as an analyst for a hundred hours a week for twenty-four months without holiday. For this the aspiring bankers get paid £40,000 to £45,000 a year, most of which they save because there is no time to spend it. They may have a childhood or college sweetheart at the outset, but that quickly ends because, she says, 'their life is their job'. The strain is phenomenal. 'They get great money but they have to kill themselves for it. These are young adults, maybe just twenty-two, yet some are having heart problems. When one of our young analysts passed away a few years back there was an instruction not to work so hard – but it made no difference. She was running for a plane and collapsed. We've got an analyst at the moment who fainted three times from overwork last year.'

For those who make it to their late twenties or early thirties, the next step is to become a vice-president, on over £200,000 a year including bonuses. Jill says that 'nearly all of them manage to get married or into a relationship. If they do incredibly well they go on to be a managing director and then, in their forties, they might just become a partner, which means they're set, financially. By that time it just doesn't occur to them to retire and spend more time with their money or family because they don't know what it is not to work. One partner I know continues to do it because he has a wife who doesn't work and three young children, and he just wants to get out of the house. He probably enjoys being with his kids, but he commented to someone that "my money could run out if I didn't work" – even though he has quite a few million. That's not really it with him. What the heck would he do at home? That's the real question. This is his life.'

Jill has a detailed knowledge of the New York bankers' insatiable materialism. 'All of them want what they haven't got because they're surrounded by that culture every single day. Their biggest discontent is if a vacation gets cancelled because of a big deal going down, or if they don't get the bonus they hoped for. When the banker does take a vacation I don't book him in at the Marriott, it's the Four Seasons, or in Paris, the Georges Cinques, and they need a BMW or a Jaguar. It's "I need the best reservations at the best place to impress X, Y and Z." In this world you've got the haves and the have-nots, and then there's the have-mores.' As their wealth increases, their expenditure laps up the extra. It seems that they would find it impossible to retire and live off their millions because 'they need to maintain the townhouse and the housekeeper. A fair few have affairs, which can be costly. They might have separate credit cards and maintain a separate residence that their spouse knows nothing about. Some of them try it on with me, and I'm thinking. "You're in a committed relationship, get in someone else's pants!"'

In a report on burnout in female corporate lawyers aged twenty-nine to thirty-eight, the New York psychoanalyst Brenda Berger provides an even deeper insight into how corporations exploit emotional insecurities. She prefaced her account with a quote from the lawyer and novelist Scott Turow about large law firms: 'The only sure ingredients of growth are new clients, bigger bills and – especially – more people at the bottom, each a little profit center, toiling into the wee hours and earning more for the partnership than they take home.'

Berger presents the case of Meg, in her twenties, who was working sixty hours a week. At the end of her brutal day she would 'zone out' in front of the telly. Despite having had less atavistic alternatives, she had chosen her firm because she felt more 'at home' with it. She came from a home in which her mother was a fragile, self-centred woman whose love Meg could attract only by giving in to her perfectionist demands, based on having been thwarted in her own ambitions which she now wanted to live out vicariously through her daughter. Meg's father was no better, taking any signs of independence as a personal affront. Berger describes how Meg had developed a masochistic need to repeat this scenario in her work life: 'her firm's stance – "I will pay you $100,000 a year if you don't tell me you feel strained, exhausted, bored, powerless and lonely" – is remarkably consistent with the messages she felt she received from her parents'. In her appearance and the way she conducted her life, Meg was utterly chaotic, all domestic work when she lived with her parents having been taken care of by her mother. Indeed, other than when executing her tasks at the firm, she was helpless, angry and incapable of thinking for herself. Similar patterns were found in Berger's other subjects, and in summarising her conclusions she points out that the pathological need to please and to join oppressive working environments is viciously exploited by such corporations.

Like Meg, Sam and Jill's colleagues are textbook cases of Affluenza. Studies from fourteen countries reveal that people who strongly favour the key Virus values – money, possessions, physical and social appearances, and fame – are at greater risk of emotional distress. The reasons these values are so bad for our well-being were best summarised by Erich Fromm, an American psychologist, writing in the 1950s and 1960s. He presented the stark choice that the American variety of capitalism offered as 'To Have or To Be'.

'Being' is an active, vital, internal state in which we are able to see what is really around us, to engage with the world without feeling a need to dominate or destroy it. When Being, a person does not preconceive their experience. This is evident in small children before they have become infected by Having. Infants may observe a ball rolling a hundred times but still remain fascinated because they are 'really' seeing the ball roll, observing its rotations, variations in direction, different on each occasion and fresh to the infant eye. If sensation is merely confirming prior expectation, as is the case when the stultified Having mode guides our perception, we are liable to become rapidly bored. We might be hyperactively busy in our day-to-day lives, but inactive in our apprehension, like hypnotised zombies. Someone who has been hypnotised may have their eyes open, and speak and move about, but they are merely the vessel of the hypnotist's volition, not their own. Likewise, a person with a compulsive obsession to touch the floor one hundred times in a strict ritual before leaving the house is a busy bee, but they are not expressing their will by these actions. In Having mode, people are as much in the grip of external forces as the hypnotised or the compulsively obsessed.

Fromm dubbed such 'Having' people 'Marketing Characters'. They experience themselves as a commodity, with their value dependent on success, saleability, the approval of others. Face-to-face or telephone selling have become a perennial of the American Way, with the proportion employed in Sales rising from 4 to 12 per cent during the last century. The structural importance of selling in America is shown by the fact that since the 1920s, advertising has accounted for over 2 per cent of the American economy, twice that of anywhere else, four times that of mainland Western Europe. The Marketing Character is very well suited to this kind of work. Studies show that they regard themselves as objects in a 'personality market'. Career success depends largely on how well persons sell themselves, how nice a 'package' they are, whether they are 'cheerful', 'sound', 'aggressive', 'reliable' or 'ambitious'. Indeed, most corporations now use psychological tests to see whether potential employees are the right kind of commodity, have the desired attributes. Just how much this way of thinking is taken for granted is shown by the name given to the corporate departments responsible for the testing: Human Resources. It used to be called Personnel. The new name indicates how the humans who work for the company are indistinguishable from the computers or widgets or financial services that the company buys and sells, just another category of thing, a resource. Reality TV programmes such as *Big Brother* are the logical conclusion of a marketing society: popularity contests in which knowing competitors parade their most intimate aspects to win viewers' votes.

'Having' intellectualises and distances one from oneself and from others. Intimacy is destroyed if you regard another person as an object to be manipulated to serve your ends, whether at work or at play. In choosing friends or lovers you are swayed by their supposed value in the personality market, by looks or wealth or charisma, rather than by love. This leaves you feeling lonely and craving emotional contact, vulnerable to depression. There is always a feeling that you could have a 'better' partner or friend, or a fear that your value may fall, creating acute anxiety. Feeling inadequate also puts you at greater risk of narcissistic personality disorder, compensating for the feeling that you are nothing by going to the opposite extreme, 'aren't I wonderful?', a relentless 'me, me, me' attention-seeking because you feel so invisibly worthless.

The widespread depression and anxiety created by the Virus are crucial for Selfish Capitalism. To fill the emptiness and loneliness, and to replace our need for authentic, intimate relationships, we resort to the consumption that is essential for economic growth and profits. The more anxious or depressed we are, the more we must consume, and the more we consume, the more disturbed we become. Consumption holds out the false promise that an internal lack can be fixed by an external means. Compensation for personal misery is why people with the Virus are at greater risk of substance abuse (alcohol, illegal drugs), but more important, of the legal 'aholias', shopaholia (till we drop), workaholia, sex and the other compulsions of mass consumption. We medicate our misery through buying things; its purveyors have never pretended otherwise.

This was spelt out in 1957, the year of publication of Vance Packard's best-selling exposé of the advertising world, *The Hidden Persuaders*. Through interviews with marketing and advertising executives, he revealed how, after the Second World War, American business shifted its emphasis from production to marketing. He quotes an executive who summarised the rationale: 'As a nation we are already so rich that consumers are under no pressure of immediate necessity to buy a very large share – as much as 40 per cent – of what is produced, and the pressure will get progressively less in the years ahead. But if consumers exercise their option not to buy a large share of what is produced, a great [economic] depression is not far behind.' David Ogilvy, a British advertising executive, described another problem: 'There really isn't any significant difference between the various brands of whisky or the various cigarettes or the various brands of beer. They are all about the same. And so are the cake mixes and the detergents and the automobiles'. People no longer bought soap to make them clean: they bought the promise that it would make them beautiful. In the virtual world of ads, toothpaste was not to kill bacteria but to create white teeth, cars were for prestige rather than travel, even foodstuffs, such as oranges, were for vitality, not nutrition. Needs were replaced by confected wants that people did not know they had. One ad executive had this to say: 'What makes this country great is the creation of wants and desires, the creation of dissatisfaction with the old and outmoded.' Fifty years later, nothing has changed; in the words of a contemporary executive, 'Advertising at its best is making people feel that without their product, you're a loser … You open up emotional vulnerabilities.'

That advertising unashamedly fosters unhappiness with oneself and with one's possessions is now blithely taken for granted by most of us. When books, newspaper articles and television programmes suggest to us that genes are the cause of emotional distress, few of them mention the role of advertising. But far from genes being the fundamental cause, the 2004 World Health Organization study of rates of emotional distress in fifteen nations is potent proof that the kind of society is what matters (see Appendix 3). My analysis (published with colleagues Kate Pickett and Richard Wilkinson) of these results shows that the greater the inequality of income distribution within a developed nation, the higher the rate of distress (see Appendix 1). It also shows that the richer the developed nation, the more distressed its people (see Appendix 1). It is no coincidence that America is by far the most distressed, for it is the richest and the most unequal, and the one where the Marketing Character and the misery created by advertisers is most prevalent. Mainland European nations have long spent only half as much as the English-speaking ones on advertising, and they are less materialistic. In Britain, since the mid-1980s there has been a steady rise in the proportion of people who use success to bolster self-esteem. Indeed, there is now overwhelming evidence that industrialisation is a fundamental cause of distress. Its arrival has been accompanied by dramatic increases in rates of depression, and recovery from even severe emotional distresses such as schizophrenia is more rapid in pre-industrial societies. Put crudely, the more like America a society becomes, the higher its rate of emotional distress.

Of course, it is important to stress that not all materialism is 'a bad thing'. There are differences between survival materialism and the relative variety, the Affluenza of wealthy people and nations. If you are starving in Africa or scrabbling to make ends meet in a derelict part of Los Angeles, materialism is a healthy reaction because you need money to survive. Materialism is greater amongst children raised in poor homes, for if you grow up not sure where the next meal is coming from it is likely to make you focus on material goals. In poor homes the struggle for survival places a higher value on money. Likewise, women are more materialistic in their preferences when choosing a partner – are more likely to want rich men – if they live in societies offering them little opportunity to become educated and fend for themselves. Emotional distress will not invariably follow from a strong drive to have more money if it is really needed; the problem comes when the money (or possessions or appearance or fame) is a confected want, not a need.

A fine illustration of the subtleties of relative and survival materialism came the morning after I met the millionaire Sam, when I got chatting to Chet, a taxi driver. He looks to be in his early thirties but is in fact forty-seven, and arrived from Nigeria three years before. Although he now earns £300 more in a month than the £750 he was paid in a year working for KLM in Nigeria, he is adamant that although they are much richer, the people in New York are less happy. 'There's too much tension, everything is about money because there is nobody you can run to if you are short of it. You have to solve your problem yourself, nobody will help if you fail or fall. If you don't earn money for two months, you are on the street.' That would not be true in Nigeria. 'Someone would come to your aid there. If you are penniless your family would keep you going for the next six months, a year even, you could never be homeless. It's not that anybody has much money, but they are contented. All an average Nigerian worries about is food and trying to find money to send their child to school, which must be paid for out of your pocket. They don't care if they have a video machine.' This bears out the findings of the WHO study of emotional distress in fifteen different countries: in the previous twelve months, nearly six times more Americans than Nigerians had suffered (26.4 per cent versus 4.7 per cent – see Appendix 3). Whilst poverty fosters survival materialism, it does not result in illness. Materialist values cause emotional distress only when countries, or classes within them, become affluent.

Chet's father was employed in the postal service and became a middle-class, senior supervisor. Despite his dad's relative affluence, with seven offspring to feed and educate and a wife who did not work, there were still many times in Chet's childhood when he was hungry. 'He really struggled to pay for us to go to school. Sometimes his cheque would not come and we had no food to eat at supper time. That would be it – nothing, unless maybe an uncle or aunt would give us a little.' This illustrates a very simple point. To a greater or lesser degree, family relationships throughout the developed world have become less reliable as a safety net. Apart from the USA, where welfare provision has always been small, in the English-speaking nations the Welfare State net, which was developed to replace the familial one, has been slashed so full of holes in the last thirty years that no-one feels safe any more. It might suit paranoid Sam, who hates dependence and is in favour of tax regimes which enable him to hang on to far more money than any individual could possibly need, but it's hard to see how it is for the common good.

If you met them both, I would be very surprised if you preferred to be Sam rather than Chet. An important difference seemed to be the presence of religion. Whilst not as devout as when he was younger, or as his wife, Chet still goes to church regularly and is a strong believer. Indeed, wherever I went I found that religion seemed to be a powerful vaccine. I should not have been surprised, because the scientific evidence has long been there: much to the consternation of social scientists, on average, regular churchgoers suffer less depression or unhappiness than unbelievers. This is regardless of the kind of religion, or of the nationality, gender, age, social class or ethnic background of the believer.

Almost by definition, religious people are less likely to be materialistic and to have Virus goals or motivations and more likely to be preoccupied with things spiritual. One study, of 860 young American adults, showed this very clearly. Those with materialistic values, such as wanting money or prestige, were far less likely to be religious, and they were unhappier, drank and smoked more, and, in the case of the women, were at greater risk of eating disorders. Compared with non-believers, the only sort of religious people who are not protected against depression are ones whose involvement in faith is guided by self-seeking ends (known as 'extrinsic religious orientation'), seeing belief as an investment, such as hoping that prayer would be instrumental in making them successful in work or love. When such people think badly of others, seeing them as malevolent or envious, and if they use religious belief like magic as a way of coping with their perceived enemies or to deal with stress, they are as susceptible to depression as non-believers.

Chet's theology is uncomplicated. 'I believe there is a God and that Jesus was his son, who was sent to try and cleanse our sin. He had to do a lot of miracles to show us that he actually was from God because nobody would have believed him. So after he was dead he was the only true thing in a cruel world, pure and good and our saviour.' Okay, fair enough, but does God really do the business for Chet? 'When we pray to God he hears our prayer and he sees the manifestations of our life and gives us evidence. When me and my wife wanted to get married we prayed about the decision we were going to make and we had the feeling his hand was in it. And we have been married for eighteen, twenty years now, we don't have no problem, or if we do, we never tell nobody, we talk it out ourselves.' I felt sheepish about asking such a decent, honest man this question, but I went ahead and enquired whether he had ever cheated on his wife. 'Because I really love her and to me she is the most beautiful woman, if I saw another who was attractive, she would not be as attractive as my wife. I have never slept with other women since getting married because I love her and I'm satisfied by her, I get what I need from her. If I want to have good fun, it's with her.'

The differences between the Life of Sam and Chet did not end with the taxi driver's uxoriousness and contentment. Chet has a whole sackful of adversities. He is stuck working as a cabbie because he cannot get the Green Card that would enable him to work legally. 'My plan is to get a job with an airline. The work I know, but I can't get a Green Card without a letter from an employer. Really, I need someone who is rich to sponsor me. [Sam flashes into my mind – and then straight out of it.] My wife does a proper job working with old people, like cleaning out their beds and stuff, but even she cannot get one and it doesn't look like she ever will.' Chet suffers from diabetes and hypertension, the pills for which cost him a lot of money each month. Although he and his wife's joint monthly income amounts to £2,000, £450 of that goes on rent and a further £150 on utilities. By the time she has bought the food and he has paid the expenses of running his taxi, what's left has to go towards his children's education.

Let's recapitulate the differences between Chet and Sam. Chet's annual income is one thousand times less. He is contented, optimistic, sexually faithful and religious; he is courteous, friendly and open but with serious health problems and no medical insurance, and has little prospect of being able to save any money or ever own his own home. Sam is discontented, pessimistic, sex-addicted and an atheist; he is curt, domineering and unfriendly yet he has no medical problems and lives in a big apartment (in which several families of Chets could gladly fit), just one of a varied portfolio of properties between which he flits in his private jet. One suffers from Affluenza; the other does not, even though the need for money – survival materialism – figures high on his list of priorities.

Perhaps most fascinating of all, one is personally and globally paranoid, whereas the other is not, despite having every reason to be. For the worst thing about Chet's life is the daily threat posed to him by his passengers. He has twice had his wallet stolen, but far more worrying have been the many violent incidents. 'Actually, I have never been attacked by white men; it's always blacks who will not pay their fare. They realise I am African and think they can get away with it. I had to go to hospital once because one man split my lip and it needed stitches. I had to pay for that. He was taken to court and told he had to pay my hospital bills, but it's not that easy. I'm not legal here. I don't have social security or health insurance, so I wasn't going to push it. If I got had up we would be in big trouble. I have to work. How else would we survive?' Which is exactly how Sam believes it ought to be, because a sink-or-swim, Selfish Capitalist system avoids 'unhealthy' dependence of the likes of Chet on the State.

The comparison between Sam and Chet illustrates how the Virus causes distress. It impedes the meeting of four fundamental human needs: feeling secure, being part of a community, feeling competent, and being autonomous and authentic. A large body of scientific evidence suggests the following reasons why the Virus impairs the meeting of each need.

Insecurity

Constantly comparing your lot with others, especially those who have more than you, is not a prescription for feeling safe. If you are always worrying about whether you have enough money and the right possessions, or your appearance, or seeking fame, you are digging a hole for yourself which can never be deep enough – the proverbial bottomless pit. You will have a nameless sense that there is something else you should be doing, a free-floating anxiety. You will be depressively running yourself down because you do not do as well as others, moving the goalposts if you do succeed. At the same time, you may deal with your sense of inadequacy by falsely building yourself up (exaggerating your wonderfulness in a narcissistic compensation) and by desperate attention-seeking. To deal with feeling like shit – depression, anxiety and exaggerated self-love – you will medicate your unhappiness with booze, drugs or the aholias: work-, shop-, sex-, choc- and all the myriad other quick fixes that Selfish Capitalism is so adept at confecting and making profits from providing.

Alienation

The Virus prevents you from meeting your need to connect with family, friends and the wider community by relegating them to a low priority. Unless your family members assist your career, you keep them at a distance, going through the motions of family life because convention demands it, or simply having little to do with them. In choosing friends you are motivated by their use to you, not a desire to be close, emotionally, and to enjoy shared pursuits for fun rather than competition. Friendship and romantic attachments are so muddled up with professional alliances that they become indistinguishable, as does work and play. You become liable to buy friendship through expensive presents or career gifts (promotions, salary rises), and this may extend to lovers. Your values prioritise selfishness, not contributing to the wider community, so you miss out on the large satisfaction to be gained from supporting others and feeling supported. If you become rich you may set up a charity, but it is to your greater glory, not really as a way to help others. The consequent lack of intimacy leaves you feeling bored, empty and lonely, promoting depression and anxiety; you compensate with substance abuse and aholias, to make you feel better and to inject some thrills into the dreariness.

Feeling incompetent

The same features of the Virus that breed insecurity also impair your need to feel competent. However conventionally successful you are, it is never enough. With your self-focused mindset, there is only one person's inabilities to blame for this 'failure': your own. There is also only one response that you know: try even harder. In a hole, it's advisable to stop digging. The Virus-stricken, driven on by a powerful sense of their inefficacy, just carry on. The deeper they get, the higher the walls of self-criticism and rampant anxiety threatening to bury them. There is a long list of hugely successful people who had a nervous breakdown at this point. You may be regularly praised in the press or on TV as an icon of achievement in your field, yet it takes only the tiniest of criticisms to spur you to reach for that shovel. With the darkness closing in, you are very vulnerable to anything that will give brief relief: aholias and chemicals. Occasionally, these are used to end your life.

Inauthenticity and feeling like you've been hypnotised

The Virus impedes our need to feel authentic and autonomous by creating a thin, tough, impermeable barrier of false wants between us and our true desires. Most Virus-stricken people are Marketing Characters, to a greater or lesser degree. By treating yourself and others as commodities, you are deprived of volition. Being bought and sold, you begin to experience yourself not as a person but as a power-less entity whose value is wholly determined by the market, something that is ultimately beyond your control. You may have the illusion of volition throughout your waking hours, as in making decisions about who to fire or hire (ironically, you may be widely regarded as 'a control freak') and what to buy or sell, but these choices are not really yours, they are part of some virtual reality: it is not you deciding these things but a commodity with your name. The decisions concern matters unconnected with your core, true needs, leaving you with the feeling that you are an actor in a play rather than living a real life. The marketing existence is an act, a game you play. Your chamaeleonism, hyper-competitiveness and machiavellianism prevent you from telling the truth or recognising that you are being told it. If you are ever honest, it is only as part of your manipulativeness – when you tell the truth it may well be to foster trust in order to trick someone, be it a lover or colleague. This inauthenticity and lack of autonomy leave you feeling outside yourself, at one remove. It makes you very prone to personality disorders and desperate for snatched snacks of reality offered by drink, drugs or aholias such as sex addiction.

These problems are most pronounced in America, but of course not all Americans are equally afflicted. Childhood maltreatment is the crucial factor in creating vulnerability to the Virus, given that you live in an infected society. The most telling account of this, and of the marketing mentality that dominates America, came from Susan, a thirty-one-year-old lawyer who had worked in advertising.

Susan was born twenty years after her two older sisters, and her mother decided to cut loose from her father when she was aged one. He was a well-to-do member of the 'old money' upper classes, a poet living in his own world, whilst her mother was a personality-disordered (erratic, emotionally febrile, narcissistic) humanitarian with ambitions to write. Whereas Susan's siblings spent their childhoods at expensive schools and posh houses in the Hamptons, she moved school seventeen times before she was thirteen. 'My mother had come from an extremely wealthy family, at least originally so, and maybe rebelled against it,' Susan explained. 'She would just chuck all the shit in the car and head for the highway. We lived in apartments with no furniture. From a very young age I had a parental role in relation to her; she was the intellectual and I was the practical one. She was extremely disorganised, very creative but totally out of touch with reality. I was reality.' Often they would have no money for food. 'At the age of seven I was setting up businesses to sell lemonade to buy fish. My clothes were from Goodwill charity, money was from the government. I had to constantly hide that from other children. We were always moving and leaving all our stuff behind – "Let's get on the road, anything's possible."' Susan thought that was normal, and only realised otherwise much later. Since the woman now before me was manifestly a mature, sensible, sane person, I was puzzled how she had turned out so well.

The first step towards a semblance of normality came when Susan was seven. 'From then I started spending summers at my father's, which I liked, because there was food. Food! I could go to the grocery store and buy what I liked.' Emotionally, her father's parenting was not much better because 'he was always very abstract, out of it, in his own world, not aware of how mater-ially poor my life with my mother was, even though I did tell him'. The problem was just as great for her siblings. 'We had to be our own parent, nobody was going to save you, so it was sink or swim. There was nobody to fall back on; no-one would catch you if you fell, so it was better to learn how not to.'

The bizarre mixture of upper-class summers and under-class everything else continued until Susan was thirteen. Then, one of her sisters said to her, 'Look, you're smart, you could get into a good school – just do it.' She passed the entrance exams for the American equivalent of Roedean and was suddenly a boarder, surrounded for most of the year by the daughters of the super-rich. A scholarship paid part of the fees, and the shortfall was partly made up by her father and partly by loans that he insisted were taken out. But the greatest problem was that 'it was a very big shock to be suddenly at school with the wealthiest children in America. I wore shorts in November because no-one had bought me trousers, which was embarrassing. I felt very out of place for a time.' Having made the adjustment, she went on to study law at university, but the sense of financial impoverishment stayed with her.

Susan was a talented writer of short stories and could probably have made a career out of it, but she consciously chose to pursue a safe, money-making path. 'In my early twenties I was always thinking, "If only I could have or be this or that." I was very driven, constantly proving to myself that I wouldn't be homeless. When I throw my trash away, I still take care to package any food that is edible so that it will not get spoilt, in case someone goes through the rubbish looking for something to eat. I still think that way.' When I made the obvious next point, that a relationship in which she might find herself depending on a man must have been rather daunting, given her history, she smiled ruefully. 'It was a struggle for me to trust a man, I'll tell you that. In my early twenties I was very resistant to long-term relationships, always waiting for the ball to drop.' She spent time in the company of 'writers, very attractive to me, on the edge of society and a little bit like my mother', but sometimes she'd be 'scared out of my mind – I hated depending.'

Although still fearful of penury, four or five years ago Susan began to change. Having soared high in the advertising world, she decided to ease off and take a less pressurised job, in law. 'From a very early age, I felt on the edge, like I had nothing. That feeling is always with me at some level, but it means that I find happiness in bizarre things. I really do find happiness in having a full cupboard, lots of food in reserve, and in paying my bills on time. To me that's "I've made it, I've survived, I'm okay" rather than being about to lose my furniture or apartment, which was my childhood. That couldn't happen now, but in my irrational mind I'm still one step away from having the electricity disconnected. Weirdly, that makes me happy because I feel, "Great, I've got what I need." I'm pretty happy with where I am. Because I grew up in poverty I realised that money doesn't make you happy. It can definitely give you access to things, but it's only useful for fulfilling real needs, not for wants like having a Porsche rather than a Mercedes.'

One of the great triggers for this understanding was when Susan fell in love during her mid-twenties. 'He pointed out that I could have been raised in a rich home and been miserable, or in a dirt-poor one and been happy, and that's really true – look at my sisters, they're certainly no better off, emotionally, for having been in an affluent home, in fact they are obsessed with conventional success. Happiness doesn't have anything to do with that but I think I only really grasped that four or five years ago.' (Her sisters have dealt with their childhoods by becoming frenzied, materialist workaholics.) The man Susan fell in love with and to whom she even became engaged, would have led her into a disastrous repetition of her past, had they married. 'We ultimately broke it off because he wanted to go and live in Africa in the middle of nowhere, subsist on nothing and take care of people at the edge of life. He really got it about my childhood, but in the end I couldn't just repeat that, living in the middle of nowhere, starving. Still, it's interesting that I managed to find someone who understood so well about the breadline life.'

So far, Susan's story was making no sense to me as a psychologist. She seemed to have a lot of insight into her motivations, which had enabled her to avoid the pitfalls of a pathological marriage and a workaholic career. There was nothing of the 'me, me, me' about her, nor of ruthless, angry cruelty. As I explained to her, the vast majority of people who had been through a childhood like hers would be personality-disordered. Graduation from the school of hard knocks is sometimes put down to genetic 'resilience', a notion cooked up by psychiatrists, that people can inherit genes which allow them to make the most of whatever happens. However, as I explained to Susan, I doubt that this exists, or hardly ever. She also doubted it, and we explored alternative possibilities.

First off, I said, some very disturbed mothers can be fantastic with babies. Being so weak of self, they can more easily enter into the baby's world, identifying with what it is like to have weak boundaries between what is me and what is not-me, with the primitive infantile existence in which being hungry or needing a cuddle is central. 'Well,' she said, her face lighting up, 'it's funny you say that because, for all her crankiness, what everyone says about my mother is that she adored babies. My sisters and father say that she was brilliant with them, and so do my other relatives. The problems came as soon as the child was old enough to have a separate life. So long as her offspring were an extension of herself, it was fine.' If that were true, I explained, Susan would actually have had a strong sense of self established in her first couple of years, before she was old enough to feel unsettled by the chaos of constantly moving home.

I asked if there was anyone in her childhood who had provided some stability or the parenting that was missing. Studies of resilience nearly always turn up such a person, and sure enough, out she popped. 'I bonded in my early teenage years with a woman who my father was dating. She was my mother's polar opposite, very stable, grounded, practical, a "be there for you" person. I clung to her at thirteen and refused to let go. Some time after they split up, she called and said we could be friends and I could visit her in New York. She was an amazing person in my life and I started to come home to her in the summer rather than go to my father's. She helped me get an internship. She really mothered me, sent me brownies at college. She was a big reason I came here. We're still very close, and she lives nearby. She's always there for me, no matter what. She was the one who came to visit me at school and discovered I was in shorts and needed trousers.

She did things for me that I desperately needed, but had no idea needed doing, because no-one had ever done anything for me.'

By now I was in ecstasy, because Susan so perfectly fits with the idea that resilience in the face of adversity is caused by nurture rather than nature. And if that were not enough, she capped it with the following: 'In my early twenties I started to realise that my mistrust of men was sometimes of my own making, and I went in search of a therapist. The first one I visited didn't seem very good, and I went into "interview mode" until I found a woman who was really good. I went twice a week for seven years and I think it has made a tremendous difference.' This fits exactly with studies which show that people who undergo therapy often become more secure in relationships.

Finding genuine people is not easy here, Susan says. 'I feel quite apart from people a lot of the time because I would be equally happy with loads of money or just enough. Even if I had a load, I don't think I would confuse it with happiness. In New York, people are so caught up with the symbols of power and status. It's very much "What do you do for a living, where's your apartment?" You feel like saying to someone, "Hey, I'm sitting across from you, we're just two human beings." It's frustrating sometimes that people only want to be with you if you own this or have that job. It really is a materialistic society. I see that every day, and what disgusts me more than anything is "throw it away and buy another".' She gave a telling example of the importance of possessions as symbols. 'There was a guy at work who described his honeymoon purely through the goods and services they had enjoyed: "We had an Audi TS3 estate car, then we got the something something helicopter, blah blah blah," and I remember being absolutely horrified that he was using these objects to symbolise what had gone on. I was wondering why he had chosen to tell me the precise make of the car, the cost of the hotel, but of course it was a measure of how successful they were. It seemed gross and inhumane. I'm very practical about the need to earn money: I'm making a living, paying my bills; it's a means to an end, not to status.'

Susan understands how consumerism works so well partly because she used to work in advertising herself. She explained that Apple have persuaded purchasers of their computers that buying one will confirm their self-image as creative. It was the same when selling other products. 'You try to find a hook which might draw in someone on the verge of being interested, getting them to think, "Maybe that's for me." Hooks can be social acceptance, sometimes something about the actual product, sometimes the fantasy that "I am this kind of person and if I have that product I will be even more so."' We discussed the oddity of needing to invent a myth about creativity when a product really is better than its rivals, that rather than just saying 'it works better', advertisers have to pretend that it will confer identity.

Susan is largely immune to such illusions because she is so preoccupied with fulfilling basic needs for food and housing. But was it not an irony that, truly knowing what nonsense marketed identities are, she had spent so many years trying to persuade others to adopt them? 'I can sympathise with the consumer. I remember from a child what it felt like not to have the material symbols that other people had, and I desperately wanted them. I had charity clothes and they were a constant reminder that I could never be normal, and I really, really wanted to be. Now I know that it doesn't mean anything and I am more like I was as a very young kid, when it meant nothing, but I also still remember what it felt like to want something you can't have, a symbol of membership of a social group from which you are excluded.' 'So,' I said, 'in persuading others to lust after identity-conferring possessions, you were dealing with your childhood need for them?' She let out a loud laugh. 'I knew all about that desire for belonging through consumer symbols. It took me a while to realise that however much money you have, you will always increase your expectations of what you need to fit it. The goal will keep changing whether you get a hundred dollars a day or a hundred thousand. I realise now that it's vital to have a sense of what is enough.'

A New Yorker with authentic well-being might sound like a contradiction in terms, but Susan seemed to be that person, so I asked her if she had any other tips. 'I think the New Yorkers that introspect a lot are less happy. But there are things that help. One of my colleagues seems really aware that his life is drudgery and wonders if he should be doing painting, which is his first love. But he's also very religious, and that seems to give him some peace – it means he ultimately feels okay with his life. I'm not religious myself but I can see that it gives tremendous solace. I do yoga every day. It's the most fulfilling thing I do in my life because it's a spiritual thing for me. I don't care if there's a God, but I get a connection to something through doing it and am grumpy and off-balance if I don't. I do sometimes wonder if ignorance is bliss. Obviously, I don't mean avoiding the truth completely, but if you are not so aware of yourself you can just get on with living in the present, enjoying the moment that you have.' Since I do yoga every morning and rapidly become a paranoid, raging maniac on the very rare days I am not able to, I could hardly disagree.

Susan's tale illustrates the role played by childhood maltreatment in creating vulnerability to the Virus. At the simplest level it is learnt from parents, but it goes much deeper than that. Strongly materialistic people are often using money and possessions to give themselves a sense of the emotional security that they lack, dating back to childhood. They tend to have had parents who were cold, over-controlling, harshly punitive and discouraging. Where childhood love is conditional on performance – mum or dad only show affection if you are a winner – distress follows. Such children learn to look outwards for self-definition, and in very consumerist societies they are more vulnerable to the multiple messages telling them that they should use possessions and wealth to define their status. They may seek to stem their misery with quick-fix purchases, from cheap junk food to expensive status symbols. Another important factor is parental divorce and separation, to which the Virus-stricken are more prone than the uninfected. The increased materialism of the offspring of broken marriages is due primarily to the consequent decline in love and support rather than to any increase in the financial hardship that also often results. The Virus-infected have less intimate, less harmonious relationships which are shorter and less satisfying.

Susan's story is exemplary of the evidence that childhood experience can create or reduce vulnerability to the Virus. A strong sense of self from early infancy makes you more able to pick a way past the hazards thrown up by a turbulent childhood and, even in the face of considerable adversity, to seek out people who will give you what you need (Susan's mother-figure and her therapist). For the fair few of us whose sense of self is not so strong, Susan also offers clues about how to reduce the risk of infection. As you get older, you can become ever better at identifying toxins in the surrounding social ecology and activities to embrace, such as yoga or religion, which will help to immunise you against them. Perhaps Susan is able to enjoy her life most of all because she realises how lucky she is. It seems a terrible shame that one needs to have almost starved to fully appreciate food in the cupboard, or to have been on the verge of homelessness to be grateful for a roof over one's head, but the message could not be clearer: the next time you are irritable or miserable, thank God your needs are met at the most basic levels (as my mother said shortly before she died when my wife was describing her birth plan, 'Just be grateful if you and the baby are alive when it's over'), and try to see the falsehood of the wants which are probably upsetting you and which you are confusing with real needs.

However much variations in the way you are cared for as a child create vulnerability, if you do not live in a Virus-stricken society then it is much less likely that you will be infected. As Susan's insights into the advertising industry and television suggest, a great deal of the problem in America is created by artificially stimulated consumerism. This was rammed home to me when I met Consuela, aged twenty.

She arrives in a black dress and with a hangover, having been out clubbing until 6am. Originally of African descent, her parents were Ecuadoreans who moved to New York when she was eight because her dad (now deceased) was an important figure in their oil industry. Having recently graduated, she is working in public relations. She is friendly, warm and pretty. Listening to her, I am strongly reminded of the patois of the affluent young Manhattan women described in Jay McInerney's sharply observed novel *Story of My Life*. Its central character is a twenty-year-old girl who describes one potential suitor as 'a Petri dish for sexually transmitted diseases' and says that there are three big lies in life: "'I won't come in your mouth'; 'I'll call'; 'I love you'." McInerney's characters are hard-bitten and world-weary, and although Consuela avoids this bleakness a harsh realism accompanies her cheerful, laughter-punctuated presence.

Amongst Consuela's friends, Affluenza is ubiquitous. One of them is deemed happy; 'if she goes out she will change three or four times, to get the right image for where she's going; I do the same thing'. Then there's Sharon, who is definitely unhappy. 'She's very aggressive, ready to fight, very angry, walks around with a knife, looking for trouble. She's depressed but she doesn't know it. If we go to the beach she will always find something wrong, whine that there's no TV.' Another friend is only happy if she has a man, but she is not easily satisfied. 'She'll date guys and say, "I asked him to buy me this jacket and he wouldn't. It was only $500, what a loser," and then break up with him. I'll go, "You only went out with him last week, are you kidding me? Give the man a chance." She'll go, "But if he can't take care of me now, he's never going to take care of me."' Consuela shared a flat with another friend, who 'has self-esteem issues. I've never seen her without makeup, not going to the gym, not even for a shower.' This girl actively encourages strangers to catcall at her. 'When we're out as a group she'll deliberately walk behind so they pick her out, excited to get the attention, it doesn't matter who it is. I'll say, "We're supposed not to want to get harassed, remember?" She'll say, "Oh yeah, that's right." Actually, all my friends are only happy if they've got men. It's basically to validate them, tell them how pretty and great they are. They can't get it anywhere else, they must have it from men, constant reassurance. I've no idea why.'

I ask if it's common for them to want what they have not got and to be someone that they are not. 'We all suffer from that, big time,' Consuela admitted. 'Of course I do. I want to get back to when I was five, a huge house like my dad had, I want to be someone who is successful, I want kids, a happy home and a huge shopping fund. I love to get dressed up, I'm such a girly girl. Okay, I know it's always said that we're socialised into seeing our appearance as central to how every-one reacts to us, but it's actually true. If I'm walking down the street in jeans and a tee shirt there's no attention, they think, "She must be a home girl," whereas if I'm in my black dress it's "Hi, are you a model?" I'm happy with my appear-ance, I'm not a super-model – they're freaks anyway – but I'm skinny and not saggy.' None of the one hundred women I interviewed in other countries discussed their appearance in this commodified fashion.

What about her career? 'I'm going through my mid-life crisis now,' replied Consuela. 'I want to be successful in my field.' Looks play a crucial role in that success. When poten-tial clients come into her PR company's office, the staff, mainly female, young and pretty, and carefully selected from all the main ethnic groups to show the company's awareness of different categories of consumers, have to walk around the office and be noticed. 'We have a beauty bar so we can get dolled up. A hair stylist comes in, we select the right shoes, and we're told the day before the pitch what to wear, how to wear it. And it works. We just got an account worth $70 million that way. We're trying to get free coverage for clients in the media. If we can get into a teenage magazine that a particular beauty product is worn by a role model, the day after it's published they can measure exactly how many percentage points more they sold. It's amazing.' She says she finds the whole industry 'funny' and doesn't take it seriously, but she can see that it is potentially infectious. 'Some of the girls are always saying "It's so hard," but they don't really do anything. I think, "Shut up, stop complaining, get over yourself!" but I could become like that, which is the last thing I would want. Everybody there wants something from someone, they'll tell you whatever you want to hear. But I like PR now because I'm young and it's fun. I couldn't do it when I'm older.'

Consuela's father had many affairs and left her mother, a professional model, when she was pregnant with her. 'He was a horrible husband, horrible, yet the best dad in the world. He said, "I'm a good dad, but don't ever marry someone like me. Trust me, I know. I'm a horrible husband." He cheated on my mum with her best friend and he had a kid with his secretary. I think the opposite-sexed parent is very important. He used to joke, "I'll divorce my wife and be faithful to you." African men make really great dads and lousy husbands, it's part of the culture. They're spoilt, used to doing whatever they want.' Her mother never forgave her father. 'When he came to pick me up at home he was not allowed to come through the gate, never let back in the house again. A servant had to take me the last few yards. I could feel the tension between them, though she never spoke ill of him. I don't know if it really had an effect on me.' She has had three serious relationships and says, 'I guess I'm quick to cut men off, I don't take any nonsense. If I'm not happy, I'm done and I'm out. I don't take it personally like some girls. They cry and say "I really loved him," but I'm fine the next day, I act like it never really happened. I don't know if I repress it.'

I was having trouble getting a real feel for what Consuela's emotional life might be like. She seemed very honest, unmalicious and living in the present, yet she also seemed slightly troubled in her expression when in repose. A possible clue to her state of mind came when she pointed to some caged birds at the café where we met and said, 'They're really unhappy in there, it must be horrible for them, they're depressed.' She mentioned her dad again, saying, 'My fear is that I end up dating and then marrying someone like him.' She had mentioned that he had died whilst she was a teenager. I asked how he died and she replied, in a subdued voice, 'He was murdered when I was thirteen.' He was almost certainly killed by enemies he had made in Ecuador. Shot through the lung, he survived for eleven days, conscious but speechless. It must have been a terrible trauma, so how did she get through it? 'I was a mess. Time, going to church, got me through. I dealt with it little by little. I go to church on Sundays and try to go during the week. I've always felt protected by God and that it could be worse, even after my dad died. That's what always gets me through, that I don't understand it all and should be glad of what I've got. It's a huge solace. It means you have hope. For my friends there's none, just horrible, they don't look forward to things, or feel they could get better. Church gets you out of yourself, you're so renewed, so hopeful, disconnected from all the rubbish, and it challenges you to think of the big things.' So here was another case of religion inoculating someone against Affluenza: it was protecting Consuela from its depressing effect by encouraging satisfaction with what she had got.

Indeed, although Consuela works in a depressing industry in a depressing city, she has a well-conceived exit strategy. She hopes to have children in her mid- to late twenties and to move to Spain, where she has many relatives. Because she is bright, I fear she may have played down the extent of her Affluenza, realising the sort of things I was fishing for. I suspect that she is as dependent on the attraction and affection of men as are her friends, and that she is slightly more afflicted by shopping as a solace than she cared to let on. For instance, she let slip that one of her main hobbies is buying designer handbags at £300 a shot (she was carrying a Dior one when we met).

The single greatest carrier of the Virus to Consuela and her friends is the contents of American TV programmes, films and magazines, and the amount of time they spend consuming them. On average, Americans watch 50 per cent more TV than Danes, and two and a half times as many films; not surprisingly, the Danish are also less Virus-stricken. The Virus-stricken watch more TV, and heavy watchers are more likely to be dissatisfied with their lives than light ones. Asked to compare their lives to TV characters, they are more negative about the contrast. Relentless exposure to images of wealth and beauty spill over and poison their lives beyond the sitting room. Since programmes are saturated with exceptionally attractive people living abnormally opulent lives, expectations of what is 'normal' are raised – and every few minutes come the advertisements. As I pointed out earlier, advertising executives freely admit that one of their main objectives is to create a sense of dissatisfaction with existing possessions so that consumers will want to buy new, 'better' ones. In this they succeed, since heavy viewers are particularly at risk of developing a permanent sense of inadequacy, more so if they judge themselves by what they own (which they are more likely to do if they are the sort of person who watches a lot of TV). Television is also an important reason why Virus-stricken people have dangerously exaggerated ideas of what money and possessions can deliver, since its constant message is that Virus goals will make you happy. The self-critical Virus-stricken person is especially at risk of entering a vicious circle in which they attack themselves for not having 'enough' money or possessions, making them more insecure and liable to check out what others with more have, making them more self-critical, and so on.

Once, we used to keep up with Joneses who lived in our street. Now, thanks largely to TV, it's the Beckhams (or Melvyn Braggs or whatever other public figures we may compare ourselves with). In 1950, people read in the newspapers about the royal family, the aristocracy and film stars, and they watched Pathé newsreels of them before seeing the stars in the films. But it never occurred to the filmgoers that these people were anything like them or that they could ever live those kinds of lives. It would have been as unthinkable to have made a direct comparison between one's life and that of the Queen or John Wayne or Winston Churchill as it would be for Christians to compare themselves to God or Jesus Christ. Public figures were entities on a different plane, and the idea that the possessions (the Rolls Royces, fur coats, stately homes), status or fame could ever conceivably be theirs was not considered by ordinary people. Today, even the most talentless, unattractive and impoverished people hanker after such prizes. The process has been rapidly accelerated by so-called reality TV programmes such as *Big Brother* which purport to provide a democratic opportunity for anyone at all to become famous; and by memoirs of, and newspaper interviews with, famous people such as Victoria Beckham. She specifically exhorts girls to believe that if you have a dream and are prepared to work hard enough, you can be anyone or anything you want.

Depressed people make a greater number of social comparisons than the undepressed. Lacking self-esteem and confidence in their own adequacy, they spend more time checking out how they are doing relative to others. Even worse, they do so in more maladaptive ways: they choose hopelessly unrealistic upward comparison targets and attributes to compare with and fail to discount the difference by making allowances for amount of time spent practising, coaching from an early age, ability, and so forth. An undepressed average golfer, for example, can admire Tiger Woods without feeling belittled by his excellence and may be able to learn from watching him. A depressed golfer is liable to moan that they will never be able to play as well as him, a ridiculous upward comparison which leaves out all the reasons why he isn't as good as Tiger Woods. Likewise, there will be needless suffering for a women who compares their looks directly with Kate Moss or for schoolchildren who compare their school performances only with the best pupils.

A tendency towards upward social comparison is a defining feature of Virus psychology. Inevitably, someone for whom money, possessions, fame and appearances are a core value will show a keen interest in others with more or better of these, influencing the sort of magazines they read and the TV programmes they watch. By contrast, those who tend to make horizontal comparisons with people like themselves tend to be community-minded and Virus-free. This is extremely important, because not only do the Virus-stricken do more upward comparing, they are also more likely to select people to compare with who live vastly more opulent lives. The undepressed and Virus-free put themselves alongside others of equivalent income and affluence; the Virus-stricken seek to emulate inhabitants of another universe.

Many studies have demonstrated the cumulative effects of all this on our well-being. Beautiful models or actresses in ads and TV programmes have been shown many times over to lower women's satisfaction with their bodies and to depress their mood. At the same time, the models make men more dissatisfied with their current partner's appearance and the relationship they have with them.

Constant exposure to desirable people creates what is known as a contrast effect: you start judging normal people against the attractive ones. A clever proof of this was a study of rates of divorce amongst male American teachers at secondary schools and universities. They were higher than amongst men who teach in primary schools or kindergartens. Coming into daily contact with women at their most nubile and attractive was causing them to find their wives less desirable. In the same way, if you are male and afflicted by the Virus, you are that much more likely to watch large amounts of TV containing sexy women, setting up a contrast that is unfavourable to your partner.

The impact on rates of eating disorders of attractive media images of women has also been proved. An analysis of twenty-five different studies demonstrates that this is particularly so for girls under nineteen whose family histories make them already vulnerable. A particularly telling study was done in Fiji. Before 1995 there was no TV there, and a full female figure was the preferred cultural form. In that year no cases of self-induced vomiting (bulimia) were recorded, but within three years of the introduction of TV, 11 per cent of young women were bulimic. Bulimia was three times commoner amongst girls living in homes with TVs than in ones without. In the general population, dieting increased rapidly.

Equally, TV has played a direct and independent role in causing the epidemic of obesity sweeping the English-speaking world. A key American researcher summarised the evidence: 'The more TV children view, the more likely they are to be overweight. Reduction in TV viewing constitutes the single most effective way for children to lose weight.' One-third of American adults and one-quarter of their children are clinically obese – and TV is a major cause. It achieves this by a combination of discouraging exercise and encouraging, through adverts, the consumption of highly calorific food. It also lowers mood, which increases the likelihood of comfort eating ... often done in front of the telly. It is only a matter of time before the same cycle starts in populations which are currently slim. Take China, where TVs have recently become widespread. A study of 10,000 Chinese found that the more they watched TV, the more likely they were to be obese – every additional hour of watching added to the likelihood of getting fat. Greater affluence ends starvation, yet with it comes TV, which fosters self-starvation in some, obesity in others.

Regarding violence, it used to be thought that only those whose childhoods had made them prone to it would be more likely to be moved to violent acts by TV images. But it has recently been proved that TV has another, independent effect. Researchers who followed a large sample of Americans over a seventeen-year period found that the amount of time spent watching TV during adolescence and early adulthood *by itself* predicted who subsequently became violent. This was so even after you took into account other key predictors, like how aggressive they had been when small, whether they were maltreated by their parents and whether they came from a low-income family. As a cause of the massive rise in violence throughout the developed world (Switzerland and Japan excepted), TV is clearly a major one. Even increases in shoplifting and theft have been shown to be caused by TV. When the small screen became popular in America in the 1950s, there was a rise in theft that was in proportion to the number of homes in the population which had acquired a TV.

All of which suggests that if television had never been invented, crime rates in America would be lower, and the self-esteem and well-being of Consuela and her friends would be considerably higher. If that were all, those of us outside America could sympathise from a safe distance. Unfortunately, no such comfort is possible. Just as AIDS is stalking the globe, so is the Affluenza Virus.

Chapter 2

Global Infection

When I embarked on my journey, I feared that the world might have become a giant shopping mall, packed with Westernised retail outlets and goods (albeit manufactured in Asia) and populated by shoppers grazing in a consumerist haze. I was extremely relieved to find that it was not so. Although this has happened in some parts of the English-speaking world (Auckland, Sydney, Singapore, New York and London), reports of the death of national differences in the face of globalisation have been greatly exaggerated. In Moscow and Copenhagen they are not living the hazy half-life, and although consumption has its hands around the existential throats of the Shanghainese, there are very important respects in which they also diverge from English-speaking nations. But my fears were not completely misplaced, nor were the grounds for the reasoning that led to them: Selfish Capitalism spreads Affluenza; America is the apotheosis of Selfish Capitalism; the more Americanised the nation, the more Selfish Capitalist it will be and the more Affluenza-stricken.

Consider the spread of Starbucks coffee emporia. Russia and Denmark had no Starbucks at all, and they were still relatively rare in Shanghai. It was only in the cities of the English-speaking nations that specifically American consumerism, as exemplified by the appearance of Starbucks stores, had become almost ubiquitous, and likewise Virus values, reflecting more Selfish Capitalist governance. Of course, the numbers of stores in Russia and China are also a reflection of their level of wealth, but the same cannot be said of Denmark, which is nearly as rich as America. Apart from retail outlets, a further marker of Americanisation is goods from its culture. Take the amount spent in different nations on American sports clothing (tracksuits, baseball shirts, and so on) and equipment, and on American CDs and DVDs. In terms of sales of sports goods, even after allowing for differences in national wealth, Russia and China are much less Americanised than Australia, Singapore and New Zealand. Similar patterns are found for discs, with the Russians and Chinese ten times less likely to buy them than post-colonial nations. This is partly because of language barriers, but that does not explain why Danes also buy ten times less than the English-speakers – most Danes are fluent in English.

The most comprehensive study of globalisation so far was of twenty-two developing nations. It concluded that the more a nation is influenced specifically by America, as opposed to other developed nations, the more consumerist it becomes. These specific influences include American capital investment, exported products and tourists. However, there was still very considerable variation between the nations, depending on how easily they digested American values and products. These are proving extremely indigestible to the Russians and Danes, and the Chinese are very much picking and choosing from the menu.

Where I did find the Virus to be widespread was in the elites of all the nations I visited, except Denmark. In portraying the extent and form of global infection in this chapter I shall focus especially upon millionaires, although there are also many examples from the professional classes. Being enormously rich is something that most people would regard as highly desirable, even though they know from media stories that many rich people are miserable. If money engendered well-being, millionaires would be the most contented folk on the planet as well as the richest. The only studies to have specifically investigated this question, both American, suggest that this is not so. In the first, over one-third of a sample of super-rich people (those with a net wealth of £70 million or more) were less happy than the national average. The second study found no difference between the happiness levels of lottery winners and comparison samples of people with average incomes, or even of paraplegics. For this reason, I did my best to interview several millionaires in the nations I visited. That certainly paid off, for they provided me with some of the most telling illustrations of just how severely Affluenza interferes with enjoyment of life.

Britain

Almost a quarter of Britons suffer serious emotional distress, such as depression and anxiety, and another quarter are on the verge thereof. Put bluntly, half of us are in a bad way. Whilst there are many reasons for this, Affluenza is a significant one. Two-thirds of Britons believe that they cannot afford to buy everything they really need, which shows how widespread the confusion has become between wants and needs. Remarkably, nearly half of all people with annual incomes over £35,000 felt this was true of them, as did 40 per cent of those earning over £50,000. Men with this latter income were recently shown to be more prone to depression and anxiety than ones earning less. They were also by far the most desperate to get a better balance between life and work, perhaps because they are so chained to expensive lifestyles that it's all work and no play. The extent to which we have lost the consumption plot is brought home when you consider that nearly all of us now have a TV, video or DVD player, washing machine, central heating and telephone, much of this affluence having arrived only in the last thirty years, yet we still think we don't have enough to meet our 'needs'. We are also rapidly disappearing down the plughole of conspicuous consumption. Sales of luxury fever cars and domestic appliances (flashy fridges that do exactly the same job as basic ones costing a tenth of the price, wide-screen TVs, and so on) have mushroomed, as have sales of those most conspicuous of all purchases, new breasts or faces: around 2.5 million cosmetic surgery procedures were carried out in 2002, and a face-lift costs around £5,000. In terms of possessions, we accumulate so much stuff that we are finding that there is nowhere to put it: self-storage facilities have been growing by 30 per cent a year, and there are now three hundred such depots.

The extent to which consumerism and extreme wealth do not promote well-being in rich Brits was brought home to me when I met Sandy, an ex-army thirty-five-year-old. He has been personal assistant to the fathers of some hugely affluent families, most with assets of well over £100 million. Whilst the very wealthy might be reluctant to talk about their mental travails, their servants are sometimes willing to speak off the record. Sandy was interested in talking to me because he wanted to know why the super-rich he had encountered were mostly, as he put it, 'so unbelievably fucked up', and I have it from several independent sources – not just the friend of mine who put us in touch – that Sandy is a reliable witness. A serious hunk of a man, with the biceps and chest of a shot-putter, he was also emotionally sensitive, happily married with three children and quite distressed by the scenes he had witnessed. He began by telling me about Julia, the third wife of Jim, an entrepreneur in his late fifties.

Jim is 'a big, fat, cigar-smoking slob who has property, women and children all over the world'. Because Jim was often travelling abroad, Sandy was employed 'to make sure Julia didn't spend all his money, sleep with anyone or fire too many drugs into her body'. Just turned twenty-four, she was from a middle-class family, her father a lawyer. In appearance she was 'the classic blonde, big chest, something to squeeze, although she wasn't stupid, good head on her shoulders. Her sisters were just as beautiful, but she was seen as the big success in the family because of all the money. They were terribly dysfunctional too, but that's another story.'

Keeping Julia on the straight and narrow proved a major challenge for Sandy. She took a lot of cocaine and drank heavily, so that he frequently had to carry her home and put her to bed. 'I had to enforce the husband's law, so I had to get rid of any guys who she might have got involved with. I was constantly watching like a hawk. If she went to the loo in a nightclub I would check that it wasn't with a guy, and if one seemed to be following I'd warn him off. I would go through her clothes, her jeans, her address book, to check what she was up to. If the husband had ever found a number we'd both have been in the shit.' Julia's life consisted of shopping, taking drugs and going to clubs. 'In the morning I would ask, "What's the plan today?" She'd want to go shopping, ask me to phone some of her friends, fix a car to pick them up, close a whole shop down and they would buy whatever they wanted there. I'd carry all the cards and the cash, and give the owner a couple of thousand for letting us have it to ourselves.'

At first, imposing Jim's Law caused major friction with Julia. 'We used to physically fight, especially when she and her friends were craving some coke. At the end of the night I sometimes had to defend myself.' Jim was one scary man, and his relationship with Julia was, to say the least, uncongenial. 'There was no love, she was his plaything – and you've got to remember he had the same in quite a few other countries.' What she hated most was having to sleep with him and the abuse, sometimes physical. 'There'd be bruises, scratches on her arm. She was also there for his friends to cop a squeeze. Once I was outside a room in London and towards the end of the evening she disappeared to a room with one of his friends. I was outside the door, and they weren't screams of pleasure she was making. You could call it rape. Afterwards, her makeup was running and she'd been crying. She said she could not stop him because she had too much to lose.' If she complained, Jim might throw her out. 'He was perfectly happy about her being used in that way. No wonder she wanted to get off her face and spend his money.' Jim also used to humiliate her in front of his friends. 'He'd like making her feel younger than she was. A lot of his friends were older, with seriously glamorous, high-powered wives, and he would enjoy putting her on the spot.'

Sandy got to know Julia well. 'On a number of occasions she would be in floods of tears. Jim would be away, and I'd ask, "What's the problem – you don't have to sleep with him, to touch him now, you've got everything." But she'd say, "What life do I have?" I pointed to the luxurious apartment and said, "Well, look what you've got." On one occasion she went to a Porsche dealer and bought one there and then. She didn't have a driving licence so I had to drive it back. I asked "Why did you do that?", and she said "Because I can. I hate him, I'm not happy and I've got the money."' I asked Sandy why she hadn't simply left Jim, and his answer was sinister: 'He would threaten her with violence. It's very easy for powerful, rich people to play mind-games with you. Women like her come across as very confident but they're not really, they're scared and feeble. I wouldn't put it past him to actually kill her, because of his friends – even I would be nervous about leaving him on bad terms. I've met two professional hit-men in London and I believe their claims that the M25 is full of gangland bodies. Jim's easily nasty and mad enough to employ someone to do something awful. She'd be bagged up and disappear for eight or ten grand at the most. Her friends and family would want to know where she is, but she could be in another country, and it might be a long time before anyone realised she was really missing.'

Sandy's next story concerned Ian, an outwardly very congenial family man in his late forties, from a public school background, albeit now on his fourth marriage with the inevitably much younger wife and, in this case, two small children. 'To begin with I thought he was a lovely person, very down to earth, normal, clever, hard-working.' The first time Jim twigged that this was not the whole story was when he arrived slightly early one morning at Ian's country estate. 'A young lady of Spanish or Brazilian appearance was being bundled into a Range Rover to be taken back to London. He just said, "Uh, she's a friend who's been over." But I soon got to know that she would have been some girl he'd picked up – not a prostitute, but perhaps from a strip club. Money's thrown at them, they get whisked here and there, flown around the world, but not actually paid, as such. There would be parties at the country house, and after his wife'd gone to bed, he'd be outside having sex. Then his friends would get involved.' Sandy was no feminist, but even he disliked Ian's attitude to women. 'It's very sleazy, slimy, I was shocked. Once I told him about a man who had spat at his wife and he said, "I'd have done the same, the bitch is taking all his money." It's that "She's a woman, she's only good for one thing." The women'd be invited to a party for two reasons only, as eye candy and a squeeze at the end.'

These women and Ian seemed to inhabit a grey social area centred on London nightclubs such as Tramps and

Stringfellows. 'It was a power thing to fill his Roller up with girls from there, go home to his London pad and share them with his friends. That would be Friday night, but come Saturday morning he'd be in the country being the family man, making scrambled eggs, holding his kids. Very deceiving, upsetting, because I liked his wife. It felt like I was cheating on her, knowing about his other life. She'd be devastated if she knew. I wanted to help, but how do you help a man with £100 million? Boy, was he playing with fire. But I can't work out why he'd risk losing all that. He never talked about being unhappy, but it was obvious he was. He had a lot of stress, ulcers, bowel trouble, body failing – not happy.'

Sandy's final example of life with multi-millionaires was an utterly chaotic family. 'The first time I went into their enormous house, I thought I had entered a bombsite. There were so many people sitting round the kitchen table I didn't know who was the owner, the wife, the nanny. I could smell marijuana and they offered me a joint. When I got to know them, it was like *One Flew Over The Cuckoo's Nest*. You've got the dysfunctional stepson who's hiding away; he won't look at you, scruffy clothes, smoked too much dope, sleeps all day, never at night, a fruitbat. Then you've got the beautiful little fairy daughter, she's probably going to be a model, skipping round singing, with the younger son firing catapults at you, breaking windows. You've got the older fourteen-year-old stepdaughter, who's jealous of all this and has a severe eating disorder, totally fucked up. I worked with her and now she's in a hospital on a drip. She couldn't get out of bed. I had to teach her how to walk, had to teach her to get her bloody jaw moving so she could speak. I remember looking at this girl, very beautiful, very bright, used to be a talented dancer and actor, and thinking it was just insane. She had every kind of help – flown to the States, taken to Harley Street. I remember thinking, "The problem is that the world you live in is fucked. You can go and see every shrink and it won't make any difference, it's that family that's got to change." The mother's been in the Priory twice for drugs. How can you expect your daughter to get out of bed if you don't until midday? They depend on their hired help so much that they can't deal with their kids. We are their lifeline. The husband just comes and goes, here, there and everywhere; the mother doesn't look after them, they pay others to do everything. There's a United Nations of cooks, his and hers PAs, nannies, gardeners, every kind of alternative therapist. It was far too upsetting, I had to get out.'

Having met quite a few very wealthy people in my time, I know that the families Sandy described are extreme examples. Most are nothing like as dysfunctional as them, although I am confident that their huge wealth does nothing to improve their emotional well-being, and in some cases has probably reduced it, especially if inherited. The point is that the rich have everything they want, yet significant numbers are miserable because their needs are not met. Our principal goals, nationally and individually, are to be richer, yet once we have achieved a basic level of affluence, this will do little to make us emotionally better. The key is not how rich you are, but how Virus-ridden are your values.

Australia

In recent years Australia has become heavily infected with the Virus, especially in Sydney, and distress has increased considerably in recent years. Over a fifth of Australians are now emotionally distressed. Between 1997 and 2001, according to studies of two nationally representative samples, the prevalence rose by half. Intriguingly, the authors of the second study dismissed the increase as resulting from a greater awareness of emotional distress and an increase in available treatments. They gave no consideration to an alternative explanation: that during those five years, Australians have been widely exposed to the Affluenza Virus by Selfish Capitalism, which grew substantially in that period.

Two-thirds of Aussies now say that they cannot afford to buy everything they really need. Amazingly, nearly half of top earners are confusing wants with needs in this way. As in Britain, luxury purchases have increased rapidly, from cosmetic surgery to yachts to flashy cars. Infection with these values accelerated at precisely the time when rates of psychological distress grew. Nowhere has that been truer than in Sydney, which has become hugely affluent compared with the rest of the country, with rocketing property prices and all too conspicuous consumption (Ferraris, and so on). Whilst I was there, I met a particularly vivid example.

It was Easter weekend. Sydney drowsed beneath a hot autumnal sun and the roads were clear, presumably because most people had headed for the beach. Nonetheless, Will, a multi-millionaire businessman who, incongruously, also works as a psychiatrist often treating what he calls the Worried Well (i.e. patients without a full-blown mental illness who are unhappy or anxious), was eager to meet up even though everyone else was on holiday.

Will is in his mid-thirties, small in stature and dark-haired, and of Italian blood – his ancestors were Sicilian Mafiosi. He lives in an opulent house overlooking Sydney Harbour and drives a gold Range Rover. Speaking very fast and occasionally running his words together and murmuring, he began, 'I'm a psychiatrist who's got a practice just up the hill and I'm a businessman who's a High Net Worth Individual [i.e. rich]. I've been obscenely wealthy but lost it all and then made it again, up and down.' Being up and down was to be a persistent theme in his account of himself.

Before long we were engaged in a potentially fractious debate about the relative contributions of nature and nurture in causing emotional distress. Will was emphatic in his view. 'Depression is a genetic, biological disorder, like asthma … it is not related to upbringing, not related to wealth, to money, to comfort, to your love life, to stressors, it's nothing to do with any of that.' Having not exactly got off on the right foot, and all too aware of my own partiality for disputation, I frantically tried, and eventually succeeded, in moving him on to the subject of happiness and wealth. 'I made a lot of money after being a medical student, but in 1996 a crooked colleague bankrupted me. My money was pretty well reduced to zero, for two or three years. In terms of my moods, there was anticipatory anxiety during my bankruptcy proceedings. I was thinking, "What will this do to me?" But it was largely minimal, made me depressed in my mood, but not very, no disturbed sleeping pattern, or reduced energy, libido, it only made me unhappy on an hour-to-hour basis.'

I wondered if Will's sense of personal value had become linked to his financial one. 'I don't think my feelings of self-worth had got connected to owning a certain sort of car. But I think your sense of self-identity does shift if you are rich, there's no doubt about that. It moves, attached to your possessions. I had periods when I thought it was my fault that I had lost the money, even though it was due to the bank collapsing. When you had those thoughts you'd feel sad maybe, but they were inaccurate thoughts so I could master them. In terms of minor depression or anxiety, I believe that "what you think is what you feel" is very true. I teach it in my therapy, I believe in it, use it myself. I rigidly and fastidiously try to prevent myself sitting on negative thoughts. It's like hygiene. The two things I do to try and retain my dignity and well-being are: one, I don't allow myself to sit on negative thoughts for very long, not for more than a few minutes; two, I try and remain active, do lots of sport, outings, things that keep me occupied.'

I asked Will if he had suffered negativity in his childhood. 'Since early in my life I've been slightly hyperactive, slightly hyperkinetic, slightly speedy,' he replied. 'I find if I slow down it's not a pleasant state. I actively stay active. I don't like the notion of relaxation and peace, don't feel comfortable sitting around, don't like going on holidays, going to resorts, I like "full on".' His mother died when he was fifteen; his father was a farmer. 'My upbringing was characterised by my father: sport and a lot of activities. We used to go surfing, beaches, camping, sailing, all that. Not an academic life at all.' However, despite this stereotypically anti-intellectual Aussie upbringing, he trained as a doctor. He had five siblings, none of whom went down a similar path, but when I asked why he had chosen a different one, he seemed at a loss. 'I don't know – genetic, endowed with a good memory? Actually I wasn't interested in medicine, it was haute cuisine, but then I got a good enough pass to do medicine, so I did that to keep Mum's memory sweet.' This sounded like the classic picture of the kind of childhood that creates vulnerability to the Virus. Eschewing the subject that really interested him, one that might have provided pleasure through the doing of it rather than motivated by rewards and praise, he chose one to please a parent. Before I could pursue the matter he asked, 'So is this a biography of me or ... this is for your book, right?' Worried that he might become anxious about my motives, I changed the subject.

Further signs of the Virus emerged when Will told me about his attitude to his working life. 'I work eighteen hours a day, get up at five in the morning and go surfing or running with a whole bunch of guys, half colleagues, half businessmen. I surf or run from six to eight and it's a lot of fun, but to me it's work. My accountant goes, my banker goes, all sorts of buddies go who may or may not be colleagues, but it's work for me. And then you do your practice all day, you have lunch with someone, you do dinner with someone, drinks with someone, and you don't stop working until you go to bed.' As happened frequently in our conversation, when referring to himself he swerved between 'I' or 'me' and the second-person, 'you'. I asked if it was hard to keep friendship and work apart. 'Friends and colleagues are all merged together in the sense that some you don't recognise are going to be a colleague. You don't circle around them like a shark trying to entertain them, but your whole persona is work-oriented. So when you go out for drinks with someone, the next week you might be going to see them in the bank, get some broking advice or doing a float [of a commercial corporation] or something, so you end up with your working life and social life almost merging. Maybe there's a twenty-year-old you go surfing with and you might give them some money to sponsor a trip to Europe, and you might find that five years later they are working in a merchant bank and can be of use. [This seemed a bit strange – that he would give money to unrelated people for their holidays.] You're cognisant of that, obviously. It's not "networking", a pejorative term, but it is part of the bigger picture of you always being at work, and I'm [note the switch here from you to I] always aware of that except when I go away on holiday, which I hardly ever do.'

I wondered what the goal of all this work was. 'Very good question. "What are you trying to achieve?" people often enquire. If you go and see some wise old soul for therapy, they ask, "So what's motivating you?" I can't explain it, except I never say what they want to hear, which is "I want to get rich and powerful" – it's not really that at all. I think it's related to arousal, my whole life is down to that: my sex life, my sporting life, my recreations, my business life, my psychiatric work. I don't like seeing people in one-to-one talking therapies. [He meant both that he does not like going for long-term therapy himself and that he does not like having patients of his own who come for years on end.] I get bored, restless, fancy a change. I don't like being a passive investor in a company, I don't like stockmarket shares. I want everything in my life to be geared to arousal: surfing, go-kart racing. I prefer my archaic midbrain rather than my frontal lobes. If I go round a corner in my car I like to do it fast, arousal – that's not the way you're brought up, you know what I mean? It's this issue of whether a person is suffering attention deficit hyperactive disorder [ADHD] or bipolar disorder [large swings in mood].'

I was not sure whether Will was talking about himself now, since he regards himself as 'slightly hyperactive'. I asked, 'You mean whether a state that could be pathological gets channelled into something healthy, a sublimation?' This proved inadvisable, returning us to our nature–nurture dispute, and he reiterated his previous view: 'The era of nurture is long gone. If you still believe that the way you're brought up as a child influences your adult life, you're way out of date'. I countered that there is a large body of evidence proving the impact of parental care on subsequent emotional well-being, and he promptly performed an astonishing intellectual back-flip, without the slightest sign of being aware that he was contradicting himself: 'Well I don't disagree with that at all. To me it's vital, the care of the child when very young ... I totally agree with you if you're saying that you need mirroring from your mother in early life, to have your needs understood and responded to ... can we stop and adjourn, we're getting close to agreement, we probably agree about a lot of things?'

Very suddenly, the interview was ended. Now affability itself, Will arranged to meet me the following week to continue the discussion in his car on the way to visit a patient. Clutching a bottle of champagne, he headed off at speed towards his yacht.

What are we to make of this eccentric man? You may dismiss him as weird, but on the surface he seems normal, highly successful in his careers, and married with two small children. His self-diagnosis is hyperactivity or tendency to mood swings; I believe that he perfectly illustrates the rise of Erich Fromm's Marketing Character in Sydney during the last decade.

Marketing Characters experience themselves as commodities whose value and meaning are externally determined. Fromm believed that although capitalism has increased our economic and political freedom, few of us have been able to take advantage of this and fulfil our unique potentialities (one of his books had the title *Fear of Freedom*). Because most people lack identity and find it too painful to face up to the basic questions of life, like 'Who am I?' and 'What am I for?', consumerism has found it easy to offer distractions and false individualism, supplied by possessions. People differentiate one another by what they own, not who they are, by Having rather than Being. The self of this *Homo consumens* is experienced as a thing, to be bought and sold just like a car or house.

It so happens that the first studies to test this specific theory were done in Australia, and published in 2000. They revealed the Marketing Character as having the following traits: eager to consume, wasteful of goods, disposing and replacing them frequently; having conventional tastes and views; uncritical of themselves or society, un-insightful; agreeing with the statement 'having makes me more'; a tendency to publicise and promote themselves; experiencing themselves as a commodity whose value is determined by possessions and the opinions of others; and with values portrayed in television advertisements. The studies found that people with a Marketing Character were more prone to be materialistic, authoritarian, conformist, unconcerned about ecology, expressive of anger, anxious and depressive. Business students were more likely than arts students to be like this.

A subsequent study showed that Marketing Characters place little value on beauty, freedom or inner harmony. Their main pursuits are social recognition, comfort and having an exciting life. They are extremely individualistic in their values and do not regard social equality as desirable. They compare themselves obsessively and enviously with others, always hoping to have more and better things than others, believing inequality to be man's natural state. As one observer puts it, for them 'things, experience, time and life itself are seen as possessions to be acquired and retained'.

However much Will may claim that he is not motivated by money, his need to possess high-status consumer goods is all too visible (his yacht, his Porsche). He might counter that it is their design, beauty or efficiency that made him choose them, but if he did I would be sceptical. Even if he is not primarily motivated by money in working his eighteen-hour day, there is no doubt that he defines himself wholly through his work, and that he is eager to live in the public eye. He mentioned no relationships in his life that are not in some sense professional. Other people are indeed commodities or pawns who exist purely as potential sources of further income, even when he engages in seemingly altruistic acts, like sponsored runs or financing young people's travels. His ideas about psychiatry are conformist, with little sign that he has really thought them through for himself. Will has adopted a very strict reading of

Positive Psychology to help keep his nose to the grindstone and ward off the intense feelings of loneliness and desperation that such a materialistic life might create, for he does not show any sign of having had truly intimate relationships. One clue to this is his need to be with people at all times and his discomfort if there is no external competitive challenge, like when he is lying on the beach. Perhaps most telling of all, when asked what he hopes to achieve by working all his waking hours, he seems to have no idea at all. This is the uncritical state in which the life of the mind plays little part and emotion is regarded as dangerous, to be caged through 'rigid and fastidious' thought-control. Whatever the truth of these speculations, there is a broader question as well.

In Fromm's Marketing Society the consumer must be permanently dissatisfied, or gratified only for the shortest possible time. Satisfaction would stop consumption, which would stall economic growth. This society needs people with an exaggerated sense of the importance of work, a false need for things and an endless desire to consume, no deep feelings or convictions, standardised tastes, suggestibility and uncritical minds. In many commentators' views, this sums up America, the nation that most heavily influences Australia.

Rather ironically, on returning to my apartment after the interview with Will, the following email awaited me:

Dear Oliver,

We are interested in using you in some upcoming TV commercials for our client, Bloggs [a car company – not its actual name, of course].

You would be featured visually as well as used as in the
voiceover. The general brief for the idea is ... we as individuals are able to make our own decisions without the influence
of flashy advertising or luxurious brands.

Caption: Bloggs – move on.

I would love to hear your feedback by tomorrow afternoon
...

Since I have railed against advertising in various media for
ten years, it would have been impossible for me to take part
in this plan. Nonetheless, I made some enquiries, and it
seemed that I would be paid a minimum of £50,000 for very
little work if I did it, and that it was more likely to be
£100,000. Whilst it would be nice to be able to use this
money to pay off some of our mortgage, it would be out of
the question for me to lend my implicit support to advertising, even if the campaign was a savage attack on the whole
genre. Intrigued to learn how they imagined I could be of use
to them, I asked to see some scripts. An example appeared a
few days later:

We open in a smart restaurant. Our spokesperson
[i.e. me] sits with some friends waiting for their
food. The meals arrive.

Our spokesperson has a sandwich and they have steaks
and racks of lamb, beautiful elaborate meals.

```
            Spokesperson [me]
        Envy is not a positive emotion and yet
        without it humans would probably never
        have come down from the trees.


Our spokesperson beckons the waiter over.


            Spokesperson
        We stop envying something the moment we
        realise we can have it.


We cut to the Bloggs range of cars.


CAPTION: The Bloggs range, from £6,995


CAPTION: Bloggs. Clear thinking.
```

A prime example of how the Marketing Society nurtures the Marketing Character? The spokesperson's initial claim reinforces the idea that wanting the possessions of others is what has led us to evolve as a species, and is inevitable and ultimately healthy, albeit not a positive emotion. Presumably satisfied with the idea of a sandwich when the food was ordered, the spokesperson is stimulated by the lavish meals of his peers to trade up to a 'better' one. The implication is that the best way to overcome envy is to obtain the possessions that are envied. That it might be better to stick with what you really wanted is rejected, as is the possibility that it does not matter what others have.

Shortly afterwards, before I had contacted the company

to let them know that I could not participate, another email arrived:

Dear Oliver,

Many thanks for this email the other day.

I am afraid to say that Bloggs have decided to review the route that would have involved you. At the moment they are looking to pursue an alternative route that does not involve a personality. Many many thanks for your enthusiasm on this and I hope another project will come up in future that we can work on together.

A major flaw in this wheeze seemed to me to be that whilst I do like to think I have a personality, I am not A Personality. I do not think of or talk of myself as a commodity, although it is interesting that some famous people do actually refer to themselves by their names, as if speaking of a product. For example, instead of saying 'I', Kevin Keegan will say 'Kevin Keegan does not let his team roll over and allow the opposition to win' (this is not dissimilar to Will's flipping between 'I' and 'you' when referring to himself – perhaps the flips are from himself as an existential being to himself the commodity). But if I were A Personality, a famous name and visage, that commodity could be bought for £50,000 to £100,000, just like a Bloggs comes 'from £6,995'.

When Will and I reconvened a few days later, I was feeling mildly nervous as I hopped into his gold Range Rover, thinking of his penchant for going fast around corners. Once we had got onto the motorway he said, 'I'll tell you what I think is interesting. I'm writing a paper about it at the moment: subclinical bipolar disorder [i.e. big swings in mood between ecstatic excitement and deep depression within a day]. You might feel fantastic in the afternoon but down in the dumps in the evening. The next day you might wake up feeling great, expansive and talkative, but two hours later you feel miserable. Next day you might feel up again, be a bit uninhibited, say a bit more than you should, stay like that for a few days, then down again.' His use of 'you' to describe such people made me wonder if he was talking about his Marketing self – why did he not speak of 'they'?

During this speech, Will had pulled the car over to the side of the motorway on a quite sharp bend in the road, coming to rest almost on the grass. Lorries and cars thundered past. 'So that's pretty cool, a pretty hot area. The other area is adult ADHD, states of increased arousal [the words he had used last time to sum himself up]: when are you just highly aroused, revved up, versus when do you have a condition, adult ADHD, a brain disorder?' Whilst saying this he had opened his door and now he got out and opened the boot to get a map. Although pretty fearless myself when it comes to bad driving, I could not help recalling that a large proportion of motorway deaths involve stationary cars on the hard shoulder.

Will continued to talk whilst consulting his map. 'It's this issue of …' then, in a very rapid burst of words, 'when is a speedy person, a revved up, hyped up individual disordered or when are they just a person? When does it get to a level that it's a treatable condition? I think that's very topical.' It certainly was for me at that moment on the bend of that motorway. He suddenly chucked the map onto the dashboard and accelerated out into the traffic. 'I get a lot of ADHD adults. I get a lot of famous people who have been full-on, cranked up, highly productive, highly motivated people. [This was spoken in what might be called verbal onomatopoeia – illustrating what he meant by the manner of its delivery; that impression was enhanced by the rapidity with which we sped past the other cars on the road at twice the speed limit.] I see them when they are suddenly exhausted or bored and asking, "What the hell is going on?" They run on no sleep, are often very uninhibited, very grandiose, very expansive. Most people with these symptoms are unsuccessful but a few harness their hyperactivity to make them very productive and do very well. It makes them what they are, charismatic, quite stimulating, very popular, centre of the crowd, fantastic sales person, always asked everywhere.'

I asked whether the drug Ritalin, the pill usually given to children with this diagnosis, would make them less hyperactive. Will said, 'You wouldn't want to take that away from adults by giving them Ritalin, it's what makes them what they are. I've got a girl patient at the moment, she's twenty-eight, a beautiful creature, she's got it really badly. She can't hold down a job because she's so hyperactive, always rushing around, always late, quite unreliable, doesn't get up on time. When she gets there she talks punchy, a bit too fast, gets a bit uninhibited, all that sort of stuff. You think to yourself, "She might have undiagnosed subclinical bipolar disorder." She's never been hospitalised, never been grossly depressed or technically manic, but her day is dictated by her moods: she is a bit up and down, she gets really sad, next day she's fantastic. But now I'm thinking more and more it might be ADHD. Does Ritalin work with adults? Yeah, it works fantastic but at a cost because it changes personality.'

By now we had left the motorway and seemed to be lost. I asked, 'Do you want to break off for a moment?' but Will continued speaking as if he hadn't heard me. 'You can treat it. This girl would be a candidate for Ritalin. Life's not going well for her, she's from a wealthy family who semi-disown her for seeming too mad.' Then he said, 'Whereas for someone like me, at my age in my life, it might make me less speedy, less driven, but it also would take away the essence of me. Dynamic, busy, overactive, lots of different things each day. It's how it is, would you do it? [i.e. if he were one of his patients, would he prescribe Ritalin to himself]. No, probably not. So for a lot of people who are quite successful in life, I just like to manage them, keep them ticking over.'

I decided to try to discover who Will was really talking about – how much did all this apply to him? 'Yeah, I certainly think that I'm at that end of the spectrum, not calm and quiet, annoyingly. I wish I was.' 'You could take Ritalin,' I suggested, 'but then that would be the "essence" of you gone, as you said?' 'I think so, yes,' he replied, firmly and clearly enunciated, as if he was giving it very serious thought. Then, running the words together and speaking so quietly that I had to listen to the recording afterwards many times to make it out, he said, 'I've never worked out whether my personality is mood-driven or not.' He was now lost, in every sense; but regarding our geographical location, I consulted the map and we eventually arrived at our destination (a psychoanalyst might interpret these exchanges as suggesting that he was searching for a clear understanding of who he is, trying to use me to help him find his way, a map-reader).

When we left an hour later, Will seemed rather subdued – his patient was at death's door. As we left the car park he began, 'Now, where were we? Let's get back to it, change the subject, because that was pretty depressing.' At that moment, for the first time since we had met, I felt that he had actually noticed I was really there. I mean that, until now, he seemed to have been relating to me only as someone who held various theories which he found threatening or irritating or wrong, and trying to manipulate my perception of him by hopping about between them, sometimes disagreeing, sometimes pretending to hold my theories himself, sometimes actually adopting them and believing they were his. At other times he seemed to be relating to me as a quasi-therapist, trying to work out who he is by using me as a sounding board or psychological map-reader. Above all, his default position for speaking with me seemed to be to regard me as a 'journalist', someone who was going to represent him to the general public through a newspaper article, just another of the pawns in his eighteen-hour working day to be used to further his goals. But as we set off back down the motorway, he seemed to wake up to the fact that I was a person writing a book. 'So what's your hypothesis,' he asked, 'that money doesn't make you happy?' At least briefly, he really did seem to want to know what I was doing there, from my standpoint.

It soon emerged that Will hadn't thought about this at all. I suggested that modern life makes people who are vulnerable to anxiety or depression (whether because of their genes or their childhoods or both) more at risk of suffering these problems. I put it to him that affluent female Sydneysiders who were at risk of feeling negative about their bodily shape would be more so because of the pressure to be a babe. For the ADHD or bipolar person, the pace of life had hugely increased (oddly enough, that very day there was a newspaper report of a study showing that children who watch TV for two hours a day before the age of three are much more likely to be diagnosed as hyperactive at the age of seven). I suggested that the huge increase in the gap between rich and poor in Australia in general, but most conspicuously in Sydney, with its Range Rover-driving millionaires, is a problem because everyone is told that they too can be rich if they work hard enough. Whereas in 1950 poor people regarded the rich and famous as remote figures who had nothing to do with them, now the press and, above all, television, make these people's lifestyles visibly accessible, and modern values encourage them to believe that they too could be rich. Money seems to have become the main way in which middle-class Sydneysiders evaluate each other's status, and there is strong evidence that such materialism tends to corrode intimate relationships and contributes to the collapse of the sense of community. Finally, I pointed to the dramatic rise in property prices. Many young people I had spoken to, already shackled by large debts from paying their way through university (half of Australian students do paid jobs for more than twenty hours a week), doubt they will ever be able to afford a house. With the older generations, the necessity of paying the mortgage often forces them to work long hours at jobs they do not find fulfilling, damaging their marriages and reducing the amount of time available to be with their children.

Will listened lugubriously to all this, occasionally making interjections which suggested that he couldn't really see what I was driving at. He had heard of an Australian survey which had asked people of various incomes how much more they would need to be happier. Whether they were earning £20,000, £200,000 or £2,000,000, the respondents all said that it would take one-third more, proving that we move the goalposts regardless of how much we have. But Will said that his patients did not talk about these things. If they had a disease, these factors were nothing to do with its cause and if they were Worried Well, the cause was some reverse in their life, like a divorce or being sacked, not any wider malaise. If they thought that 'I'm fat, I'm lazy, I'm stupid' when they were not, it would mean that they had the disease of depression. 'You wouldn't be well if you were having those thought-schemas,' he said. 'They take a toll, they do on me. If I was to let myself have those thoughts I would get depressed.' This was a rare reference to his depressive side. Presumably he does not talk about it much because 'rigid and fastidious' patrolling of such thoughts would forbid it.

In Will's view, patients were either diseased or they had suffered a reverse, got depressed and the negative thinking followed. I suggested that what is defined as a reverse might have changed since 1950 (extended to include not being able to afford a swankier house, not having a beautiful body) because expectations have risen. His responses were not combative or hostile – he simply did not understand how these very broad trends could influence the course of 'a disease', nor cause being Worried Well, in an individual case.

We were fast approaching the city centre, and I still had not asked Will about his business career. It had begun when he was aged nineteen and at university, when he started a restaurant. When asked about the more recent money-making which has led to his substantial wealth, he reverted to hushed, jumbled diction mode. 'I buy sites all over the country and get their usage reassigned so that I can build hotel complexes. I buy a home or land owned by private individuals and try and get it rezoned so that hotels can be built. Another company I own builds them; my key skill is in knowing the council officers and politicians [who do the rezoning] and also in finding the individuals who own the land and persuading them to sell it. Most people are risk-averse, I'm the opposite. There's not too many people who want to buy it before I've got it rezoned. It suits me to be in the niche between the private individuals and the people who do the rezone classification.'

I presume that this Will, the wheeler-dealer Marketing Character who makes millions, saw me primarily as a source of publicity for his business activities, although such characters also enjoy being in the public eye just for the sake of it. This Will had exploited his persona as Will the psychiatrist and quasi-scientist to present himself as an authoritative figure who dispenses wisdom to the Worried Well. Then there had been Will the troubled person, someone who is not sure if he has a 'disease', which disease it is and what to do about it.

It would be facile to ask which is the real Will: is the Marketing Character more real than the psychiatrist or the troubled person? Clearly, his mood swings are often a problem to him throughout the day. His wired, manic defence leaves him tired and unsatisfied – but then being depressed would not be much fun either. A psychoanalyst would argue that this incapacity to confront his depression is what fuels his manic or hyperactive or speedy or whatever-you-want-to-call-it side, that this perpetual action is a defence against depression. His work as a psychiatrist is frustrating because however well he 'manages' his patients, he does not get better, even if they do. Being the Marketing Character probably gives him the greatest satisfaction because he gets quick hits of excitement and boosts to his (probably very low) self-esteem, even when deals go wrong (such entrepreneurs love a challenge). He is also living at a time and in a social place where the Marketing Character seems the only option, a sense that There Is No Alternative. I put it to him that there might be large differences between Sydney and less competitive regions of Australia, that the yuppy chasing of gold in Sydney was now all-important. He baulked at the word 'yuppy', rightly pointing to its pejorative connotations: 'What is a yuppy except someone who is socially mobile upwards? We're all yuppies in that sense, always have been, what else is there? You're in the system chasing success, that's what motivates all of us, always.' As far as this book is concerned, that blinkered conviction (often served with lavish helpings of evolutionary psychology) is close to the heart of the matter.

I tried raising some alternatives to upward mobility as a goal. I reminded him that he sees his whole waking life as work, except his rare and brief holidays. We were getting near Will's house now, so I asked him about the most obvious alternative to achievement, something he had not mentioned yet at all: his family life. The Marketing Machiavel clicked in. Seamlessly and charmingly, he did his best to rezone the subject three times, but I eventually pinned him down to having had a childless first marriage and four children from his present marriage, the oldest aged seven. He said he was keen to have more, his wife less so. But that was all I managed to find out, nothing about his feelings for these people. So my final question as we turned into the road opposite the entrance to his house, was this: 'Presumably you don't regard your relationship with your family as work. How would you characterise your intimate relationships as different from that?' He thought for a bit, struggling to find the right words. 'Umm, you love your wife, children, your brothers.' This was said just as the car came to a standstill: saved by the bell. With a wide smile of relief, he said, 'Well I hope you got enough data there. I'll look forward to reading it, send me a copy. I should read your books.' Next, please.

That Will is both a psychiatrist and a millionaire hotelier neatly combines two key elements of Sydney's current malaise. Greater focus on share price, deregulation of Australia's economy and other Selfish Capitalist developments since the 1990s enable him to pursue his rezoning property career more easily. It may also explain the sharp rise in emotional distress since 1997. But of particular interest, during that period the proportion of Australians who believe that emotional distress has a genetic cause has risen from half (in 1995) to two-thirds (in 2004). This is significant because other studies show that people who believe that genes are the major cause of who we are, are also more likely to prefer pills as the way to treat emotional distress, and if they do suffer it, to take longer to recover. They see the problem as a destiny that they are powerless to influence. They are also more likely to hold Conservative political beliefs and to regard childhood nurture as largely unimportant as a cause of distress. This makes them less likely to support political policies aimed at reducing distress.

A test case of Will's genetic view of the causes of emotional distress is the young women of Sydney. These female canaries in the cage of Selfish Capitalism enjoy ever increasing independence and material opportunities, and in Will's worldview they should be much less prone to distress as a result. In fact, just like their sisters in the rest of the English-speaking world, they are much more likely to suffer than their mothers and grandmothers, and twice as likely to do so than their male peers. Will's model is hard pressed to account for this.

Holly, aged thirty-four, is an attractive woman who has had a very successful career. Raised in Sydney by wealthy parents, she did a degree at an American University, and very soon after graduating became a producer of television current affairs programmes there. Four years ago she was head-hunted to a senior position in a pay-TV company in Sydney, lured by a salary of over £60,000 a year (large by Australian standards) and by the fact, as she saw it, that the serious investigative programming she had excelled in was no longer possible on American networks. 'Now I basically repackage stuff from the States, making it almost impossible for the locals to compete, sucking away any talent. My job doesn't even involve making selections of which American garbage to transmit, we just put slightly different titles on or a new logo and whack it out. Everything is controlled by sponsors and their brands.' Her feeling about the work is negative, to say the least. 'I've got to get out of this, I really hate it. I'm being well paid but I'm not contented. I'm thoroughly pissed off by it. My job is not intrinsically satisfying at all. I've just got to get the courage to make a break, but I'm not sure how.'

Holly used to be motivated by the intrinsic fascination of investigative TV journalism. Now, like so many TV executives I know in England, she has been promoted into a managerial role which is far less satisfying and geared to a totally commercial world of which she does not feel a part. 'I went to an awards ceremony just last night, it was excruciating. As soon as I could I fled. All these tanned, rake-thin women in skin-tight *Come Dancing* outfits just lapping it up, believing it, whereas I feel as if I'm in *The Matrix*, not really there. I've got used to people looking through me, not actually speaking to me. It's staggering how easy it is to get pulled away from the things that you know are important, caught up in peer groups, needing to be accepted.'

Possibly Will would regard these as inaccurately negative thoughts that require 'rigid and fastidious' policing, signs of depression. To me they are signs that Holly has been sucked into the Marketing Society. 'I'm not very materialistic, but I have this fear of not being employed – which is ridiculous because I am pretty employable – but that drives my life. I think, "I can't possibly stop, I can't get off the treadmill of earning money," and for the last four years I've been doing a job I hate. I've gone into a bit of a decline, my stock is down, I've gone into a big sulk, don't attend meetings, don't have that much status, and in terms of what I actually do now, I'm ridiculously overpaid. It takes great energy just to walk into work. I'm staggeringly bored, I sit on the internet reading articles about yourself or the next book I need to read, I'm just desperate to find the next thing to do. The irony is that I resigned eight months ago and they said, "You can't possibly leave!" Now they don't know what to do with me, even though they've extended my contract. I give too much attitude, sit there sizzling at the uber-yuppy who's my boss. I sat there last night and watched him, someone who has done basically nothing but shout at people and is ignorant about our genre, win the "achievement of the year" award. His social X-ray blonde wife was sitting there, with an obviously fake tan. The whole thing was just appalling, if quite funny.'

Given Will's view that upward social mobility is an inevitable and fundamental motivation, presumably he would regard Holly's lack of interest in it as further evidence of 'inaccurate' thinking. I would interpret it as the consequence of having allowed herself to become a commodity that has been bought by a pay-TV company, the switch from work that is intrinsically absorbing to that which has purely Virus goals. 'Working for my employers is a very cynical exercise of taking their money so that we can buy our first home and pay the mortgage. I do need to be doing something that I believe in, I can't just take money. And I have taken a lot [said with an unwitting pride]. I was in floods of tears about having to take this job but it was such good pay. So like a little rat running through the right gate in the maze, I thought, "I can't turn it down," and I've never been so unhappy in all my life.'

Will would say that Holly is one of his Worried Well. In her account the cause is lack of money because she has decided it's time to have a baby. The problem is that she has a partner to whom she is committed but who would never earn enough to pay the mortgage. 'The idea of having a baby is something that calls you, you can't really help yourself. If you'd asked me four years ago I would have said, "You've got to be kidding!" Then I was going out to clubs all the time, going nuts, sex, drugs and rock 'n' roll like my life depended on it, a rollercoaster. But now I've got a partner I like, and I've made a huge decision not to throw that away. He's not had any of the moneyed middle-class background that I had, he's not acceptable to my mother. I realise I can't depend on this person financially, but I need security, to the point where I was about to walk out on him. Then I had to say to myself, "Don't worry about all the material things, just resign yourself and give it a try." It's a difficult phase, being thirty-fivish.' She is not alone. Rates of distress amongst Australian women in her age group have risen enormously in recent years.

Holly doesn't feel that she has spent her time since university in a truly productive way. 'I realised recently that I've been a salary-earning gerbil on a wheel, and I thought, "Why have I wasted so much time?" It made me very angry to realise I had been persuaded somehow that there is no value to family or friends or home life and it's considered despicable to want children. We daughters were supposed to put off kids as long as possible and earn as much money and be as successful as possible, though it's probably lucky I didn't have them until now because I was way too confused.' The reasons why might elude Will, but they seem clear enough to her. Her mother, an alcoholic divorcee who remarried to a millionaire, drove her on. 'I have this permanent thing that I'm about to be fired, be chucked out. It's an irrational fear from my background that's stopping me. I can hear my mother saying, "You're a failure."'

In my schema, Holly is someone whose childhood made her insecure and very vulnerable to the glittering ornaments of success that the fragile use to distract from their true feelings of unattractiveness and insignificance. However, I would be reluctant to place all of the burden of her unhappiness on her childhood. I daresay she would have suffered in any era, but there is much about modern Sydney that is causing her pathological potential to be fulfilled. Unlike Will, she certainly believes that the social environment she lives in has become toxic. 'Unfortunately, this city is now driven by surface things, the show of wealth. It's the Dolly Parton of cities in Australia, the most vacuous, the city of conversations about real estate. Melbourne is more Meryl Streep, a bit more depth, more cultural resonance, with a lot of people who are creative and have an intellectual life beyond "What car are you driving, how's your house?"'

Holly recalls life on the beaches as a nubile teenager as having been much easier, because today she is no longer able to compete. 'My snide view would be that the glamorous women don't read a lot, don't have a wider reference for finding their individuality. The life of the mind is replaced by the life of the body – look at the meat market on the sand at Bondi. It's an appalling place. I've parted from a whole clique of friends who spend all their time there. If you want to get carcinomas from prancing around on the beach, go for it, great.' She regards Sydney as sexist. 'You could turn the clock back a few decades in terms of male–female relationships. In America I was treated as an equal, but I try to ignore the maltreatment you get here at work. It's pathetic: "Fluffy Bunny, could you help with this?" Seriously, that's how I get addressed.'

But the problems are not only for women. 'I look at my men friends, and everybody's searching for happiness, for belonging, or a dream of a lifestyle where they go down to the beach all the time. Like my friend Colin, who has a studio on the beach, a grim little building but on the bay. He works forty-eight hours without a stop, and never gets to the beach ever; he's got very pale and interesting, produced vast amounts of really good work but he's desperately unhappy.'

It seems strange to me that Will does not accept that Sydney has changed dramatically in the last fifteen years or that these changes are making people who might have been fine, or just a bit neurotic, very distressed. What would be the 'accurate' way for Holly to think about the issue of being able to afford her mortgage and care for her children: perhaps develop even more of a Marketing Character? Find a rich husband?

Russia

The Virus is rife amongst the New Russians who control the country, many of whom have attended American and British universities, although they are but a tiny minority of the population. However, it does not seem to have much infected the indigenously educated classes, perhaps because many of them are hostile to American values.

Since its helter-skelter rush towards capitalism in 1989, Russia has endured two massive financial collapses (in 1991 and 1998). It is these upheavals, combined with the rapidity of change from a totalitarian regime, rather than Affluenza, that explain the very high rates of distress. Although there have been no surveys based on a nationally representative sample of Russians, there have been four sizeable ones. The most recent was of over 900 forty-five- to sixty-four-year-olds in Novosibirsk, thought to be a 'statistically average' Russian city. Nearly half the women and a quarter of the men were found to be suffering from depression – but one would expect to find higher rates in this age group, since they are likely to have been hardest hit by the seismic changes of recent decades. The safest guide to the current national rate is the recent WHO study of neighbouring Ukraine, whose population and political economy are said to be equivalent in all important respects. There, 21 per cent of the population had been suffering emotional distress during the previous 12 months, putting it behind only America and New Zealand and five times higher than Shanghai (see Appendix 3).

That this is not due to Affluenza is suggested by the widespread antipathy to Virus values. One survey, done in 1990 before the first economic crash and in the afterglow of the escape from totalitarianism, showed that Russians were still considerably more hostile to consumerism and to people who wanted to make loadsamoney than a comparison group of Americans. Three years later, Caroline Humphrey, an anthropologist, provided an insight into Muscovite consumerism. She pointed out that Soviet society had created its own kind of consumer, very different from the Western variety. There were two sorts of commodities: those allocated by the State as your rightful dibs, and those battled for through hard graft on the Black Market. Before 1989, Western goods were status symbols, as well as signs of implicit dissent from the status quo, especially during the 1980s in the youth culture. Under Communism, procuring anything that was not allocated by the State was regarded as a triumph. In the period immediately after 1989, when foreign goods suddenly became freely available, the children were loose in the toyshop and bought just about anything, hardly able to believe it was possible. But within a very short time the novelty wore off, and Western goods lost both their glamour and their dissenting symbolic value. The mafia and the government between them soon took control, and after the massive economic crash of 1991, 30 per cent of the Russian population were thrown into absolute poverty. Hardly anyone could afford Western goods, and even for the middle classes the real issue was where to find some bread each day.

Perhaps most significant of all, Russian Americanophobia, originally stoked by the Soviet government, had endured amongst the people, and the deep suspicion engendered by decades of being messed about by the State was transferred to foreign goods. There was a superstitious feeling that something must be wrong with them because they came via the hated speculators (the New Russians) and just because they were foreign. Consumer lethargy and disinterest set in. Humphreys quoted how the dissident Vladimir Bukovski felt after he had got used to shopping in Western supermarkets: 'I stood before a counter with twenty-four kinds of salad oil and I couldn't choose one, I only got tired. What is oil, after all, one can live without it.' A recent survey of attitudes to America shows that the hostility has not diminished. Over two-thirds of Russians take a very dim view of its recent military ventures. Despite an improving economy, nearly half of people still remain hostile to the Selfish Capitalist reforms which took place after 1991 and only a quarter are in favour of them. Russian cinema attendances are less than 3 per cent of American levels, and American television programmes are not yet ubiquitous, so the spread of the Virus through these agents of cultural imperialism has yet to occur. It is interesting that no Starbucks have yet opened in Russia – surprising given how large a potential market it is – although the company has recently announced plans to rectify this lacuna.

Nonetheless, amongst the tiny elite who control Russia, I did find examples of the Virus-infected. Boris is the head of a huge department in one of Russia's largest banks. His company's office block soars above the city, a gleaming statement of the new power of money in the nation's affairs. He is dressed like a British merchant banker preparing to take his labrador out for stroll on a Saturday morning. He wears a yellow and blue Turnbull & Asser-style shirt, his sandy-coloured corduroy trousers look expensive, his brown leather shoes even more so. His English accent is so markedly Sloane Ranger that for a moment I think he is a Briton. When he drops back into a Russian accent it seems doubly strange, as if you were talking to Boris Johnson or Willie Whitelaw and they suddenly started to add 'ski' to the end of words. His sentence construction is partly Waugh and Wodehouse, but mostly *Yes, Minister*. He speaks with Sir Humphrey's slow, tortuously deliberate, evenly spaced diction. Unlike him, there is little change in tone or volume, and the face is impenetrable and static as concrete. Boris has a tedious tendency to

go into too much detail, but what he has to say is pretty interesting and delivered with a good deal of spin – the raised
eyebrow, the slight hesitation or change of emphasis to cue a
big point. Listening to him, it occurs to me that if I did not
know differently, I would swear he had been educated at
Winchester public school, where they turn out chaps with the
same dry wit, cleverness and understatement. He is also like
practically every merchant banker I have ever met – as judicious and cautious in his utterances as the narrator in a Jane
Austen novel.

I start by explaining that I am studying the oddity of rising
emotional distress amidst increasing affluence. He says immediately, 'It's interesting. The probable explanation is that the
more choice you have of things to desire and the more you
compare what you have with what others have, it makes you
unhappy,' a pretty sharp answer from someone who says he
has not considered the problem before. However, he adds,
'You have lost me with the definition of Affluenza.' I explain
it, and he nods. 'I do notice this. The beggars are not jealous
of the millionaires, they worry about the other beggars who
are getting more money. Amongst my friends, when we were
in the university at the beginning of the nineties we were more
or less equal. Some were more equal than others but we didn't
care. Then, suddenly, some people became more successful,
their status rose in their jobs and their material affluence
increased, and relative jealousy arose. It was like the beggars
but at a higher level of wealth. Some of it is luck. I would not
expect in the UK in my wildest dreams to be the Head of
Resources at the equivalent of Barclays at the age of twenty-
nine, managing tens of thousands of people, yet here I am,

because I am Russian at a particular moment in history, rather than English.'

I gasp at the idea that Boris is that young. I had assumed he was at least in his mid-thirties, although his face is of indeterminate age. 'I have a friend a few years older who was an employee of mine for a time. He is deranged by his hardships, as he sees them, relative to others. Now he is launching into all sorts of extremes. He flirts with fascism, believing the Jews are responsible for all the "privations" he suffers. He runs a very small company with small profits, maybe makes £750 a month, much more than the vast majority of people, yet he feels he is failing.' Boris then explains that he has recently seen the latest figures for the proportion of Russians who are middle class, now nearly one-third, earning £225 a month. He seemed rather pleased, since it meant that more people will be able to afford one of his loans. He was also rather excited at being the bringer of these glad tidings, wanting to give me a printout of the graphs and adding, with exactly the kind of exaggerated faux-concern of a Sloane Ranger, 'If I forget, please *do* remind me.'

By now I was gagging to hear how this wunderkind had managed his rapid ascent. When he started university in 1992, everything was whirring around so rapidly that the dean of the university encouraged students to start up businesses. Boris was one of the few that did, setting himself up as a stockbroker at the age of eighteen. He has just sold the business, beginning this job only three weeks ago. He says that 'most people who are very successful now started businesses then. For instance, the CEO of one of our biggest banks today started his own one at the age of twenty-one. It was a time when all sorts of things could happen. The senior management of many commercial organisations are about my age. The next generation have missed this opportunity, and we shall see if the youth thing continues.' Presumably, he did his law degree at Moscow State? 'No, at a more specialised university,' he said, adding with a positively Old Etonian semi-irony, 'obviously a more superior one. You would not want to do law at Moscow State, perhaps physics or mathematics, but not law. Of course, I am biased towards my old school' – this last remark delivered with a drippingly complex mix of languid self-mockery, sarcasm and superiority.

To put it mildly, Boris did not strike me as the kind of man who would take kindly to probing of his emotional life, but readers would not expect their heroic mind tourist ('he visits places only LSD can reach', etc.) to bottle out at such a moment, so I gave it a go. His father had been a key figure in the Soviet military, and his mother worked for the KGB, both members of the Party elite. She gave up work to care for him when he came along. When I asked how long she had cared for him, he looked amused and said, 'Do you know, I never realised that I have never thought about that, or that it might have been of importance, so I do not know the answer. I think it must have been until I was at least three.' He has a stepsister, although it is some time since they met: 'Because I have been so busy with my company, we have only talked on the phone in recent years.'

He is not married, and this topic ushered in a matey 'we're all lads together' phase in our acquaintanceship. He definitely does have girlfriends. 'As a senior manager I have an open door policy here [nudge, nudge, wink, wink, pointing to his literally open door] and there are three whole floors of distractions here. Inevitably, one day something will distract me from my work – under which I am currently snowed – sufficiently for me to get married. It's correct to say that the women here are absolutely unbelievable. The beauty seems to grow as you move east from Poland and Czechoslovakia. In England, I guess it's also correct to say – although I can't possibly comment – that it's easier to concentrate on one's work, there is less female distraction, shall I say?'

I asked about Russia's sky-high divorce rate. 'I don't know why divorce is a problem,' he answered, 'because I have not been married. If I have a girlfriend I get bored in about three months. I suppose you could say I divorce every three months. Why? I am a very busy person who tends to put my work first, and that drives my girlfriends crazy. I'm just the kind of person who likes structure, numbers, effectiveness. I would see my achievements in doing something, rather than in relation to girlfriends. Sex is like food: you have to have it once a day, but it's only once a day, then you move onto something else. It will probably get worse rather than better, I don't know, I guess I'm coming to the sort of age when one starts thinking about a family and a long stable relationship will come eventually.' So, would he say he is happy? 'Sometimes I am, umm, you can only realise you are coming out of the trough when you are coming up and that you are going into one and were happy before, when going down. I've never thought about this. I can't say. It's always a snapshot of how I am at a particular moment, I can say that there were times when things were better or worse. But I cannot see this very clearly because there are no numbers involved, no plus or minus, er, calculations of mathematical signings, number basis, no bottom line, that's what I understand. My long-term goal is to achieve more and more, not so much for money, it does not come first. I become happy when I have achieved something that is useful, like in my present job we are going through a transition and if I have played a significant role in making it successful perhaps I will feel happy.'

During this five minutes Boris had lost his previous eloquence, emerging as immature and emotionally illiterate. Otherwise highly sophisticated, he was astonishingly at sea when it came to considering the most basic questions, such as whether he is happy or why he splits up with girlfriends. It was not even that after years of agonising he could see how complex the problems are, it was that he genuinely had never given them a thought, having been so wrapped up in his work. He may possess a very charming, strangely aristocratic veneer, but when he was talking about only understanding numbers he was seriously flailing, his words flopping about incoherently, only just audible, for a moment completely different from his poised, assertive self.

With Boris, we see the ubiquity of the Marketing Character. He regards himself and others as instruments for the advancement of profit. Women are like food – things to be consumed in order to satisfy an instinct, necessary once a day but only in order to be able to keep one's own machine functioning. His new job gives him access to a warehouse full of these woman commodities, three whole floors of them, objects to be discarded for a new model every three months. The really important matter of being a senior manager in the business of selling financial products can then be pursued uninterrupted by tiresome, distracting sexual urges, using the (more or less educated, selected on merit) producer-machines who work for him to persuade the consumer-machines out there to buy them. The feelings he has for others or that others have for him seem to have been extinguished from his consciousness. He is oblivious to the possibility that he may have emotional needs for intimacy and love, for a child or a wife; he knows only that around his age a man-machine is supposed to contemplate reproduction. Because he is a commodity, a thing, and because others are more or less educated commodities too, he has no emotional relationships. It's really quite extraordinary to imagine that such a person as he can exist, yet here he is.

For a few moments before we parted I glimpsed at least the possibility that he is lonely, perhaps even very unhappy. 'Actually,' he said, 'I must thank you for having made me think about all these important things that I have not had time to think about.' This was said with feeling, but even before I had begun to reply he disconnected from me, looking down and waiting for me to go through the door. I said, 'I would be happy to send you a copy of my last book, which discusses these things. There's a lot of interesting scientific evidence ...' but I had already lost him, he was a commodity again. 'Goodbye,' he said, not responding to my offer, as if he had not heard it, and he closed the door beside the sleeping guard. It's frightening to think how many of the people who run our businesses and countries are like Boris. The very people to whom we entrust control of how we lead our lives are so often completely ignorant of the most important aspect of human living: our inner, emotional existence.

They are both the best educated and the most emotionally illiterate.

Perhaps you feel as remote from the Marketing Characters I have described as people of this kind are, themselves, from their feelings and true needs. The next morning I lay in bed uneasily pondering the extent to which Boris and I truly differ. At least superficially, it would seem to be a lot. Intimacy is important to me and I seek it, unlike Sam (the millionaire New Yorker), Will or Boris. I have many friends and relatives whom I care deeply about and who I would like to think feel similarly towards me. I am definitely not primarily motivated by money and usually do not work very hard at all. Normally, I find plenty of time for golfing and loafing about doing nothing very much at weekends, when I almost never work.

So far so good – except that if I dig a bit deeper it's not that simple. The truth is that my work is incredibly important to me. I like to think that most of the stuff I do has some ultimately altruistic purpose (making the world a better place, etc.). But really, I also do it because I have to. I'd soon go bonkers if I couldn't channel my feelings and thoughts into it. The theories, statistics and analysis of others makes me feel in control and is a playful, amusing challenge. But more than this – and something I prefer not to think about – I suppose that I do gain self-esteem from the fact that what I do may sometimes lead to others seeing me as important or admirable or clever, or whatever. I certainly do not crave power, in the way that Boris does, but I would like to have some influence on how others feel and think, and what they do as a result. Is that so very different from Boris's strong desire to directly control his staff and, indirectly, the people his company lends money to? Regarding money, whilst I did not inherit very much from my parents, it was enough to cover half the price of my first flat, which subsequently enabled us to afford the house we now live in. I have had a tremendously privileged upbringing, and some of the friends I have been brought up with are very well off – I am used to being around money. Although my parents' healthy disregard for it is the primary reason I do not care much about it, that might not have been the same if I had been raised in a low-income home.

Much as I would like to think of myself as putting relationships first, here I am sitting in Moscow on a Sunday morning writing these words a thousand miles away from my family and friends, and for the next seven weeks it will be the same. There is definitely a part of me that misses them, but there is another, as with Boris, that sees myself as a man on a mission who will not let anything get in his way. I see my friends far less often than I would like, and in some cases our relationships are tinged by complex mutual professional assistance. In this sense, to what extent do I share Boris's view of others as necessary instruments for fulfilling basic needs in order to free me to work? I don't really know, so perhaps his emotional illiteracy is not as far from me as I would like to think. Finally, I am sure that my relationships with women are different from his because I have never been any good at quick flings, nor do I get bored like he does. (It was interesting how muddled he was about this: first of all, the problem was with him, that he gets bored, then it was with them, that it drives them 'crazy' that he works so hard.) Yet the fact is that I did not marry until in my forties, and I am not convinced I have been the most emotionally available person on earth to the women with whom I have been involved. But then again, is any writer, or for that matter, any man?

All in all, whilst I may be more emotionally mature than Boris (and at twenty-one years older, so I should be), there are not a few motes that need to be pickaxed out of my eye before I start seeing him as a Martian compared with me. I am pretty sure I am not as much a Marketing Character as him, but is it possible to be at all successful in the upper echelons of a developed nation without being one to some degree? With the exception of Denmark, my experience in all the countries I visited is that it is not.

Singapore

In Singapore, shopping is the favourite, and in many cases the only, leisure activity. The government has fostered the exclusive pursuit of material goals, very systematically, for fifty years, creating English-speaking rates of emotional distress in a largely Chinese-descended population.

When Singapore became independent of Britain and self-governing in 1959, it was plunged into high unemployment and looked as though it might be absorbed into neighbouring Indonesia. So Lee Kuan Yew, the father of the nation, went to the United Nations and asked, 'What do we do?' With the help of a Dutch economist, Albert Winsemius, he hatched a cunning plan. Its object was nothing less than premier-league economic status within thirty to forty years. They would create a city-state that attracted foreign capital for manufacturing at low wages, exploit the huge harbour (it is now the second busiest in the world) and become a hub for trade and finance, akin to Hong Kong. Every feature of the society would be planned towards these ends, completely at the service of economic growth. Quality of life was factored in, but only as a necessary element for creating more productive citizens and making the city attractive to foreign visitors.

They succeeded in their economic goals, spectacularly so. Singapore is twenty-four times richer as a nation than it was in 1960 and lies seventh in the global league table of per capita average incomes (Britain sits in twenty-seventh place). Such figures are misleading in all sorts of ways, but it is undeniable that on average Singaporeans are a lot better off materially than their peers in adjoining countries. The Singapore government website is awash with statistics attesting to the success of Singapore plc, including:

- 2nd most globalised nation in the world
- 2nd most profitable place for investors
- least corrupt country in Asia
- 5th best offshore location globally.

Rather less publicity – in fact, none – is given on the website to the findings of a representative nationwide study of minor depression and anxiety rates amongst 3,000 Singaporeans, published in 1998. It reveals that 16.6 per cent of the population suffer this way. The highest rates (21 per cent) are found amongst thirteen- to twenty-year-olds. If other problems, such as substance abuse and impulsiveness/aggression were added, this would make Singapore considerably more prone to emotional distress than continental European nations and in the same league as us English-speakers. Whether amongst the averagely successful or the super-rich, I found plentiful evidence that the Virus was breeding misery.

Mark, a forty-year-old, slightly podgy, unmarried man with two degrees in chemistry and a smattering of grey hairs, still lives with his middle-class parents (his dad is a middle-ranking civil servant). His two siblings have flown the nest, but he gets on okay with his parents 'apart from occasional nagging about getting married'. He seemed a bit inhibited, and I wondered if this had to do with his upbringing. 'You could say that it was a strict one,' he said. I asked how he would describe himself, and he replied 'reasonably happy but not overly emotional'. He has a 'fair number of friends' and is 'thinking of taking up golf, but it'd be a bit of a strain'. He has had 'nothing too steady in the way of girlfriends' because he is very worried about the damage marriage could do to his independence.

Mark suspects that there is a good deal of unhappiness in Singapore. 'If I look at my friends and colleagues, I don't think they are particularly happy, judging by their comments about how hard they work, and how they wish they didn't have so many liabilities – school fees, mortgages.' He thinks he's managed to stay happier than them by avoiding 'liabilities', especially a mortgage. I tried to sell him the joys of teaching my daughter to swim, but after politely hearing me out (and as though I'd said that I enjoy cleaning toilets), he said, 'I'm just wondering – wouldn't it produce other pressures? Now, I could just tell them at work that I want to walk out and could get up and go, but with children I would really have to think twice. Having friends like mine doesn't help very much. I have one who takes Friday afternoons off and doesn't tell his wife so that he can go to the arcade and play video games with his old school mates.' Err, see what you mean mate.

His job as a sales manager contains a lot of 'mundane, repetitious elements', but he chose it over his true love, academia, because of the money. If he had enough money he would do a doctorate and go back to the study of how chemicals behave when mixed together, for chemistry is what really rings his bell. At present he works sixty hours a week and fears redundancy. There was a strong sense of resignation about him. Strictly disciplined by canings as a child, he appeared to feel equally policed by his society. Most of all, he seemed to me like someone who just wanted to be left alone, preferably without a wife or parents to nag him.

In contrast to Mark, Sarah, a thirty-five-year-old management consultant, is a true technocrat, a dreamer of Lee Kuan's Singapore dream. An engineering graduate, she feels satisfied by her work because 'every day I pick up new things, I'm kept on my toes'. Her only criticism of the system is that the educational pressure has become excessive. 'When I look at my nephews and nieces, I worry about how much they have to do.' Singaporean schoolchildren are sorted at a young age into gifted, average, and so on: 'I think that's not good when so young.' She has never met anyone she would like to have children with and 'would not be too worried if I never do. I would work if I did, partly because of the money, partly because it's important to have challenges and social interaction.' This need for challenge was her main theme. 'It seems as if our economy has reached its plateau. There is another significant incremental jump we will have to make in the next phase. We are a country with limited resources, and you see other countries nearby beginning to catch up. We have a lot of pressure to keep ahead, which is a good thing.'

Regarding Affluenza, Sarah commented, 'People here are entirely happy. Most are content to just jog along and be contented with what they have got, but they are not exactly happy.' 'What about fun?' I asked. 'Having fun is important,' she replied, 'you need a balance to achieve the most that you can. My friends do try to take time out sometimes but many of us are too caught up with competition, they need to catch their breath.' Although she does occasionally get to the gym (apparently this is a form of fun), at the moment she is doing a further graduate degree in a legal subject during the evenings to give herself an edge over the competition in her field.

As far as I could see, everything in her life and her society is directed towards greater economic performance. Even the having of fun is only 'important' inasmuch as it serves this purpose. Personal fulfilment must take second place to the creation of a more efficient machine for creating wealth, and that machine is a me who has been commodified by herself primarily out of a sense of duty to parents, at the command of Lee Kuan. What started as traditional collectivist values have been manipulated to create a nation of wealth-creating machine-people whose individualism is expressed by buying this rather than that brand.

I met few Singaporeans who seemed to have any life outside work. Most are doing jobs that entail very long hours (sixty or more a week), dedicating their minds and bodies to the selling of services or commodities rather than to activities they find intrinsically absorbing. All had been caned as children by parents and subsequently put under tremendous pressure at school. This surely means that they are more easily coerced into subservience to authority and its goals in the workplace, and a sense of filial duty (originally based on fear of the cane) anchors the people-machines in place. Until they are married they remain in the family home, where parents can continue to monitor them; it is barely thinkable for them to take off for other countries where they would have greater freedom.

These examples, and that of Singapore as a nation, were the purest that I encountered on my mind tour of the damage done by the Virus to the playfulness and sense of volition which are so important for well-being.

New Zealand

By all accounts, in the fifties and sixties New Zealand was about as clement a society as could be. Equitable, economically flourishing and relatively untouched by the world wars, it seems to have been genuinely jolly, truly classless. However, in 1974 Britain's entry to the Common Market cast a socking great shadow over this alleged utopia. With the loss of guaranteed markets for its wool, meat and dairy products, it ceased to be Britain's South Seas Farm and had to get to grips with global competition. This took ten years, and it was actually a Labour government that began to turn it into a Selfish Capitalist economy. A decade before anyone had heard of New Labour in Britain, a supposedly socialist New Zealand administration set about scaling down the Welfare State. In just six years they laid waste to many cherished publicly owned institutions, such as the railways. New Zealand spread its previously tightly closed legs (which had prevented floods of imports) to welcome insemination from any passing foreign investor, and today's New Zealand is the most trans-nationalised country in the world. Practically everything you can think of – the grass, the mountains, the water, virtually the sea and the air – is liable to be owned by foreign capital. In place of governments encouraging cheery relaxation have come a succession of administrations which – regardless of political complexion – have urged the citizens to 'modernise' and become entrepreneurial.

The advent of Selfish Capitalism in New Zealand might have destroyed immunity to the Virus, especially if the culture had been Americanised. The inequality, consumerism and dog-eat-dogism that go with it might have replaced the relaxed mentality of former years. However, fascinatingly, this does not seem to have happened amongst much of the population. Most New Zealanders have not been seduced by Selfish Capitalism, and indeed are strongly antipathetic to it. Surveys show that they want much stricter regulation of trans-nationals and much tighter limits on imported foreign goods, to protect local jobs. Over two-thirds feel that the country 'is being run by a few big interests looking out for themselves', and only one-fifth believe that it is run for the benefit of New Zealanders. Equality of opportunity was a sine qua non for those who created this country, the first to have a woman member of parliament, and the gap between rich and poor was kept to a minimum. Even today, despite the huge increase in inequality, the highest paid only get ten times the average wage, a far smaller disparity than in the rest of the English-speaking world (there are also far fewer millionaires, per capita). Here is a country with a government doing its best to infect its citizens with Affluenza, but with a long-standing culture that may have provided a measure of immunity.

The results of a huge nationwide survey of New Zealand mental health were published in 2006. With 20.7 per cent of the population having suffered a mental illness in the previous twelve months, the nation goes straight into second place in the league table of mental illness (see Appendix 3). It would seem that, despite public opposition to the Selfish Capitalist governance, the Virus has taken hold and distress has spread, especially in urban areas. Infection was widespread amongst the ruling elite when I visited Auckland, where one-quarter of the poulation live. Outside that city, I was mightily impressed by the authenticity and integrity of the people. But when it came to the top of the pile, it was an all-too-familiar story. I was given a breakneck tour of their miseries by Gerald, a media lawyer.

We had arranged to meet during his lunch hour at a Starbucks (Auckland has one of the highest concentrations of these coffee bars in the world) in the commercial centre, where he specialises in foreign ownership of New Zealand's newspapers and television companies. Well over six feet tall, beefy, handsome and impressively coutured in a pinstripe suit, Gerald came very quickly to the point (as lawyers tend to when not being paid for their views). We had agreed on the phone that he would not talk about himself in any detail, but would instead give me a thumbnail sketch of his friends, all of whom come from the same stock of well-to-do Auckland elite families as he does. Whilst he is not unhappy himself, he told me, he knew a great many Aucklanders who are. 'I truly believe that most people I know are clinically depressed, not just in a down trough. Over half would say, "I'm just having a bad time at the moment," but it's not the truth. I have to say that I don't know that many happy people. Outwardly they're all really fine; they function, but they're not happy.' Gerald is certainly an emotionally intelligent man, as well as highly articulate, and to a Londoner from my similarly privileged background, their stories were eerily recognisable.

First there was twenty-two-year-old Judy, a model who switched from anorexia to bulimia in her late teens, obsessed with women's magazines and celebrity. 'She adopts every fad and diet that comes along,' said Gerald, 'constantly on detox yet eating buckets of ice cream and sugar. She's the most funny, delightful person you could hope to meet but completely bonkers. She's a chatterer, permanently wired, permanently thinking about food or the lack thereof. All she wants is to be famous – that is her sole motivation in life – or to be attached to someone who is famous. She dresses that argument up, but that's the real truth.' Then there was Jerry, thirty, a hugely successful actor and theatre director, keeping depression at bay by 'consuming large amounts of drugs at every opportunity. The comedowns from that are vicious and awful, he just gets angry, angry, angry, that rage where you think he could actually kill somebody. Oddly enough, a lot of my friends have that same level of volcanic fury.' Like Paul, thirty-two, a TV presenter who has moved to Australia to escape his over-controlling mother. Despite four days a week of therapy, he also gobbles cocaine and has 'a drug-induced inflation of ego. He can't not be with company, has to be with people 24/7. He needs to believe that where he is in the world is above others, a cocky kind of fragile self-regard. He was actually a big star in New Zealand, and the reality is that he is secretly quite happy that no-one in Australia knows who he is from a bar of soap. He's able to be depressed and alone without people who know him seeing him like that, especially as he's not getting any work. But in the long term, it's very, very, very important to him to be successful.'

Seamus was the only person Gerald described who is not in the arts or media, but this does not seem to have helped him. He is doing a doctorate in engineering at Harvard. 'He suffers from a strangely cinematic depression. He's made it kind of funny, part of his personality, which isn't so clever, very Woody Allen. He has a chromatically black darkness. The most exciting thing in his day is when he wakes up in the morning and he's trying to make a list of what he will do – it's a control thing. He's a rationalist who finds it impossible to be happy. It's strange. He has scholarships coming out of his ears and comes from the perfect family. His parents genuinely are happy, yet his brother's the same. They're both deadbeat in comparison with his upbeat other two siblings. His mother is a writer of children's books. They're all genius-clever, appallingly bright; she must have had the book on how to create geniuses on her shelf. Seamus will certainly rise to the top of the ranks of engineering professors in this country, yet he can only email about the weather and "I am so depressed". So you think when you see him, "You're great-looking, you're bright, you're wealthy," yet he just wants to reduce his life to the safety of a spreadsheet.'

Back in media-land, Claire, twenty-seven, is head of publicity at a major media organisation. 'She is a maudlin person,' says Gerald, 'very serious and earnest. She was raised alone by her mother, an only child. Her mother was an incredibly stubborn woman who had insisted on refusing any help from her wealthy family, so they lived on state benefits in a poor ghetto in South Auckland. However, one of her uncles persuaded her mother to allow him to pay for Claire to attend a flash private school, which gave a very confusing message – most of her friends came from wealthy homes, yet she returned every evening to a slum. That made her resilient, but she is also very angry and suffers a lot of depression. The pursuit of career success is everything to her, it's instrumental in her building an image of herself, it's what keeps her going.'

Gerald finished his recitation just within the hour he had taken off from his work of checking the contracts of the New Zealand companies he helps to flog off to foreign owners. I only just had time to thank him before he merged into the crowd of tourists, mall-rats and business-people to return to his desk.

Denmark

In Denmark, even the rulers seem Virus-free. You could say that, just as the Singapore elite has done its very best to create a system which would spread it, the Danes have done the opposite. This is reflected in lower rates of emotional distress than in English-speaking nations. As we shall see repeatedly in the coming chapters, Danish social policies and culture offer some of the most potent vaccines against the Virus yet to have been tested.

When my wife and I were on holiday there in 1997, we were startled by how well organised the place was, designed to the hilt. The Danes embrace modern furniture and architecture with the enthusiasm of a film critic discovering an unknown Hitchcock movie. Even their bus shelters are stylish. They may not be the greatest painters or novelists, but their aesthetic impulses flow into the arts and crafts. A comparable love of ordered modernity has been lavished upon their social system. For seventy years they have gone to tremendous lengths to fashion relationships between their 5 million citizens in order to maximise well-being. Whereas the Singaporean regime has striven for material comfort at any human cost, the Danes have put relationships first. To this end, they have virtually abolished poverty, and when criminals come along they see them as troubled people in need of help, not of censure and incarceration (quite rightly – studies show that a staggering 80 per cent of convicted criminals suffer emotional distress in Britain and worldwide). In the developed world, only Finland, Norway and Iceland imprison fewer citizens, per head of population. In common with their Scandinavian neighbours, the Danes foresaw the problems that female emancipation would bring, and to forestall them they have given mothers of small children heavily subsidised substitute care in kindergartens, and before that a year's paid maternal leave plus the option of two more years of State benefits, per child. When the mothers return to work, they are usually guaranteed re-entry to the workforce at the same level they left it. This means that, unlike almost everywhere else in the developed world, the Scandinavians do not have a collapsing birthrate. On top of all that, their economy is extremely successful (think Carlsberg, Lego and Bang & Olufsen) yet they do not work our ridiculous hours. Only 6 per cent live on half the average income or less, the gap between rich and poor is tiny, and their ecological policies are exemplary.

Confronted by these facts, sceptical Brits mutter about them all being drunks or depressed or suicidal because of the cold climate, but none of these myths are true (in fact, Denmark's climate is much like Edinburgh's and their suicide rate is not so high). Confounded by the evidence, Brits start claiming that the economy is collapsing (untrue; again like the other Scandinavians, it has not been out of the top ten economies for decades) because it has such high taxes (but not prohibitively high – the top rate is 65 per cent, which can rise to 72 per cent for a tiny minority; true, VAT is 25 per cent, which raises the cost of living, making Copenhagen the fifth most expensive city to live in), and anyway, 'Denmark is such a small place that it would never work over here'. Finally, deep in a hole, the Brit's last-ditch retort is that they are 'a racially homogenous population' which makes it so much easier (usually meaning that they do not have many Afro-Caribbeans, an argument hardly deserving a response).

There have been no nationally representative surveys of all Danish emotional problems, but there has been a survey of rates of major depression, finding that 3.3 per cent of Danes had suffered in the previous two weeks, half the European mainland average. When rates of psychiatric disturbance amongst representative samples of eight- to nine-year-olds have been measured in Denmark, they are found to be at the low end for that age group in the developed nations.

This suggests that the splendours of its social system have been converted into lower rates of emotional distress. When happiness or life satisfaction is rated, Denmark consistently comes out as one of the best countries in the world. Indeed, it is one of the very few developed nations in which these ratings have increased since 1950, rather than remaining the same or dropping.

Studies comparing Denmark with other developed nations show it to be relatively Virus-free. Tøger Seidenfaden, editor of *Politiken*, their equivalent of the *Guardian* newspaper, believes this is because of their 'very strong, real life gender equality'. The men actually want to make a huge commitment to their domestic lives and if they did not put in the hours, their wives would soon leave them. An alpha workaholic in the classic American Donald Trump mould would be very hard-pressed to find any Danish woman prepared to serve as his trophy, Barbie Doll housewife. Unless they remain single, neither the men nor the women can become work-dominated killer-drillers because their spouses will not stand for it. Said Seidenfaden, 'Men simply cannot go all out for materialist goals because you have to pick up the children, get back and make sure the cooking and the washing-up are done.'

Perhaps equally fundamental is the economic equality of Denmark, the lack of a gap between rich and poor, almost implausibly small by the standards of the English-speaking world. 'I'm a very well-paid individual,' says Seidenfaden, 'but after tax I am not more than three or four times richer than the lowest 5 per cent of the population. The gap in other countries is five or ten or a hundred times more than that.'

Because being richer than the other guy is very actively discouraged by the tax system and the culture, it is not a source of status ... and status cannot be bought by conspicuous consumer goods. 'If no-one is going to care how rich you are – in fact, would despise you for flaunting it – why would you work a sixty-hour week for decades on end?' The answer might be a need for power, but that does not operate in the same way here either. 'Our sameness is emotional as well as financial – it's positively reinforced that we should be similar.' This is expressed in the absence of hierarchy within families, schools and organisations. A very big effort is made to avoid authoritarianism, people are not bossed about by one another at any point in the system. 'Studies of inequality, even when you take out economics, show that hierarchy is a serious source of frustration and unhappiness, one's relative rather than absolute position in a system. Ours is hostile to individuals who want to dominate. In terms of deference and acceptance of being ordered around by our superiors, we have probably become even less hierarchical than twenty or thirty years ago.' This is about as alien from most societies in the rest of the world as you can get.

But, given that seeking status must be, at least to some extent, inevitable for all humans, what criteria do the Danes use to measure themselves against one another, to mark themselves out? 'Of course, all the usual mechanisms exist here, but they are much weaker because of the gender equality – we do seek power, status and wealth, but not to the same degree.' Then how do men attract women in this system? 'They cannot use money, cars, houses and hierarchically founded access to resources to persuade women that they will be good provider-cavemen. Instead, they must persuade the women that they will pull their domestic weight.' Equally, how do women attract men who are not looking for a homemaking dolly bird? They must be interesting rather than overtly sexy, Seidenfaden replies. Men are not looking for a clothes horse or a domestic drudge, they want a person they can communicate with.

As we shall see, although far from being a utopia, Danish society has many of the clues to where the vaccines against the Virus are to be found. I had expected this to be the case, but more surprising was the number of top tips to be found from visiting China. In the 2004 WHO study, Shanghainese were found to have the lowest rate of emotional distress, yet the Virus is rife in their city. If there is evidence that it is possible to have the Virus without getting distressed, it is there in Shanghai. That makes it the single most interesting destination from the standpoint of a searcher after vaccines, and it is where I begin Part 2.

Part Two
The Vaccines

Chapter 3

Have Positive Volition (Not 'Think Positive')

On hearing my theories about Affluenza, the managing director of a financial services company in Shanghai tells me that if I really want to understand its penetration here, I should interview what she called 'my Shanghai Gals'. They are in their twenties or thirties, university-educated and in executive roles. According to the MD, they are all infected by the Virus, yet none is distressed.

In her mid-thirties, the first Gal's assessment of Chinese well-being is that 'we are extremely optimistic and progressive. People here are very excited, tomorrow will be better than today.' However, this Gal knows where I am coming from and addresses my next question before I can ask it. 'That does not mean that people are totally happy because there is competition between peers. Some are doing better than others, and there is competition to keep up with the Joneses. I was reading an article in *Newsweek* about millionaires from the internet boom, and surprisingly a lot of them say they are not happy because "I see my neighbour is buying a new Mercedes every month, I am not doing as well as him." I am slightly having that pressure. At present I am doing okay, but some of my friends have set up their own businesses and they are doing better. When I graduated ten years ago the trend was to work for a global corporation. Some of my schoolmates did less well than me at school and could not get a job with one, and now they are much richer than me because they set up their own company.' This kind of social comparing is a recipe for Affluenza distress, yet she is manifestly not a depressed person.

Her next step will be to set up her own business. 'There is another life outside a corporation, where I can be in control. I want something that will make me money – everything in China is money, money, money!' I remind her of the implication of the *Newsweek* article. 'Yes, but money is the most concrete, tangible validation of your contribution.' But why does she need such external evidence of her worth? 'It's proof to yourself that you are creating value,' she replies with the logic of a Marketing Character who has elided her self-estimation with her economic one. Even if she is very successful and becomes massively rich, will she not always want more? 'Of course, greed. But the challenge will keep me going, the challenge to overcome ever new problems. I will still feel good as I reach for the next big money target.' She also says she is bored by her current job and wants something that is interesting. I ask what really interests her, whether it be knitting or fishing, and she asks, 'You mean hobbies?' I try to explain that I mean anything which absorbs her, has flow, has an intrinsic motivation. 'It's the elation that I'm the first amongst my friends and peer group,' she replies, 'it's having the competitive edge over them that gets me going.'

This woman is riddled with the Virus. In New York or London such values would put her at grave risk of being distressed, yet she is not. Something is keeping her immunity high enough to prevent symptoms from developing.

The next Gal is a tall, thin and rather remote twenty-seven-year-old. Her face is exceptionally pale (highly prized here; you see women walking down the street with raised umbrellas in the sunlight, anxious to remain pale-skinned). Only occasionally during our meeting does she respond to me in a personal manner, for most of the time she seems distant, sizing me up, insofar as she can be bothered at all. Her father owns a factory and is rich enough to have sent his daughter to university in England, where she did an MA in media communications at London University. Her observations are acute, if very detached.

She seemed to be reeling from her English odyssey, to have lost her cultural bearings. 'The values are totally different back here. I would use the word "aggressive" to describe them. They know what they want exactly: to be rich, to have a husband, to have a car, a beautiful wife, lovely kids, the need for social status is clear.' In her account, Affluenza values are more rampant in Shanghai than in England. 'The English are more considering what is right for them in partic-ular, they think about human nature, "What will make me happy? Exactly what should I study?" Most Chinese will do business-related courses, but in England you might do art or sociology. They have time to be in touch with what they want and who they are. Here, everyone around me complains about work: too long hours, boss not as capable as them, a lot of problems. I can tell that some people are unhappy, but I don't know if they are aware of it or not. I know I am, "I'm fed up with this company, this country, I want to move." A friend warned me that wherever I worked it would be the same. But money is driving people here more. That's what I hate. Even girls will check where you live, where you work, what's your position, what's your background, trying to find out how rich you are. You can see them coming up with different questions to dig this out of you. But it's up to you to find the right friends who are not like that, you should make yourself happy, that's the rule.'

I encounter some version of this final thought from everyone I meet in Shanghai, that you must take responsibility. Her colleagues may complain, but rather than a culture of complaint in which everyone is looking for an excuse to sue doctors or to blame the System, there is still a very genuine sense that it is both possible, and your duty, to make the most of your environment. Nonetheless, if this Gal is to be believed, money-grubbing is even more important here than in Britain.

Another twenty-seven-year-old Gal had also been to university abroad, spending two years in America doing an MBA. Like the others, she works twelve-hour days during the week and lives with her parents, yet she is not saving any of her quite large (by local standards) salary because she believes that you have to spend to accumulate – in her case a rich husband, a goal about which she was remarkably open. 'Penny wise, pound foolish, they say. If you only go to work or your home you do not find opportunities. Living the good life you meet quality people. It's not only by work that you can make money. To speak frankly, if you come across a good guy who's rich it doesn't mean you have to only look for his money – it's very good for me to be independent – but if he has good financial status, it can be a plus.' Rich bachelors of Shanghai, beware: there's a Gal after you. Except that her next comments provide a completely different view of what she hopes for, again displaying dissatisfaction with her culture.

'I don't think I want to have a baby. I used to think so, but not now. To be honest, I think the baby today lives a much harder life than what we had. Even my mother, who looks after my nephew, says she would not have a child if she had to work as hard as my sister does [indeed, 20 per cent of young Chinese women say they will never have a baby, the same proportion as British women]. There's too much pressure on them to study, go to a good school. You have to have a good career, and the society is, I hate to say it, more selfish and ruthless. Old people used to be given a seat on the bus, now they will be ignored. I saw it last week: an old lady was sick on the street, and a cleaner cleaned it up and then walked by the lady, she didn't say a word to her. The world is really, really upsetting me. Like my nephew, he can speak a lot of words but he has a big temper, if he is not satisfied with something he shouts and he does not like animals. We had two birds at home and we were so kind to them, but my nephew will kick the cage. People are far from their natures. I don't know if I have become like that. Lots of people say the Cultural Revolution was awful, but I'm not sure it was so bad. People are paid so differently now. My dad and mum were both graduates of best universities, yet their salary was only slightly higher than that of a worker. Now there is big gap between rich and poor. Women as well as men are getting so stressed, feeling pushed by the crowd, dare not hang back. I don't resist it. I take it as I choose, I accept this as the real environment that I must live in.'

This Gal felt, every bit as much as so many of her Western contemporaries, that her society's values are wrong, that it is a crazy system. The huge difference is that she does not feel trapped in it, with no choices. She asserts that she chooses to accept it and make the best of a bad job.

If these Gals, and the others I interviewed from the same company, were representative of their ilk, then the well-to-do young women of Shanghai would seem to be intriguingly different from their Western contemporaries. They certainly have the Virus, but none of those I spoke to had the distress. They are blindly Doing rather than Being, aware of their discontent but seeing no alternative to the pursuit of status through money. It seems plausible that their equivalent in twenty years' time will be more like British students, agonising over whether to do arts or sociology at university, and after their degrees (where the recently established counselling services will endeavour to help them agonise over their drinking, drug-taking or bisexuality) whether both to take antidepressants and go to a therapist, or to do only one of them, as they battle with the mid-to-late-twenties blues. But for now, whereas these Gals were not exactly brimming with optimism, they are not depressed – at least, not yet.

The impression provided by this snapshot of the Shanghai Gals is borne out by the broader picture from the scientific evidence: Shanghai has the lowest prevalence of emotional distress amongst the fifteen countries in the WHO survey, at 4.3 per cent of the population, one-sixth of the level in America. At the same time, the Virus is rife and has been spreading at a rapid rate ever since 1978, when Deng Shaio Ping originated the Open Door policy to foster a commercial mentality, opining that 'to get rich is glorious'. To the transmission of Affluenza, such an injunction is the equivalent of what someone sneezing in your face is to flu (Deng also promoted the slogan 'look towards the future', the Chinese for which is a pun that also means 'look towards money'). Since then, material expectations have mushroomed. In terms of consumer goods, the cost of what is regarded as fundamental for a household has increased tenfold every decade. Before the Open Door (from the 1950s to the 1970s), there were 'Four Big Pieces' that every family regarded as essential: a bicycle, a sewing machine, a wristwatch and a radio, costing 100 yuan. In the 1980s these became a refrigerator, colour TV, washing machine and tape recorder, costing 1,000 yuan. In the 1990s it was air-conditioning, a computer, mobile phone and car, at 10,000 yuan.

Shanghai now has dozens of shopping malls and nationwide, in the last six years, 400 have been built, many of them twice the size of British ones. International luxury goods retailers are licking their lips. Armani's chief financial officer says that 'China is certainly the most prominent and most important market we have in front of us' (and I can give him the name of a teenage girl I met who specifically stated her ambition of being his CEO in ten years' time). At the moment, only 30 million Chinese can afford such luxuries, a very tiny minority of the 1.3 billion, but the American bank

Merrill Lynch estimates that within five years 20 per cent of worldwide sales of top-end goods, will be made in China. Credit Suisse First Boston predicts that by 2015 'Chinese consumers will have displaced American consumers as the primary engine of global economic growth'. On top of all this, property ownership has grown rapidly: by 2000, 77 per cent of urban families in China owned their own home. Although the prices are still affordable in relation to wages, even in upmarket Shanghai it is only a matter of time before mortgage-slavery becomes widespread as property prices rocket. The average cost of a home in Shanghai rose 19 per cent in each of the three years from 2002 to 2004.

What, then, is the vaccine that is preventing the Virus-infected Shanghai Gals from becoming distressed? Maybe it would work for us, too. Ethel, a marketing expert, thought so. Her office was lavishly modern, with laminated wooden floors, flashy sofas and all the accoutrements of the market-ing sorority. Ethel herself was pretty shiny, as well as extremely brisk and confident. Dressed in black, with thick, groovy specs, she must have been in her forties. She has worked for several years in Hong Kong and Singapore, well placed to make useful comparisons.

'Absolutely, the people here really are happy,' she said, 'extremely optimistic about the future, which is why they don't get stressed. If something goes wrong they still believe it will come right eventually.' Part of the reason was the pace at which things have improved. 'If people have not got much now, materially, they believe that the future will be better. A small home is not an issue here because they grew up in one. If they have a bigger one, that's a bonus, but it's not a big priority. School fees are taken as a way of life, something you have to live with. The important thing is that the income keeps coming so you will be able to find a way to pay.' But surely that is stressful? 'No. The way we think is, "Things are good now, they will get better and they are considerably better than they used to be in almost every way imaginable."'

Beyond this sense of relative prosperity, Ethel believes that a key reason why the Chinese are so cheerful is that they do not engage in introspection. 'Even compared with other Asian countries, the Chinese tend to be less reflective on themselves, are less emotionally in touch with their feelings. In a way, if you know less, it *is* better: gain some material thing and you are happy, this world is all there is. Maybe the more you probe, whether through religion or psychology, the more confused you get and the more confused, the less satisfied with what you are. The thinking pattern is simpler here. An entry-level executive of mine admired my shirt the other day, which she cannot afford, but she thinks, "I'll get something like that when I have more money." She does not feel depressed because I have got it.' Another example was an account manager who had moved to Shanghai from a small town. 'Her living conditions at home would have been not that bad, but very small. She had a small apartment here and when she visited mine she said, "If I had an apartment like this I'd do this, this and this." Now she is married and her husband has bought an apartment like mine. She has got in an interior designer, has done it as she would like, and she says, "That's it" – she doesn't ask for more. She has to pay off the mortgage for the apartment, so she doesn't shop so much, but she is happy. All she thinks about is getting a dog.'

This may be all very well, but surely when she has got used to her new surroundings and sees friends in even more sumptuous ones, she will start to make comparisons with her lot and feel dissatisfied? 'No, she will not be envious, she will just assume that she has the ability to achieve what her friend has in the longer run. She does not worry that her friend has got something she has not got.'

Whether Ethel is right about this is debatable. There are strong grounds for suspecting that in only twenty years' time, the Shanghainese will be as distressed as the English-speaking world. According to Professor Mingyuan Zhang, China's most distinguished psychiatrist and the head researcher for the Chinese part of the WHO study, that is how long it will take Shanghai to come to resemble the New York which it aspires to supplant in more ways than the height and number of its skyscrapers. When I asked Zhang what the prospects were for a city of Woody Allens, his reply was 'how long, rather than whether'. His conclusion was that 'in twenty years the mental illness rates will be very similar to England and America'.

Ethel's counter-argument is that Chinese culture will always keep the population from thinking too deeply about their emotional state and that this will protect them. Shanghai reminds Ethel of Hong Kong in the eighties. 'They did not know they were unhappy. They kept going, going, going, it's just a way of life, they don't stop. Maybe if they don't know they are unhappy there is no point telling them.' I doubted that. I suggested that they would be locked into Doing rather than Being in order to Have, and it would leave them feeling very empty. 'If they don't realise it, does it matter?' came the reply.

I encountered this idea repeatedly in my interviewees: that ignorance of misery is bliss. It raises some important questions for those of us afflicted by the Affluenza Virus. For one thing, is it really possible to be unhappy yet unaware of it? Could such suppression explain the low recorded rates of distress in China? Finally, assuming that it is possible to think you are well but be kidding yourself about it, is that a good strategy?

Regarding the first question, it seems clear that all of us sometimes do suppress negative experiences, and that someone can believe themselves to be happy as Larry whilst actually being depressed. For example, about 15 per cent of people in Britain and America have what is known as a repressor personality, systematically avoiding negative information. Asked how they are feeling, they will put a positive spin on it almost regardless of whether their life is heaven or hell, even though physiological measurements, like how much they sweat and other signs of stress, suggest that they are not conveying an accurate picture of their mental well-being. In many cases, they are deeply distressed but simply deny it to themselves and others. Once you accept, as nearly all psychologists now do, that we have preconscious and unconscious thoughts and feelings, there is no theoretical reason to assume that Ethel is wrong: you can simultaneously believe yourself to be fine whilst at a deeper level feeling terrible, suffering physical and mental symptoms.

There is also some evidence to suggest that Ethel is right, that the Chinese do suppress depressive feelings, although this probably does not explain their low rates of depression. In this respect, China is something of a *cause célèbre* amongst social psychiatrists. For twenty-five years now they have been debating the question, 'Do the low rates of depression found in China accurately reflect the citizens' true emotional state?' It goes back to 1980, when an American medical anthropologist called Arthur Kleinman began a series of studies of psychiatric patients at the principal hospital in the Chinese province of Hunan. He repeatedly encountered cases like Lin Xiling, a twenty-eight-year-old primary schoolteacher. She had suffered chronic headaches for six years, had bouts of dizziness, was easily fatigued, felt weak and had a ringing sound in her ears. Extensive checks for physical causes had revealed nothing, so Kleinman probed a bit deeper: 'Gently, sensing a deep disquiet behind the tight lips and mask-like squint, I ask Mrs Lin if she feels depressed. "Yes, I am unhappy," she replies. "My life has been difficult," she quickly adds as a justification. At this point, Mrs Lin looks away. Her thin lips tremble. The brave mask dissolves into tears.' It emerged that she had suffered a series of great misfortunes, including a sister driven to suicide by the Red Guards, a forced marriage and a stillborn child, and that by Western psychiatric definitions she was suffering from a major depression. She could not sleep, had lost her appetite, was joyless, anxious and felt it would be better to be dead, desperately and hopelessly regarding her life as a failure.

A Chinese psychiatrist did not dispute that diagnosis when Kleinman suggested it, but he explained that the correct Chinese term was 'neurasthenia', a syndrome of exhaustion and diffuse bodily complaints which the Chinese believe is caused by inadequate physical energy in the central nervous system. Kleinman subsequently discovered that neurasthenia had been diagnosed in around 40 per cent of all Chinese psychiatric patients. Widely recognised in South-East Asian nations and the countries of the former Soviet Union, neurasthenia was originally identified in the West, at the end of the nineteenth century. Kleinman offers evidence that in much of the developing world, people we might regard as depressed usually talk about physical symptoms, such as tiredness or aches and pains, rather than their emotions or thoughts. When Kleinman gave his Chinese patients antidepressants, the depressive symptoms did decrease, but they would still maintain that their condition was physical. This was partly due to the social ramifications of the different labels. Emotional distress carried a huge stigma in Maoist China because it implied criticism not only of one's family but of the State itself; effectively, this made it a dissident political act, whereas neurasthenia was not regarded in this way. Kleinman discovered that most of the patients were suffering extreme loss of autonomy under the regime, and concluded that in many cases neurasthenic symptoms were one of the few sanctioned ways of gaining support and a measure of control over their circumstances.

He followed up his findings by questioning whether it was at all appropriate to describe most of the patients as having any illlness. Their problems could instead be seen as healthy and natural reactions to severe psycho-social stresses. As Jung Chang has famously since chronicled, virtually all aspects of the material and mental life of the Chinese under Mao were tightly policed. For the vast majority, to perceive oneself as hopeless, powerless and helpless would be accurate reflections of their true circumstances, an argument much like the one advanced by Erich Fromm in *The Sane Society*, only

applied to China: it's the society that's mad, not the person
feeling distressed as a result of its madness. Notably, however,
Kleinman did not follow through the logic of this argument
to apply it to his own society, filled as it is with hopeless and
powerless African-Americans having medical, psychiatric
labels applied to them. That would not have gone down well
with his peers. Instead, Kleinman kept his focus on China,
concluding that to identify their malaise as symptoms of a
medical illness (whether labelled neurasthenia or depression)
rather than as healthy responses to a sick environment would
be a misuse of psychiatry. If they showed up as physical
symptoms, like tummy aches and dizziness, and if the social
system made such categorisation a safe means of showing
dissent, then it would be quite wrong to slap Western psychiatric tags on them.

Whatever the merits of this part of Kleinman's argument,
regarding the actual prevalence of depression in China, more
recent, thorough studies have suggested that the Chinese really
are less prone to suffering it. It is true that when depressed,
they are more likely to attribute the problem to physical
causes and express it initially in physical symptoms, probably
because of the stigma attached to being categorised emotionally distressed. Until 1980, under Mao, psychology was
officially condemned as '90 per cent useless' and '10 per cent
distorted and bourgeois phoney science', so it paid not to call
your problems psychological. Somatisation, a condition in
which physical complaints are caused by psychological problems, is compounded by the Chinese language, in which words
for emotions and bodily states are similar, and by Chinese
philosophy, which conceptualises distress very differently

from the Western scientific mind-body dualism. However, the lower rates of depression are also believed to be a reflection of fundamental Chinese cultural values, long preceding Mao. There is a potent tradition of quiescence and stoicism in the face of adversity, an uncomplaining endurance of traumatic events and severe hardships (such as bereavement or starvation), whereas it takes much less to produce howls of complaint from Westerners. The very strong and abiding commitment to family networks has survived Maoism and provides important succour in times of material hardship or emotional suffering. Perhaps above all, optimism, determination and purpose – what I term 'positive volition' – are strongly encouraged by the culture: a person is expected to be hopeful, self-directed and resilient in the pursuit of goals, whatever the obstacles.

Oddly, the scientific evidence seems at first to contradict what I was told by my Chinese interviewees, all of whom describe themselves and their peers as optimistic. It does not find high levels of optimism, as defined by (usually American) social-science criteria, nor of happiness and life satisfaction. In studies comparing Chinese with Americans, the Chinese consistently score lower on these counts, as well as on self-esteem, and the same is true for other Asian countries. But there are compelling reasons to doubt whether these studies are a true measure of what either Americans or Asians actually feel. One is that the Chinese report much less depression. If they really were as unhappy as the studies suggest, it would be odd if they were not also depressed. Even greater reason to doubt the results of these studies comes from investigations of the way the Chinese think. These demonstrate a self-critical, modest and un-narcissistic mindset which is totally at variance with the American mentality that underpins nearly all the well-being research.

In America, it has been claimed, emotional well-being is actually better if one lives in an optimistic bubble of positive illusions, deceptively rose-tinted. Americans who think that their friends like them more than they really do, who believe that bad things are less likely to happen to them than is statistically the case, or who have an exaggerated notion of their abilities, are consistently found to be less prone to depression. The depressed, according to these researchers, suffer from 'depressive realism' (a curious formulation: those who distort reality by painting it pink are healthier than those who perceive it accurately). Some American researchers have gone so far as to propose that positive illusions are a universal foundation of emotional well-being.

A major shortcoming of this research is that it does not take into account the fact that around 15 per cent of Britons and Americans have repressor personalities. In one study, repressors accounted wholly for the bubble of positive illusions: all the bubblers were distressed but didn't know it; measured separately, the illusions were absent in the 85 per cent of us who are non-repressors. On top of this, it is important to remember that artificial boosting of self-esteem is a huge industry in America, with school programmes to increase it and government task forces targeting it (indeed, there is currently talk of fostering this faux-happiness in British schools and of using a national network of psychologists to foster it in adults through cognitive behavioural therapy). Thousands of American pop psychology books and tens of thousands of scientific papers are devoted to the subject. Partly as a consequence, when Americans are asked about their self-esteem, the great majority will score theirs as high rather than moderate because their culture encourages this kind of self-appraisal. When asked to rate their 'interpersonal sensitivity', half of Americans saw themselves as in the top 10 per cent, nationally. By definition, of course, that cannot be so.

In contrast, the average Chinese person when asked to rate their emotional state would describe it as only moderate. In general, in collectivist Asian societies, to claim to be better off than your peers is frowned upon because it could upset group harmony. Visibly exhibiting high self-esteem is contrary to the Confucianist emphasis on modesty, and in some Asian societies positive illusions are hardly found at all. If anything, there is a bubble of negative illusions, because a sharp focus on one's shortcomings is strongly encouraged from early childhood. Instead of being continually boosted by parents, as happens in America, Asian children are exhorted to search for their inadequacies and weaknesses so that they are able to correct them. When seeking out evidence on which to base self-regard, Asians are more likely to turn to failures than to successes, to try and learn from mistakes and evaluate esteem from them.

This way of thinking could result in a very negative existence, a state of 'accentuate the negative, eliminate the positive, don't mess with Mr In-Between', and an ignoring of successful outcomes when they do happen. One reason why it doesn't is that what is prized highest of all is effort, perseverance and endurance: your best is good enough. So long as you have tried as hard as you can, that is sufficient, as far as your parents and society are concerned. No-one will castigate you, and you are under no pressure to castigate yourself, so long as you have tried your hardest. In America, only the outcome is accepted as the basis for self-esteem – the good exam result, the successful deal; in Asia, you can fail and still feel good provided you gave your all.

How deeply this is pickled into the Chinese psyche is shown by studies of the values which their children possess from a young age. One study presented Chinese and American four- to six-year-olds with two stories, as follows:

1. 'Little Bear watches his Mommy and Daddy catch fish. He really wants to learn how to catch fish by himself. He tries for a while but he cannot catch any fish. Then he says to himself, "Forget it! I don't want to catch any fish!"'
2. 'Little Birdie is learning how to fly. He jumps off a tree, but falls down to the ground. Daddy Bird and Mommy Bird bring him back up again. He tries again and again, and he falls down again and again. After trying many times, Little Birdie finally learns how to fly.'

Asked about these stories, the American children showed much greater interest in the methods by which Bear or Birdie could improve their performance, in the creative strategies that might work. By contrast, the Chinese children focused on the virtue of concentrated persistence. Nearly all the children in both groups liked the Birdie after his valiant efforts. However, after the Bear story, nearly all the Americans liked him despite his failure, whereas nearly two-thirds of the Chinese said they disliked him, critical of his lack of perseverance.

Underpinning Confucianism are three primary tenets: the principle of contradiction and paradox, so that there are always two opposed propositions to be sought, both of which may be true; the principle of change, positing a universe that is constantly in flux; and the principle of holism, by which all things in the universe are seen to be connected. This fosters a dialectical mentality in which the same object may contain both yin and yang, good and bad, masculinity and femininity, strength and weakness. Whereas Western thought tends to be linear and less concerned with emotion, with both sides of an argument being considered but incongruities resolved, Asian thought permits a great deal of bad to reside alongside the good. With regard to the self, failure is as readily acknowledged as success. Negative emotions are not excluded in the frantic attempt to play up positive ones advocated by most American pop psychology books; they are tolerated. For this reason, when the Chinese are asked to rate themselves on a scale from 'very happy' to 'very unhappy', or from 'very likeable' to 'very unlikeable', they are far more prepared than Americans to countenance the negative or intermediate ratings. Acknowledging negatives is correlated with depression ('depressive realism') in America, whereas in Asian countries it is not.

Another vital difference is that the very concept of individual self-esteem is alien to the interdependent Asian self: it is the group's standing that matters, not the individual's. This version of collectivism is crucial for immunising against depression, even though, from an American perspective, it should be disastrous. When they fail, the Chinese are more likely than Americans to attribute it to their own lack of ability or flawed character, in order to protect parents and their wider group from humiliation. In America, that would lead to wrist-slashing desperation because they would take it very personally, but in China, since one does not think of one's capacities as one's fault, there is a get-out clause: 'I am the way I am because of my family and community. It's not my fault that I lack abilities.'

On the other hand, when the Chinese succeed they are much less likely than Americans to beat their own drum by attributing it to their cleverness or diligence, implying instead that credit should go to their teachers, parents and support groups. Again, this could be a toxic prescription for despair. You could end up never feeling that your achievements were yours – it was the group's success – and taking the blame for failures that were not your fault. It is the polar opposite of the American Way, advocated by countless 'Think Positive' and 'How to Be a Leader' pop psychology texts: in individualistic, corporate America, you are supposed to grab as much of the glory for any successes as you can, then play them up, and to blame peers for failure. In China, blaming yourself for the group's failures is done from a different position which provides two crucial escape routes: in the end, the fact that you have let the side down is ultimately due to the family and community that created you; and so long as you have done your best, though you may take the blame for stuff that is not your fault, you can still feel good about yourself.

Confucianism explains why blaming yourself for failures and not taking credit for success does not depress the Chinese. It makes for a culture of a group shame rather than individual guilt. In the West, with its Christian tradition of 'thou shalt not' from the Ten Commandments, the norm is moral censure, in which we look upon ourselves as bad and wrong. It makes depressive self-attacking (saying 'I'm fat, I'm stupid, I'm lazy' when you are not) a common response to adversity. In Asia, it is dutiful attitudes to parents and maintaining face that are crucial – face being the avoidance of disgrace for your family or by extension, your society. One of the Shanghai Gals provided an example of this which would be almost unimaginable in a person from an English-speaking nation. She told me that during her time as a student in America, she was so concerned about her role as a representative of the Chinese nation that she held back from sexual relationships. 'When a man was interested in me I would think about how it would seem to others before I did anything. I did not want people to think that Chinese people care about the man's attractiveness or status, I would worry a lot about how our nation would look because of my behaviour. I would prefer my classmates to think I am a good, popular girl who gets on with all her classmates, instead of getting a reputation for approaching an American guy, which some Chinese girls did do, hard. I would not do that, I would show American guys that Chinese girls are not so cheap.' This also exemplifies the different way in which collectivist values define what is good or bad behaviour. It's hard to imagine the characters in *Sex and the City* regarding putting America's prestige first when evaluating an opportunity for sex.

Because shame-avoidance is so important in the collectivist setting, lying is not seen as bad, and putting on a mask is regarded as essential. Yet again, this would be alien in the West – a prescription for falsehood and the empty bourgeois existential void so vividly portrayed by the likes of T.S. Eliot and Tolstoy. But the mask adopted is not of the 'Look at me, aren't I great?' variety so commonly worn in America (disastrously so, in the case of some violent men: several studies have now shown that the most aggressive Americans are ones who have grandiose self-esteem; they are particularly dangerous if this false esteem is challenged, liable to behave violently). Rather than brassy bravado to shore up insecurity, the Chinese mask is designed to protect one's group from shame.

It would seem, then, that Ethel and the Gals' claim that many of their peers are unhappy but do not realise it is a misconception. More likely is that the Chinese succeed in acknowledging reality accurately, compared with Americans, but at the same time their culture encourages them to feel shame and to put on masks to protect their family and community. Above all, the Chinese culture allows you to feel good if you do your best and encourages you to accept that, whether things go right or wrong, ultimately your background is the reason.

The implications are momentous for people in the English-speaking world. Rather than live in rose-tinted bubbles of positive illusion, we would do better to face reality. Whereas the Chinese do not score highly on American optimism scales, they are positive about the future, but only realistically so. Allied to this, they are almost fanatically determined to wrest control of their fate from destiny, and to take responsibility for it. Put the two together and you have positive volition. To the extent that you have an (American) unrealistic, inaccurate notion of your capacities, or of the likelihood of misfortune befalling you, you cannot change your experience or behaviour for the better to function more effectively and evade disasters; on a wider scale, nor can you alter the world you are in so that it is less harmful to you. Spin, at least on a personal level, is not going to be good for your emotional well-being, and calling realism depressive is a grotesque distortion of the truth.

In Britain, academic or professional success is not primarily the consequence of individual capacities but of social class and schooling. Oxbridge students are deemed 'bright', meaning that their success is the result of individual ability. Far more, it comes from social class background. Only 7 per cent of children attend public schools, yet nearly half of Oxbridge undergraduates went to one, and there are similarly disproportionate percentages of public school students at other top universities. Children from high-income homes are far more likely to have well-educated parents who have a greater input into their academic performance. This, combined with the smaller classes, better teachers and well-developed links to Oxbridge colleges enjoyed by public schools, is why more of their alumni go to top universities. In fact, since 1970 there has been no increase in upward social mobility in Britain as a result of education. Your family background is still by far the strongest indicator of whether, and where, you will go to university. Rather than patting themselves on the back for getting into a top university, it would be far more emotionally sustaining for the privileged students to give due credit to their family and the class system for the high grades that got them there, which is what would happen in China. Equally, if such a privileged person does not get into a top university, far better for us if the Christian tradition of blame plays no part in the response. It would be much more accurate for that person to identify their own shortcomings as the reason, as the Chinese do. Only then could they improve performance (if they so wished).

All these points were strikingly exemplified by the only Chinese person I met who had suffered a major depression. On first meeting Tai, I assumed that she was in her mid-thirties, but she was only twenty-five. Her face was drained of colour. A few inches taller than the average Chinese woman, she had the standard trim figure (I hardly met a single person, of either sex, who could be described as overweight).

She described her depression, as follows. 'Two or three years ago, when I broke up with my ex-boyfriend, life was nothing to me. Every day your sky is grey, there is no sunshine. I was very depressed, actually. The worst period of the day was after work. I had no friends and the only thing I could do was go to the university library and watch videos, two or three in a row. It was a very unforgettable period. I would go to bed at around ten or eleven and only fall asleep for two hours, at about four. Yet I had to work during the day, as the secretary to a general manager. That was why my health was under the weather.' Psychiatrists would term this a reactive depression because it was clearly triggered by an external event, the end of her relationship with the boyfriend. 'It only lasted for one year [she gave a nervous cough, her eyes glistening]. We broke up because he will want his wife not to be very independent or very strong in her career – a proper wife. However, I was definitely not that kind [laughter]. On Christmas Eve he told me that he wanted to end it, very cruel to do it then, and I cried for the whole night. He was very sorry, he said, "Can't you forget? Can't we keep our relationship?" I said, "No, you have told me the truth." I didn't sleep and had to take an exam the next day. Actually, I did very well. Now we do have the relationship of friends. He has his girlfriend and I have my boyfriend.'

I questioned Tai closely about the feelings she had during her depression, checking that it was different from the sadness that afflicts most of us when a relationship breaks up and to see if there were any culturally distinct features. 'I did not feel bad about myself, only that I was not his type in appearance or character. His girlfriend now is very lovely, very woman, I was not.' That she did not start attacking herself is a significant difference from much Western depression, where guilt and failure are common themes. In accord with her culture, she had carried out a thorough inventory of how she might have tried harder, and concluded that it was not her fault. More important was her loss of face. 'To speak frankly, I think I would have been much less upset if it had been I who said we should break up. That's why I cried. It was for many reasons, but maybe that was the most important: that it wasn't me who raised the question, he did it first. Anyway, it passed.'

A key issue was that she was not good enough for him, in terms of status; whereas he was doing a degree, she was doing only a diploma. 'Once, he told me that although I was a student with only a diploma, I was much smarter than the degree students. I was very sure I was smart but you have to face the facts. In China there is a saying, "You have to match door to door if you're going to marry," match the status of the two people. He was a BA graduate whereas I was doing a diploma, and I guess to "match" I needed to be a BA as well. We communicated very well, talked about everything, and sometimes he was surprised that I could talk about things he thought only he understood. But still, in reality I suspect he was taking my status into account. He thought he could see what I would be in the future, though if he were to meet me with my status now [she is about to get her BA], he might choose me.' It sounded a bit like what sometimes happens when a public school-educated student splits up with a state-educated one at a British university, a feeling that the class system has got in the way. The difference here might be that loss of face is a big issue, whereas in Britain a spurned state-educated, lover might put it down to personal traits, like not being attractive or clever enough. Tai blamed social rather than psychological attributes. The sense in which she was 'not good enough' was in status, not personal.

So far, we are looking at a reactive depression; however, it soon emerged the problem ran deeper. 'I get depressed sometimes now, but I try not to think about those things too deeply. Every night when I close my eyes, the worries that I have no time to think about during the day come: my future, what I should be, my career, my life, everything. It's not that I want to think about those things, it happens automatically. I hate that. I think I'm lost now, lost again. I don't know what I should do for the next step.' Her career featured as the main element in her sense of being lost. 'My current boyfriend and I bought a house and we are planning to deco-rate it in September, but the most important decision is my career. I don't know what kind of job is suitable for me. I don't know what I am good at. In this big city, everything is measured by money. My brother tells me I've changed – "You've become so money-oriented' – and it's the truth, it's a fact that you work for money. I think now I work for money because I have a house.'

I asked if she gets on well with her boyfriend, and she smiled broadly, her face creasing as she grappled with the fact that it was imperfect. 'Umm, it's hard to say. He's a very good man, very nice, very kind. I know that he loves me much more than I love him. He wants to keep everything inside himself, but it would be better if he communicated with me more. With my ex-boyfriend I can communicate very well, even now, but he didn't love me – I always compare the two. So everything has not been decided yet between us, even though we've bought a house. My colleagues say, "Are you going to marry?" and I joke, "Why do I need to marry?" I just want to have my-self. It's very simple.' A Confucian admission of contradiction immediately followed: 'Yet everything is also foggy, in the wind; I'm lost, again. I guess I need to be further educated, to do a masters. To some extent then, I will feel secure. I'm not sure what in, maybe psychology or if I want to make money, an MBA. Life is tough. It would be better if I didn't come into the world [laughs]. But I will live very well. I said to myself once, "My parents give life to me so I must survive myself very well, not just waste my life." I will try my best. By the age of sixty or seventy I will look back and I will not regret.'

Those last thoughts are startlingly different from what a Western young woman might voice. Despite feeling under the cosh, Tai is genuinely positive in her hopes for the future, and instead of feeling helpless she demonstrates an admirable determination to make the best of what she has got: positive volition, and this despite being depressed. It is very different from the 'call black white' school of positive psychology fostered by Western cognitive psychologists. Whereas they would advocate a crude deletion of negative thoughts and painting your bubble rose-coloured, Tai is facing up to reality first of all, and only then declaring her intention to change things for the better. Her declarations of intent do not have the hollow ring of the American positive psychology which our present government seems to be embracing with such enthusiasm. They are based on experience – Tai has already overcome many adversities – and on a truthful appraisal of her situation.

However, what is most interesting about Tai is that she is depressed, and despite possessing the Shanghai vaccine of positive volition, her moods are often black. The reason the vaccines did not confer immunity in her case emerged when I asked about her background. She was not raised in Shanghai, but came here from a small fishing village to attend university, having risen through the system by educational success. This is a rare event. Until very recently, most citizens did not move, either geographically or socially. The values from which she came were quite different to the ones she found in Shanghai, and she was able to provide a distinctly detached account of the Big City. 'The Shanghai girls seem to be very good at survival of the fittest. They measure everything by money and won't think about deep, crucial things. They will enjoy their life, have very full days, working hard, have holidays, have a nice place to share with friends, every fashion trend – they will enjoy it. I've been here ten years and started to become more that way about a year or so ago. If I told a Shanghai girl I am depressed, they will not have this subject discussed very deeply, just not want to talk about it, too painful for them. They would think, "Why are you talking about that? We want to talk about happy things, fashion, clothes I bought, where we can enjoy our lunchtime. Across the road is a new coffee shop." Very material, I guess. They will say they are unhappy about a phone call that was annoying or if their boss was not listening to them, but it is not like my deep, fundamental unhappiness. I think they were taught by their parents from when they were born that you have to learn to smile to survive in the city: "Don't think about those depressing things, it won't work. You have no choice, you are living in this society with one government and they control all, you are not allowed to have these ideas, they will do you no good, so just forget about them."'

When Tai first came to Shanghai she did not see things that way, but she says she has gradually come to realise that the only way to stay sane is to adjust. 'Maybe I will compromise to the material world because I have no choice. If I can find another choice then I will take it.' Whereas the Shanghai Gals are completely pragmatic, Tai is a harsh critic of the growing materialism. 'We are victims of the Open Door policy. When the door was closed, the people lived in peace, got on with their work, not caring about material things. The door was opened and it all rushed in – new ideas, rubbishy objects, good and bad things.' Yet having said this, as ever, she balanced the comments with realism and optimism about the future. 'You can't avoid one generation having to undergo this, but I know that one day all the people will go back to the spiritual things that concern the developed countries. [If only this appraisal of the West were accurate!] Right now, here, you have to worry about money, I have to make money. That's not the most important thing for me but I don't want to live a very poor life. I still have to care about my inside things, my spiritual things, so they always conflict. How to balance it? It is difficult. That's why it has taken me more than eight years to understand why the Shanghai girls look so happy and find it so easy to live. For quite a long time I could not get used to it but now I am. That was maybe why my brother was saying I am changing. You need a thick skin.'

Tai's depression appears to have been caused by a conflict between her inner needs and the materialism that surrounds her. Her peers feel no such conflict. However much they may also criticise contemporary materialism, none feel torn by it, whereas Tai, from her simple rural background, does.

Her story has important implications for all of us: to what extent should we ignore or suppress depressing truths in order to keep the show on the road? Obviously, it is best not to be in social or work settings which conflict with your core values. If, deep down, you want to be a painter but are a merchant banker, you are liable to feel torn, like Tai (who would like to write novels). If you prefer understated authenticity in people, do not marry someone who wants to spend their time at cocktail parties, nightclubs or on arriviste millionaires' yachts in the Mediterranean. But whatever you choose, there is always liable to be some measure of contradiction between your ideals and reality, and some measure of self-deception is essential if you are to cope with this lack of 'self-concordance' (having a good balance between your life and your values). In a study comparing levels of self-concordance in four different nations (China, Taiwan, South Korea and America), it was found to be a strong predictor of well-being in all of them. In the Asian cultures there was much more pressure to conform to parental and societal demands. However, Asians who had actively adopted, rather than blindly accepted, these demands and made them their own were just as likely to have well-being as Americans who had been given far more choice and had done so. The authors of the study concluded that 'it is possible for people to "own their own goals" everywhere, regardless of their cultural membership, their income, family education and the concrete focus of their goals'. Although putting on 'a face to meet the faces that we meet' (in T.S. Eliot's words) is essential to some degree for all of us everywhere, the more it resembles what lies behind, the more likely it will lead to the expression of our authentic needs (rather than confected wants), and not just the biological ones, like food or sex, but for relatedness to others and playfulness as well.

One could argue that Tai should simply adjust to her circumstances, develop Shanghai values. However, the evidence is that she has a far better chance than her contemporaries of leading a fulfilling life, even though she gets depressed and they do not. Because she does not easily accept blind Doing and hankers for Being, the face she presents to the world and the career decisions she will make are far more likely, in the long run, to express her inner life, to be self-concordant.

To a considerable extent, Tai's depression would seem to be caused by the absence of the immunity to distress that her peers seem to have developed (the 'thick skin'). In Shanghai,

Fromm's consumerist insanity seems to have replaced Mao's totalitarian lunacy. In Tai's account, the Shanghai Gals equate money with freedom and strive for it through their profession or a rich man. It seems that if they get the dosh through work, they cannot hope for intrinsic motivations to be satisfied because they must put their selves at the service of their employers. If they do it by attaching themselves to a rich man, then, equally, they must be his servant in exchange for the freedom to buy expensive watches and clothes. But unlike Tai, they believe in these goals and have not started to strive for more intrinsic satisfactions – they are self-concordant. Tai longs to be a writer, but she cannot see a way to achieve this intrinsic goal while staying part of the money-seeking world. Whereas the Gals live on the surface, Tai believes in something deeper. With some justice, Ethel would argue that this is why she gets depressed, that she is asking too many questions which is making her self-discordant. If she would only keep her nose to the grindstone and stop seeking more profound gratification, she would feel okay, as her peers do.

The trouble is, once basic, survival material needs are met, we start seeking something else. That could be still greater material comfort or luxury, or, as in Tai's case, something inner, but whichever it is, self-discordance will be liable to follow. Shanghai will soon be full of Tais, and the Gals' immunity will soon wear off – positive volition will not be enough. Indeed, the seeds of self-discordance were already very evident in some of the Gals' comments. There was the one who had felt culture shock on returning from Britain and bemoaned the materialism of her peers; and there was the one who is hunting for a rich husband but is so disenchanted that, at the same time, she feels it would be wrong to bring a child into her world. In the end, once the struggle for material needs is won, we can move on to meeting other intrinsic, authentic needs. That is why, in the long term, Tai is ahead of the game: she is already wrestling with the problems that will be the norm in her society twenty years hence.

A crucial reason for the lack of discordance amongst the Gals is that the improvement in material conditions and civic freedom in China is still so recent. Until a few years ago, only a tiny proportion of Chinese had a standard of living which we would regard as adequate, and today, two-thirds still have a relatively low one (the average annual income only recently topped £500). Just twenty-five years ago, the rural population were five times poorer in real income than at present, and the urbanites were three times worse off. At the same time, although China is not a democratic nation and the Communist Party still keeps a close eye on anyone who dissents from its dictates, freedom of movement around the country, opportunities for self-expression and restrictions on living have hugely improved.

In Ha Gin's novel *Waiting*, to take one example of what life was like under Chairman Mao, a married man who has not lived with his wife for years is unable to get a divorce because the local town judges refuse to grant it. He has to wait eighteen years before marrying the woman he loves, with whom in the meantime he dare not have an affair for fear of severe retribution from the authorities. Where he works, how much he is paid, where he lives, are all completely out of his control. In that curious mixture of feudalism, communism and traditional collectivism which was Maoism, practicality and being grateful for what you have were good for survival. The choice was not between Having and Being, as in a developed, consumer society; it was Do or Die.

Although the State still controls life here to a significant degree, with two-thirds of Shanghai residents having government-paid jobs, the worst excesses of totalitarian tyranny no longer affect the vast majority. Compared with the conditions under which they were brought up, or with those of most compatriots who still live in the countryside, middle-class Chinese are still rubbing their eyes with disbelief at their good fortune. In terms of relative deprivation, if you are only one generation from poverty and extreme totalitarianism, what has happened since 1978 must seem miraculous. Just as paracetamol suppresses fever if you have the flu virus, that upbeat feeling keeps at bay the symptoms of the Affluenza Virus.

The most perfect embodiment of all this during my visit was George. Despite his forty-nine years, he still has a full head of jet-black hair and only a slight paunch. He is a tremendously engaging chap, amusing and amused. Most Chinese people I have met are outwardly unemotional by Western standards, with a seemingly steady mood. George was unusual in this respect, more like a stereotypical Italian. When he makes a point he waves his arms, his voice reaching contralto as he squeaks with amusement at some folly of Mao's regime. At other times his face goes black with despair, and his voice is as sad as an operatic tenor bemoaning the suicide of his beloved. He occupies a senior position in a corporation, but doesn't need to work because he managed to make a few bob on the stock exchange with some cunning wheezes.

As a child, he had endured considerable material adversity. 'My childhood was terrible, so tough. My parents were extremely poor and uneducated. When I was born, in 1954, there were a lot of poor people, but at least they usually had food. My family was often starving. I can remember sharing a tiny bowl of porridge with my brother for breakfast. Food was always short during Mao's days, there was never pork or beef or fish, it was rationed. An adult was allowed 14 kilos of rice or noodles a month. In our home there were five kids, my parents and grandparents: eight people living on a total of £2.60 a month. I still remember vividly how, when I went to school, I could not pay for my food so I just did not have any. It is quite incredible to think of it.'

When he was nineteen, as part of the Cultural Revolution, George was sent off to be a labourer. 'If there was more than one child in the family, then one had to go. At the beginning, my elder sister was sent to the very far north, near the Russian border; it took four or five days by train. I was lucky, sent to the suburbs of Shanghai. One time we were set to digging irrigation dykes to reclaim the land. That was in winter. It was so hard. After only two or three days one of my colleagues went crazy and had to be sent to the psychiatric hospital. We left our dormitory at six and walked for an hour to get to the job site. Then began the digging and carrying of the soil. We were from the city and not used to that. The sludge was so slippery, people often did it in naked feet, so cold. You did that until lunch, then back to work, then leave for home around five.'

Rebellion was not an option. 'I have to say that China is a feudal country. People here will not stand up and question authority, say no to the government or the boss, they will never think of that. Very, very few people would leave the farm. If they did escape, they would live by thieving. People who objected would be forced to criticise themselves, depending on how extreme had been their protest. They would be put under very extreme trouble.'

The extremes of poverty and totalitarianism that George endured illustrate a fundamental reason why the Affluenza Virus has not yet produced high rates of distress in Shanghainese: in his generation there is an acute awareness of how much better things have become. Although the younger middle-class Shanghainese I interviewed did not suffer directly to the same degree, they are aware of how fortunate they are (as well as, paradoxically, bemoaning the increased materialism and speaking longingly of the past). In being pragmatic and materialist, they do not feel much discordance – not yet, at any rate. Over the next twenty years, Shanghai will be a fascinating natural experiment into the causes of emotional distress. The buzz that comes from relative prosperity – compared with the recent past and the relatively poor majority of Chinese citizens today – will soon recede. After that, only positive volition will be there to ward off relative deprivation; studies show that, ironically, the sense of relative deprivation will be felt most keenly precisely when things are getting better, just as they are in China today.

Five necessary and sufficient conditions have been proposed for creating the resentful, combustible variant of relative deprivation that results in revolutions:

1. wanting something (such as a pay rise or promotion);

2. seeing that someone else possesses it;
3. feeling entitled to it;
4. feasibility that you could obtain it;
5. the absence of a sense that it was your fault that you did not get it.

If a person passes through the first four stages but not the last, they are liable to self-blaming depression rather than the resentment that can lead to mass unrest. In the fourth stage, you conclude that it was because of your own inadequacy that you did not obtain what you wanted. This fourth stage is the one in which most of us live in the English-speaking world. For example, a study of American twenty-five- to forty-year-olds found that those 'who felt there was a gap between what they obtained from their job and what they wanted ... expressed significantly more self-reported depression'. The depressed were more likely to feel that they were not getting what they were entitled to, to regard themselves as doing worse than others in a similar position and, above all, to feel it was their fault (the fourth stage).

Despite Ethel's conviction that her employee who has got the home she longed for will be happy to stick with that as her aspiration, it seems unlikely that she is right. Far more probable is the view of Mingyuan Zhang: that widespread depression will set in at being unable to achieve ever-higher material goals. However, there is another possible outcome. When people pass into the final, fifth stage of deprivation, they cease to blame themselves for the lack of improvement. Studies of protest movements and civil revolts suggest that it is often precisely when people begin to get what they want that they start to want even more. Thus, although an individual or group may be objectively better off, after, for example, being granted some (but not all) new freedoms or improved living conditions they were demanding, they may feel subjectively worse off because their expectations keep being raised, beyond whatever is the present level. The conviction endures that these ever greater expectations are their entitlement, however high the expectations go. If this evidence is correct, the Chinese leaders may be sitting on a powder-keg.

Vaccines

1. Your best is good enough

The cornerstone of Chinese emotional well-being is that, if you fail, then as long as you really have given it your best shot, you are not culpable. It removes the necessity of beating yourself up, and others will accept your performance if they believe you did your best. It also removes the need to discuss what might have been because it's irrelevant if there was nothing else that could have been done.

2. It is not your fault that you are who you are

Recognising the extent to which your individual characteristics, whether good or bad, are the product of your family and society also protects against unmerited self-blame or exaggerated notions of your own value. Whereas many Western thirty-something singletons are prone to wild fluctuations in their self-esteem, awareness of what 'caused' you creates a much more balanced, stable basis for appraising your performance.

3. At the same time, you must accept that the particular situation you are in is chosen by you and that you are a free agent, with volition

Perhaps aided by a Confucian acceptance of contradictions, it is important to always take responsibility for your life. Yes, your background and society determine your options and capacities but yes, also, within those constraints you must make choices and live with their consequences. This is not Gloria Gaynor shrieking 'I Will Survive', it is Tai asserting that only she can decide what course her life will take.

4. Form as truthful and accurate an assessment as possible of yourself and your society, rather than living in a rose-tinted bubble of positive illusions

Unless you make an unsparing diagnosis of yourself and your situation, you will be incapable of changing them for the better. Warding off depression with dishonest or fantastical assessments will not build you a solid platform from which to progress.

5. Hope for the best, expect the worst

Chinese optimism – the abiding conviction that if I try hard I will be able to improve matters – is far more valuable than that fostered in America by positive psychology, which is largely concerned with removing the negative. It is always helpful to believe in your capacity to achieve goals, however modest they may be and so long as they are realistic.

6. Don't be scared of examining your failures as much as your successes when searching for clues about what to do

You can improve your performance only by looking at what went wrong, as well as what went right. Western positive psychology focuses exclusively on the successes to keep your pecker up, but that is at the expense of realising what needs to change.

7. Don't take responsibility for what is not your fault or for others' achievements

As long as you have done your best, you cannot be faulted if things go wrong. Equally, if you grab glory that is not yours, sooner or later it will catch up with you – apart from the risk of exposure, it will make you feel a fake.

8. Avoid black-and-white simplification, embrace complexity and tolerate contradictions

Complexity and contradictions create confusion for Westerners because they want a right answer. Almost always, there is no definitive one. If you can live with the foggy nature of reality, it is less worrying because oversimplifications for the sake of clarity will be constantly upset by contrary evidence.

9. Be as self-concordant as possible

We are always going to be self-contradictory to some extent, but the more you can align your values with the life you live, the better it will be. To take an extreme example, it's no good being a stockbroker who longs to be a social worker or if you are a novelist who writes obscure texts but also wants to be rich and famous, you are obviously going to have a problem.

Better to be a stockbroker with a social conscience (perhaps making donations to charities) or a novelist prepared to compromise in the name of entertainment, if money and fame are also important to you. If your values and your life are at odds, you need to scrutinise what really matters to you and be prepared to live with the consequences of your decisions.

Chapter 4
Replace Virus Motives (with Intrinsic Ones)

Virus motives are more distressing than Virus goals. A motive is the reason we do something; its goal is the outcome we seek as a consequence of doing it. Virus motives are reward and praise, looking for others' approbation in order to feel pleased or disappointed by what we do. Virus goals are money, possessions, good appearance and fame.

Most of us have some such goals, to some degree, but as long as our motives are not Virus-infected, that is not necessarily harmful. It is possible to be a merchant banker, pursuing money as the outcome, but to do so for non-Virus reasons, like finding the work fascinating. As we saw in the last chapter, the Shanghai Gals have heavily Virus-infected goals, but several did not have Virus motives. The only depressed Gal had adopted Virus motives and could clearly see that this was what was distressing her. But the best illustration of the damage done by Virus motives during my mind tour was an undergraduate at Oxford University, a young man called Simon.

Dressed rather like a country squire, in tweed hacking jacket, and with a fruity upper-class accent, Simon surprises me when it emerges that he was educated at a comprehensive, and has serious political aspirations. He holds senior posts in the Oxford Union and the National Union of Students, and has already made it onto shortlists for selection as a parliamentary candidate for one of the main political parties. Handsome, with curly red hair, he speaks with great confidence and a good deal of splashy flourish, full of ironies and complex unexpectedness. For instance, when I asked him about his father's profession, he said, 'I'm not entirely sure, because I don't like discussing it with him. But you know when they put pylons up in the countryside? I think he's the person who stands beside them and tells them where to put it, having moved up from the one who actually clambers up the pole, to the one who tells them where it goes.'

He came across as a bit affected, impersonating a character from Evelyn Waugh's *Brideshead Revisited*. 'I like the ideal of what Oxford could be and occasionally have had spells cast upon me, something I know I could never have anywhere else. In Oxford I see very brief glimpses of what life could have been like.' In his first term he embarked on a drunken binge. 'Getting drunk in a white tie means you're behaving like a base human. But trying to live up to some kind of romantic 1920s estimation of what a man ought to be, doing it in the context of an ideal which I can sympathise with, excuses the behaviour. I'm given permission by being here whereas if I get drunk at home I usually end up having a lazy slash in the local dog pound and collapsing drunk in front of the television: pointless, sordid and silly. I think it's not what you do, it's how you do it. I'm a great believer in a 1950s standard of behaviour.'

He seemed to be someone acting the role of a Hooray Henry but with eccentric differences – his 'lazy slash' in 'the local dog pound' (curious place to choose to illustrate his point), his moralising (1950s standards alongside 1920s *Brideshead* ideals). The signs of greater complexity multiplied. 'When I got here the number of people who asked, "When did you first read *Brideshead*?" was ridiculous because I'd never even heard of Evelyn Waugh. It so angered me, first of all because I hated the book when I did read it, and secondly, that people assumed I had made up my personality. That's one of the worst aspects here. Everyone is so insecure about who to be that when they see someone who is genuine, they assume it's an attempt to imitate something they've seen on the telly. And its just riaaally [he drew out the word in classic Sloane Ranger fashion] frustrating, a plagiaristic society in which you just speak the lines someone else has written for you. I spend my life feeling that I'm being perceived as someone pretending to be someone they're not, which I'm not. That's Oxford failing to be something it should be.' On the one hand, he seemed to be someone who was seeking authenticity; on the other, his whole persona, something to which he made repeated reference (including his strong sense of being a prominent undergraduate figure), smelt of imposture.

The person who had suggested that I interview Simon had said he was enjoying Oxford, but I was becoming doubtful. When I asked if he would like to have children a whole new vista of distress opened up. First there was high-pitched, hysterical laughter. 'Err, ha-ha-ha, no, I won't. Because of a wide range of sick psychological factors, I must never have children.' He said he would not be able to trust himself not to sexually abuse them. In describing his sex life, he oozed self-disgust. His first relationship had been with a man who he believed had laced his drink with ecstasy and raped him, after which they had become lovers, 'a very sick, twisted, horrid, revolting, all-those-things relationship'. For some time after it ended, he took antidepressants.

I wondered if it might be an idea for Simon to talk the rape through with someone. 'No,' he replied emphatically, 'because that's what weak people do. I'm quite a good writer and thinker, and a very good public speaker, and I'm getting on in politics in a very good way, and I believe that is due to my particular psychology. I'm frightened of tampering with it, of waking up as if a body snatcher has been.' I pointed out that other clever people, such as Stephen Fry and Clive James, had expressed the same fear that therapy would let the creative genie out of their bottle. However, that there were plenty of others, equally clever and eccentric, from Woody Allen to Hugh Laurie to Ruby Wax (and not forgetting Lou Reed), who have had therapy without losing their magic ingredients. Therapy might help him to acquire weapons of increased volition, and he could be storing up a lot of unhappiness by not having them. 'I don't have too much trouble with unhappiness. Three very good friends and I have decided we will eventually become priests and live in Deal, with pictures of *EastEnders* stars on the wall and bottles of whisky beside our chairs; once a week we'll go out to the Rat and Parrot, from which we get banned so we have to go back in the taxi and throw up on the beach. That's our plan.' This answer neatly illustrates the extent to which he deals with his difficulties through clever and entertaining fantasies which distract him and his listeners from uncomfortable emotions.

Although Simon is not motivated by money, nor sees wealth as a long-term goal ('seeking the status of wealth I find one of the most vulgar things in the world', he says, with an assumed upper-class disgust at the notion of Trade), he is motivated to become a famous public figure, wanting the praise of his fellow-man and the reward of people thinking more of him because of it. Having fame as a goal would not in itself be damaging, but having Virus motives for it is.

His rationale was as follows: 'I want to be honest to The People, that's what I prize most in the whole world, intellectual honesty. Whether it's professional or personal, people lie so consistently in the smallest ways, and I would like very much to shock the world, to grab it. There's a wonderful phrase Joe Orton used: "I must rage correctly." I want to get attention, which means doing something vaguely respectable and at the same time, I want to goose the public – politicians can do that, challenge their populace.' I did not say so, but I suspected that there were two elements of self-deception or unawareness here: Simon is so annoyed by the lies of others because he lives a lie himself; and he wants to upset others because he is really angry with his parents, whilst at the same time wanting to be the centre of their attention and compensate for feelings of self-loathing. Since he was clearly someone who did not want to consider his relationship with them (genes caused him, he told me), I concentrated on the potential problems of having such a false self, with which he readily engaged.

'I say shocking things which are sometimes really quite abnormal to create still further distance – oh yes, I've had a very long time to analyse my own thoughts. That way I can both lie to myself and say, "I've been honest" and done it in such an offhand, offensive, ill-judged manner that I make people no longer want to question me or get to know me in any way.' I told him I had interviewed many famous people who found that fame was no substitute for intimacy and that it usually impeded it. Inevitably, he responded with a humorous comment. 'My father once said, "You do realise you are going to become Ted Heath?" I loved the fact that as an insult he chose a prime minister.' But was there not a danger of loneliness? 'Oh, I'll just have lots of cats,' he replied, with a sad, mirthless chuckle.

At other times, however, Simon was able to seriously address the problem of public image destroying intimacy. 'It has happened here. People literally can't speak to me, only to my image.' He was also aware of the virtual, removed nature of his existence, which he explained without facetiousness. 'When I had my relationship, just as I didn't really believe in God when I went to church, I didn't believe in this human being who I was with. But for a certain period, although I'm ashamed to admit it, during the act of sex, I was able to switch off and I've never had such a wonderful time, even though it was little bits of gold in the middle of shit. For a brief period I was able to stop thinking, but unfortunately the experience became corrupted and I was able to think my way out of it. Finally, as a last resort, I was able to stop thinking again by a very brief experiment with drugs and then by taking antidepressants.'

Regarding his fellow students, he despised their money-grabbing Virus motives and goals. He spoke of the pointless consumerism of a friend of his who now has a job as a management consultant. 'He loathes it. He said to me recently, "All I do is read brochures, I'm covered in brochures. I do all this work to be able to afford to go to Hungary or Venezuela. I don't see anyone there, I just do it because it's all I can do." It's not even greedy, all this law and accountancy and banking, it's just what you do. Oh for the days of Thatcher when you had the Hard Left moaning and yuppies who applied an ideology, said "Fuck you!" and had big phones to prove it. Now it's the simple, cosy assumptions that are most offensive, and a certain pattern of consumption that is essential to them.'

Despite some unattractive characteristics, Simon has a passion and warmth that is endearing. He is amusing and has considerable adolescent sagacity. Although his lust for fame requires some manipulative elements of the Marketing Character, his greatest problems are his narcissism and living 'as if' he is Simon, an imposture that makes authentic relationships impossible, a problem that will grow as he gets older. Added to this, he is severely neurotic about sex, which will prevent him from being able to form stable relationships. He strives not to speak of himself as vastly superior to everyone else, constantly making attempts not to put himself above them, but running the risk of being patronising: 'It's not fair to characterise my peers as automaton-consumers ... I have tremendous respect for nine-to-fivers, envy them even.' But superior is how he truly sees himself, so that his drive to be famous is to take up the position that he feels is naturally his. 'I don't want to be the centre of attention but I can't stand boredom in any way. If I'm going to be forced to live with other people, I at least want them to be interesting [because they will also be famous].'

As a narcissist he seeks fame to compensate for feelings of self-disgust; he wants to bathe in the high regard and admiration of others which he does not feel towards himself. The political party he belongs to seems largely incidental. He did not really seem to care which might bring him fame and he had no ideological beliefs to inspire a desire to make the world a better place. What mattered was to be famous, and this example is very important for identifying vaccines that protect against the Virus.

The opposite of Virus motivation is known as intrinsic motivation. Here, you do things for the pleasure of the activity itself, the getting there rather than the arriving, the process by which a result is achieved rather than its completion. Typical intrinsic goals are supporting others, beauty and self-expression.

The studies prove that, overall, people with intrinsic motives and goals tend to be emotionally better off than those who have exclusively Virus ones. However, it's not a simple case of 'Virus bad, intrinsic good'. There are also people who manage to mix and match, without becoming distressed. Nearly all the citizens of English-speaking nations worry about one or more of wanting more money, new possessions, better appearances and achieving celebrity. But having these

Virus goals does not, in itself, spell distress, for the studies also show that people who have intrinsic motives for pursuing them are less likely to suffer.

Motivation is at its most intrinsic where interest, enjoyment and the stimulation of a challenge are paramount; they are done for their own sake. The purest illustration is children's play, witnessed by me, daily, in my four-year old daughter. Most of the time, she couldn't care less what I want her to like, which is fortunate since her most joyful pleasures entail following her own nose. Yesterday, some acquaintances came to visit. She decided we needed to make 'pwepawations' by taping flowers from the garden to doors, chairs and curtains. There was no practical purpose to the activity, she just liked doing it. The same can be said of the half-hour we spent this morning crashing her Thomas the Tank Engine trains or putting her Bear-Bear in a chair and covering him (or her, depending on whim) with a blanket. Small children effortlessly make up words, throwing out streams of poetic thoughts. Like many children of her age, she says things such as 'London is a big water lung'. Their absorption, excitement and passion in their activities are in marked contrast to what they will later experience when having to do their homework in preparation for GCSEs, or what the average call centre worker will feel while doing their job, which are reward-motivated activities with externally ordained goals.

The state of mind during intrinsically motivated activity has been characterised as 'flow', a strong connection and oneness with the activity, done for what it has to offer in the doing of it, rather than for praise or reward. During such activity people become so deeply involved that they forget themselves, and afterwards they find that much more time has passed than they would have expected. They feel most themselves, and experience a special freedom emanating from pursuing authentic interests and needs.

A particularly striking example of intrinsically motivated activity was apparent in a recent TV documentary about Bob Dylan. In the film, Dylan brilliantly kept his balance on the tightrope of sanity that is walked whenever an artist speaks whatever comes into his mind out loud in the public domain, and at the same time, paradoxically, does so with phenomenal rigour. Dylan was standing outside a pet shop, circa 1964. The camera cut between a sign listing the products and services on sale, and Dylan's extemporisations. The sign said: 'We will collect clip bath & return your dog. Cigarettes and tobacco. Animals and birds bought and sold on commission.' Speaking very rapidly, Dylan went into a rhythmic incantation: 'I want a dog that's gonna collect and clean my bath, return my cigarettes, give them back my animals, return my cigarette and give my birds a commission.' This relatively concrete stream then flowed into abstract surrealism: 'I'm looking for a place that's gonna animal my soul, mitt my return, bathe my foot and collect my dog.'

The state of mind of people with Virus motives and goals is a very different story to this. Their flow is fractured by an overriding concern to meet external demands. Focused on the reward, they get disconnected from the pleasures of the activity that produces it. This has been proved many times in experimental studies. When a reward is offered for performance of an initially intrinsically satisfying activity, there is not only a measurable drop in interest and enjoyment, but also in motivation to do it at all. For example, students were given three-dimensional cubes to play with. One group was paid to do it, the other was not. The paid ones lost interest sooner and were more likely to stop and read magazines that had been left lying about. Money changed the focus. The unpaid volunteers reported playing with the cube because it was fun or because they chose to; for the paid students the interesting, enjoyable, challenging aspect of the activity got lost. In the context of work, people with intrinsic motives and goals have been shown to seek intellectual fulfilment, creative self-expression and a sense of mastery in completing tasks. The Virus-infected look for money and see work as the way to get it.

The Virus even penetrates the dreams of the infected. An in-depth study of students' dreams found that nearly one-fifth of the infected dreamed of death, whereas it barely figured in the dreams of the uninfected. Likewise, falling – being out of control, with nothing to hold on to, suggesting insecurity – featured in 15 per cent of materialists' dreams, whereas it was present in only 3 per cent of the dreams of the uninfected. And there was an intriguing difference in how the materialists and non-materialists dealt with frightening objects in their dreams: the non-materialists might turn a dangerous-seeming rhinoceros or giant purple poodle into an unfrightening character by attributing a benign motive to it; the materialists never did this, always seeing threatening figures as unalterably so.

A novelist friend of mine, though successful enough to be published, earns little from the years of painstaking work that writing his yarns entails. I encouraged him to start a newspaper column as a bank balance-boosting sideline, but he said it was not that simple for him to activate his (phenomenal) literary skill. If he was only doing it for the money, the words would not come to him freely and he would find it hard to be inspired. When he is writing his novels he is totally immersed in expressing himself through his fictional characters; churning out a thousand words for a newspaper would not release the same creative juices. Another friend gave up his job in the City to write feature film scripts. Unfortunately, just producing brilliant ones is not enough: he must also devote a lot of energy to cultivating key industry figures to promote his scripts, but that is not something he is particularly good at, or enthusiastic about, because it is all about money.

A major pollutant of the Virus-infected person's inner life is their self-consciousness, triggered by excessive concern about what others think of them. By definition, they are preoccupied with recognition and status, conferred upon them by others. Their fragile self-esteem needs constant bolstering from outside, so they tend to agree with statements such as 'I'm self-conscious about the way I look' and 'I usually worry about making a good impression'. It's hard to go with the flow if you are focusing on your faults or inadequacies, fearful of feeling foolish for something you have said or done, excessively alert to the danger of seeming incompetent to others. People with such high levels of self-consciousness are at greater risk of depression, neurosis and narcissism.

The Virus prevents flows by the nature of the activities and goals it entails. The infected tend to watch a lot of TV, which has been shown to create an apathetic, passive state rather than the joy and excitement of more challenging pursuits. They work longer hours and amass more debt, risking the sense of being trapped on a hedonic treadmill: working to earn the money to buy the possessions by which they measure themselves against others. When asked to name their most important possession, they are more likely to mention its monetary value and the impression it gives to others. Virus-infected business students and entrepreneurs asked about their motives for making money were more likely than the intrinsically motivated to want to afford things that would enable them to keep up with the Joneses and to thus demonstrate their intelligence or ability to others.

Whilst not all the infected are compulsive shoppers, studies of people with this aholia shed light on Virus psychology. Shopaholics talk about being on automatic pilot, having no choice when in shops, having to have the goods even though they don't actually want them. Their anxiety mounts until, like any other kind of addict, they just have to get out there and buy as the only way to dispel their unhappiness. Some shopaholics are motivated by a desire to please the sales personnel or even the drivers who deliver mail-order goods, actually saying that they want to please the retailers. There is considerable overlap between characteristics of such addicts and the Virus-infected, not just greater emotional distress but also an irresistible drive to possess unneeded products, which removes the sense of autonomy so vital to the flowing experience.

The Virus-infected also tend to place a low value on the self-expression and autonomy necessary for flow. They disagree with statements such as 'I will choose what I do, instead of being pushed along by life' and 'I will follow my interests and curiosity where they take me', unlikely to feel that 'understanding myself or being true to myself no matter what' is important to them or that 'I want my work to provide me with opportunities for increasing my knowledge and skills'. They agree with 'I'm less concerned with what work I do than what I get for it' and 'I am strongly motivated by the grades I can earn' (in exams). Asked to list their commonest work and leisure activities, and the two friends they hang out with most, they more frequently mention boredom, feeling trapped and unengaged in connection with these things.

The distinction between Virus and intrinsic motivations helps us to see the base elements from which vaccines against the Virus are compounded because it defines what to want and to be motivated by, as well as what not to. Above all, people who have both Virus motives and goals are the most prone to emotional distress, as we saw in examples from around the world in Chapters 1 and 2. We began with Sam, the millionaire New Yorker in his one-bedroom, five-storey apartment, who regards women as instruments of pleasure and 'friends' as people to be insulted and humiliated. There were the more or less disturbed British multi-millionaires and their families described by Sandy, the personal assistant. There was Will, the Australian millionaire psychiatrist and property tycoon who cannot decide whether he suffers from subclinical bipolar disorder or hyperactivity. There was the high-flying Boris, the Sloane Ranger Russian who shares Sam's attitude to women and is equally emotionally sealed off. Then there were the sundry distressed professionals of New Zealand and Singapore. In most of these people, both motives and goals were Virus-infected and the consequence was emotional distress.

However, the scientific evidence suggests that Virus motives do more harm than Virus goals. One study of the issue, which had the subtitle 'Is it what you want or why you want it that matters?', suggested that people with Virus goals could have well-being as long as they had intrinsic motives. Other studies have shown that pursuing money in itself is not harmful – it's the motive. Provided the motive is intrinsic, like meeting basic material needs, supporting a family and self-efficacy, people were not made unhappy by wanting money. That goal becomes problematic when you start to believe that money can buy you what it cannot, like love or a better character or higher self-esteem, as in Simon's case. Specifically, the pursuit of wealth becomes harmful if it becomes a material substitute for the life of the mind, Having rather than Being. A recent study bears this out: it found that purchasing experiences, such as trekking in the Himalayas, tends to make people happier than purchasing material possessions, such as an iPod.

As long as your motives are intrinsic, you may be able to get away with having some Virus goals, and on my tour I met many who've managed to do so. In Singapore, for example, I met Miranda, the calm and relaxed twenty-five-year-old only child of a multi-millionaire entrepreneur. She is close to her father, whose interest in economics she shares. Eventually she would like to work in the Singapore Treasury because applied economics really does light her up. Miranda's intrinsically motivating activity happens, accidentally, to entail Virus goals. In the same way that wealth and fame can be accidental, unanticipated by-products of a compulsion to write novels in a few cases, this woman happens to enjoy making sense of stocks and shares, which happens to make her rich because getting absorbed in that process has that outcome.

Of course, our values can change. Some of the people I interviewed had started out with both Virus motives and goals, but in later life, the motives had shifted to intrinsic, with an accompanying improvement in well-being. A prime example was Ross. The moment I knew I was visiting New Zealand, I phoned Ross from London. I had seen him only once in the last thirty-three years, and then only briefly, but until he left for New Zealand at the age of seventeen we had been good friends, living near each other in London. We went to different secondary schools: mine boarding, his in the City. This was one bright guy, so I was shocked to learn that he had been summarily withdrawn by his father from his expensive, highly competitive school after he failed an exam. I remember being very puzzled that he had been sent to New Zealand to work on a farm, as if he was in disgrace. I managed to spend a few hours with him and his fiancée in Britain in the 1980s, but there was no real chance to talk intimately, and anyway, he seemed to have become a rather tough-skinned, buttoned-up person. I received only occasional scraps of information about his doings, from his sister, whom I ran into from time to time. Apparently he had established a successful tourist business and bought a farm near Russell, a pretty coastal town near Auckland in the North Island.

When I called him from Britain, after the usual pleasantries of long-parted friends he revealed that he had recently separated from his wife. They had children, and I was about to weigh in with commiserations when he said, 'I guess I am happier today than I have ever been'. 'Oh-oh', thought the psychological I, it could be tricky spending much time with a man in denial at the distress of separation, especially since he might be upset by the contrast in our situations, what with me just starting out on married life, with a small child 'n' all. I was quite wrong.

Ross's farm turned out to be huge by British criteria. His front gate was about a mile from his house. The building was elegant by the architectural standards I had so far encountered in New Zealand, having seen very few houses I would want to live in. But in even better nick than his home was Ross himself. Despite having recently turned fifty-three, his body was athletic and toned. His tanned face had a ruddy, red apple complexion, his balding pate set off by fair but greying hair, shaved short. Over the next few days he displayed tremendous energy, switching between competitive recreations, like tennis and golf, and his many business interests, including the farm. Whether he was authoritatively and unsentimentally groping sheep (in search of mastitis; the infected got a blue crayon cross, meaning imminent death) or on his mobile phone organising various business deals, he seemed to be enjoying his work. Equally, he was courting a potential girlfriend, display-ing considerable emotional intelligence.

My wife and I were feeling pretty shagged out after spending two months in a camper van, and did as little as possible. Despite this, we found his company most uplifting. He was playful, he was jolly, yet he was as eager as a teenager to get into debates on subjects from the most emotionally charged to the abstruse, with no holds barred, from the prob-lems of love to the question of how to come up with a new letter to add to those in our alphabet. Keen to catch up with my sleep, I missed out on some of these debates, but he engaged my wife in them, to her great enjoyment, although they had only just met.

To me this was all the more remarkable when I heard the facts of the recent break-up of his marriage. His wife Julie had become increasingly friendly with the husband of a couple they knew well. After a while, Ross could not help wondering whether there was more than friendship, and several times he asked her outright if there was an affair going on. She hotly denied it, and as they had been married for many years and thinking he knew her well, he had assumed that she was telling the truth. It came as a considerable shock to learn that there really was an affair, and he quickly fell into a deep depression. How had he managed to get from there to here? He told me the story sitting on his veranda one evening, to the backdrop of a glowing sunset and the lapping of the Pacific Ocean.

'My current happiness started with Julie having the affair and me going to the bottom of the hole. I felt dreadful, certainly suicide crossed my mind. Now, I can't think why and I certainly never went close to doing it. But I had taken my whole marriage for granted and just assumed that it would be fine.' Apparently, the catastrophe was a springboard for his renaissance. 'It started with survival, we've all got that instinct. That's why I addressed the whole thing, not just my marriage, everything about me. A lot of people are just grinding their lives out until they die, and I think the only reason I did anything about it was because I got to the bottom of the hole. I'd had it.' Unusually for a New Zealand male (as he undoubtedly now is), Ross went to see a counsellor within two weeks of learning of the affair. From England on the phone, his father was somewhat less than enthusiastic about this. 'He was banging on at me, "Be careful of these shrinks, they'll keep you locked in and you'll be paying them for the rest of your life," but after about three or four months Jan [his counsellor] said, "I think I've done all I can do for you, I think you're all right, you need to get on with it yourself."'

Jan's method seems to have been a mixture of positive psychology and conventional therapy. 'She encouraged me to look at myself, literally. She would say, "Go and sit in that chair opposite yours and tell me what you see in yourself. What are the good points, what are the weak points?" She taught me that you can change, reduce your levels of anger or frustration, and increase your levels of kindness, humour, those sort of things. She convinced me we've got levels of humour and generosity that can be increased or decreased, worked on.' He explained that positive psychology, which encourages us to accentuate the positive and give the negative a kicking, was at the heart of her approach. 'It comes down to whether you see the glass as half-empty or half-full. Throughout my life, until I had met Jan, the negatives were hitting me in the face rather than the positives.' Jan taught Ross how to deal with banal frustrations. 'We don't get many traffic jams in New Zealand, but when we do, one of my challenges was to get a positive out of it. Like I was sitting in a queue two months ago and I thought, "What can I achieve that I couldn't achieve if I wasn't in this situation?" And one is to ring my mother-in-law – because I've built up a good relationship with her – just be kind to someone and have a good chat. You end up, when the traffic moves, almost wanting to pull off to the side and continue. Half the battle is to realise the state of mind you're in. If you stay in a glass-half-empty state, that can cost a day of negativity. I'm in business with a guy who always turns up late and it just destroys the other guy we work with, wrecks his day. He just goes on and on and on about it, can't correct.'

Another tactic he developed was to meditate. 'Jan encouraged me, but it was self-taught after I read some books. It plays a key role if I'm feeling down, it balances and calms me, just convincing yourself that certain thoughts and feelings need to be reduced.' Jan also encouraged Ross to explore the effect of his upbringing. 'The level of communication at home [with his parents] was very light, no meaningful stuff, no depth, no talking about feelings at all, they were very peripheral. It made me insecure and feel powerless. That made me a control freak who hates things to be less than perfect. Much of my anger and frustration stems from being a perfectionist and presuming that everyone else is. In my business I would assume that my employees would give 110 per cent and do everything as well as they could; that's so far from the truth it's not even funny. Jan taught me simple but effective ways to curb my frustration, like if I saw something an employee had done that really annoyed me I'd leave it for twenty-four hours and bring it up after that. Obvious, but it works well.'

As an enthusiastic convert to Jan's techniques and his self-taught use of meditation to keep depression at bay, Ross has been teaching his children how to be more positive and seems keen to spread the word. Occasionally this reached a consciously religious fervour: 'I guess I'm a believer, I'm an apostle, it's just been fantastic for me. I don't talk to many people about the details of my meditation, but I wonder if you're not being a bit selfish if you don't pass it on. Why is it not taught at school – how tough would it really be for them to teach these things?'

Many British readers will be wondering if Ross has not become a bit of a cult follower, buying into an all-encompassing ideology which creates a false positivity. The psychologically clued-up will be wondering if he is able to relax: what with such a vigilant attitude to his mind and very busy life of work and play, perhaps he is keeping his feelings at bay through action. They might also wonder whether the meditation is a form of dissociation, a mental escapism from what is really a state of despair and rage and fear at having been betrayed and had his world turned upside down. There may be some truth in all of these reactions, and in other possible objections, like the fact that he seems tremendously preoccupied with winning at sport (and I am not just talking about the fact that he thrashed me at golf). But two particular aspects of him did suggest to me that his well-being has an authentic core and that there are lessons for those striving to be more contented.

Ross's honesty about himself and others was remarkable for its fine calibration. He says that his relations with others have been transformed by being more open, but when I asked about this in detail, he showed that he had not collapsed into a boundary-less state of pathological honesty, the gruesome self-disclosure that is so often passed off by distressed people as insight. The empirical, realistic, British boy I once knew is very much still there: 'Sure, I can still deliberately lie if I have to, in all aspects of my life, but I've got huge rewards from being honest. The key for me is that I haven't been burnt by it, although I'm very aware – and accept – that I will be at times.' Evidence that he has not embarked on a deranged programme of honesty at all costs comes when he qualifies it. 'I find that the best response is from females, you have to be a bit choosy with the males, it's just too much for many Kiwis. They don't want to know.' The Ross I used to know would not have found this kind of thing at all easy. 'I wasn't open: I was the opposite, bunched up and tense.' Being able to express yourself to others and to listen to them is crucial for intimacy, and since intimacy is one of the main predictors of well-being, this augurs well for him.

The second striking feature was his capacity to make choices. We like to think of ourselves as free agents, but even a moment's deliberation reveals how hard volition is to achieve. Ross is almost visibly engaged in a second-to-second, moment-to-moment endeavour to decide what he is feeling and its implications. You can see him tuning out of a conversation that makes him uncomfortable and changing the subject, constantly alert. Again, you might wonder whether that is a good thing, but he is very conscious of the problems. 'I seem to be in touch with my emotions, and I've become very aware of what space others are in. At times I think I'm way too over-sensitive; occasionally, I wish I didn't realise this or that thing about someone else. But that's fine, it's just a case of learning not to overreact, because everyone goes up and down. If you get very close to someone you can drive them mad if you're constantly saying, "You're very pensive." I've still got to learn how to manage the information that's coming in.' Bearing in mind that emotional awareness of self and others is pretty new territory for Ross, it is hopefully only a matter of time before he strikes the right balance. The fact that he is so actively wrestling to be the organ-grinder rather than the monkey of his experience is a sure sign of psychological vitality.

That he had not lost his edge was shown when we talked about his mother, who died a few years ago. 'Mum was certainly my role model. I chat to her on hills, she's a huge influence.' I recalled how witty she had been, albeit with a black humour. 'Yes, her glass was not even half-empty, more like one-tenth. But then it got filled up pretty regularly,' he quipped, in a humorous reference to her love of a drink. Since it was exactly the kind of joke she would have made if things were getting a little heavy, it proved that she is still alive and well and living in New Zealand in Ross.

As we waved goodbye and made our way back down the drive (to an accompaniment of 'Sheeps! Sheeps! Sheeps!' from our daughter, silenced only by a rendition of 'Old Macdonald Had a Farm'), I pondered what had been crucial about Ross's transformation. He had been trundling along, gaining wealth and status, living and partly living, when struck by disaster. In most people this would trigger a depression from which recovery is hard. One way of conceptualising how he avoided this norm is to regard him as having made the transition from Virus to intrinsic motives, with the introduction of some intrinsic goals as well.

Whilst he still pursues Virus money goals, he does so for fun, having long since ceased needing more (not that he had ever 'needed' it, having inherited a fair amount). Originally, I suspect that he was making a success of his business in order to prove his father wrong – a Virus, people-pleasing motive; now he does it because it is absorbing and stimulating. He had become inured to intimacy, but his divorce had set him off in pursuit of many intrinsic goals, such as involvement in the emotional lives of others and helping out at his children's school.

What should be clear is that our motives and goals are not set in stone: in the case of Ross, it was possible to retain some Virus goals whilst shifting to intrinsic motives. What is also clear is that hardly anyone probably has exclusively one or other sort of motive or goal. In most cases we have competing values coexisting within us. We would like to be rich in order not to be so worried about the mortgage or to be able to afford a larger home, but we also want not to have to work all the time, preferring a job which leaves enough time to hang out with friends and family.

Each of us is different, and generalising is difficult. Nonetheless, the overall message from the research is crystal clear: combining Virus motives and goals is least likely to result in emotional well-being; combining intrinsic ones is most likely to. There is no escaping the fact that individuals with the greatest well-being are most likely to be the ones with the combination of intrinsic goals and motives. Hence, whereas it is possible to get away with mixing 'n' matching, overall, *it's best to be intrinsic in both*. What is more, if intrinsic goals are good for your health, the research shows that they are not as good for it as Virus ones are bad: Virus goals foster unhappiness to an even greater extent than intrinsic ones increase happiness.

Vaccines

1. Audit your motives and goals

To a certain extent, nearly everyone works for the money. The key question is *why* you want it, not that you *do*. If it's to buy possessions that give you status, it's Virus-motivated; if it's to put food on the table and a roof over your head, it's not. Hardly any of us, in getting ready to go out on a date, does not seek to maximise our sexual desirability by making the most of our appearance. What is critical is whether you are doing these things in order to please others or for yourself. You may say, 'I get dolled up to go on dates so that the other person will like me, to please them, but ultimately, it's so that I can get close to them physically and mentally, so it's really to please myself.' In which case your motive is intrinsic. The problem is if your dolling up is in order to feel better than others, or to show off, or to manipulate and use.

2. Identify work activities which have intrinsic motivation

The fact that you are a unit of labour whose mind and body are purchased for an allotted time to be at the service of an organisation does not in itself preclude intrinsic motivation. If you write down all the different tasks you perform in your job, you will find that some of them give you more flow than others. If you can, angle for them. Of course, you may be stuck in a job which has no flow whatsoever. If so, you need a new career, which may entail some retraining and a major change. However, this is often not necessary. Once you start going with the flow, the surprising thing is that often you start doing better in your work, giving you more options for what you do next, moving steadily towards posts with greater and greater elements that you find intrinsically satisfying.

3. Identify play activities which have intrinsic motivation

Think back to when you were a child. You loved going to the park or playing football or drawing. You have to find leisure activities which provide the same level of absorption. First and foremost, that almost certainly means that they are not self-improving. If you have always wanted to read Tolstoy in the original Russian because it would bring you joy, join that evening class. But be very wary of such plans, for they can easily seem to be intrinsic but really be closet people-pleasing, unwitting attempts to curry favour with past authority figures in your mind. In doing these activities, your sole arbiter should be whether they are absorbing, exciting, stimulating.

Chapter 5

Be Beautiful (Not Attractive)

Valuing beauty is a defining feature of the intrinsically moti-vated; using physical attractiveness to gain praise or manipulate others is what the Virus-afflicted do. A significant portion of American economic activity is devoted to pressuring women to preoccupy themselves with how attractive they are to others, through magazines, films, television and advertise-ments. An even larger slice of the economy provides the means for conforming to these norms, from fashion to cosmetics to cosmetic surgery. On my travels it was brought home to me that in the matter of our external presence – the bodies, clothes and haircuts that others see when they look at us – there is an important distinction to be drawn between a Virus concern with appearance and an intrinsic concern to be beautiful.

Appearance-driven women are prone to an obsessive concern with their weight, a love of cosmetics, elaborate hair-dressing, and socially valued, expensive clothes, and are willing to countenance cosmetic surgery. By contrast, women who seek beauty are largely immune to these ways for corporations to make money out of them. They develop their own notion of what constitutes a pleasing external presence and then measure it against that, doing it for their own pleasure, not that of others. They make themselves up rather than necessarily wearing makeup. They select clothes primarily because they like them, not because they are fashionable or they will 'look good' to others. They define for themselves what they like about their body's shape or their face or their hair, rather than feeling under pressure to conform to a norm. They may be dissatisfied with aspects of what they see when they look in the mirror, but their reason for wishing to change it is in order to look more like their own internally created notion of beauty, rather than an externally generated norm of how to be 'sexy' or 'sassy' or 'pretty' in the eyes of others.

My impression of the elite women of Virus-infected China and Singapore, and the English-speaking countries, was that confected appearances far outweighed the pursuit of beauty. Many of the middle-aged women aspired to look like teenagers, using cosmetics to make their skin look young, surgery to make their bodies look young, and carefully contrived clothing to reveal their carved, teenage-slim figures. Ironically, many of their daughters sought to seem older than their years, by wearing expensive clothing. Of course, there were local variations. In Sydney and Auckland the style was naturalness. In New York, it was unnatural but sexy. In Singapore and Shanghai, keeping skin as white as possible was prized, with designer clothing ostentatiously used to designate wealth. But these differences were only variations on an underlying theme: seeing oneself through the eyes of others. Moscow and Copenhagen revealed a completely different approach to external appearance: a concern with beauty – although, fascinatingly, the two countries sought it in diametrically opposite ways.

Anyone who has visited Moscow (or St Petersburg) will tell you that the city is host to a remarkably high concentration of startlingly beautiful women. Arguably, they are sexually desirable too, but it took me some time to realise that this is not the message the women are trying to get across. On the whole, their primary intention is not for men to desire them or for other women to envy them, but simply to look beautiful. Exactly the same goes for the women of Copenhagen. By Muscovite standards the Danes are two stone overweight and give short shrift to the tight-fitting, short-skirted clothing which a proportion of Muscovites sport, but their goal is identical: meeting their own criteria of beauty, not competing with one another, or attracting men.

The Muscovite approach was typified by Sonja, a twenty-four-year-old trainee executive in an American merchant bank, six feet tall and thin as a model, yet full-breasted. Her face is delicate-featured, with a snub nose (most Russians have quite long ones) and a relatively wide mouth, a pale complexion, clear blue eyes and short, blonde hair, worn in a pageboy style covering her forehead. Her clothing was simple and plain, a pink cotton dress.

Like virtually all the young women I met in Moscow, Sonja had read Helen Fielding's book *Bridget Jones's Diary* (Russians are avid readers, dating back to the Soviet era when Russian classics were a central part of the curriculum) and has welded it into her vocabulary. For example, she still lives with her parents and brother, and if she wants a bit of privacy with her TV producer boyfriend, 'we go to a dacha or for a mini break' (a mini break is one of Fielding's satirical indications of how commodified Jones's attitude to romance has become). I asked how relevant Jones is to the Moscow single girl. 'Some of it is. Her relationships with her friends, how they take care of each other, their theories about "singletons" and "smug marrieds".' What about the unhappiness of Bridget's life? 'She only does her job to be able to buy the things she doesn't have, which is not a good way to live, worrying about what you can buy. We don't live like that. We have problems with our love-lives, boyfriends, jobs and stuff, can see ourselves in that, but we are less upset about them, not taking things so emotionally. Bridget sees many things as problems that we do not take to heart. Luckily my mum is not like hers at all.' Do she and her friends share Bridget's worries about dieting, smoking, drinking? 'Personally, it's not a problem to be slim. We are not obsessed with going to a gym. I guess it's genes. I don't eat bread, but I'm crazy about cakes and chocolate. I knew a girl at university who constantly talked about doing yoga, going on a diet, but to my mind there was nothing to improve. She had adopted some American ideal of how she should be, but that's unusual.'

I asked how the women here manage to be so much better-looking than women in other countries. 'It's true,' Sonja replied, 'women here are much better-looking and better-dressed, that's a fact. Every time a Russian girl travels to Europe she sees unattractive women who are hand in hand with a handsome guy and thinks, "Whooo, what's he doing with her?" It's a common joke here to say that it would be a better fit if all the Spanish men came here and all the Russian men went to Spain – that would be a fairer combination of looks. It's a cultural thing. For some reason the men here don't go to the barber or look for nice clothes to attract girls. They lack style. But here we say it's finding a nice person that's important, not how he looks. The women don't care much what the man looks like, as long as he takes care of his woman, that's the thing that is wanted.' It struck me that life must be pretty tough here for women who are not pretty. 'Are there any not pretty women in Russia?' she joked. 'If you've got something about you, are confident, calm and don't care about the impression you are making on men, that indifference makes them want to be the hunter, it makes you more interesting, a challenge. The women expect the men to take the first step, to do all the running. It would be an insult in America if a man let you through a door or offered to take the bags, but here it is perfectly all right. It might even be a man you don't know, it's okay for him to help you off the bus.'

Another young woman I interviewed was Janna, also aged twenty-four. She wore a long flowery skirt of the kind I imagine working-class women used to buy through the Littlewoods catalogue in the early 1960s, a white tee shirt and a grey, zip-up cardigan – again, more reminiscent of outdated British working-class fashion. When I asked her about her clothes, she explained that there are no chain stores in Moscow so that there is a much greater variety of styles compared with Britain and America, both of which she has visited. She had shoulder-length black hair, a round face and, as far as I could tell, a model figure. Her face was beautiful in the classical Russian style, although for much of the time, in repose, it was hidden behind hair and distorted by downcast eyes and a mournful expression. The reason for this melancholia turned out to be that she had recently been badly let down by an American boyfriend.

I asked whether women here were as despairing of men as in the West, in the style of Bridget Jones (which Janna had read). She said that her female friends certainly do not expect to rely on their men solely 'to buy us cars, apartments, clothes and jewellery. There are a lot of jokes here about blondes who do expect that.' She told me one. 'Two blondes are on a bus – I don't know why because normally their boyfriend would have bought them a car – and they do not know when to get off. One asks the driver if he can let them know when they reach the right street, and he says he will. The other says, "Will you let me know too?" These women are seen as too stupid to earn their living, obsessed with their appearance, buying designer clothes. Most of us like to make our own clothes or adapt ordinary purchases to create our own appearance. We are more concerned with expressing ourselves than with being clothes horses for designers. We like to do it for fun or to invent something which is lovely-looking, but more for ourselves than for men. You don't bother what men think – or other women, come to that.'

Her point about blondes who snag rich boyfriends was made repeatedly by other women I spoke to. Only a tiny, Virus-stricken minority used their looks for this purpose; for most women, their appearance was a source of intrinsic pleasure. Unlike in the other countries I visited, none of the women I met in Russia tried to ingratiate themselves to me with charm or flirtation. Whilst their clothes can be tight-fitting and some wear very short skirts, they do not transmit the 'come and get it' messages which similar fashions transmit on Friday and Saturday nights in British city centres. In the absence of fashion retailing chains, the clothes are very diverse in styles, fabrics and colours, partly reflecting the continuing practice of making your own.

I spoke with only one example of the New Russian, the small minority who have got rich. This was the delightful forty-three-year-old wife of a successful entrepreneur. She looked about twenty-five, was dressed in fashionable clothes and spoke with tremendous vivacity (reminiscent of the French; with characteristic eccentricity, my dad always used to say that if he is ever reincarnated, he would like to come back as a middle-aged French woman – good luck dad, I hope you did). The women here have long been beautiful, she said. 'When I was at university, in 1980, there were many girls who were beautiful. Russian women looked special, their figures were always fuller than in much of Europe. We used to think the women a bit plump, the slimness is a new thing. I have noticed when I go to London that the women here are nicer looking, but I can't say the same about the Russian men. The stereotype that the Soviet men drank, gambled, and were usually useless is absolutely true – the system made them so.'

Whilst it can be only speculation, I suspect that the beauty of modern Russian women may have something to do with their lack of opportunities for self-expression. Under Communism there was some degree of emancipation. Sixty per cent of doctors were women, although in that profession, like most others, men occupied the senior roles. In 1970, 49 per cent of adult women worked full-time, higher than in the West at that time but not as high as China's 90 per cent. Whereas in Communist China the grandmothers were usually there to care for the offspring, in Russia the grandmothers were forced into the workforce too. Russian mothers have always been expected to take virtually all the responsibility for child-raising. This was exacerbated by the massive numbers of men killed by various disasters (21 million Soviets were killed during the Second World War, for example, and large numbers of troops were executed or consigned to life-threatening gulags on their return to the USSR). Today, amongst forty-five- to sixty-five-year-olds, there are eighty-four men for every hundred women; a lot of widows were left to care for their children without the help of a partner.

A big difference between Russia (and Eastern Europe) and China is that capitalism has ushered in very substantial gender inequalities in earnings and educational opportunities. From a relatively equal baseline under Communism, by 1993 women's wages had fallen to half those of men. Mothers' maternity rights have been cut and so has State-sponsored childcare. Without State support or a high income, parent-hood spells a broken career path, and birth rates have plummeted. Put this together with a divorce rate that has been one of the highest in the world for several decades, and it should not be surprising that studies show modern Russian women to be emotionally distressed.

A study carried out in 1999 by Richard Ryan and colleagues compared American and Russian undergraduates. The Russian women, compared with the men and with Americans of both sexes, had significantly lower levels of self-esteem, life satisfaction and self-actualisation (self-expression and ability to fulfil oneself). Whereas expecting to fulfil their goals improved well-being for the Americans and the Russian men, doing so had no effect on the Russian women. They were anyway bordering on the goal-less, with very low ratings on both Virus and intrinsic goals. The study concluded that they are 'facing particularly difficult personal times' and that they may have simply given up on hopes for the future as a way to avoid being disappointed. Subsequent studies support Ryan's conclusions, and it is reasonable to suppose that these difficult personal times have not affected Russian women's attitudes to their appearance.

There is specific evidence that social conditions do profoundly affect women's anatomies, even the age at which they enter puberty. On average, an English-speaking girl whose father separated or divorced from her mother before she reached the age of ten comes into puberty six months before one from an intact family. Girls who are not close to their fathers come into puberty significantly younger than ones who are, even if the parents do stay together. Coming at it from a different angle, during the twentieth century the 'thin standard' (waist-to-bust-to-hip ratios) varied according to how much women were aspiring to male roles. During periods when they were competing most fiercely with men, at school and in the workplace, the models in magazines resembled men – flat chests, narrow hips. Women who competed most vigorously in this competition were less likely to favour full-figured, classically feminine shapes.

Given that social forces mould attitudes to the body, I would contend that in Russia they have spurred the women to concentrate a significant part of their creativity into being feminine *in a beautiful manner*. Perhaps it is because there is nowhere else for their creativity to go, conventional routes for emancipation (education and profession) having been largely blocked. As Ryan's studies show, Russian women are especially lacking in 'self-actualisation' compared with the men, let alone with people from other nations. If beauty provides an area of self-expression, that would explain the individuality of their looks and why the pleasure of achieving beauty is more important than competition with one another or pleasing men.

The twenty-three Muscovite women I interviewed in some detail are in no way a representative sample. However, the results from a survey of sixty-one sixteen-year-old school-girls are remarkably interesting. Compared with samples of girls in the other countries I visited, they were the most likely to agree or strongly agree with the statement that 'it is really important to be physically attractive'. On the other hand, they were the least likely to agree or strongly agree either that they would like to have a prettier face or that they would like to lose weight. It is possible that they took 'physically attractive' to mean 'beautiful'. Whilst it may also reflect the importance of looks in order to thrive in a sexist society, the fact that they do not want to be prettier or thinner could indicate that their notions of looks are not Virus-driven, compared with infected peers.

Although they may not realise it, young English-speaking women's notions of what is attractive are tremendously influenced by commercial forces. The main purpose of fashion magazines and advertisements is to sell clothes and cosmetics, which boosts the markets for weight-loss (diets, gym membership) and plastic surgery. Although the directors of mainstream Hollywood movies might prefer not to think about it, their choice of leading actresses has the same result. The portrayal of affluent lifestyles and products is also a hugely significant (in terms of stimulating consumerism and ultimately sustaining economic growth) subtext of the movies' stories. The same is true of most television programmes, many of which are now barely concealed advertisements for classes of product (houses, cars, food, travel), tales of how to consume and slightly more entertaining versions of the nakedly commercial shopping channels. Indeed, one sign of the shift away from the artistic or social motives that originally inspired British television and film is the growth of product placement in films and calls for this to be accepted on TV. Perhaps the only thing that prevents these media from becoming exclusively devoted to sales pitches is that hardly anyone would watch because it would be too boring. When you consider that Americans visit a cinema thirty-seven times more often than Russians and the British seventeen times more often, that must have an effect on how Russians consider the importance of appearances. Add to that the fact that Americans and Britons spend far more time watching TV, and what Russians do watch is far less Virus-infecting.

Whereas Bridget Jones frequently uses brands and consumer products as adjectives, the Russian women do not, and find it rather sad or pitiful that she does. The ones with whom I spoke read serious fiction, and for all their angst were both playful and eager for intellectual debate. They did not come across as perceiving themselves as (sex) objects at all, in the way that the women in *Sex and the City* do. Every one of them seemed interested to form a relationship with me, but they wanted it to be with my mind, perhaps as a foreigner or a psychologist who might be able to impart some interesting information, and as a person with whom they could discuss ideas. In these discussions they were not out to win the argument or grind ideological axes or show how clever they could be, or, for that matter, to be compliant. They actually seemed interested in exploring ideas. However beautiful the woman, none seemed to want that to distract me from communicating with them as a person or to use it to impress or control me.

Exactly the same can be said of all the women I met in Denmark. Looking out of the taxi on the way into Copenhagen, a very remarkable contrast with Moscow is all too visible. The men actually seem more overtly attractive than the women. Indeed, insofar as I am capable of assessing such things, the numerous tall, slim and very handsome men seem as startlingly good-looking specimens of their gender as the Muscovite women were of theirs. Not that there is anything wrong with the Danish women. Although the stereotype of blonde Scandinavian bombshells has always been incorrect – most are dark-haired – the raw material has the same potential as the Muscovettes. The difference is that the female form is less in evidence, as are any other indications of a concern to be overtly feminine, such as makeup. During my time in Copenhagen I saw few skirts worn above the knee, even by the young women, even in a nightclub on a Saturday night, and their clothing was very rarely at all revealing of their bodies. Rather, they aspire to looking well-fed without being fat, wear natural-looking clothes and go for unaffected, simple designs that do not accentuate the female form.

Some art goes into achieving this naturalness, as Helena, a thirty-four-year-old housewife, explained. 'The women here have to look good, not glamorous or getting men to tremble with desire, but the fashion is for natural beauty, although a hell of a lot of work goes into creating it. They do want a perfect body, but perfect is not incredibly thin here. There are a few teenagers who don't eat but that's not the main thing. Sure some teens are pretty hot, but looking like that is not the aim of their mothers.' On the difference with Russia, she said, 'I went to St Petersburg a year or two ago and I was sitting there thinking, "Oh my God, they're totally out of my league." They were just so perfectly figured and beautiful, and coming back here you really noticed the difference. Our fashion designers produce very different styles, much more relaxed. We aspire to a different kind of beauty, but that's the goal.'

This was further explained to me by Tøger Seidenfaden, the editor of *Politiken*, who agrees that for most of the time Danish teenagers definitely do not dress to maximise male lust towards them, and that older women do not seek to plagiarise the slimness and smooth-skinned nubility of teenagers. Cosmetic surgeons whose task is to create the semblance of eighteen-year-old breasts, thighs and stomachs, and of even more youthful snub noses and stretched-smooth skin, have thin pickings in these parts. He confirms that, though by no means fat, the women are perfectly happy to have big bottoms (I rather doubt that a book with the title *Does My Bum Look Big in This?* would sell any copies in Copenhagen) and unflat stomachs. Indeed, some fairly plump

Danish women seem very comfortable wearing those crop tops which display the midriff. By no means are they aiming for asexuality. Says Seidenfaden, 'A woman might like to be desired on a Friday night when she goes out dancing, but it's not something that's important to her at the office on Monday; in fact, the opposite is true. It would be an irritating distraction to her if the men were constantly flirting aggressively with her. I know that she doesn't mind being chatted up by a handsome Greek man on a beach on holiday, but she doesn't want that in a lot of other contexts. It would be a hassle that doesn't give her any of the respect she wants. This is a society where a woman is far more valued for her performance at work than her looks. I don't want to sound like a propaganda book for feminist seventies values, but I think that is really true.'

Evolutionary psychologists, nearly all of them male and American, would argue that it is contrary to our genes for women to have this attitude to their body and for men to accept it. According to them, back in the primordial swamp, the most successful hunter-gatherers attracted the prettiest wives. In this picture, prettiness is a genetic indicator of fecundity and of good 'feminine' homemaking and mothering skills. (Never mind that there is no evidence at all that a woman's looks and these skills correlate or have ever correlated; but then, fascinating though its speculations may be, evolutionary psychology's urge to universalise often makes it run the risk of being (American) ideology, not science.) The evolutionary ideologist's woman looks after the children, sweeps the cave and keeps the home fires burning to cook the sabre-toothed tiger stew for when daddy gets home from his hunter-gathering. She will maximise her desirability in order to attract men with the best hunter-gatherer genes. In not playing up their secondary sexual characteristics with revealing clothes and nubile figures, the Danish women are going against their natures, and in not favouring women like that, so are men.

I put this to Seidenfaden, asking him if men here sitting at pavement cafés really don't, as they do in the English-speaking world, go 'Phwoar, get a load of that!' when a strikingly sexy girl walks past. He replies that 'the men say a little bit to each other that women are attractive, but not very much. I have internalised the value system so much that I wouldn't do it, but maybe other men would not have [internalised that value system] as much as me.' This may be true. I put the same point to a father in his mid-thirties, who is less of a pillar of the Danish establishment than Seidenfaden – in fact, is something of a rebel. He commented that 'of course, when we are all just lads together we will make chauvinistic comments to each other if a pretty woman walks past, obviously we like sexy women. But we would never say that if a woman is present. The women are very strong and the men know there would be hell to pay if it was overheard.'

On reading this, American evolutionary psychologists might say, 'Danish men are having to suppress their instinctive, natural desire for dominance; being pussy-whipped by domineering women into domestic servitude is bound to depress them, which is why more Danish men are depressed than the women, who, in turn, nonetheless, in playing down their sexiness, are going against their natures.' They base their claims about the universal, genetic nature of gender differences on surveys of patterns of attraction around the world. One survey has shown that in the matter of sexual jealousy, whereas men worry about sexual infidelity, women are more anxious that their man will become emotionally attached to another partner. Another (of fifty-two nations) shows that men are more driven by a search for sexual variety than women. Most important of all was a thirty-seven-nation survey showing that women are attracted to dominant, wealthy, high-status, older men, whereas men everywhere seek youthful nubility and do not care about the status or wealth of women.

The trouble with these studies is that they blithely assume that genes explain these patterns without testing the social alternative. When that is investigated, the genetic foundations look rather shaky. Two re-analyses of the thirty-seven-nation study, for example, have shown that in societies where women can gain access to wealth and status through education and a career rather than marriage to a man, they are less likely to be attracted by those characteristics in a potential mate. Denmark would seem to be a prime example of this: the women do not aspire to nubility; if anything, it is the men who have to use appearance to attract women.

Most recently of all, an analysis of the forty-six studies that have surveyed this issue challenged the notion that men and women are all that different, psychologically. In the great majority of traits (78 per cent), differences between men and women are either non-existent or small. It turns out that there is no difference in how good girls and boys are at maths. Girls' self-esteem is widely believed to be lower because it nosedives on entering puberty: in fact, boys' self-esteem falls just as much. In most respects, the genders communicate in the same way: forget about men interrupting much more than women and being much less self-revealing. Only a handful of the cherished nostra of evolutionary psychology survive this analysis. It is true that women do not masturbate nearly as much and they are not up for casual sex to anything like the same degree. They physically attack others dramatically less often. But the conclusion is that, overall, to a very large degree, when it comes to gender difference we almost do start as blank slates.

There was certainly considerable support for this view in the 'femininity' of the Danish men. Rolf, now in his mid-twenties, had lived for a time in America as a teenager, and confirmed that laddish bravado does exist in Denmark during the teenage years. 'They do brag about sleeping with girls here. There's a trophy culture around it to some extent – it's still something to be proud of.' However, overall, he felt that the gender balance here was very different. For instance, he believes that sex starts much younger because the girls are more assertive. 'They are definitely more confident, will make an approach if they like the look of you. There's a sense in America that there must be something wrong with a woman who does that, but here there's no stigma. The women will come up and ask you if you would like to buy them a drink in a pub. Actually,' he added, 'I prefer it that way.' Rather than replying 'Yeah, phwoar, what red-blooded male would-n't?', I sensed that something more sensitive might be required. It turned out that Rolf is not a man who enjoys one-night stands. 'I don't know how to express this in the right way, but sexual intercourse has never been the important thing to me, it's always been more emotional intimacy and the talking that I was after. Not that the sex is not important,' he says, but what he is really after is 'having someone I have confidence in, someone I trust, who takes care of me. I would not like intercourse with someone I don't relate to closely on a mental level. I don't like the one without the other.'

I found this kind of sensitive, New Man's comfort with talking about emotions in all the Danish men. Take Stig, aged twenty-five, who split up with his long-term girlfriend a month ago. Can you imagine many British men talking about a break-up like this? 'Last summer we went to China together, and on an eight-hour bus trip I remember thinking a lot about us. I tried to recall when I had last bought her flowers, or done the washing for her or said I loved her and, actually, I found it had been a long time. I also realised that when she had done the washing I didn't really feel I owed her, or that I was grateful and wanted to do the same for her. So I concluded she was better off without me. She wanted us to stay together but I thought it wasn't good because I was not putting in as much as I was getting out – it was unfair. It would drag her down, and in a year's time we would break up anyway. So I felt it was best to end it now.' That was very considerate of him? 'I hope so. We discussed it a lot and I think she saw my point of view. She could understand but she didn't agree. So we broke up when we got home, and soon after she went to Australia to work. It was best to clear the lines before she did that, it would have been much worse over the phone or by email. We still chat over the internet and I think she is all right. I'm sure she can cope, although of course it's much easier for me because it's me who thinks it's for the best.'

Although Stig has trendy modern hair arrangements (complex facial hair and a weird pattern carved out on his cropped skull) and wears youth culture kit (baggy jeans showing the crack of his bottom), they are belied by his character. Like all the Danish men I met, he is just so sensible, decent and willing to see both sides of an argument. It's not that he is unemotional or cold. He finds many things amusing and ironic, is passionate in his loves and hates. If there is anything dubious about the Danish male, it is his lack of passion and irrationality, though this may be merely a sign of my skewed English-speaking mentality. I could not help feeling that Stig is a million miles away from the complexity of the characters in the songs of David Bowie ('Baby, I've been breaking glass in your room again') or Lou Reed – such a perfect day, but what most people seem to ignore is that the perfection in that song is only perfect for perverse old Lou because of its imperfection: 'You just keep me hanging on', he repeats at the end of each verse, revelling in being tantalised. On the first side of his *Berlin* album there is a song which begins 'Caroline says that I'm just a toy, she wants a man, not just a boy'; by side two this has become 'Caroline says, as she gets up from the floor, you can hit me all you want to, I don't love you any more'. Okay, a wildly dysfunctional relationship with Caroline might not be many people's cup of tea, but you can picture the total incomprehension on Stig's face in trying to make sense of it. 'Maybe they have problems,' you can hear him saying sympathetically, but leaving it at that (and maybe that's not such a bad way to be).

Indeed, the rules of attraction seem to be very different in Denmark from those prescribed by either evolutionists or by

American culture. One man explained what it takes to be an alpha male here. 'Women realise that if a man is to have a big amount of money or an important job he will have to work all the time, and that's not going to be much fun. They also are doubtful about anyone who stands out too much from the crowd, careful not to dress too sexily for the same reason. My wife really likes to see me on my bike with our daughter, says she finds that sexy. That sums it up, because she's only partly kidding. Is he a good father? That's the question for women.'

If it is true that signalling to a Danish woman through career (hunter-gathering) success that you can be a good provider is not going to attract her, since she intends to do half the providing herself and will expect you to do at least 35 per cent of the homemaking, then how does the Danish man attract a woman? The answer is by being physically good-looking and emotionally sensitive. That is the diametrical opposite of the usual way it works in most of the English-speaking world. In America you need to have lots of money to attract good-looking women, and to get it, unless you inherit it, you must be a killer-driller workaholic. Danish women use other criteria, like emotional literacy and what many Brits would regard as politically correct values. A chap like Stig would stand no chance of attracting women if scripted into an episode of *Sex and the City*, but then the men in that series would not do too well with real-life Danish women. Denmark may pose a major challenge to the theories of evolutionary psychologists and to the American assumption that there is a one-size-fits-all human nature (which just happens to knit neatly into the economically neo-liberal, atavistic one found in America).

In their very different ways, Denmark and Russia demonstrate how powerfully societies influence a woman's attitude to her appearance. I would guess that Russian female beauty is a response to a lack of other channels for self-expression and creativity. Danish women's greater concern with beauty than attractiveness is heavily influenced by the gender politics and economics of their society. Although pushing in the opposite direction, the other countries which I visited also controlled the female form. What seemed abundantly clear was that it is far better to have the attitude of the Danes or the Russians than the others. The pursuit of beauty is a much more satisfying, fulfilling and less emotionally distressing enterprise than the Virus-driven obsession with how you appear to others that is found in the English-speaking world. Regarding yourself as a commodity which needs (but really, wants) bedecking in other commodities is not conducive to emotional well-being.

Vaccines – For women

1. Rediscover the meaning of beauty by observing small (three- to eight-year-old) children

In the first place, purely to look at, most people would agree that small children of both sexes are often beautiful. Despite our widespread horror of paedophilia, it is still a very common occurrence for someone, on seeing a child, to say 'Isn't he/she beautiful,' referring to their physical appearance. What exactly has triggered our use of this adjective, rather than, say, 'attractive', 'handsome' or 'gorgeous'? Although there are many elements involved (the unblemished skin, graceful movement, etc.), perhaps the critical one is that the speaker is not assessing the child in terms of its sexual desirability, and in speaking of 'beauty' can feel completely protected from being interpreted as doing so. This should provide a strong clue as to how to be beautiful: having the intention of being desired will not enable it. Indeed, part of the beauty of small children lies in their innocence of sexual desire as a means of manipulating the perceptions of others. For most of the time, their appearance is not something to which they have given any thought. Of course, as they move along the spectrum from three to eight or so years of age, they become more or less aware of clothing as an issue. But this also provides a vital clue to adults who seek beauty for themselves. When they have made an effort to select particular garments and to combine them with others, it has usually been done purely for their own gratification, without a thought for how it will appear in the eyes of the onlooker.

I see this in our daughter with increasing frequency. Depending on whim, she will insist on combining the most bizarre (to adult eyes) garments, both in terms of colour and style, perhaps insisting on adding a pink skirt to her mauve pyjamas with red wellies and a purple cardigan without vest. In making these choices, she shows not a sign of caring what others might think or whether they conform to accepted convention. The end-product is beautiful to her, and that is the lesson for adults: forget about how you look through others' eyes, concentrate on what you find pleasing and amusing. Whether you look beautiful to others depends on who is beholding, but the fundamental rule of being so deemed is that you feel beautiful yourself. The result will be a much more personal, self-expressive appearance.

Not valuing beauty is one of the defining characteristics of people who have the Virus, appreciating it defines the opposite. Beauty is closely allied to art and truth. Regardless of how successful an artist may be in creating beauty, truth is always a goal. However conventionally ugly the sitter for a Lucian Freud portrait, faithfulness to the original plays an important part in its beauty. The motivation to create beauty is evident in children's play, and in that respect there is little to distinguish my daughter's goals in painting a picture from those of an artist. Most small children have a powerful aesthetic impulse. For example, my daughter is very specific about the point at which her picture is finished. In painting barely recognisable group portraits of mama, dada and herself, a particular red daub may be very important to her, in order for her to feel it is now 'done', that it satisfies her aesthetic sense. In adults, appearance, as opposed to beauty, is a social signal of concerns with status or power or wealth, with aesthetics relegated to the secondary role of supporting that signal. Appearances and deceit are closely allied to advertising. Despite advertisers' protestations of performing a public service by providing information about products, and however much they may employ beauty as one of their stratagems in doing so, their real object is to promote consumption through purveying lies.

2. When trying on clothes in a shop and looking at you
   self in the mirror, forget altogether about what others
   might think

Whether or not your bum looks big in the garment should be an issue only if you think that runs against your notion of beauty. If your goal is to get men to want to sleep with you, it may be important in a society where most men have been turned against big bums. But before you go down that road, remember that there are any number of large women who have no difficulty in finding men who desire them because they feel confident of their beauty. Just as English-speaking (but not, as we have seen, Danish) men are often fixated on the appearance of potential partners, young women are becoming increasingly picky about how men look. But one of the great strengths of women has long been that they are less concerned about it than men, so if you decide to follow Sonja the Russian banker's philosophy, and concentrate on what the man is like as a person, maybe he will do the same with you.

3. When considering cosmetic appearance-enhancing purchases, ask yourself, 'Will this make me more beautiful?'

If you find yourself about to fork out £50 for a jar of skin cream, pause and ponder whether this purchase is truly consistent with your notion of beauty (and also remind yourself that countless scientific studies have shown that a tube of E45 will add moisture to your skin just as effectively, and for a twentieth of the price). The cosmetics industry is concerned with making you believe you can look younger or sexier, not with beauty (despite their mendacious use of that word to designate the section in the shop where the cosmetics are sold). In your mind, you need to disconnect being desirable from being beautiful.

4. If you are middle-aged, ruthlessly interrogate any desire you have to look younger

It's one thing to want to be physically fit and not be carrying more weight than is physically good for you; it's quite another to adopt a fanatical training regime designed to make your body approximate to your twenty-year-old daughter's. At the risk of descending into a Hades of cliché, beauty, as Lucian Freud's portraits have proven many times over, is both ageless and unrelated to the raw material with which you are starting. To resent your body for ageing is a prescription for misery and means that, like so many of us, you have not matured out of the grip of consumerism.

5. Stop reading women's magazines!

They are the devil's work! Their articles on 'beauty' and the adverts on the facing pages only make it harder for you to understand what being beautiful might mean for you.

For men

1. Learn from the Danish men

As a lover of the lyrics of Lou Reed and David Bowie, I would not suggest that you become level-headed, indiscriminately friendly, bland and limpid. What was hugely impressive about the Danish men was their genuine interest in the kind of person they are with and sensitivity towards them. At the very least, although the sexual allure of a partner is the reason you desire her, it is a ludicrously random basis on which to choose someone to share your life with. If someone looks like Britney Spears or Madonna you may become aroused, but you might just as well use the letter of the alphabet with which their name begins, or the colour of their eyes, as a criterion for their suitability to have your babies. Like the Danish men, you need to cultivate your appreciation of beauty, not of tight-fitting clothes.

2. Become more emotionally intelligent

Again, at the risk of sounding like an editorial from *Spare Rib*, circa 1970, the truth is that the Virus not only gets in the way of your appreciating what a woman is like as a person, but of what you are like yourself. If only for selfish reasons, you need to know what you feel. If you don't, or can't even talk about it with anyone, you are an emotional car-crash waiting to happen.

Chapter 6

Consume What You Need
(Not What Advertisers Want You to Want)

Affluenza replaces our true needs with confected wants. We *need* emotional security or to be part of a community, we only *want* a newer iPod or car. In no single domain is this better illustrated than that of property ownership and home improvement.

More than anything else, our personal finances are dominated by the 'need' to pay the mortgage on a residence whose purchase price is nearly always many times greater than our true means. The insatiability of the Virus means that, as well as having mortgaged ourselves to the limit, we never seem to be content with what we have, although for many of us a less expensive home would be perfectly adequate to meet our needs. There is always a better house, whether in a more fashionable area or street therein; we constantly hanker to improve what we have, the conservatory, the new kitchen or the sculpted garden; we may seek a second home and, on getting it, soon want a better one; even those who have acquired more homes than any individual could possibly need are liable to desire still more or better ones. We talk of 'needing' these things, but really, we only want them.

Modern Australia is the embodiment of these trends. Sixty-year-old multi-millionaire Brian lives with his wife June in a large mansion a few miles down the coast from Sydney. This is the largest domicile I visited in the Antipodes. 'There aren't many old houses left around Sydney, they just keep knocking them down,' says Brian proudly, because it increases the exclusivity of his 1920s residence, illustrating how relative the notion of 'old' is. His has a good-sized hallway with a wide staircase leading up to the first and only upstairs floor. It has five bedrooms and reasonably high ceilings. Paintings of beaches and boats hang on the walls, intermixed with bits of what I presume is aboriginal art, fairly crudely designed wooden figures: incongruous trophies of wealth, wrenched from their original context.

Brian looks exactly like any of the several dozen British captains of industry I have interviewed over the years. His hair is slicked back in a distinguished manner, his clothes look casual but expensive. His wife, who is also immaculately turned out, with a powerful perfume that even my nicotine-encrusted nostrils can detect, makes some coffee, asking us, 'You can pour it, can you?', apparently without a trace of sarcasm. Brian pours one for himself first, fixing me with a piercing look.

He is doubtful that Australians today are any less happy than in the past and he uses his recently purchased house (which he spent a year doing up before moving in) as illustration that things have only got better. 'We employed a researcher to look into the history of this house and they uncovered two elderly ladies who lived here. They came from privileged families. In those days there were staff, the children went to certain exclusive schools. Back then, the privileged were quite jealous of their position and it was hard to break in. Nowadays there is much less old money, and I live here when once that would have been impossible – anyone who can afford to, can join the [golfing and millionaires'] Club now. Next door, we have a Pakistani gentleman who is spending 10 million dollars doing his house up; there's a couple of Indians doing the same in this street. They come over here for drinks, we go to their houses.'

Although Brian portrays himself as having come from poor beginnings, his father actually ended up on the board of an international conglomerate. 'Of course, we were not rich because in those days you did not make as much money from industry' – unlike today, where executives in the Selfish Capitalist nations get a far higher stipend in relation to the average pay of their workforce, and unlike Brian. He also started out as a corporate man, making very tidy sums, before accruing absolutely pots from setting up companies which he grew and then sold, sometimes buying back the shells a few years later when, by Brian's self-aggrandising implication, some plonker had let it go to ruin.

One of his companies makes materials for plastic surgery. He was sent a video about it and was 'not in the least interested until June happened to see it by accident and said, "That's fantastic!", so I went for it. It's spectacularly profitable.'

Apparently Australia is 'way ahead' of Britain and France, in terms of the amount of such 'enhancement', about the same as Spain, although still behind Italy, America and, oddly enough, Brazil. There are 500 specialists in Australia doing 350,000 'interventions' a year, including 10,000 breast implants and 5,000 facelifts. Just as Australians are now obsessed with improving their housing, so they are with their bodies.

At first, Brian doubted that women today were more preoccupied with their appearance than in his youth. However, on further reflection he said, 'Well, perhaps they are. We go out for a walk early in the mornings and you see them jogging away. Women have much more disposable income than before, they can make themselves look younger. When you see photographs or cine films of women in the 1950s, the thirty-year-olds look like today's fifty-year-olds. I think it's a good thing that they can look younger, its making them happier, not unhappier.' I could see little point in regaling him with the evidence to the contrary, especially the finding that women are depressed by a diet of beautiful models in the media. It is also of more than passing interest that Brian's profits from plastic surgery coincide with a period (1997–2001) in which young Aussie women's rates of severe psychological distress doubled. The distress drives the surgery, more so than the higher disposable income.

Turning to the problems of Aussie men, Brian did feel they had more stresses today, but doubted it is making them unhappier. 'There's much more pressure to perform. Having done quite a few sales of companies I have seen how hard those lawyers in the commercial companies work. You go into one of those buildings at nine at night and you'll find people still slaving away in half the offices. Thirty years ago you would go out to lunch at least twice a week, waddle back to the office at 4.30 to sign a few bits of paper and waddle off home.' When I wondered whether it might not lead to unhappiness if these young people spent their twenties and thirties working such long hours, rather than waddling through short ones, he doubted it. 'They can have fantastic holidays nowadays: skiing, Bali, Fiji – it's unbelievable. Of course, things used to be simpler when there were fewer reasons to have a high net worth or a strong cash flow [a euphemism for a large disposable income, presumably American]. There certainly are enormous pressures at work now, but people aren't any less happy because of it, or certainly not in my generation. None of my friends have retired: we're all still at it and don't intend to stop. Personally, I can't contemplate not working. I'm bored shitless if I haven't got anything to do.'

The main reason for needing a 'high net worth' is the cost of housing. 'Property is a national obsession. The only subject for discussion at dinner is who's bought what, how much did they pay, what's it worth, boom, boom, boom. I'm glad to say the government have just changed the tax rules. This house was one of just 1,300 which were subject to a special tax based on land values which meant I had to fork out 25k a year,' he said, with unmistakable pride. I asked about the problem I had heard repeatedly from younger people who thought they might never be able to afford a home. 'Well you can see it. The entry point for a half-decent property for someone who is on a good income is going to be one million dollars [£400,000]. You need 10 per cent for a deposit up front, the stamp duty is 4 per cent, you need to do it up a bit, so you are looking at 200k to buy – and then you have to meet repayments on an 800k mortgage.'

As he walked me to my car I used the words 'middle class' in reference to unhappiness, and he became quite animated. I assumed that his objection was to the British class obsession, but it was a different one. 'It's such a horrible expression. "Middle class" seems very ordinary, dull. June would have a fit if you called her that.' Duly admonished, I headed for the hills.

In Britain, the possession of homes as a source of status is nothing new. That night I had a variant of a recurring dream, one which doubtless says a lot about me but also illustrates just how profoundly the middle classes' inner lives have long been affected by property prices, albeit increasingly so in recent decades. Some preliminary explanation of my property history is required to make this dream intelligible to the reader.

In reality, rather than the dream, I used to own a rather beautiful two-bedroom flat in Notting Hill. It had high ceilings, and one very large room, and was similar in the grandeur of its stucco white exterior to one of the houses in which I was raised. We sold this flat when we moved to Shepherd's Bush, a cheaper nearby suburb, in order to afford a house with enough space for us to accommodate a family. This house is actually rather nice for what it is, with a largish hall, a quite spacious stairway with a bare pine wooden wall along one side of it. Even so, it is far less grand than the homes in which I grew up.

The basic gag in my recurring dream is that I purchase a second flat in Notting Hill, a very large one that I never actually occupy but bought as a property investment (this is something I would never have done in real life because I am not especially farsighted, and in any case nowhere near rich enough). In the dream I have contrived to completely forget about the second flat, but on recalling its existence I pay a visit. In various versions of the dream – it has been a bit like a soap opera in which there are plot developments each time – I have discovered that it has been rented out and that there is an extremely sinister man who now pretends to be its landlord. Further investigation, through the estate agent which markets it to potential renters, has revealed that it is now very valuable. However, I am powerless to realise my asset because I have lost the deeds, and anyway, when I confront the sinister man who pretends to be its owner, he subtly indicates that he will have me killed by a hit-man if I pursue my interest. In early versions of the dream I doubted that this was possible – surely people do not get rubbed out in this way? However, in succeeding dreams I have become convinced that this man really would do as he said, so I am powerless to gain from my investment. In some dreams I have tried threatening the man so that he will at least share some of the large rents he is collecting with me, but always to no avail.

In last night's instalment, I was passing the flat and decided to investigate it again. I go up to the door and see a pair of potential renters being shown around it by a menacing thug employed by the impostor who is claiming to be the landlord. The thug slams the door in my face. Eventually I extract the particulars of the flat from one of the renters, and yet again am reminded of my predicament: I own a valuable flat but can do nothing to benefit from it. Yet again I threaten action, but the thug sees me off.

I need not trouble the reader with the myriad unconscious resonances that echo for me in this dream but I relate
it as an example of how profoundly property dominates the
lives of the British middle classes – it fills their very dreams.
In my case, property has very particular associations, for it
scarred the last decade of my father's life, as illustrated by a
second recurring dream that I have. Again, before describing
it I must crave your patience whilst I present some more biog-
raphical background.

My father's father, Warwick James, was a tyrannical,
driven man, not averse to saying, 'Let's compromise and do
things my way.' The son of a successful grocer in
Northampton, he trained as a dentist and established a very
fashionable practice in London, making enough money to
rent two huge stucco-fronted houses overlooking Regent's
Park (in Park Crescent). His practice drew many of the rich
and some of the famous of that era (at public school, my one
claim to fame was that he did the teeth of Lawrence of
Arabia, a pathetic brag even for a schoolboy). For all his
faults, Warwick was a dynamic man, the inventor of some of
the equipment still used to this day to meddle with our teeth,
and I believe he was something of an expert in the field of
physical anthropology, with a detailed knowledge of the jaws
of our ancestors. He was also a mountaineer, perhaps styling
himself a gentleman explorer. In his old age he paid a heavy
price for his pretensions, because he had never actually
purchased his homes. In order to live in ones normally occupied by the aristocracy or successful businessmen, he had
rented; when the lease became due, in his mid-eighties, he
could no longer afford to live there. He was forced to vacate

the premises and to move to the more modest residence in Taunton, Somerset, where he eventually died.

Considering that my father was a psychoanalyst, analysed by no less a figure than Freud's daughter Anna, you might suppose that he would have avoided following in his father's footsteps. Unfortunately, Anna Freud was not a terribly good analyst. It seems unlikely that she ever had a sexual relationship, despite being a very vigorous proponent of her father's famously sex-dominated theory. (She does seem to have had some knowledge of sex, though. My dad once told me that he had been going to his analysis with her when he felt an inexplicable urge to leap over the garden wall outside her house; when he told her this, she asked, 'And did you have an erection at that moment?', which he did – God knows how she could have surmised this if she had never seen an erect penis.) Sadly, my dad contrived to repeat his father's dire property error.

In 1967 he sold our freehold property in Knightsbridge and bought a tremendously grand home nearby. The new house was every bit as splendid as the one in which he had been raised himself, even more so, but the trouble was that it had only a twenty-one-year lease. To be fair, at that time the 'charity' that owned it seems to have been largely serving the purpose of providing cut-price accommodation to the rich, although its stated aim was to raise money for the poor. My father reasonably assumed that when the lease became due he would have to pay only a small amount to renew it. However, in the early 1970s the charity altered that policy and he was given three months to pay a substantial sum if he wished to renew the lease for a much longer term, after which the sum would rise even further. Perhaps he could have just afforded the new lease if he had sold his second home in Cornwall and every share he owned, but, never a worldly man, more a scholar, he did not do so – with grim consequences. As the end of the twenty-one years approached, he suffered terrible anguish, some of which he shared with me. Eventually, just as his father had done, he was forced to sell the rump of the lease and move to some far more modest lodgings (the extremely noisy Earls Court Road, no less).

I am sure that this explains why he was so unhappy in his final years. Having to go down in the property world was painful to him because, again oddly for a psychoanalyst, a good deal of his self-esteem rested upon living in a posh house, a prize-hunting pillar in the psyche of an otherwise vocally, and usually exceptionally convincing, advocate of the non-material in life. Furthermore, I am sure that he felt a failure for having lost a considerable sum of money through his dealings. (I am not alone in having had a father who made this mistake; when I did a newspaper interview with Sir John Harvey-Jones, the enlightened business guru, he told me that his father was 'the only man to have managed to lose money in the London property market'; I was able to assure him that he was not alone.)

Having risked the reader hurling the book down in disgust at all this autobiography, I can now recount my further recurring dream. My parents have sold our posh house but, mysteriously, my father is still living there because the new owners have only bought it as an investment and never bothered to live there or rent it out. My mother, meanwhile, has taken herself off to a new flat somewhere by the river. It seems that they are still perfectly affable in their dealings with each other but just prefer this arrangement. There have been many plot developments in this dream, but it is essentially a very sad one.

Of the numerous problems my dad suffered in his child-hood, his father's social aspirations played a big role. My dad was sent to one of the most prestigious private boarding preparatory schools (i.e. for his primary education) of his era, St Cyprians. Although I never discussed his time there with him (except that he said his life revolved around his personal Marmite jar, apparently a rare luxury permitted to the pupils in an otherwise Spartan regime), George Orwell described the place with characteristic lucidity in his essay 'Such, Such Were The Joys'. Orwell was a pupil there a few years before my dad (along with other famous artistic alumni, such as Cyril Connolly and Cecil Beaton). In Orwell's account, prox-imity to the royal family via aristocratic inheritance was a crucial determinant of how you were treated by the monstrous tyrant who ran the place. Boys with a handle (The Hon, Lord, etc.) were pandered to, people like Orwell and my dad had to get by as best they could in a savage status system not based upon merit at all. Unlike most St Cyprians gradu-ates, my dad did not go to Eton but to Marlborough, a public school of lesser status. That he was not bound for Eton (and I wonder why not, given his father's contacts and social ambi-tions) was yet another sign of his inferiority. To top it all, dad went on to Magdalene College, Cambridge, which was then awash with Bertie Woosterish Old Etonians swanning about, apparently having a whale of a time.

Going back to my dream, it should be obvious from all this how my dad's sense of status might have become so strongly tied to his homes. Despite being a determined advocate of the importance of authenticity to fulfilment in life, and despite being highly skilled at nurturing it in his patients, he somehow contrived to be a property snob as well. He paid a very heavy price for this, in every sense.

Meanwhile, my mum was much more mixed in her feelings about property. Also raised in grand residences, she had good reason to know that where you live has little to do with happiness. She always claimed she would be happy living in a council house (my father used to joke that 'she would get out of her Rolls-Royce to go and vote Labour'), although she did go along with dad's property adventures. So my dream is partly about the divide between them regarding the importance of your home as a sign of status: she moves out of our posh residence and into a more modest one.

The dream's wider significance is the way in which home ownership is easily confused with identity (a property fallacy). People whose childhoods leave them insecure are very vulnerable to it, and there are a lot of them. My dad was no dolt, far from it. He knew that outward signs of status cannot compensate for an inner sense of inadequacy. Yet even he fell into that trap, despite his impressive scientific and clinical understanding of precisely this issue, when it came to his patients. His travails occurred before Thatcherism had created the massive gap between the richest and the poorest in Britain. Think how much greater the problem must be today, with its several hundred thousand more millionaires than in 1979, not to mention the large numbers of foreign investors in London property. Like my grandfather, some of these newcomers hail from relatively modest origins, and many have been motivated to succeed by insecurity-inducing childhood relationships with their parents. How easily must they unite the size, number and grandeur of their homes with their fragile identities?

Applied to contemporary Sydney, these ideas are even more poignant. In the last twenty years Sydney has gone from being a relatively egalitarian society to one in which wealth and its trappings are everything to a large proportion of its inhabitants. The number of people like Brian, living in their pink cakes, oblivious of the true causes of fulfilment or of the state of their wider society, must be considerable. So must the dissatisfaction and emptiness.

This was brought home to me by another Sydney millionaire, Cyril, fifty-one, who although still very rich had been chastened by the decline in his fortunes from the billion-dollar level – he was once amongst the richest of Australians. He hardly knows anyone who is not deeply dissatisfied with their life. 'Almost without exception, they are obsessed with craving ever more material affluence, to the exclusion of all else. The concern with housing is completely weird, especially renovation. I was recently round at a friend's for dinner and he asked me if I would like to come and see the refurbishment they have done to their toilet – their toilet! Just to see what would happen I said, "Well, no, not particularly," and he looked as if I had just slapped him in the face. Not being willing to admire his toilet was like refusing to say "Good shot!" if he served a winner at tennis or had hit a hole in one at golf.'

A deeper insight into the lives of the Australian wealthy came from Sarah, a thrice-married forty-five-year-old. Slender, with short black hair neatly coiffed and set off by a pair of what looked like pricey earrings, she wore a pristine white sweater and slacks. She is not really my type but I warmed to her rapidly. An only child, she had been to Cambridge to do her first degree before working in a bank, and then after two years as a missionary in Argentina she returned permanently to Australia in 1987. For the last nine years she has been a headhunter of top business executives. Along the way she had managed not to have any children, was in her third marriage and seemed full of well-being.

Much of Sarah's work over the years has been low-paid and concerned with the welfare of others – intrinsic goals. Her present job gives her a bird's-eye view of the Australian executive because she has to select candidates for the very top jobs. Of them, she says 'the word that comes to mind is "hollow", The Tin Man from *The Wizard of Oz*. They come in confident and full of their achievements, but their locus of control [i.e. how people conceive of the forces that motivate them] is somewhere over there [pointing to the garden], back with their maths teacher or parents. I almost feel you could tap some of them and it would ring hollow. When I ask them how they see their role in the wider community, you can just imagine the look I get: "Whaaat? What's that got to do with me?"' I was reminded of the T.S. Eliot poem 'We are the Hollow Men'. When I asked how happy these people are, she replied, 'I don't think the matter arises. I've got a horrible feeling that, asked for adjectives to describe themselves, the vast majority would choose "successful, driven, ambitious", but confronted by the word "happy", at best they'd say "I'll be happy sometime" or 'I'll catch five minutes' happiness later on". As for the word "fulfilled", the response would be "Wanker!" – that would be the Australian response: "What do you mean, fulfilled? I'm cashed up, I've got money in the bank."'

Sarah has witnessed tremendous changes to life in Sydney. 'The rush hour has got earlier and earlier, it used to be 8.30am, now it's 7.30. People tend to be working much later as well, there's just not the room to do the things like going for a picnic, playing little footy games on the beach, just messing around together. People go to the gym now for exercise, to do it in a nice manageable hour, instead of more leisurely, over the course of a weekend.' This is borne out by the evidence: Australians now work the longest hours in the developed world, even more than Americans.

The hollowness catches up with these men, it seems, when they retire. 'I'm finding that men coming to the end of their careers as CEOs are looking inside themselves and finding nothing there,' said Sarah. 'You ask, "What do you want to do now?" and you have to peel away, peel away, peel away, until you get anywhere near something that is theirs, let alone how you help them to do something with it. These are people who are used to "What do you want to do? Let's make a plan."' Having has replaced Being, intrinsic needs supplanted by wants.

We discussed the Australian character. I had hoped to find a nation of jolly, uncomplicated fun-seekers who might not read deep books but who knew how to enjoy themselves. Instead, middle-class Sydney seemed to be packed with career-obsessed workaholics. Sarah said, 'They're almost not Australian, just the global overworked citizens you see everywhere. Americanisation has only really happened in the last twenty years, before that there was a distinct culture.'

Which was? 'Playful picnickers.' Had there ever been an interest in the life of the mind, in intellectual debate? 'I don't think the life of the mind was ever big here, perhaps because of the pull of the sun, but it is definitely done down if anyone shows such inclinations. [Former Prime Minister] Bob Hawke was an Oxford Rhodes Scholar and a very bright guy, but all you ever hear is "he was a good lad, he drank a yard of ale, a bit of a womaniser", all those larrikin bits. It's as if they are embarrassed that he was a scholar, a bit like how in previous generations a bright woman had to be pretty and cook well to avoid being threatening. There's not a lot of pure Australianism left, just a rather diluted English-speaking something.'

I asked about the housing boom that now echoes across Australia and deafens Sydney. Sarah told me that 'there is a total obsession with renovations, very competitive: '"What's everybody else doing? We'll copy that," rather than doing what they really like. It's so much about status, literally keeping up with the Joneses. It leaves me cold. Their status is invested in their property, and they pay fortunes to designers to decide what fashion to follow. If they have to change jobs they can't be seen to be downsizing to a smaller place because it suggests they're not successful. They all want an older house because that seems to make them feel more substantial, to be part of history.' It struck me that the need to pay someone else to design the inside of their houses might not be a bad symbol for the emotional emptiness of her corporate, hollow, tin men. Just as they seemed not to know who they were when considering life beyond their career, they were at a loss as to what to do with the inside of their houses.

If Sydney has caught a particularly vicious strain of property fever, similar strains were to be found almost everywhere, an addiction to wanting more and better housing. In America between the 1950s and 1970s, housing replaced food as the largest single expenditure for middling consumers. After that, in real terms, the cost of housing increased during a period in which male earnings stagnated for the great majority. This fuelled the shift towards dual-earning households and increased the extent to which housing became a crucial indicator of status. As more households earned more, the cost of housing spiralled ever upwards. At the same time, liberalisation of financial markets enabled more and more people to get larger and larger mortgages. In the battle to sign up house-owners, mis-selling became widespread, with endowment mortgages becoming a disastrous investment. Between 1950 and 2000, mortgages went from accounting for half of household consumption expenditure to 89 per cent, whilst saving dropped to nearly zero. There were similar trends in other English-speaking nations. Young people and those on a low income now find it increasingly impossible to get onto the property ladder, and home ownership is now what chains the middle classes to the hedonic treadmill.

Curiously, on my travels I usually found the millionaires to be the most revealing of the emotional damage done by the new obsession with housing. In New York I met Jerry, the owner of numerous homes on various continents, a very decent, deeply thoughtful man in his sixties who got a first in sociology at Harvard before doing a law degree. He managed all this despite coming from a blue-collar background: his dad was a postman, his mother a school dinner-lady. The friend who introduced us had told me that when Jerry was taking his finals he did very little work and was confronted by this question about the inventor of sociology: 'Was Emile Durkheim a conservative?' Hazy about the dates but knowing that he had to mention the famous Dreyfus case of that era, Jerry put 'Writing as Durkheim was in the shadow of the Dreyfus Case ...', neatly evading the fact that he did not know which came first (the shadow could have been cast forwards or backwards in time).

Although he completed his legal qualification, Jerry was a communist activist during the sixties and, rather than become an attorney, he decided to write a legal textbook. It immediately became a bestseller, and that was pretty much it as far as money-making efforts went. Every autumn, without fail, a hundred thousand law students have bought a copy, and Jerry has done no work for the last twenty-five years, apart from revising it a couple of times. He now lives in a huge flat on the top floor of a beautiful brownstone house overlooking the West Side river (he had a grandstand view of the 9/11 attack, witnessing the second plane crashing into the tower). Settling down on his roof terrace, Jerry tells me about New York Affluenza. 'Many years ago, when I was in Haiti, one of the poorest countries of the world, I was struck by how extraordinarily happy everybody looked, full of joy and laughter, bursting into song. When I came back here I noticed the peroxide blondes on Fifth Avenue hopping in and out of their husbands' limousines with drawn faces and worried frowns. It struck me then that there's very little connection between affluence and happiness.' A high proportion of the people he knows are either on antidepressants or have been, and he has had his problems too. 'The textbook has meant I've been on vacation ever since leaving college, as anomalous a situation as you could imagine.'

The trouble was that being rich was completely against his principles. 'There was actually a period when I was really depressed.' What was that about? 'Um, it's a good question. Durkheim talks about how a change in status can cause suicide, and I found the change from being a radical communist student to an affluent person incredibly disorienting. I suppose most people would have said, "Oh wow!" and just carried on, but I didn't. Having all this money made me incredibly guilty. I would get six-figure royalty cheques and feel literally sick. I let all kinds of characters borrow money that they never paid back, I suppose because I felt guilty that I had it and they didn't. I felt disgusted that I had pots of money, kept getting these cheques which I would simply not know what to do with. I'd leave them lying about the house, wait a month before paying them in. I'd been a radical student leader, for God's sake, spent years opposing people like myself, railing against rich people and their tax dodges, and suddenly I was the person I had been hating. For a less sensitive soul it wouldn't have mattered in the least, but it upset me no end.'

An added complication was that he was gay. 'It was only about five years after the money started pouring in, in the mid-seventies, that I grasped that I was extremely unhappy. Then I mostly isolated myself, which turned out to be a good thing. I went without sex for eight years from the start of the 1980s, which probably saved my life. But I suppose I should have seen that the absence of any relationship was a sign of depression, or at least malaise.' From 1975 until 1982 he had been addicted to sex. 'It was all I did, wild and uncontrolled, multiple partners, sometimes several in one evening. By the early eighties I was feeling sick of it. Looking back, I was depressed, and the empty sex probably contributed to it. It was utterly meaningless, an anomic searching for the perfect partner. Each chap I would go with, no matter how gorgeous, was not quite perfect, so I would search out an even more gorgeous one, a dreadful searching. Of course it was a depressing time. Most of the people I was close to in the eighties died, including many I'd had sex with. I only stopped in the very nick of time.' Indeed, when he did get back into a relationship with 'the love of my life', it ended in a tragic death from AIDS.

Jerry owns five other residences, in Naples, London, Wales, Ghana and Barbados, and stays in New York for only a couple of months a year. In London he goes to art galleries, in Wales he spends a lot of time gardening, in Ghana he enjoys walking alone through wildernesses, in Barbados he hangs out on the beach and in Naples he laps up the exotic culture. He has friends in all these places who he sees when he is there, but I cannot help wondering whether it's a bit lonely to live such an itinerant life. For instance, how does he decide where and when to go? 'It's entirely a matter of fancy, wherever the whim takes me. I can't say that it makes me happy, but shall we say it keeps unhappiness at bay.' Whilst he no longer gets depressed, he is well aware of the modern feeling of dislocation and of its causes. 'Durkheim argued that once the "collective conscience" [social cohesion] is shattered, [along with] the shared values about what is acceptable, then the goals expand indefinitely and infinitely in the absence of constraints. You can never be satisfied, no matter what you get – there's always something more. That's what he meant by "anomie". It explains America's paradoxical religiosity – no other society is anything like as pious, 40 per cent attend church weekly here – which somehow coexists with our fanatical individualism. You're on your own here, exhorted to be an individual in a way that no society in history ever has been, without any collective rudder.'

In an email thanking Jerry for speaking with me, I wrote that 'I was very struck by what a good job you have done in making the most of your life, down to finding some decent therapists. That's more than I have managed, despite knowing quite a few.' Rather sadly, Jerry responded with the following: 'I'm not sure at all that I've "made the most" of my life – I believe I could have done a lot more and enjoyed life a lot more, actually. It's that old anomie, I suppose.' On reflection, it is hard to see how his life could really be very happy if he is so footloose, constantly globe-trotting to 'keep unhappiness at bay', as he put it. Perhaps his life would have been more fulfilling if his textbook had flopped and he'd had to work at a university or a law firm for money, had not been so affluent. Having vastly more money than you need increases the risk of inventing wants or being seduced by them.

As described in Chapter 1, when it comes to the conflation of needs with wants, Jerry has been living (well, at least, for two months of the year) in the heart of darkness. This is the city of Madison Avenue, home to the offices of the advertising executives who consult psychoanalysts about how to stimulate consumerism by plugging into our deepest impulses, by lying to us. However, this toxic process has not yet emulsified everywhere. In Moscow I met Fyodor, a hard-working, twenty-seven-year-old PR executive and family man whose only wish was to spend more time with his small children. Having done an American MBA, he had some intriguing observations about his profession as applied to Russia, where it has existed only for twelve years. 'The first agencies were purely middlemen, trying to pass bribes from commercial clients to journalists. That probably still exists.' I tried to picture how it would go down at any of the newspapers I work for if someone bunged me £250 to write about their company; it was not a pretty thought.

Fyodor was meanwhile explaining another important difference. 'It's not necessary to excite Russians with consumption, as such. Russia is so young as a consumer society that it's usually straightforward to sell goods. Gadgets are novel and are often the first purchase: for instance, if you try and sell a PC in America you assume your target person has already got one, so you have to persuade them they need something better, which can be hard. Here you just have to tell them about PCs in general because they don't already have one [in 2002 it was 20 per cent]. All you have to say is "A PC is a really useful thing to have." You don't need to explain how it differs from its predecessors.' This is a very important point. A major element of Affluenza is consumers feeling that their possessions, bodies, even their minds, are inadequate. That Russian advertising does not yet attempt this could be a major reason they are less afflicted by the Virus. A further reason is that encouraging social comparison is still not required for advertisers. 'Most of the stuff people are buying is state-of-the-art, so it is much harder to persuade them what you are offering is newer and better than their neighbours.' They are liable to be satisfied with their first PC or iPod. We had an American client who makes software for call centres. They were amazed that the programs we have are already very advanced. It's because they are pretty new, and that's true of most consumer products.' This gives Russia a few years grace before Virus-inducing marketing becomes essential.

Similar considerations applied in Shanghai. A marketing expert there told me that 'consumers here are still very much driven by practicality, take things very literally. Strategically, campaigns here must be absolutely straightforward and bene-fits-driven. In a more developed nation, if you were selling toothpaste you would talk about a smile and how it affects your day. Here you couldn't make that the platform of the campaign, it is still about keeping teeth white.' A study comparing trends in advertisements in Taiwan, Hong Kong and China bears this out: practicality was much more empha-sised in Chinese ones.

It seems hard to believe that Shanghai or Moscow will have long to wait before the arrival of the massive distor-tions which come from the sophisticated modern advertising, marketing and PR we now take for granted. These are lucidly enunciated in Avner Offer's book *The Challenge of Affluence*. In order to persuade, selling messages must be credible to establish trust. Because few products are genuinely superior to the competition, the truth about the product's relative price, efficacy or other merits must be distorted. The more distortion there is, the less credibility is given by the public, forcing even greater distortion. As 'deception inflation' multiplies, the whole genre becomes incredible. For this reason, from as long ago as the 1930s in America, the great majority of the population have believed that advertising is misleading.

Offer itemises the methods by which the deceptions are achieved. The most basic 'value approach' provides an 'honest' account of the 'facts' about the product. In Shanghai and Moscow, these facts are generally honest, but the technique is now rarely employed in Westernised societies because they are simply not credible. Much commoner is 'appetite appeal'. This is literally employed in the case of foods. One magazine ad presented such convincing images of sweets under the words 'please do not lick the page' that it brought letters from parents complaining that their children had been caught doing so. Applied to other products, like cars, two appetites may be stimulated at once, one by a sexy woman, another by a false claim about price. Pretending that the car is cheaper is achieved through 'anchoring', with words like 'just' or 'only' preceding the claim that the car can be obtained for £99 a month. Reading the small print reveals that such payment would only account for one-fifth of the true cost. Such downright fraudulent practice is a commonplace in retailing. A classic example is to briefly mark up the price of a product, then to mark it down, claiming that it is now cheaper.

Another tack is to acknowledge the buyer's scepticism and to claim your message is a special case of honesty: 'SOME ADVERTISERS WILL SELL YOU ANYTHING: most computer suppliers sell first and ask questions later'. The opposite strategy is the puff, a preposterous claim, such as 'Nothing acts faster than Anadin' or 'Hands that do dishes can feel as soft as your face'. Because these are so manifestly absurd, the regulatory authorities do not deem them deceptive, since no reasonable person could believe them. The key to the puff is that the claim is impossible to test, such as that a cigarette is 'measurably long ... immeasurably cool'.

As credibility inflation devalued the coinage of trust, ever greater deviousness was required. Devices which created what Offer terms a 'mask of intimacy' were employed, with the human smile taking centre stage, simulating false bonhomie, happy associations with a product and a personal link to it. Although most people believe themselves able to detect such false friendliness, studies prove that they can certainly be fooled. The prime method is the testimonial. This testament to the wonderfulness of the product may come from a real member of the public, an invented one, an expert (usually a doctor or scientist) or from an admired public figure. Also commonplace are narratives about families or children. Although all these remain hardy perennials, from the 1960s onwards, novelty and visual surprise have had to be employed. The boundaries between art and ads became increasingly blurred. Warhol's soup cans became both a comment on consumer culture and part of it. Although newspaper editors claimed to be fiercely protective of the distinction between journalism and ads, PR became ever more sophisticated at feeding messages into the bits between the ads. Faux-scientific surveys commissioned in association with a new product are now a staple of editorial content. Although wholesale muddling up of the two is avoided, this is only to prevent the complete collapse of the whole system. As Offer points out, 'editorial material provides the bread of credibility in the advertising sandwich. This boundary is respected by advertisers, because of its value to readers. But the brighter the boundary, the more tempting it is for advertisers to free ride and exploit editorial material for their own purposes.' In television and film, product placement has become common practice, with the camera paid to linger on it.

It is conceivable that the Chinese and Russians will hear the most devastating message in Offer's book: namely, that all this artifice does not actually work. America has long spent 2 per cent of its gross domestic product on advertising, other English-speaking nations spend 1 per cent. Continental Europeans spend only 0.5 per cent. Offer demonstrates that these differing advertising spends do not increase national economic performance: it is an unnecessary as well as a corrosive fraud, one which damages public trust. Most harmful of all, there is a direct relationship between how much a country's population agrees with the statement 'people can be trusted' and its advertising spend.

Whether or not China and Russia will soon be heading down the same marketing plughole as the English-speaking world, they differ from developed nations because they are still influenced heavily by survival materialism. More directly relevant to us is the example of Denmark, where they have managed to avoid becoming swamped by conspicuous consumption. Tøger Seidenfaden, the newspaper editor, explained that 'Multinationals have learnt that there is no market for luxury goods here. When a new type of product comes out, for a few years it does not penetrate at all because it's too expensive and we don't like to be ostentatious, so only freaky playboys have one. But when the price comes down, so that middle-class Danes can afford it, then within eighteen months it reaches 70 per cent of the population.' Danish consumption is based more on need, not just because an advertiser has created a confusion with wants. Along with the necessity of hanging onto your wife by getting home in time to do your bit, the relative unimportance of luxury consumption as a source of status for Danes also splinters the main plank of the male workaholia found in the Americanised world. If the sign of your alpha status for women is nothing to do with flashy cars, the size of your wedge or the prestige of your home, there is little reason for you to work your balls off to earn more than the other guy. But for all that, Denmark has not escaped the property fever that has gripped the world. In 2005, Copenhagen was the city in which prices grew by the largest amount, fuelled by low interest rates and scarcity of housing stock.

We feel as if we have very little choice in the matter of this most costly of consumer decisions. Whereas in much of the world people are grateful for a roof over their head and utilities (water, gas, electricity) that work, we in the developed world have completely lost track of the connection between the practical need to have a home and what it communicates about our social significance to others. To a remarkable extent, the price we pay for our inflated borrowings is far greater than the monthly direct debit. Suppose for a moment that you had no mortgage, and no-one else you know did. You would have a great deal more capital at your disposal, and so would our national economy. But much more important, you would be freer to choose how and where to live your life. You would be able to walk away from jobs or careers that had no intrinsic value to you. You would be liberated from the pressure to keep up with the Joneses by having a home in the right street, decorated in ways that will impress them.

The conversion of something as fundamental as your home into an investment is emblematic of the blurring of the personal and the professional that happens to Marketing Characters in Marketing Societies. This extends into almost every aspect of our lives, from the straightforward commodities we buy to the shape of our very bodies. You may not think that this applies to you, but you may be surprised how deep it runs. Without necessarily realising it, nearly everyone in the developed world is concerned about what their possessions say about them. The same may have been true of pre-Neolithic (before 10,000 BC) hunter-gatherer groups and was certainly true from the time that settled agriculture arrived. What has changed is the extent to which we are concerned about these things, and the degree of penetration of the ethos in all sectors of society.

Vaccines

1. Keep it real when it comes to the size of your mortgage

Borrowing up to six times your annual income (as some first-time buyers are now permitted to do) is, by definition, not a true reflection of your wealth. Fifty years ago, 'living on the never-never' was regarded as morally dubious as well as dangerous; today it is normal. In theory, the growth in the value of your home will, at least in the long-term, be as great as the cost of your interest payments. Leaving aside the risk you are running – what happens when, rather than if, property prices decline? – and leaving aside the fact that for most of us, when we sell, we pay as much more for the new home as we made out of the old one, borrowing such enormous sums of money disconnects you from reality. The truth is that it is the rich who mainly benefit from so much of our capital and income being tied up in housing. They can afford to buy homes for their children and benefit far more than the rest of us from inflated property values, because they have the most expensive ones. Only 4 per cent of the British population earn more than £52,000 a year. For most of us, it is strongly advisable not to allow our self-esteem to be attached to how our home appears to others. If you allow that to happen, you are trapped on a treadmill you will be too scared to leave.

2. Back to basics: be grateful for what you have got

In buying and decorating a home you can actually afford, however unfashionable it may be, it will almost certainly give you a number of amenities that were lacking to most of the population of the world until very recently, and still are for a significant slice. Give thanks for having an inside loo, a bath, a cooker, a fridge, central heating and utilities that work. Having properly realised this, be extremely cautious about purchasing new commodities to fill your home with. Why exactly do you need a flat-screen plasma telly to replace your perfectly good one, a DVD when you have already got a video, a new sofa instead of your battered but comfortable old one? If you think hard enough, you will see that these things simply do not matter, they are not needs. Your life is about much more than slaving away ever harder at your job in order to be able to afford them.

Chapter 7

Meet Your Children's Needs
(Not Those of Little Adults)

Why do siblings from the same family differ in their susceptibility to the Virus and the distress this causes? Here is depressive Jimmy Jones, with his BMW, designer clothes and longing to be famous – yet look at his brother John, a happy-go-lucky schoolteacher who could not care less about these things. There are two reasons, both to do with the way a child is cared for in early life. Indeed, since child-rearing methods vary between societies, they also go some way (but, of course, by no means all the way) to explaining why some nations are more vulnerable than others. The first reason concerns just how depressive Jimmy's parents inculcated their values in him, compared with how they did this with John. The odds are that Jimmy will have been browbeaten, whereas John was given freedom to adopt what values he wanted to. The second reason concerns the extent to which basic needs were met in early infancy, and subsequently. Jimmy's constant hunger for more is most likely to be his way of dealing with not having got enough when tiny, or afterwards; John's capacity to be satisfied by life comes from having had his early needs met.

The contrast between patterns of nurture in Shanghai and in Singapore that I found on my travels was the most telling illustration of these points. In many respects they are similar societies, yet the Shanghainese have one-quarter of the emotional distress of the Singaporeans. This cannot be down to genes, because 70 per cent of Singaporeans are of Chinese genetic stock. Indeed, studies of Chinese emigrants to English-speaking nations have shown that within a few generations they duplicate the rates of emotional distress found in their adoptive nations. A key cause of the difference between the rates in Shanghai and Singapore would appear to be the care provided in the first few years of life.

During my time in Singapore I did not meet a single person who had not been chastised with a cane during child-hood. Listen to these voices of middle-aged Singaporean women answering the question 'If you were naughty, what happened?' One replied, 'I would get caned, but I know they did it for my own good'. Another said, 'The very fact that my father reached for the cane meant I had done a really, really terrible thing. Just reaching for the cane is so frightening, it becomes enough in itself. I have friends who say that caning is barbaric but they still have one, to frighten the kids. They might whack the table, or actually use it on the occasions when their children have really, really, really screwed up, to make them remember. If I had kids, I would do it, depending what age they are; there's no point in trying to reason with a two-year-old.' A third said, 'I know it's fashionable to say the caning is bad, but as I grow older I appreciate what my parents and the government have done for me'.

At a nursery school I visited, there was a collage of paintings the children had done. One was of a child being caned, with the words:

> MY MOMMY USE A WHIP TO BAT ME.
> ?WHY. BECAUSE I WARS NAUGHTY.

When I asked the (very warm, as it happened) male teacher there about beatings, he said that in his day, 'if the teacher asked us "Are there any questions?" we all stayed silent. If there was something we hadn't understood we would only ask each other afterwards because we were so afraid to speak up.' He believed that modern parents were less cane-happy than his own had been. There were those who still believed in the saying 'Spare the rod and spoil the child,' but this was increasingly uncommon. I have little doubt that the vast majority of Singaporean adults today had frequent corporal punishment, and it is this experience that underpins the lack of creativity, sense of obligation to parents and obedience to authority that enables the system to run without opposition (almost literally, in the case of the politics). This may be what ultimately enables the father of the nation, Lee Kuan Yew, to get away with his pronouncement that 'We decide what is right. Never mind what the people think.'

I interviewed some sixteen-year-olds whom the British Council had lined me up with. It turned out that all six of them had been caned. I asked, 'What would have happened when you were three or four or five if you said to your parents, "I don't feel like doing my homework today."' Some excerpts of the answers they gave were: 'They would shout at me ... I'd get beaten with a cane ... If I didn't get good results at kindergarten I would be beaten ... I would be caned if I misbehaved badly, like lying or not working hard ... Now it would be a smack around the head, then it was the cane, which stops about thirteen. You learn not to do the things that would lead to being beaten but it would still happen.' I also asked, 'Did you feel angry with your parents when they did this?' All said they did, yet when asked if they would beat their own children, they thought they probably would (with one sparky exception: 'Seeing all the trouble I caused, I might not even get married,' he joked).

I repeatedly encountered a rather sad, unplayful deadness in Singapore. In moments of repose, the mouth of Amy, a thirty-year-old senior corporate woman whom I interviewed, was at a strange angle, high on one side and lower on the other, making her look rather miserable, but when she started talking she became animated, speaking rapidly and very succinctly. I asked if she'd had to work hard at school. 'Singapore is a very competitive society, always pushed, have to do well in the rat race, study very hard. If you drop out you are seen as a failure, which most people do not want to be. At school it's study, study, study, all the time. There is not much time for enjoyment. When you get home from school there is a massive amount of homework, assignments, work all the time. We have a few weeks' holiday, but even then there is a lot of schoolwork. You have to cope with it. You don't have much time for watching TV.' This had not changed on joining the workforce. 'We don't have any time to go out and enjoy ourselves, we have to keep working so hard, chasing money. A lot of people are getting depressed, I have friends who are. At times I feel unhappy, we do a lot of crying. When I get like that I still have to go to work even though I am asking, "What is the meaning of life?" I just have to do what I have to do. You cannot put your job out of the way or you will be a failure.'

Amy spoke with a child-like innocence, mixed with a certain dark humour and rueful smiles. Asked about whether she would like to have children, she joked, 'We have to, the government says so,' referring to Romancing Singapore, a government campaign to get women to reproduce. 'Having a child would be a bundle of joy. You would be happy if you had a kid, I'd like to give up work if I can, to look after it.' She has been with her boyfriend for seven years, but she did not seem convinced that he was the man to impregnate her. 'I would like to have more time to develop my personal life, get to know more people, I don't have much time to interact outside my work circle.' The cry of the educated thirty-year-old woman across the world – where have all the sober, solvent and sane men gone? If Amy were to have her child with him she would have to work because he is a social worker and their mortgage is three-quarters of the apartment's £140,000 price. Her advertising-executive father would be glad to help her out, but she felt it would be wrong to take any money. When I pressed her about it, she said, 'I'm in Singapore! It doesn't work like that here. Your parents have high expectations – it's our culture.' She says she is close to her parents, although they were strict (and used the cane). If she did not do her homework as a child, they 'would heavily scold me, say that when I grow up I will thank them, appreciate what they are doing.' 'Good Lord,' I said, 'what a difficult situation. You don't really seem to feel you have much choice.' 'It's very hard,' Amy replied. 'Don't really have a choice. It's the rat race: work hard, have a good job, not much social life.' Her British equivalent would have been having a good moan by now, blaming the System, but she would have none of that, perhaps partly because she is a practising Catholic. 'I don't think we have a resentment towards the government, we don't really think like that.' I said, 'But your employers are getting very rich as a result of all your work,' and she replied, 'Life is unfair. When things get tough I blame myself for not getting good enough results, working hard enough, I would never get angry with the bosses, I just keep praying.'

Evidence that authoritarianism is still the norm in parenting came from Gemma, a merchant banker with two small children. She had been caned as a girl and at first used it on her children. 'The older one was more sensible: when she did wrong, she understood. This one, Ned, is very defiant. The more I cane him, the more defiant he becomes, he does not respond to it at all, so that's when we decided to change the method. But I'm still considered avant-garde in my circle of mothers; most of them still believe in the cane. Many will still cane both siblings even if the older one encourages the younger to come and jump on the bed when it's forbidden – they make no allowance for the fact that the younger one was led astray.' When surveyed, Singaporean parents may say that they disapprove of corporal punishment, but I suspect that the proportion who still do it is high.

The scientific evidence shows that the methods employed for the transmission of values from parent to child in Singapore are a prescription for Affluenza. Parents do it in two main ways. A controlling pattern uses rewards, threats, deadlines and hectoring words, pressurising them to think, feel and behave in conformity with parental dictates. Love is conditional upon achievement of goals laid down by the parent – there is no love for the child that does not achieve them. By contrast, supportive care takes the child's perspective, minimising pressure and encouraging the child to find out for itself what it wants: self-determination by the child is valued. These two patterns result in very different types of engagement with parental wishes and are liable to lead, respectively, to Virus and intrinsic values.

At the extreme, controlling parents directly coerce the child, regardless of what it feels or wants. They insist that the offspring does exactly what is required of it, immediately, and failure to comply results in harsh retribution, from angry words and threats to physical punishment. This is very ineffective since, as soon as the parent ceases to apply pressure, the child stops the desired behaviour. Such coercive child-rearing, often with escalating use of physical force, amounting to abuse, has been shown many times over to result in delinquent and moody offspring, especially if it is done erratically and as an expression of passing parental moods. If done consistently, it produces highly conventional, compliant offspring.

Less extreme, but also controlling, is if parental love is made contingent on the child adopting a particular pattern of behaviour. This seems to be increasingly popular in the middle and upper classes of the English-speaking world. Whether combined with corporal punishment or not, it results in 'introjection' of parental values, where the child rigidly adheres to the injunctions without truly accepting them as their own. The child may learn, for example, to seek approval by working hard or being scrupulously well-mannered. It will carry this out in a robotic, literal, unimaginative fashion, sometimes verging on the parodic, because the behaviour is not infused with the child's own personal juices. A child raised this way may well become an excessively diligent pupil, and the parents will say, 'We're always telling her not to work so hard, we really don't pressurise her. She's always been like that,' and the child will say the same. The child does not realise that the demand has been introjected because the process by which parental dictate has become child's compulsion has been going on from before it had words with which to question or analyse it.

It was, in fact, my own father who identified how this process starts in early infancy. He explained that infants who do not have their primitive needs for food, physical comfort and love met at the time they arise suffer 'premature ego development'. Because they can do nothing to meet their own needs, such infants learn to look outwards for a definition of their internal state. Their pangs of hunger or feelings that they are too hot or cold are neglected by themselves as well as their carer, and instead they look to the carer to tell them if they have these needs. The result is a weak sense of self and an ego which is falsely predicated on what the carer wants, not what their body is telling them. In later life, they transfer this external sense of self-definition to teachers and to employers, increasing the likelihood of confusing needs with wants.

Introjection of parental wishes also results in a fragile self-esteem because of the constant pressure – now from within, when once from without – to live up to the introjected standard. The child enjoys its successes only briefly because it is not really its own wishes it has fulfilled, but its parents', and because there is a constant moving of the goalposts to create an ever harder target. Frequent failure – inevitable if the standards are high, as they usually are in controlling families – is followed by shame and guilt. The most accomplished of pupils will not always be top of the class in every subject all of the time, nor always do their classwork perfectly, so even coming second in one subject, or the occasional correction by a teacher, will trigger self-criticism. There is a perpetual fear of failure, leading to non-specific, free-floating anxiety that can become attached to anything and everything. Self-esteem fluctuates constantly in response to the small victories and defeats of daily life if one's worth is so shackled to one's performance. It's a roller-coaster of self-disgust and fear of failure, with only brief respites. Such individuals are dogged by feelings of shame, an excessive preoccupation with what others think, which can easily turn into depression.

Controlling parenting puts children at a high risk of both anxiety and depression. Depressed people can be divided into two main types. The 'dependent' kind are plagued by feelings of loneliness, helplessness and weakness; they chronically fear being abandoned and left uncared for by loved ones, and are desperate to be comforted, nurtured and protected. The other category of depressive is called 'self-critical' (or 'introjective') because they are afflicted by feelings of unworthiness, inferiority, failure and guilt. They are plagued by a fear of disapproval, criticism and lack of acceptance by others and are prone to harsh self-scrutiny. They may set themselves impossible standards, strive for excessive achievement and perfection, are often highly competitive and hard-working, making huge demands on themselves yet never feeling lasting satisfaction, even if they succeed. Dozens of studies show that this often results from controlling parenting.

Although it is possible that vulnerability may be caused by genes in some cases (although an intriguing study of 109 adoptees suggests not), there is a great deal of evidence that distinct patterns of child-rearing are the main cause of self-critical depression. Only achievement was rewarded by their extremely damning, insatiably demanding parents; the children used high marks and outstanding performance as a way to ensure acceptance. They were more likely as children to be subjected to a torrent of negative words such as 'bad', 'stupid', 'inadequate', 'useless', 'unwanted' (at least one in ten of all British children are exposed to such hyper-criticism). Whereas the dependent type of depressive uses fantasies of a relationship in which they are loved to derive feelings of self-worth, the materialist prospect of glittering prizes is the means for self-critics.

The international ubiquity of these findings was recently suggested in a carefully constructed study of the impact of controlling parents in large samples of teenagers from eleven very diverse nations, or ethnic groups therein, from across the globe. It found that in all cases, if parents (especially mothers) were intrusive and manipulative, there was a significantly greater likelihood of depression. Conversely, if parents – everywhere – were supportive, the child was less likely to suffer depression.

Supportive nurture has a completely different outcome. Whereas the controlled child has adopted un-metabolised parental wishes, the supported child has accepted the principle behind the behaviour, comprehending its necessity to itself, rather than to its parents. In place of pressure, there has been affection and encouragement for what the child wants, and into its own chosen mix the child has welcomed some of what the parent wants. For self-regulation, it has 'identified' with them, rather than introjected – made an active choice. A further integration of parental wishes may occur subsequently, so that those parts which fit with the child's wishes have been customised to its particular needs, beyond those intended by parents. If this child is a hard worker and high achiever, it has chosen to be so of its own accord; its self-esteem does not depend on how it is ranked against other pupils, or on living up to parents' or teachers' standards. The inner compulsion driven by introjection is absent, as is the fluctuating and fragile self-esteem, because nothing is contingent on the performance of externally provided goals. The child may be upset if it does not live up to its own standards, but at least they are its own, not someone else's.

For a number of reasons, then, children who have introjected rather than identified with parental values are at much greater risk of developing Virus values and subsequently of distress. First and foremost, many of them will have suffered infantile premature ego development and will look outwards for self-definition. Subsequent experience will have taught them that the price of love is success, starting with school performance, and usually involving an equation between money and exam success, as in 'work hard to be able to get a good job and earn a good salary'. On top of this, the kind of parents who are controlling are also more likely to have Virus values themselves and to seek to pass them on to their children. Finally, if the family is living in a Virus-stricken society, these values will be even more likely to be inculcated in a people-pleasing child who strives to conform to them.

This wholesale adoption of parental values of the strictly raised and physically punished child has been extensively researched in studies of what is called the authoritarian personality. This was identified shortly after the Second World War as part of research to discover the causes of fascism. As the name suggests, authoritarians impose the strictest possible discipline on themselves and others (the sort of regime found in Bush's White House, where prayers precede daily business, appointments are scheduled in five-minute blocks and women's skirts must be below the knee; Bush rises at 5.45am, invariably fitting in a 21-minute, three-mile jog before lunch). As children they have almost invariably been inflexibly and corporally punished with a fierce rigidity, and they do the same with their own children. Their personalities are organised around rabid hostility to 'legitimate' targets, often ones nominated by their parents' prejudices. Intensely moralistic, they direct their hatred towards despised social groups. They avoid introspection or loving displays, preferring toughness and cynicism. They regard others with suspicion, attributing ulterior motives to the most innocent behaviour. They are liable to be superstitious and they crave strong leaders, as well as being overpowering and unilaterally insistent when in authority themselves.

The reason they do not rebel against their tyrannical parents, and instead try to be like them, is fear. Trapped in an inescapable family system which is usually linked to fundamentalist religious or other ideologies, they deal with their deep loathing of their parents by feeling intense hostility towards despised minorities (this explains George Bush's passionate desire to rid the world of 'evil'; the real darkness in his life was his overbearing mother and perfect father). In Britain and America the hated groups are most commonly homosexuals, people of colour, foreigners and Jews. All of which raises the interesting question of what happens to the rage of the sixteen-year-old Singaporeans I interviewed. Perhaps it is redirected into the Virus goals that Singaporean parents set their children, imposed, in turn, upon them by Lee Kuan Yew's totalitarian body politic. Caned into compliance, the children identify lock, stock and barrel with them. The rage they felt towards their parents for treating them in this way is directed against any aspect of themselves which fails to live up to these values, and against a group who were repeatedly referred to during my stay, the 'failures'. Being a failure in Singapore is as despised as being a Black or a gay is in some sections of American society.

If the results of a 1994 study are to be believed, low self-esteem is actually normal in Singapore, and is much lower than in America. Singaporean girls suffered the problem more because their self-esteem is so heavily vested in academic performance, so they are constantly living with fear of failure. As we saw in Chapter 3, these findings have to be treated with some caution because recent studies have shown that American self-esteem is largely bogus, a cultural posturing as feeling good about themselves rather than based on authentic emotion, an attitude they get from the 'me, me, me' culture. However, it would hardly be surprising if the low self-esteem in Singapore is a real phenomenon, given the childhood caning, educational pressure and lack of positive emotion expressed by parents to children. I have been told repeatedly that it is extremely rare for parents to say 'Well done'; unlike in China, the child's best is never good enough.

Another important trend amongst Singaporean youth is loneliness: 87 per cent had experienced it. They were loneliest when not at school – at weekends, in the holidays (the loneliest months were June and December, the main holiday periods) and when at home. The report stated that 'They seemed to need company in order not to feel lonely ... on their own at home they were not able to occupy their time productively, unable to create their own pleasures ... many did not have friends or other activities outside school.' The loneliest were also those with the lowest self-esteem.

This search for companionship might explain the curious scene that greeted me when I had to visit a library right across the island from the commercial centre in a quest for a book. I arrived around 5.30pm, and each floor of this spanking new building, spotlessly clean and with every sign of being well-ordered, was packed with children of all ages. In the unlikely event that any British library were similarly flooded, such a large number of children would be making a fearful din. The older boys would be chatting up the girls, the younger children would be eating and gossiping, and very little work would get done. By contrast, in this library in Singapore the children were all diligently swotting. A few could be seen texting friends on mobiles, but there seemed little need for the periodic reminders on the tannoy, 'Please do not make a noise. Be considerate to the other library users. Thank you'. But behind such scenes of industriousness there lies a good deal of unhappiness. In a study of eighteen- to nineteen-year-olds, over one-third suffered neuroses such as phobias and general anxiety, and 16 per cent were seriously depressed. In another survey, over half of a large sample of schoolgirls saw themselves as too fat, although even minor corpulence is extremely rare in this society. The number of under-eighteens who have been seen as outpatients at psychiatric clinics has doubled since 1990.

Such trends are found throughout the developed world amongst children, but where Singapore is very different is in its low rates of drunkenness and crime. The reason seems to be a continuing respect for authority. As one researcher put it, 'the young people express a tremendous sense of obligation to meet parental expectations and an unquestioning respect for parental values and wishes. In the hierarchically structured, usually authoritarian families in Singapore, young people perceive their respect for parents and grandparents as natural and automatic. They do not express any sense of oppression or resentment about this.'

Many would argue that the job of family and society is to raise children to be citizens whose fundamental psychological needs are satisfied. The Singaporean system seems uniquely well equipped to do the opposite, and in some respects the same might appear to be true in Shanghai. It could be argued that if China wants to see its future, it has only to look at Singapore, another Mandarin-Chinese dominated, one-party state with great economic vitality. However, the similarities go no deeper than that. Singapore is as individualistic as America and even less collectivist. China is still strongly collectivist, with neither its government nor its citizens embracing every feature of Selfish Capitalism. For example, whereas Singapore offers minimal regulation and maximum profits for foreign capital, China does not allow businesses to be wholly owned by non-Chinese. (A young British toff merchant banker I met in the departure lounge on the way to Shanghai commented, 'You can have a flutter with those companies, but there's bugger all you can do if they run off with the money.')

Unlike the countries of the former Soviet Union, China has not jettisoned Communism, and the ruling elite still has a strong commitment to broadly socialist goals. Indeed, although many hen coops full of civil-rights eggs were smashed in the process (it is estimated that 70 million Chinese died at Mao's behest), it must be admitted that in the long term the population benefited hugely in many vital respects from the Communist regime: life expectancy doubled, housing and transport were transformed for the better, and starvation, child slavery and destitution were abolished. With the liberalisation that began in 1978 have come some of the vices and virtues of globalisation and consumerism, including elements of Americanisation. At least some of the younger generation of city-dwellers adhere less firmly to the Confucian principles which endured beneath the Maoist surface and are veering, albeit gradually, in the direction of individualism. But overall – socially, politically and economically – Singapore and China are very different, despite their common genes.

There is four times as much depression and anxiety in Singapore than in Shanghai, an interesting demonstration of how tiny a role genes actually play in causing them, since over two-thirds of Singaporeans come from the same genetic stock as the Chinese. As noted above, studies show that when Chinese move to America or Australia, they begin exhibiting indigenous rates of emotional distress within a couple of generations. As we saw in Chapter 3, there are many reasons for the low rates of Chinese emotional distress, but their pattern of nurture may be a crucial one, fostering identification rather than introjection – choosing parental values rather than adopting them robotically. The most important element here may be the remarkable fact that a considerable proportion of Chinese citizens were not raised during their early years by their parents, and yet, as far as I can tell, often received excellent care.

When I was in China, I met only one person who had been looked after as an infant or toddler by their biological mother. In every other case, it was the grandmother. Annoyingly, there are no published figures about this specifically, but the proportion of Chinese not raised by their mother can be inferred from certain official statistics. In 1975, 90 per cent of women under forty-five worked full-time. Maternity leave was just two months, and since state day-care nurseries were not common, it is highly probable that the great majority of small children were being cared for by grandmothers. This pattern continues today, although amongst the new rich the custom of using a nanny is gradually taking hold.

In the case of Ruth, for example, her parents were shipped off to a distant province during the Cultural Revolution and she was given to her grandmother in Shanghai, almost at birth. Her mother could only manage two, occasionally three visits a year, and 'each time she told me that I would go back to the country with her, and I told my grandmother "I'm leaving you," and she would cry.' Her grandmother may have cried, but how did Ruth feel when she discovered that her mother had lied to her? 'I cannot remember how I felt, but I know that I never cried when she left. I did not cry but I can't remember the feelings. I would have appreciated it if she had told me the truth, maybe that's why I always try to tell it to my son' (who is now cared for by her mother). When I explain that many Britons would be rather angry with a mother who abandoned her, she claims to feel no resentment about it, only understanding.

Indeed, Ruth professes to feel nothing but enthusiasm about the care she received. 'Grandmother was a very nice grandmother; although she would never spoil the child, she taught me a lot, poems and housework, for example. If I did something bad she'd talk to me. She said, "I can't spoil you because you will go back to your mother some day, and I hope that your mum will feel it is easy to look after you." It was a good thing that she was strict.' This account is broadly in accord with scientific studies of Chinese parenting. Confucianism advocates being loving to infants and toddlers, but subsequently strict training is advocated, including the use of shaming to teach the disobedient child lessons. Whilst the loving early care should lead to identification with parental values, this later care sounds like a prescription for introjection.

Compared with American parents, studies of how Chinese parents care for their children show that, at least from about the age of four, parents espouse more authoritarian styles and practices. They become keener on corporal punishment and strongly advocate curbing the child's individualism, imposing their own values. They are quite likely to humiliate a child's bad behaviour by imitating it sarcastically for general amusement. Given that primary school classes often have over forty pupils, a fair degree of obedience to authority must be inculcated by that point, or else chaos would ensue. The child who has not learnt to obey could expect a rough ride from fierce teachers. The purpose of parenting the older child is not so much to give love or to foster creativity as to train a virtuous citizen and, especially today, to succeed in the educational system. Fantasising or using imagination for no practical end is very actively discouraged. Studies comparing Chinese with American children show that they are strongly pressurised to inhibit themselves and their creativity, and to develop maximum self-restraint from the age of four. Play is regarded as a waste of time.

This care results in widespread and wholesale acceptance of both the filial ethos and parental values. There is a much greater desire amongst Chinese teens to assist and respect their parents, and commitment to provide financial support for them in the future, compared with American peers. Indeed, in one study, Chinese teenagers were actually more committed to filial values *than their parents*. Despite numerous articles about spoilt Little Emperors in Chinese newspapers, many studies show that Chinese only children are no more unfilial (or aggressive, materialistic or selfish) than those with siblings.

This strongly suggests that, like the Singaporeans, the Chinese have introjected parental values. However, it ain't necessarily so. Whereas such parenting and pressure to conform to parental dictates after the age of four would be experienced as authoritarian by Western children, it does not necessarily work like that within the Chinese cultural setting. In Western homes, such an upbringing is usually accompanied by a cruel, hostile parental attitude, but not so in China. It is possible to be pressurised to conform, within a family or a society, without the result necessarily being Affluenza distress. If the environment is warm and supportive, as the research suggests that Confucian parenting often is, even after the age of four, then the child may enjoy actively adopting parental dictates, may truly make a choice in the matter and be autonomous, even though it has conformed. There is a world of difference between a child who beavers away at learning the piano to gain a parent's love and one who does so with equal diligence because they are in a culture where their interdependent self is strengthened by being concordant with parental wishes – not a false self based on empty people-pleasing. Perhaps in this common East Asian situation, the Virus can become intrinsic. Recall the repeated comment of the women in Chapter 3 – very unlike what one would hear in the West – that, however much they may deplore the money-grabbing mores of modern China, they have *chosen* to make a go of it, that they must take ultimate responsibility for their careers and the lives they lead. At the very least, they think of themselves as autonomous. A typical example was Sidney.

Having scored myself a coffee in the Starbucks where we have arranged to meet, I immediately run into m'man, who is out of the top drawer of Shanghai's educational system. Sidney is a calm and warm person. He was cared for from birth until the age of five by his grandma in Shanghai; his parents lived three days away by train. Although it takes a bit of getting him to admit it, he is far more attached to his grandma than to his mum. Asked 'Would you be more upset if your mum or your grandma died?' he was quick to reply, emphatically, 'My grandmother. She is my dearest people [person]'. Apart from the three years between five and eight, he has never lived with his parents because after that he went to a boarding school. Despite all this, Sidney exhibited many signs of self-determination. Having spent some time with an American corporation, he courageously overrode advice to the contrary from his intimates to set up a business which is based on an abiding love of music, expressing an intrinsic motivation. His ambition is not for it to just get bigger and bigger, but to 'make enough money that I can decide what to do with my time'. Very contrary to the prevailing culture, he hopes to share the childcare with his wife when they have children. He appears relaxed rather than driven and is well able to think for himself. He shows every sign of having identified with, rather than introjected, parental values.

The warmth in the Shanghai family, despite authoritarian parenting after the age of four, may be an important factor in facilitating identification. Studies show that introjection occurs only if conditional love is combined with coldness and with cruelty. However, although it can only be speculation, I strongly suspect that even more significant in separating Sidney and his Shanghai peers from their Singaporean equivalents is the quality of their early care. I saw little sign of the consequences in adulthood of premature ego development in the Shanghainese – the weak sense of self, lack of autonomy, fear of intimacy. It may well be that having the undivided attention of a grandma is critical in helping the Chinese to colonise the filialism which is so widely subscribed to as a value.

Along with the strong importance they place on an optimistic taking of responsibility, and recent memories of hard times (described in Chapter 3), this may be what is enabling the Shanghainese to be so widely infected with the Virus without becoming distressed, but it seems unlikely that this will last. For one thing, the tradition of grandmaternal care is gradually being replaced by nannies (and day care). For another, although impossible to predict with confidence, it seems very likely that individualism will supplant collectivism and Confucianism, as it has in Singapore. Whatever the future holds, the most instructive message, from an English-speaking standpoint, is that vulnerability to Affluenza distress is strongly connected with introjection.

In America, New Zealand, Britain and Australia, as well as Singapore, cold, controlling and intrusive parenting weakens the ability of the psychological immune system to resist the Virus and thus to ward off distress. In these countries, this kind of care is on the increase. Signs of this in Britain include the popularity of strict regimes for regulating infant's sleeping and eating, the spate of parenting programmes on television for disciplining out-of-control families using rigid behaviourist principles, and the tendency for successive governments to clamp down on parents who do not clamp down on their children. None of these trends are primarily motivated by the needs of the child. They are driven by the increased pressure for parents to work long hours and for nurture that tames the beast in the nursery.

For our children, the vaccine against introjected values is supportive (but not permissive, boundaryless) nurture. For adults, it is to audit how your values came about and to colonise the ones that meet your needs, rather than confected, introjected wants.

Vaccines
1. Disentangle your parents' values from your own
One way to do this is to run through the 'Have you contracted the Affluenza Virus?' questionnaire at the start of the book, but this time doing so on behalf of each of your parents, separately. Having done so, you can contrast your views with theirs – how much do they overlap? It's worth running through the basics of your and their attitudes to the following: money; conspicuous or expensive possessions, including housing, cars, furniture, holidays, electrical goods, clothing, food, art; your physical appearance; your social importance; and any desire for fame or association with it. In itself, of course, a high measure of agreement does not prove that introjection has occurred but it's a strong indicator. At its simplest, if your parents come out as having had the Virus strongly, it's very likely that they passed it on to you.

2. Identify introjected values

To tease out introjections, you need to take each value in turn and ask yourself whether your adherence to it is compelled, something over which you feel you have no control, or whether it was chosen. As part of this stocktaking, you need to check that you have not adopted a value as a reaction against a parental one – if so, although it may seem like a self-determined one, it is quite likely to be something you feel compelled towards. Although it is not the same as your parents' value, in effect it has been introjected because you have had no choice about it. (To take a clichéd example, perhaps your dad was a sexist and so you are verdantly in favour of sexual equality; if your position is an unreasoned passion, rather than a view to which you came independently of your dad's prejudice, it is equivalent to an introjection.) Working this out is extremely hard, but you will be helped by the next vaccine.

3. Scrutinise how you were persuaded by your parents to accede to their wishes when you were a child

After reading this chapter, you will probably have recognised whether your parents were cold and controlling, and will be able to remember whether they beat you on a regular basis. If so, you have done a good deal of introjection. But that is an extreme; most of us will have introjected some values and identified with others. To find the black and white amidst this grey, it's worth asking what specific issues would evoke authoritarian, 'because I say so' responses, or the harder to spot, intrusive, interfering, manipulative reaction. Some classics are: homework; stealing; showing off; showing them up in front of others; good manners; eating at the table when a toddler; going to bed when told to; tidiness; cleanliness; being allowed to watch TV; being home at the time they said; and, in teenage years, sex, drugs and rock 'n' roll. If you are a parent yourself, there are also certain to be clues to what you have introjected in how you respond to your kids' behaviour. At its simplest, ask yourself which aspects of their behaviour really get your goat. More complex is to ask yourself about the areas where, if you are really honest, you are too lenient – they could be a compulsive reaction against a parental value.

4. Now colonise your inherited values

Having disentangled what you really care about from what you were forced to value, you are finally in a position to choose. This may well take the form of realising that it's unimportant whether you replace your car with a brand new one, just like your dad always did, or that keeping the house spotlessly clean was what your mum thought was important, not you. However, not only Virus values are introjected. There may also be some surprising ways in which you are overly anxious about spending money or valuing your appearance. Just as parents can inflict Virus goals, in some cases they may inhibit desires for them that are true to you. Maybe you fear asking for higher pay at work because your parents were puritanical about money; perhaps you see it as inherently bad to have a well-heated house, living in a freezing one because your mum was so neurotic about spending money on heating; whatever the details, the key is to start the work of finding out what really matters to you, not your parents, and colonise for yourself.

Chapter 8

Educate Your Children
(Don't Brainwash Them)

In most of the developed world today, you learn in order to earn. Especially in English-speaking nations, education has been hijacked by business. The goal is to create good little producers and consumers, whereas it should be an enquiring mind, capable of both scholarship and of a playful, self-determined and emotionally productive life. The result is Virus distress, and in no group is this clearer than in British mid-teenage girls from the top social classes.

Eleanor, aged seventeen, attended a highly competitive all-girl London comprehensive (Lady Margaret's) and got top grades in almost all her GCSEs. Yet she recalls that 'I wasn't pleased when I got my results. All of my friends got better than that and I felt terrible.' 'You're such an idiot because you did really well,' interjects her childhood friend, Jessica, sixteen, who knows plenty of other similarly high-achieving girls. 'I've a friend who's incredibly stressed-out, yet she got ten A-stars in her GCSEs. There's just so much competition between girls in all ways: how you look, the way you dress, how clever you are, everything.' Sitting in Eleanor's mother's West London sitting room, they chronicle an alarming new trend amongst their cohort of girls, a counter-intuitive leap in rates of distress amongst British schoolgirls from high-income families. You might suppose that their greater freedoms and higher achievements would be good for their well-being. In fact, a study published in 2003 reveals the opposite.

The study looked at levels of anxiety and depression in two very large (5,000-plus) representative samples of fifteen-year-olds, one in 1987 and the other in 1999. Amongst the bottom social class, girls' rates rose only a little but in the top class, the rise was from 24 per cent in 1987 to a startling 38 per cent in 1999 – more than one-third of the most privileged and successful. Contrary to popular perceptions of a teenage male emotional apocalypse, there was no significant increase in problems amongst boys, but for the girls, rates of the kind of distress that can require hospitalisation rose threefold (from 6 to 18 per cent).

The period between 1987 and 1999 was one in which girls began to outperform boys in almost every academic subject at every educational stage. In 1987 there was virtually no difference in how well the genders did at GCSE, but by 1999 a gap had opened: whereas 43 per cent of boys got five or more at grades A to C, 53 per cent of girls did so. This greater success of the girls precisely mirrors their increased emotional distress. The study provides strong proof that girls find the time leading up to exams more stressful, and that this difference from boys has arisen only recently. In the three months before exams, distress was more likely only amongst the high-income girls, and only in 1999. In fact, English fifteen-year-olds are the most stressed by exams in the world (at ages eleven and thirteen the English were in second place, after America).

The excellent academic performance of the high-income girls correlated with ill-being. The increase in distress could not possibly be caused by genes, and is strong evidence that environment is the main cause of emotional distress. Something toxic had entered the social ecology, and this study identified it as Virus-related. The main worries that were increasingly troubling the high-income girls were family problems, schoolwork, exams and their weight. Virus-infected children are more likely to come from disharmonious or broken homes. A strong concern with academic perform-ance and weight equate with placing a high value on social and physical appearances – Virus values.

Eleanor's mother Joanna, a fifty-two-year-old senior lawyer, can scarcely believe how things have changed since she was a girl. 'The pressure on girls to perform academically is a zillion, trillion times greater than it was when I was fifteen. I went to a convent, where very few girls would be expected to go to university. They really did used to say to us, "We are training you to be the wives of ambassadors."' The greater vulnerability of girls in general and high-income ones in particular to academic pressure, whether at state or at private schools, may partly result from a greater desire to please. Joanna remembers that 'watching other parents when Eleanor was small, docility was prized in girls whereas it wasn't in boys at all. "That's a good girl" was said only to obedient, docile girls, from a very, very young age.'

Messages of this kind, repeated throughout childhood, create a markedly greater tendency amongst girls to want to please authority and to be compliant. They become far more law-abiding as teenagers and adults, whether in terms of obedience to traffic regulations or committing fewer serious crimes. Above all, this people-pleasing makes them much more vulnerable to school cultures in which academic success is highly valued. Placed in a competitive GCSE school environment, it seems to be harder for girls to avoid worrying. Jessica recalls that 'the school put me under so much pressure. They used to say to me, "We've only had one B in the last five years, don't be the second." We were just, "Aargh! How can we ever live up to that?"' Eleanor became part of an intensely competitive clique. 'I had genius friends and we'd work incredibly hard to be the cleverest. We'd predict who was going to get what score before a test. I used to get really upset when people got better marks than me.'

These kinds of cliques, focusing on academic performance, do not seem to be nearly as common amongst boys. Parental pressure, specifically on daughters rather than sons, may have increased. 'You do see an awful lot of parents who are very, very anxious about their daughter's achievements,' says Joanna. 'We went round St Paul's Girl's School [which is consistently at, or near the top of, the exam results league table] with Eleanor in mind, and I thought nothing would induce me to send her there because of the parents. You'd go to the chemistry lab and the fathers would be asking how many Bunsen burners there were, incredibly intense anxiety.' Partly as a result of such high anxiety, there seems to have been an outbreak of perfectionism amongst high-income daughters.

The perfectionist feels that her best is never good enough. She sets impossibly high standards, rigidly imposed with a fanatical intolerance of mistakes. She has an intense fear of failure and is plagued by self-doubt. Even when she does achieve goals she feels dissatisfied, focusing on what she got wrong or belittling the scale of success. Her main concern is to do better than others rather than the pleasure, in itself, of carrying out a task. Her self-esteem relies heavily on winning, whether at work or at play. She is prone to depression, despite her successes, and to obsessive thoughts. As we have seen in previous chapters, these ways of thinking go with having Virus motives and controlling parents. It is also of interest that several studies have found an association between excellent school performance and schizophrenia. Indeed, the most able schizophrenics are four times more likely to commit suicide than less able ones. Since schizophrenia can be caused by parental maltreatment, it is possible that, in some cases, pushy parenting really does drive offspring mad.

Charlotte, aged sixteen, goes to St Paul's. 'I became anxious and depressed from about the age of thirteen,' she confesses. 'I was always worrying about other people's opinions: whether they liked me or thought I was attractive.' She is a classic perfectionist: 'If I do something less than perfectly I will think about it for quite a long time. It's petty, but in my mock GCSEs I got two As and A-stars in the rest. One of the As was in maths, and I cried for so long. It was my best subject and I didn't get the top grade: "Why not?", I obsessed.' Studies show that girls like Charlotte are very likely to have had perfectionist mothers from a generation that were frustrated by not being allowed to attend university after leaving school. Discouraged from fulfilling their career potential, they poured these unfulfilled ambitions into their daughters rather than their sons because they identified with them more. In some cases this has simply righted the wrongs of previous generations, but it has also created many perfectionists. Although such a mother only wants the best for her daughter, in practice they unconsciously tend to treat the girl as an agent for satisfying their own thwarted ambitions, by making their love conditional on performance and by being excessively controlling. On top of that, the girl gets a double message: 'Do as I say, not as I do.' The mum is saying 'Do well at school to get a high-flying career,' but when the daughter looks at her, she sees a full-time mother. In other cases, where the mother is herself a high achiever, she may have high hopes for her daughter because she is conscious of her own mother's lack of opportunity. Joanna recalls that she 'was brought up by a mother who had no choices. I have this vision of a fifties woman who had none because she was still economically dependent on a man. I wanted to encourage Eleanor to do well enough to have choices.'

There is good reason to believe that girls in most nations are increasingly likely to be the object of perfectionism-inducing parental care. In all developed nations with the exception of Japan, governments have gone to considerable lengths to encourage female academic and career success. But whereas some of today's disturbed high-income girls may have had perfectionist or over-controlling mothers, it would be very unfair to blame it all on them. For one thing, British fathers now do one-third of childcare, so they may be contributing (although their impact tends to be more on boys than on girls – in what studies there have been of this issue, girls' perfectionism is largely unaffected by their relationship with fathers). For another, the care that mothers provide is heavily influenced by social pressures and it only creates the potential for a problem; what happens in the wider society determines whether that potential is fulfilled. A crucial change from 1987 for high-income girls is the sheer number of criteria against which they now judge themselves. Eleanor's friend Jessica has noticed this: 'Girls try to have it all: be really, really clever, and have a great social life and lots of friends, and be really pretty and thin. What leads to really high stress is juggling all of them.'

Perhaps the greatest increase since 1987 has been in concerns about weight, a major worry for high-income girls. It has become normal for young women to be irrationally critical of their bodies. But if this is a general problem, girls from fee-paying schools are more at risk of eating disorders than those at state schools, and high-income girls are even more likely than others to long to be slimmer (whatever their actual weight). This preoccupation extends to academic high-flyers. In a sample of women at an Oxford University college, over one-third had suffered an eating disorder at some point in their life, and 10 per cent had one currently – both far higher proportions than in their less academic peers (and their less wealthy ones: nearly half of Oxbridge students attended a fee-paying school). Perfectionism, academic success and eating disorders very often go together. In Charlotte's case, it became a serious problem. Although she is back to a normal weight now, for a time she was bordering on the anorexic. 'I never felt like getting up in the mornings, tried to avoid mirrors. People told me I was underweight but I didn't believe them. I saw fat where others saw very thin.'

That the pattern of high rates of emotional distress amongst women from the top social class continues into higher education was confirmed by the students I interviewed at Oxford University. Typical was Amanda, aged twenty, at an all-girl college, of average build, weight and looks, dressed in a long skirt and a slightly hippyish, ethnic top. She described her college peers as 'insipid, terribly conformist, just do what the lecturers tell them, don't think. They're very nice, very good girls who should all be at a vicar's tea party.' The girls in other colleges are no better. 'They're much shallower than I expected, conversation about shoes, having the right skirt and going to the right clubs. I still get quite shocked by the need to be cool and part of the scene here. They're not interested in their courses, apart from exam results, although they have to pretend not to care about those. There's a lack of passion; the focus is on afterwards and their very carefully structured career.' Apparently, Oxford women do not call themselves feminists: 'I only know men who would call themselves that. In my college it means getting a "man's job", banking or consultancy, competing with men on men's terms rather than looking at what those terms are. I don't know if it's legitimate to reject those careers or whether the system has just suckered women into seeking them because it doubles the potential number of applicants for employers to choose from.' This was a clever observation. Between 1979 and 2000, the proportion of the UK workforce employed in the gender-neutral financial services industry nearly doubled (from 10 to 19 per cent). It hoovered up graduates from the elite universities, as well as welcoming women at lower levels, offering the highest graduate pay. I would argue that Selfish Capitalism was all for women getting a slice of that action, since it increased the number of potential employees, increasing employer power.

The men Amanda knows are cautious about the commitment those city jobs require, nervous of the heavy demands. However, 'The women are much more open to the idea of twenty-hour days, which I can't see as anything other than buying into the worst elements of the system. They don't ask what they are trying to achieve or whether it's right or wrong, it's just there and held up as an ideal, so let's go for it. There's no-one asking what women specifically have to give the world.' These observations also show that the culture of long working hours, imported from America, is something of which students are aware. Since 1998 the number of people in Britain working more than sixty hours a week has more than doubled (from 10 to 26 per cent), and full-time Brits work an average of forty-four hours, the most in the European Union.

Amanda feels that babies might be the starting point for a debate about what modern feminism could offer. 'Feminism here does not incorporate the idea of motherhood at all, almost a denial that any of us are women. We want to believe that babies can't happen to us, that we have this big barren space which we'll suddenly rediscover when we are thirty-five – I suppose that's hypocritical of me, since I refuse to think about children until then myself.' What the women students do think about is consumption. 'They justify their forthcoming careers by saying, "I need to sustain a lifestyle"; when pressed, they mean the Gucci tights, luxury goods to look good in the office.' Intrinsic job satisfaction is sacrificed on the altar of Virus motives. 'I know a girl who is obsessed with shoes and name-dropping. She's only interested in PR and New York, like so many people here she lacks self-awareness, says she will be happy effectively organising canapés – it's an oddly anti-intellectual mentality. It's "I'm going to adopt these masculine goals so that I can afford to buy things which will make me more sexually desirable to men."' The problem exists in the present as well as the future. 'It's a status thing, the very expensive make-up, very predominantly displayed in their rooms. It's somehow cool to indicate that you've spent twenty quid on eyeshadow.' Even though women are now much more successful at most exams than men, and should therefore be being valued for their brains, looks remain crucial. 'It's amazing how much everyone focuses on their appearance. In my first year I was very active in the Union. I was in competition with this other girl for a senior position, and it was all about who is prettier, so I was "Ooh, I'm not pretty enough, I don't want to run." It was going to come down to who was prettiest, that was made clear – absurd! There was a play last year in which the only thing anyone talked about was an actress's hairy armpits.'

When I was at Cambridge University (1973–76), exam results did not play much of a part in creating status. Quite a lot of students were content with a 2:2 or worse. Sure, when the results came out we would check out what our peers had got, but hardly anyone seemed very concerned by it. According to Amanda, those days are long gone, and the colleges are putting a lot of pressure on. In hers there is something called the Thirds Committee, before which any student getting less than a 2:1 in their exams must go, a 'mark of shame' (a 2:2 is now seen as a third in her college). Amanda got a First in her initial exams but a 2:1 in her second year. 'I was very upset by it, stupidly upset – absolutely gutted, to be honest, even though I knew it was only my second-year results, which don't count, an insane achievement thing. I still feel bad about it. My boyfriend's friend used to joke about me as the "Scholarship Girl", and when I lost the award I said, "Don't make that joke any more!" The status that hurts here is not social class but how intelligent you are, measured by your exam performance.'

As you may have guessed by now, Amanda is not a happy bunny, although at first she enjoyed the excitement and new freedoms of being at university. 'I didn't have a gap year, so my first just continued the momentum from school, but in the second I crashed. I felt completely miserable, didn't see anyone or go to lectures. I was depressed, really didn't have any fun, could have quite happily dropped out.' She visits a counsellor once a week, and is on and off antidepressants. She describes her father as having been 'a bit of a yuppy' in the 1980s, but now unemployed. 'He isn't a child person, and I definitely didn't get any approval from him until I got into Oxford. My reaction to my 2:1 was to do with him: "Oh dear, sorry dad, that's what I got." Because neither of my parents were here they don't know what it's like, though I think both always assumed I would get in, which was weird.'

Her exam performance fits with research undertaken by the Cambridge Student Counselling Service. Women students with high levels of neurotic personality traits – not emotionally distressed but prone to worrying – are four times as likely to get a First than averagely neurotic ones (for men it's twice as likely). By contrast, female students suffering severe emotional distress are one-tenth as likely to get Firsts. It seems that people who are at risk of emotional distress (which neurotics are), but who manage to channel it into achievement, do well. Severe emotional distress impairs achievement. In Amanda's case, her neuroticism may have fuelled her exam results in her first year but turned into severe distress in her second, impeding performance.

Amanda has opted out of two main dimensions of Affluenza-inducing comparison with her peers: consumerism and looks. However, she is unable to avoid the social appearances derived from success in exam competition as a vital way of defining her self. Presumably, a major reason for that was her parents' desire that she go to Oxford and, once there, that she become one of the best.

The key questions about high achievers like Amanda are the extent to which their childhood deprivations or maltreatment would have disturbed them as much had they gone to non-Oxbridge universities, and whether it would have been any different had they been at university during a less atavistic, relatively Virus-free era. It seems very likely that Amanda would have suffered problems whatever university she attended. However, being in an environment where most students feel under pressure to be 'best' increased the likelihood of students like her, with a potential for distress, fulfilling it. In a status hierarchy in which exam performance is crucial, all but the top performers will have an accentuated sense of failure. At the most obvious level, if your Oxbridge peers are the most motivated, able students in the country, it would be that much harder to succeed, meaning that you would have to push yourself more, creating more stress. American studies have confirmed this.

One study related the average ability level in several different types of school to self-esteem. Self-esteem was lower in schools with pupils of higher ability, suggesting that if you are surrounded by very able people, you tend to regard yourself in a lesser light. Another study found that high achievers in top universities had lower views of their value and career aspirations than did high achievers from less exalted universities. What is critical is perceived social status and power, and the level below which a person feels it must not be allowed to fall. This may help to explain why levels of emotional distress in American students are now found to be highest amongst the most affluent, academically competent social classes.

The common experience for educational high-flyers is a transition from being the biggest fish in a small pond to being in a shoal of equally big or bigger fishes. First of all, they must do well at their primary school. They may get a scholarship to a top public school, but on arrival there, unless they are extraordinary, they will find plenty of other pupils as able as them. If they succeed in rising to the crème de la crème at their public school (always remembering that there can be only one – putting other pupils in danger of feeling subordinated), they will move on to a university where there will be students who are just as good. Even for prodigies there is no escape. The major public schools have all had even more prodigious prodigies than you in the past; being this outstanding, you will rapidly be assigned to university-level teachers, upping the ante; in mathematics, for example, you will quickly find yourself compared with the great minds of the past and sooner or later, in almost every case, be found wanting.

These problems have existed for a long time (see Hermann Hesse's novel *The Prodigy*). But whilst it is obviously a matter of degree(s), I feel reasonably confident that the academic and consumer pressures were far less when I was at university. I do not doubt that Amanda would have suffered problems in my time, but they would not have been exacerbated by the present-day Virus-filled social environment. Amanda summed this up when she told me of her feelings about her future career. 'I'm very tempted to take a gap year after I graduate but there's such pressure and momentum to keep going. If I take a year out, all my friends will have moved on and I could fall behind. Everyone feels it's a race for the prize, you can't stop – the gap year's got to be before university. If you take one afterwards, are you doing it legitimately or are you just scared? If I'm honest, it's probably because I want to go under the duvet for a year.'

What a very, very silly education (and subsequently, career) system if its main impact is to leave even the highest achievers feeling like shit. Amanda's despair at the way in which her female peers ape the males' chase for glittering prizes epitomises how little progress there has been towards anything resembling the emancipation that feminists originally had in mind. Far from setting women free, the system propels young girls into a destructive competition for grades and, very ironically, heavily pressurises them into competing with one another to appear the most attractive.

Elevated rates of emotional distress amongst children from high-income families are not restricted to Britain. American children suffer the same problems, at both school and university. A particularly telling study of university students followed their emotional vicissitudes from the start to the end of their first year. The ones whose self-worth depended on academic success were much more stressed than ones for whom it did not. They felt short of time, fell out with peers and teachers, derived little pleasure in the actual performance of the work and, however good their grades were, felt less satisfied on learning their results. As previous studies had found, their grades were in any case not improved by their esteem-driven concern to do well, with them apparently hampered by cumulative stress and handicapped by anxiety during exams. The study concluded that 'Students who base their self-worth on academics are caught in a compelling but ultimately unsatisfying quest for self-worth. They believe that good grades will validate their worth, they study long hours to obtain that validation ... [B]ecause they have so much at stake they are stressed, and the motivation they have to do well in school does not increase their grades. Pursuing self-esteem through academic performance does not increase their self-worth; although they do get a boost to self-esteem on days they receive good grades, the boost is temporary and a grade that is lower than they expected makes them feel worthless.' The final conclusion is that low esteem does not in itself cause poor performance. Rather, students tend to do badly when they worry too much about results.

Coming at it from a different direction, in a sample of 14,000 Americans, people with a degree were twice as likely to be fans of rock music than those without one, and the reverse was true for country music. This difference in musical tastes correlated with different values and educational level achieved. Degree-holders defined independence as expressing and expanding the self, and achieving uniqueness; the degree-less defined it through integrity, such as being honest, reliable, loyal and consistent in approach. The implication was that degree-holders are much less authentic ... perhaps because their self-esteem is not grounded in the meeting of real needs.

Wherever you look in the English-speaking world, a new obsession with exam performance is to be seen. Compared with previous generations, schoolchildren are menaced from ever-younger ages by assessment. Whether in Notting Hill, Manhattan, Sydney or Auckland, there is extremely fierce competition for entry into the nursery schools that feed the primaries that prepare pupils for the most prestigious second-aries, from which disproportionate numbers of undergraduates go to the best universities. As soon as the child is old enough to understand, the message is rammed home that only by obtaining good exam results will it be able to succeed in its career. A London private nursery school was recently exposed in a newspaper as doing tests on two-year-olds to see whether they would be suitable for entry at three. The test was to leave the toddler alone in a room with five others; the ones that failed were deemed to be those who went after their mother when she left the room – scientifically speaking, a hilariously inappropriate predictor of success.

The yoking of the wagon of education to business and to money-making, once limited to America, is now found throughout the English-speaking world. In Britain, businesses are permitted to sponsor classroom materials in return for the right to display their logos. The legislation for the new city academies, personally promoted by Tony Blair, effectively permits wealthy individuals to run state schools, often with strongly Selfish Capitalist values and sometimes tied to strong religious convictions. The curriculum in the State system is being increasingly divested of subjects which will not contribute to the economy, and school sports fields have continued to be flogged off under New Labour at a rapid rate. The introduction of undergraduate tuition fees, and loans to pay for them, is a brilliant wheeze for keeping students' noses to the grindstone. Not only does it saddle them with large debts when they graduate (unless their parents are wealthy), it also obliges them to sign up for jobs and become good little producers as soon as possible; it is unlikely to have escaped Mr Blair's attention that it greatly increases the size of the unskilled cheap labour market, since most students now have to do low-paid jobs to fund their studies, often during term-time as well as in holidays. On top of all that, the trend towards vocational subjects started by Thatcherism is strongly encouraged by New Labour, with explicit public exhortations from successive Education Ministers for universities to tailor their courses to what business wants and to make their research more focused on commercial goals.

Elsewhere in the English-speaking world, similar developments are fostering the Virus by putting prize-hunting high on the list of ambitions of parents, as well as children and young people. The key message is that the purpose of education is not to find out what has intrinsic interest for you, but to work hard at school for long-term financial reward. As we saw in Chapter 4, that is a prescription for the absence of flow during work, for low self-esteem and a host of other problems. Ironically, on top of that it is death to the capacity to think imaginatively – the foundation of our economic future if the 'skills economy' is as important as politicians are always telling us it is. This was driven home to me with vivid clarity in China.

There, long before communism, educational qualifications were vital for ascent to power and wealth. For thirteen centuries prior to this one, literati competed for office in the Chinese State by taking civil service exams which tested their mastery of classical texts. It was believed that absorbing the works of Confucius and other Chinese luminaries would create moral and proper personages. (Much the same thinking was behind Britain's strange reliance on Latin and Greek to prepare our toffs for ruling the world during the second half of the nineteenth century and the first three-quarters of the last one; quite how a rote knowledge of '*amo, amas, amat*' would help in judging the best way to keep 'natives' under control in Africa or in working out the most effective means to swindle them of their natural resources has always eluded me, but then I scraped through Latin by the skin of my proverbials; perhaps if I had studied harder I would know the answer.) The legacy of this Chinese history is a system which places a very high premium on rote learning and diligence, and the cultivation of personal virtue. However, since 1978, with the expansion of the university system and the adoption of economic growth as a national objective has come a comprehensive downgrading of non-vocational subjects.

Students now do courses which are highly practical, such as engineering or business studies (courses which aren't career-oriented barely exist, and hardly anyone even thinks of doing them, unlike in Russia). In addition, the intellectual tradition in China is unsparingly pragmatic, and I could not have had a clearer illustration of this than when I interviewed seven Shanghainese sixteen-year-olds, three boys and four girls.

In doing so, I employed the same basic gag as I had used with groups of teenagers in all the other countries I visited. I asked them to imagine that they had a job and were being paid the national average wage for a graduate, in China around £200 a month. Six months later, the salary is doubled without any additional work or responsibilities being required of them. How would they feel? The Chinese reaction was fascinating because, unlike in the other countries, they immediately got bogged down in doubts about the scenario. 'What extra work would we have to do?' one asked. I repeated that there would be no change at all in their tasks. 'Maybe I would feel more pressure because if I didn't do well enough I wouldn't deserve it,' said an earnest girl with spectacles, looking rather worried. I stressed that there was no need to be concerned with that: they would still be paid for doing the job, as long as they performed just as before. 'No pain, no gain. You must only get more money for more effort,' said the fiercely moralistic daughter of two music teachers whose ambition was to be a composer (although, 'I don't think that will come true; I'm sure my parents don't want that, they would prefer a banker'). I reminded them that they now had twice their former salary. Were they not happier? Finally, they agreed that they were. What about six months later – would they still be excited about it when they woke up in the morning? 'I will give up the job. I want a challenge. Maybe I get another job,' said the daughter of an entrepreneur who says she wants to be the CEO of a foreign clothes designer in China, like Versace. They had the greatest difficulty in engaging with a hypothetical situation.

The boys were not contributing at all, so I asked a couple of them directly what they thought. Both had fathers with lower-status jobs ('worker' and 'clerk') than the girls' dads, and wanted to be teachers. One said, 'Money is not the most important thing,' and the other said, 'I wouldn't be any happier after six months.' The girl entrepreneur butted in (the boys barely got a word in edgeways throughout this, not that they seemed to care – they looked bored stiff): 'Maybe I would work for five months to save the money, then I would set up on my own and do my own project.' The would-be composer still didn't get it: 'I'm still confused by this situation. Twice the money for doing the same work?' I tried asking them how they would feel if their salary were increased tenfold. 'For the same job?' queried the would-be composer, incredulously, finding it hard to see what the point of this unimaginable situation was. 'Are we dreaming?' asked another, expressing the implausibility of what I was saying. The practical entrepreneur said, 'I will do it for one month and then leave the job and never come back.'

On the one hand, compared with the teens in other countries, these ones were proactive and felt confident enough to challenge the premise of the scenario. They were impressively practical in doing so and not in the least reticent with their objections, making it seem faintly ridiculous. On the other hand, there was an incapacity to stay in a hypothetical situation. Because it was not real and was unlikely ever to happen, what was the point of discussing it? The teens from the other countries were much better at grasping the idea as a sort of game, and seeing that contemplating a theoretical situation could shed light on actual ones. Although the Chinese could grasp what was being suggested, they were hampered from learning anything from it by constant worries that it could not happen. This is consistent with the evidence that Chinese carers do not play with children, because play is regarded as a waste of time. Fantasising or using imagination for no practical end is very actively discouraged. Studies comparing Chinese with American children show that they are strongly pressurised to inhibit themselves and their creativity, to develop maximum self-restraint from the age of four.

In some respects, this lack of imagination and inability to contemplate hypothetical situations bodes well for China as an economic force. It should make the Chinese more malleable employees and more easily brainwashable into believing that the pursuit of Virus values is all. This has already happened in other Asian societies, notably Japan and Singapore, whose populations have been shown to be quite unimaginative. However, it carries with it the penalty of lack of originality of thought and a risk of unquestioning Virus motivations, which may be less provident in the long term.

I gained a deeper insight into the demands of the Chinese education system when I went to meet Qua, a very rich petrochemical executive, and his wife Soo, a marketing manager. Their three-year-old son Chi spends his Saturday mornings at Early MBA, an American-inspired course for three- to six-year-olds billed as 'enrichment education for tomorrow's leaders'. The subjects include mathematics, economics ('business becomes real as children explore products from around the world'), astronomy ('explore spatial and abstract thinking') and team-building. Chi is mostly cared for by a nanny. His day starts at 6am, and at 7.15 Soo drives him to school, catching up on what he has done educationally the day before. In the last week she has been home only once before he has gone to bed, and she usually manages this only three times a week. Qua is similarly busy, so it is vital for Chi's parents to see him first thing if they are to keep up with his doings. Remember, this boy is just three years old. He plugs away at school until 4pm, when the maid collects him and takes him to his evening class – learning English two days a week, Japanese and mathematics on the other days. At the weekends he gets to do his piano lessons and painting class, so it's not all maths and foreign languages, lest that make Chi a dull boy. His parents believe that his creativity is fostered by such subjects ('This will be crucial if he is to be a top leader,' says Qua) and are glad that he has the chance at the Early MBA to interact with other children, because China's One Child policy means that the little Ones get too few chances to play with one another. At the weekends Soo and Qua spend some time playing with him, although as far as I can see from observing him with them, this consists mostly of getting him to read out the English words in picture books. Today is Saturday, and they have brought their son to the country club for the interview.

After a lightning tour of the club's many-splendoured amenities (I could not help wondering to myself what John

Lennon would have said to George Orwell on seeing this capitalist enterprise in the midst of a quasi-communist state), Qua explained that their goal in educating their son was to create 'a useful person', meaning one who would become 'a leader in a globalised world, who would maintain the traditions of the Chinese people'. To achieve this, it was necessary for Chi to have his mind trained. Individuality and creativity were also important, but only to make him more able to succeed. I commented that if he was having to worry what teachers and parents wanted him to think and say from such an early age, it might not work. Qua begged to differ. They were not raising him to live in America, where Qua had spent several years, but in China, where they did things differently. A balance had to be found between individuality and duty. I sensed that the scale was a good deal more heavily weighted on the duty side.

Soo did wish that she could spend more time with her son. However, she had great difficulty in understanding a series of questions I asked about his emotional needs. The main reason she wanted to see more of him was to have a greater direct effect on his educational progress but she believed that 'EQ [emotional intelligence] is important for IQ', a slogan that sounded as if it had been lifted from a book. Perhaps her lack of empathy for her son was connected to the fact that, when she was only three, she had been sent to a boarding kindergarten during the week to free her parents to work hard. 'I can remember crying when I left them at the end of each weekend. I was very sad. But I would soon be happy again after a day back at the school. We considered doing the same with our son because we are also very busy, but we felt that it would be better to keep him at home. So he is much luckier than I was because he sees us during the week.' The impetus for his incessant tutelage was a savage exam he will have to take at the age of seven, one it was vital to pass if he was to enter a top primary school. This was crucial to get into a top secondary, which was crucial to get into a top university, which was crucial to get a top job.

I wondered whether it might not be possible for Chi to go to a less-top school and then to put his foot on the gas when he was fourteen or fifteen, but Soo had her doubts about that plan. I pointed out she had not been to a top university, and neither had her husband, but they were doing all right. 'I want him to do better than me. In our generation, going to university was not so hard to do, now there is much more competition. The other parents will all push their children to do well and he will fall far behind, so we must force him to compete as well.' I wondered whether this kind of hothousing might not be rather bad for him emotionally, leaving him feeling like a failure even if he did well. She surprised me by replying that she knew what I meant and wished that the system was not so competitive. I also wondered whether she would consider scaling down her job for a year or two, or even giving it up to care for him herself. 'But I enjoy my work,' she said, 'and I would get depressed if I only cared for him,' which was fair enough – that would hardly be much help to him. However, at the end of the discussion both parents said they would discuss the idea of her taking more time off work, although I was not sure that it would be a very long debate. (Much to my surprise, when I spoke to her again a week later she had decided to rearrange her workload so that she could spend more time with her son.)

There are two sinister aspects to Chi's story, from the standpoint of the emotional well-being of China's future leaders. One is that Qua and Soo have rejected the traditional practice of handing their son over to his grandmother, part of a growing trend amongst the very rich. From infancy, he has been cared for by a succession of nannies. As noted in the last chapter, the high quality of care from grandparents which the present generation of adults received and which provides some immunity against distress, if not against the Virus, will be absent in many of Chi's cohort. But the second worrying aspect is the frenetic, fanatical pursuit of educational success as the only goal they seem to have for their child.

It is perfectly understandable why academic prize-hunting is so valued by Chi's parents. Survival materialism is a natural response to the material scarcities which, until only very recently, were the lot of much of the Chinese population, and still are for two-thirds of it. It is also easy to see how the extreme pragmatism could have been so pickled into the sixteen-year-olds. There is not much space for abstract thought, children's play and imaginary situations if you are not sure where the next meal will come from, which is the position in which some of their parents may have been. What is worrying is how vulnerable this makes China to English-speaking workaholia and exam-fever, making it even easier to see why Mingyuan Zhang is so confident that the Chinese will have New York's rates of emotional distress within twenty years.

If education in China and the English-speaking world has become little better than a systematic method for spreading the Virus, the Danish approach offers the vaccine. As in much of Northern Europe, there is no formal education there until the age of seven. Although some Danes think that the system has too little structure and is too pupil-centred, there is good evidence that the pupils enjoy it. A large study comparing twelve- and thirteen-year-olds from Denmark, France and Britain found that the Danish children were by far the most positive about going to school and the least likely to be in a hurry to leave. They did not regard school as something that got in the way of their lives, perhaps because they were much less likely to say that their teachers put pressure on them to work hard. Classes averaged eighteen to twenty in size and were of mixed ability. The official rhetoric is that education is for creating good citizens rather than economic performance, very different to that of the other countries. This rhetoric was reflected in the pupils' emphasis on learning to function well as part of a group. The curriculum is crafted to encourage them to find subjects that interest them and to be pursued in ways that also achieve this. In terms of fostering intrinsic rather than Virus motivation, this ought to result in confident, creative and autonomous children, and indeed, at least in some respects, this seemed to be so when I met with eight Danish teenagers at their school.

The children hanging around at the school gates look cheerful enough, as do the ones playing football in the playground. The ages range from seven to sixteen under the one roof. Two tiny girls come into the administration office and are given a warm, motherly reception from the secretary, who goes to great lengths to solve their problem; they skip off looking very happy. The teacher takes me up to the non-smoking staff room, but there is also one for smokers, which is where I set myself up. Because girls have tended to dominate the group sessions with teens in other countries, this time I have decided to do the genders separately (I am especially nervous that the boys won't get a look-in in a society where the women seem so self-confident). Four fifteen-year-old girls are ushered in, none displaying the kind of obsession with appearance so common in other countries, although one is wearing a miniskirt. Their parents are professionals – policemen, nurses, child psychologists – except for those of a very lively Indian girl, who run a café. All the girls seem at ease, lighting up a cigarette in one case, not nervous at meeting a spooky British shrink.

Unlike the Shanghai children, they have no problem with 'suppose you have an average salary and I double it'. Two say that they would only be pleased to have their pay doubled if they were doing a job they enjoyed. One says, 'I would be twice as happy. I could buy twice the things I already have.' The Indian girl begs to differ. 'I don't think I would be happier because money does not make you happy. I'd rather have ten good friends than be paid ten thousand more.' They seem to enjoy picturing themselves in this hypothetical scenario, apparently unconcerned with pleasing the adult by their responses, in fact largely ignoring me as they kick the idea around between themselves. When I ask if they are still as happy six months later, the Indian says, 'No, because you just want even more,' and the others agree – a good grasp of the dangers of relative deprivation. When I double their salary again, they find it very amusing, laughing at the idea and unsure what they would do with the money. The nurse's daughter says, 'If I didn't like the job then I wouldn't do it any more'; the miniskirt says, 'It's very important to be happy and like what you're doing. I would rather be unemployed and happy than have more money and be unhappy.' Despite her earlier observations about money not making you happy, the Indian says, 'I would do it even if I didn't like the job.' Would she still feel happier six months after the pay rise? 'If it's a job I don't enjoy, it would still make me happy to have all that money because I could use it to help my family, my friends and the people back in India. I don't like going to school but I've got to do it, it will be the same with a job. You do it because you know you have to, you just need to try and get the best out of it and be happy and crazy like I am. I'm not only helping myself by going to school, there's a lot of other people involved, like my parents' – a classic illustration of survival materialism fuelling a Virus goal, but accompanied by intrinsic motivation (like Chet, the New York taxi driver in Chapter 1). It turns out that she is the only one of the four who does not do a casual job after school ends (the academic hours are 8 to 2.30): the others work in video shops or hairdressers. Her parents want her to concentrate on her studies, which is often the case in Indian immigrant families (they came here eighteen years ago) throughout the world.

Now I jack up the amount they are paid to £400,000 a year, a huge salary by local standards. Incredulity finally rears its head. 'Is this really just an ordinary job?' exclaims the nurse's daughter. 'You must be crazy. Is there a catch, is there something else I have to do for this? I would quit my job.' The miniskirt thinks she 'would be unemployed and maybe have a garden and travel around the world to give me something to do'. The policeman's daughter says, 'I'd keep my job, buy a huge house with a swimming pool. But I wouldn't be any happier than when I had half that because money can't buy you family and friends. I'd rather have those and a great social life than the money.' Only the Indian seems to relish the prospect. 'It would be totally wonderful because I could take all that money and help people in trouble in India. I would give lots of it to charity. I might take a little holiday too.' I try to tempt the unemployed girls back into the job, emphasising the nice car, flat and clothes they could buy if they stayed in it, but they are adamant that they would not care about those.

A gentle, sweet-natured bunch, the boys were laid back and, as in all the other countries, considerably less articulate and confident than the girls, despite being a year older. Nonetheless, like the girls they were immediately at ease and did not seem apprehensive about me putting them on the spot or making them look stupid. Their responses to the salary-doubling gag were similarly anti-materialistic.

They instantly grasped that the initial buzz of being richer would not last. One of them seemed quite shocked by the scenario, saying, as the salary increments increased, 'you would just be greedier and greedier, it's horrible' and eventually declaring that he would resign unless the employer agreed to pay only the original salary. As the sums of money increased, the others had trouble working out how they would spend it. 'I would already have a big apartment so I would not need a bigger house,' said one; another (with long hair and hippy values) 'would not buy a car, I belong to Greenpeace'. Two of them had fathers who had retired because of sickness, yet they felt their families had adequate incomes – 'we have lots of good stuff in our home, all that we need'. Another boy was of Muslim, Pakistani origin (his parents had emigrated here nineteen years before) but was no more materialistic than the others, although he was 'not interested in girls, I don't really like them and it's not to do with my religion'. The three others had all started messing around with girls at the age of twelve or thirteen, but none had a girlfriend: 'Girls like boys who are a bit more mature and more brainy than our age.' They were adamant that looks were not at all the main thing when it came to girls. Said one, 'if she is cold and you can't talk to her, that would be uncomfortable, even if she looks like Britney Spears. Of course I care if she has a nice body, but a good personality is more important. She must have the ability to use her brain, good-looking is for one-night stands.' This received general approbation. Although none said so, I got the impression that these boys had not really had much sexual experience, and when asked what they got up to out of school, computer games were the main thing.

The only subject that provoked much animation was America. 'I don't like Bush and Iraq and all that stuff. There is so much difference between rich and poor there [America], you have to pay to go to hospital or a good school, it's ridiculous. It's better for the State to pay.' I did not meet anyone in Denmark who had a good word to say about the American Way. Like the girls, none of the boys was excited by celebrities or being famous.

When I asked the newspaper editor Tøger Seidenfaden about Danish teens, he explained that, when it comes to the common teenage excesses found in teens from English-speaking nations, neither parents nor teachers react with punitive prohibition. 'If a twelve- or thirteen-year-old is going out getting drunk, even several nights in a row, the parent will usually just sympathise and hope for something better.' If anything, he felt this permissiveness had gone too far: 'Perhaps we should be a bit stricter about that because we have a high level of teenage drinking compared with other nations.' He also worries that the lack of discipline or pressure in the educational system may be harmful, and that the emphasis on social and emotional skills over learning in the schools, whilst desirable to some extent, has gone too far. 'A recent report showed that fully 12 per cent of our sixteen-year-olds are functionally illiterate and a further 6 per cent have real trouble reading. That's deplorable in one of the most expensive, best-resourced education systems in the world.' Not that progressive education necessarily leads to poor performance – far from it. A recent study of American children at ages four and nine showed that ones who had been taught using the child-centred Montessori method were not only more socially skilled, they also performed better academically.

An interesting witness to the differences between the Danish and English systems was Leif, a thirty-two-year-old who had been educated partly in the English one. He believed that the twelve universities in Denmark do not have as high a standard as the best British ones, and that too many Danish students keep dropping out part-way through degree courses. His main criticism was that both school and university lacked structure and there was insufficient pressure to perform. He explained that the first serious academic evaluation is not until the age of sixteen. Weirdly, there are actually only ten grades, though the top one is '13'. (The scale goes 0, 3, 5, 6,

7, 8, 9, 10, 12, 13, but he did not know why. I told him the *Spinal Tap* gag, where the lead guitarist explains that they are louder than other bands because they have a special amplifier which goes beyond the usual 0 to 10 volume control – it has an 11. Leif did not laugh uproariously; alas, I did not find the Danes to be the most humorous of peoples, but maybe it was the way I told them.) The Danish system's strength was in its emphasis on emotional literacy. 'Social skills are very valued, recognising emotions is important. My sister hasn't done well in her exams but she is not thought of badly by her friends for that, what matters is what she is like.'

Whether or not the Danish education system has become too permissive, the fact is that its economy has been one of the world's most successful for several decades. Here is hard proof that an intrinsic- rather than a Virus-motivated system does not lead to economic failure. That the other Scandinavian countries have similar academic approaches and are similarly economically successful shows this is not a unique aberration. But the hardest evidence of all against Virus-based education comes from studies demonstrating that the idea of education being the key to economic growth is no more than a myth. Of course, both individually and nationally, basic numeracy and literacy are essential for workers in a strong economy, but once they are achieved, which is the case by the age of eleven for most of the populations of the developed world, then, incredibly, there is absolutely no evidence that a nation's economic growth benefits from further investment in educa- tion. This view is summarised by Alison Wolf, a British professor of education, as follows: 'Throughout the developed world, politicians take it for a fact that education and economic growth are linked. They translate this into an enthu-siasm for yet more education spending – and yet the balance of evidence is clearly against them. One argument after another falls apart on closer examination: there is no clear indication at all that the UK, or any developed country, is spending below some critical level, or that pumping more money into education will guarantee even half a per cent a year's extra growth.' Whereas the Chinese will certainly pros-per by expanding knowledge of 'the three Rs', and do so in the short term by crushing creativity in early childhood, the Danish approach offers an important vaccine which also serves them well, economically, and in this respect, like the other Scandinavian countries, they are imaginative and inno-vative. The grinding obsession of parents and government in developed nations with children's exam performances is unjus-tified on economic grounds, and absolutely indefensible in terms of emotional well-being. That Denmark has lower rates of depression than the English-speaking world is surely, at least partly, because of its education system.

However, despite its glories, I was very surprised to learn that even the Danish system has not cracked the problem of how to increase upward mobility for children from low-income families. Seidenfaden lamented that 'there has been no increase in social mobility since the sixties: the classes just reproduce themselves through the education system. Giving children such a lot of freedom to choose what to study and whether to work is okay for the strong, but for the weak – by which I mean the ones whose parents do not take the trouble to teach the child – it does not work. It means the lowest income groups nearly always stay there when they grow up.'

In theory, in the developed world, meritocracy was supposed to be the royal road to upward mobility. In particular, it was supposed to be the driver of female emancipation and the means by which low-income people could, through merit alone, gain access to power, status and wealth. In practice, there has been remarkably little progress for the poor, and the gains made by women are debatable – some studies suggest that a woman is far likelier to become very rich by marriage than through her occupation. Wherever I went, I was shocked to find how small a part merit really played in success.

In America it has long been claimed that anyone can be president, although it is doubtful that many believe it. The reality is that it helps an awful lot if, like George W. Bush, your dad was the president before last. About one-third of the American population are incredibly unlikely ever to ascend from the relative poverty that governs their life. In England, there has been no increase in upward mobility through education since 1970. Although the proportion of children entering further education rose from one in eight in 1979, to one in three in 1991 and is now approaching 40 per cent, the vast majority of the new graduates are from middle-class families. The same is true throughout the English-speaking world. In Singapore, although merit becomes significant once you are a member of the elite, a strict system of old school tie credentials still governs who gets a chance to join. It is virtually impossible to gain access to the primary schools that feed the secondary schools that feed the universities unless one of your parents attended them. True, the system's authoritarianism forces the children to be good little examinees. As long ago as 1995, an international survey revealed that Singaporean thirteen-year-olds scored 79 per cent of maths questions correctly. The international average was 55 per cent, with Ireland, Belgium, Switzerland and France all reaching higher standards than England's could-do-better 53 per cent. The statistics for science were similar, and have continued to be so in more recent years. But at what price? In Russia, the system is even more nepotistic. Who you know – through your kinship network – is crucial. One mother there explained to me that if you are part of the elite, you can even use it to get better grades in public examinations. She knew of several cases in which children had performed too badly to gain entry to schools and to universities, and where family contacts had been used to simply get someone within the educational hierarchy to change the grades given to the children.

Of course, compared with Victorian times there are now far greater opportunities for the poor and for women to be upwardly socially mobile. But we are a very large distance from the meritocratic ideal. The great majority of people's educational and subsequent career achievements reflect their class of origin far more than their individual efforts. Most interesting of all from my standpoint, with the emotional well-being of the majority as the main concern, even if the meritocratic ideal were fulfilled, it would be disastrous. This point was made nearly fifty years ago by Michael Young. In his dystopian satire *The Rise of the Meritocracy*, published in 1958 and set in 2034, he foretold much of our current obsession with educational performance, psychological testing of employees and micro-measurement of job performance. He also foretold the disastrous consequences for emotional well-being.

In Young's dystopia, a person's position in society is completely determined by their IQ test score and exam performance, instead of wealth or aristocratic origins. Socialism's insistence that everyone has an equal potential has been supplanted by equality of opportunity, based on evidence supposedly demonstrating that IQ is genetically inherited. Intelligence has been redistributed by meritocracy. The old elite has been replaced by a new, high-IQ one, so that children from poor homes automatically join it if so blessed. Low-IQ children from clever homes drop down the social scale. The lower classes are composed of those who were already there with low IQs and the downwardly mobile. The ties that bind family background to academic and career success have been cut.

Young followed through the logic of this scenario with considerable foresight. 'The greater the frustrations parents experience in their own lives, the greater their aspirations for their children ... Every advance towards greater equality of opportunity in education ... stimulated aspiration ... each new opportunity did something to stimulate appetite.' Where once a poor man, such as a docker, had assumed that his son could only follow the same occupation, Young states, satirically, 'improvement of communications helped to root out such wickedness by advertising the standards of the wealthy and the glittering lives of thousands of people far beyond his own community to every child in the country'. By encouraging everyone to believe that their child could be wealthy, working-class parents became as obsessed with academic performance as the rest.

The assumption that education would be an unalloyed blessing to the masses, the key to social mobility, went largely unchallenged in the 1950s, as it still does today. Through the ironic voice of his narrator, Young outlines the harm this does to emotional well-being. 'The great dilemma of industrial society is that ambition is aroused ... in the minds of stupid children and of their parents as well as in the minds of the intelligent ... everyone has to be ambitious so that no one with talents of a high order shall fail to make use of them. Yet when ambition is crossed with stupidity it may do nothing besides foster frustration.' If overheated aspirations could do this, total humiliation was an even greater risk. 'Today all persons, however humble, know they have had every chance ... Are they not bound to recognise that they have an inferior status – not in the past because they were denied opportunity; but because they *are* inferior? For the first time in history the inferior man has no ready buttress for his self-regard.' This goes right to the heart of the problem of our new obsession with assessment and its damaging effect on self-esteem. Too many teenage girls and young women, having been infected with a paradoxical mixture of exam fever and over-concern with their looks, feel like failures however well they do, and the system in which they exist leaves only themselves to blame. But they are not the only sufferers. I would contend that most people, including the model students, leave school feeling like failures.

Modern education has been sold under a false prospectus containing three untruths. The first is that it will bring meritocracy, which it has not; and the pretence of it, requiring absurdly long hours devoted to passing mind-sapping, pathology-inducing exams, is hugely harmful to our children's (and especially our daughters') well-being. The second is that by enabling people to rise up the system, it will confer well-being, which it does not. The third is that exam results are crucial for our individual and national economic prosperity, and that is simply not true.

The truth is that in all the countries I visited, except Denmark, education is used mercilessly to put the needs of employers and economic growth ahead of those of children and emotional well-being. Just as the needs of parents have become paramount in most modern childcare manuals, with the damaging regimes dressed up as being for the child's good (leaving infants to cry themselves to sleep 'so they learn independence young', authoritarian discipline because 'they have to learn to obey rules'), so with education. The education systems of the English-speaking countries, which purport to be giving children opportunities to become richer than their parents, are actively hostile to the flourishing of creativity and emotional development.

Feminism has been hijacked by consumerism, and so has the emancipation of poor people. A major method by which this has been achieved is the modern obsession with examination at ever-earlier ages, under the guise of enabling women and the poor to realise their 'God-given talents', as Tony Blair once put it. Whether, like his friend George W. Bush, he literally meant God, or 'for God read genes', is not known. But a strong clue comes from his recent statement that God was working through him in the decision to invade Iraq. Blair presents education as increasing 'opportunity' and encourages 'aspiration'. What is really meant by these words is 'to make money, become as rich and famous as the folk on TV', not to have the intrinsic satisfaction of identifying and pursuing one's authentic interests, which is the goal of Danish education. I shall leave it to Chapter 12 to develop this point; for now, I restrict myself to the slogan 'Don't believe the meritocratic hype.'

Vaccines

1. If you have a daughter, be aware that she will be much more vulnerable to prize-hunting exam fever than a son will

Because people-pleasing is commoner in little girls, you must be very careful to avoid being unwittingly or overtly over-enthusiastic at your daughters' good school performance and exam results: you could be risking perfectionism, eating disorders and depression in her teenage years, and beyond. If your daughter is already showing signs of being a high-flyer, discourage academic prize-hunting and engage with her authentic interests, many of which may be extra-curricular. In helping her with schoolwork, encourage curiosity and play-fulness, discourage excessive concerns with being right, or seeking out what the teacher wants.

2. To what extent were you the victim of prize-hunting exam fever yourself?

Perhaps you did well at school and university, perhaps not. Either way, there is a significant likelihood that you left dissatisfied with your exam results or that you still judge yourself with those fabled words 'could do better'. Even if you do look back on your academic performance with satis-faction, you may be kidding yourself about this – oblivious of the heavy price that you paid for those grades in terms of your creativity and capacity to subsequently find work of intrinsic satisfaction to you, still prize-hunting to please teacher and, ultimately, parents. For some people, the day they opened the envelope containing their A level results or discovered their degree class remains the high point of their life's achievements. If so, it shows how strongly you were sucked into that way of confusing your self-estimation with the worth placed on you by academia. Whatever results they achieved, many people still have exam nightmares, tormented by answering the wrong question, or the ink running out in their pen, or making a fool of themselves in some way in front of other examinees. Facing up to the extent to which you were hijacked by exam fever can free you to rethink what you are doing with your life. You may have to retrace your steps back to early childhood to recall the last thing you did that was truly for its own pleasure, rather than to gain rewards or praise.

3. Discourage your children from believing that the purpose of education is to launch a career

Be willing to side with your children against the dreariness of conventional schoolwork. Obviously, you are not seeking to prevent them from doing well, but you should help them to challenge the assumption that it is all that matters, and to question the system. However slothful your child at school, never try to motivate them by menacing them with the spectres of failure and penury in their adult career, the shrill cry of the frustrated parent that 'you will never achieve anything if you do not do your homework and make an effort to get through your exam'. In saying this you are the unwitting patsy of corporate interests. Far better is to ask them what they hope to achieve in life. If the answer is 'don't know', try engaging with them about their favourite activity – soccer, dancing, music, sex, it does not matter what. Then discuss with them how they would need to proceed if they wanted to make a career out of this activity, preferably with them asking the questions. If you are still finding nothing that interests them or that they will engage with, tell them that the ideal is finding something that interests them that they can also be paid to do. It does not matter whether this is glamorous or well paid, only that they find it fascinating. If they do proceed to university, encourage them to find a subject which captivates them rather than to worry about their CV. Whilst they are there, do not worry them about coursework, but see whether they are reading and thinking – say that it does not matter what they read, merely that this is their chance to really think a subject through, develop their own intellectual and philosophical positions about life.

Chapter 9

Enjoy Motherhood (Not Desperate Housewifery/Househusbandry)

It is disappointing that women have become more emotionally distressed since 1950. Their education and income have improved at a substantially faster rate than those of men during the last half-century, yet a twenty-five-year-old woman today is at least three times more likely to suffer depression than fifty years ago. Despite all the progress, women are twice as likely to be depressed as men. Alongside the new pressures described in the last chapter, a key reason is the Virus's devaluation of the status of mothering.

Virus infection is extremely harmful to the well-being of mothers. It impels them and their partners to buy property they cannot afford, creating a perpetual sense of impoverishment, almost however rich they are, and putting them under pressure to work whilst their children are small. It encourages them to regard only paid work as a source of self-esteem. It leads them to hate their post-natal appearance, if they put on a bit of weight or have stretch marks. Above all, it makes them and their society downgrade the huge importance of caring for small children – almost everywhere I went, the role of mother had a status somewhat lower than that of street-sweeper.

If this were not bad enough, the Virus has also impeded the emergence of a greater participation of men in motherhood. Men are much more involved than they were. In 1970, UK fathers with an under-five spent an average of fifteen minutes a day doing childcare; today it's two hours. But the vast majority of domestic work is still done by women, and it is still very rare for men to give up paid work, part- or full-time, to take on the role of 'mother'. There is considerable evidence that if that were to happen, many of our modern problems would be solved. If men were to feel as responsible for the care of babies and toddlers as women do, our lives would be transformed. Rather than outsourcing the care of small children to paid help, be it day care or nannies, flexible working and a high status for the role of 'mother' would mean that fathers and mothers could share the care more or less equally, depending on their particular aspirations. The Virus makes this notion seem risible. Even more than women, men must prove themselves through paid work. So long as their self-esteem and capacity to attract women derives from this, we will continue to make a dog's dinner of our children's early years, increasing their vulnerability to the Virus and reproducing the higher rates of depression found in women, because the burden falls so heavily on them. They are left holding the baby, and this, combined with the fact that they have been raised to be Bridget Jones rather than a mother, accounts for their greater misery. Consider Sandra, aged thirty-one, who cares for her fifteen-month-old daughter.

She lives in a pokey flat in an affluent Sydney suburb. Her husband is an estate agent who works six days a week, from eight in the morning until late at night. Although she has some supportive friends, and her parents and mother-in-law help out, it has still been a considerable strain because her daughter has never slept well and she has only just stopped breastfeeding. 'You get used to being permanently exhausted. It's new for the baby, it's new for you and for the rest of your life you've got someone to look after. It's hard work.' She was so tired when we met that she could barely keep her eyes open and had not brushed her hair. She is dysphoric (irritable, subdued mood and physically exhausted), pretty negative about herself and struggling to stay optimistic about the future.

The strain has caused Sandra to do a fair amount of snacking and compensatory eating. Strikingly pretty, with long black hair, she feels she needs to lose two stone to be comfortable, and although she is far from obese this has become a major issue with her. 'People say to me, "You've just had a baby and you've still got all that weight on." I started worrying about my weight straight away after the birth but there was nothing I could do. I had a baby who really didn't want to sleep, and I was breastfeeding so I had to eat a lot. I've really only got my energy back in the last few months.'

It's easy to see why she feels upset because, to judge from photographs she showed me of her before the baby arrived, she was thin and would have been described in popular parlance as a 'babe'. She cannot help comparing her present self with what she was like when she was twenty-five – when, no doubt, she was constantly admired by men, making her feel good. 'I've never been somebody to exercise, never had to, really. When I was younger I had a very quick metabolism. I used to be really, really skinny, so for me, this is fat.' Also, she is aware that she is living in a suburb in a city where there is more than the usual pressure on women to be thin. 'In trendy areas like this one, the latest fashion involves really tight clothes; to wear them you have to lose weight. I think of the figures of the women round about here as normal. But when people come to visit from outside Sydney or abroad, they always say, "The women look amazing!" I just think it's normal. The other women in my mothers' group worry about their weight big time, yet they are so much thinner than me. Actually, my husband has put on a lot of weight since we had the baby, so he can't really say that much to me. But he always says, "You'll feel a lot better inside yourself if you take off some weight."'

Sandra is no Stepford Wife, is not devoid of a critical mind; on the contrary, she is insightful. 'If I had my twenty-five-year-old body again, I don't know if that would really make me happier: back then I used to get a shock when I ran into sixteen-year-olds. I don't think you're ever happy, there's always something you can do to make it better. You see people having facelifts or implants and they're never happy with themselves.' Such dissatisfaction is a crucial element in the Marketing Society, and in recent years cosmetic surgery in Australia has boomed. But there are others who can also make money out of Sandra's unhappiness about her body. She has been following a diet which entails all her meals being delivered to the house by a company precisely aimed at housewives like her. She is not supposed to eat anything else but still has to cook meals for her husband every night, which must be a kind of torture since she is on starvation rations. To top it all, fortunes are being made by food manufacturers and retailers from the comfort-eating that so many unhappy people engage in, with ballooning obesity rates in America and Britain as well as Australia.

I suggested to Sandra that it was vital she do something *for herself* to improve her mood, and she replied that she intends to, by setting up a business 'to get some money of my own, to make a contribution to the mortgage'. Ironically for someone who is so concerned about her weight, her plan is to cook meals for dinner parties. When I explain that I meant something which gives her personal pleasure – an alternative to eating as a basic satisfaction, such as a weekly visit to a film with her husband or a friend – she replies, 'I'd love to, but we've just bought a house in one of the most expensive suburbs, and what can you do? You have to pay the mortgage.' There seemed to be no other options. 'It's hard, really hard, probably always was, but everything's getting so much more expensive. My mother was saying she could have bought four big houses for what we paid for this flat.'

Just as the governments of New Zealand and Australia (and Britain) genuinely believe that there is no alternative to Selfish Capitalism, so a great many of their populations believe, like Sandra, that they have absolutely no choice in battling on, trying to live up to the standards they have been set, whether it be the shape of their body or the grandeur of their home. Sandra's parting comment before she hopped back onto the wheel in her not very gilded cage was, 'A lot of people say to

me, "Is that all you do, stay at home with a child?" You hear
that from women as well as men, some of whom haven't had
kids. We'll see what they say when they have had them.' No-
one tells Sandra that the care she is providing for her child is
laying the foundations of its subsequent emotional well-being,
that she is performing a role which is more important than
almost any other. She lives in a crazy world where she will earn
far more respect if she sets up a business cooking dinners for
other women too busy to cook their own. If successful, who
knows, some of her clients might be women who set up the
business that delivers Sandra her diet meals.

There are many millions of Sandras in cities throughout
the developed world. The Virus impedes them from enjoying
motherhood in a number of ways. The most basic is that it
induces them and their partners to buy properties in expensive areas, just to keep up with the Joneses. This leaves them
always short of money and often living in a home that is less
than ideal as a place in which to care for small children. The
Virus also makes them feel that they have lost the physical
allure to which they had become so addicted before motherhood. But most tragically of all, it causes them to buy into the
idea that activities which do not earn money, like caring for
their baby, are worthless. It is very easy to see why so many
of them conclude that the solution is to return to work: it will
not only bring in money and help them to regain their figures,
it will reconnect them with society by providing status. It's
worth taking some time to consider the wider implications of
making women think this way.

Whilst there may be no conspiracy, having these women
in the workforce greatly strengthens the hand of employers,

as Oxford undergraduate Amanda suggested in the last chapter. The larger the available employment pool, the easier it is to control the labour force. From Amanda's female peers swelling the ranks of hungry Oxbridge graduates applying to merchant banks, to low-income mothers applying for part-time jobs on Tesco checkout tills or as cleaners, the more of them there are, the easier it is for employers to dictate their pay and working conditions. Selfish Capitalism hijacked feminism by presenting it as primarily a chance for women to have male amounts of money and jobs, rather than as a re-evaluation of what it means to be either male or female, which was its original essence. In practice, this has led to low-tax economies, with high employment but mostly low-paid workers. The vast majority of women have very low pay compared with their bosses. It is hard to imagine how this would have been possible if the proportion of women in the British workforce had been at its 1950 level of 30 per cent. If, instead, it had become the norm for men to be as likely as women to stay at home and care for small children, which is what many of the original feminists would argue should have happened, there would have been a much smaller workforce who would have been much better paid.

These points were exemplified a few miles down the road from Sandra in Sydney by Liz, aged thirty-two, who cares full-time for her six-month-old daughter. Her parents were New Zealanders with a strong public service ethos and ambitious for her to succeed in the arts. 'They felt we were immigrants and had to make our way. They gave me every possible opportunity in life so that I could make the most of myself. I suppose I am the classic oldest child of a first-generation immigrant. It didn't feel like it at the time, but now, when I look back on it, there was huge expectation on me to succeed for them. I did piano and violin every night, ballet, choir practice at eight in the morning – my whole life was structured.' Having this pressure did bring some problems. 'I think I'm a bit of a perfectionist, less so now, but I was as a child. My parents actually sent me to see experts because if I didn't get an A in something I was completely distraught: "Why did that happen?" Had I gone to a regular school it might have been different, but I was surrounded by incredibly high-achieving children.' An additional factor may have been that her father suffered a handicapping illness in his late thirties which limited how high he could go in his career as a health administrator, and Liz became a vehicle for his unfulfilled aspirations.

A talented artist who was offered a scholarship at London's Royal College of Art, the perfectionist decided that she would never be exceptional in this profession. A precocious career in government public information campaigns followed, neatly combining her parents' concerns with public service with an opportunity for her to take an interest in art. After five years spent working for the US Government in Washington, rising to a senior position, she moved back to Australia because she was ready to have babies. She took a more commercial job, not as intrinsically satisfying as her previous one, but with good maternity leave and day-care options.

Liz has cared for her daughter full-time and intends to continue to do so, but the early months were not easy for someone who had Virus motives for most of her life. 'There were moments when I fell apart without the status and safety of a job. I've had days when I've just been sobbing and in tears, thinking that perhaps day care at three months is a good idea. I was much better equipped to handle a board meeting and address corporate executives, much easier than changing nappies all day. I'm used to being applauded. You do a report – "Great report." You do a proposal – "Great proposal, you brought in 100k for the organisation." You put in the hard work, get the results, and people commend you. Looking after a three-month-old that just sleeps, eats and burps, you can't get that, the only person who sees you are doing anything is your husband. I found it a lot harder than I thought it would be.' Symptoms of obsessive compulsive disorder (OCD) developed. 'I turned into a clean freak. I had to structure my day here like I would structure my work life, meticulously planned segments of time, "having a coffee", "going to the gym", "sort out this place". I became obsessed with that, a routine with weird goals, like I couldn't be at home in a tracksuit and not feel presentable. I don't know where that stuff was coming from, it was how I coped with being at home and feeling a little bit lost.' There was also quite a bit of tension with Liz's husband, who is a self-employed commercial artist.

That she should have reacted as she did fits the evidence that pretty severe emotional problems are actually the norm amongst mothers throughout the developed world in the early months of a child's life. Indeed, most women are unlikely to experience a greater threat to their emotional well-being: 10 to 15 per cent develop a full-blown major depression soon after the birth, and about one-quarter have done so by the end of the first year. For the remaining women who do not become severely emotionally distressed, caring for the infant in the earliest months *normally* produces dysphoria. A survey of a thousand British mothers found that over half said their exhaustion left them in 'a state of despair' and highly irritated by their babies. Four hours' sleep a night was the average for those with small ones. Eight out of ten mothers of under-twos said that the infant had placed their relationship with their partner or husband under 'immense strain', with rows commonplace and two-thirds 'completely put off sex'. Whilst at times they doubtless also feel an unprecedented sense of fulfilment and achievement, until the infant has settled into stable patterns of sleeping and eating, on a daily (and especially, nightly) basis, they will be liable to terrifying feelings of loss of control, chronic desperation and even, occasionally, violent impulses towards their baby.

Most people imagine that post-natal depression is a largely biological misfortune, the flipping of a hormonal switch, but there is no evidence whatsoever that it has a primarily physical cause. Whilst all women's hormonal levels alter during pregnancy and for a few weeks after the birth, a difference has never been demonstrated between the hormones of those who become depressed and those who do not. By contrast, it is possible to predict with a fair degree of accuracy which pregnant mothers are most likely to become post-natally depressed by asking them about their psychological histories: it's not hormones or genes that predict depression, but the kind of childhood they had and their current circumstances. In most cases, the combination of these with the sheer relentlessness of trying to meet the needs of the infant tips them into depression. The fundamental problem is the total dependence of the baby, twenty-four hours a day, resulting in an equally total loss of autonomy in the mother. The great majority of mothers do not have some-one else there at all times to help them out when the grinding routine of meeting the infant's needs becomes too much. Before the Industrial Revolution, people lived in extended families and there would always be aunts, grandmothers and other relatives on hand, but nowadays when the exhausted mother of a tiny infant is at the end of her tether, all too often there is no-one to give her a break.

Having money certainly reduces the risk of depression, because it buys support, both mechanical (cars, washing machines) and human (maternity nurses, nannies). In the definitive British study of the subject, whereas nearly one-third of the mothers from poor homes with a child under six suffered from full-scale depression, only 4 per cent of middle-class ones did. But it is not only a matter of money. Women who breastfeed are at greater risk, since they get less sleep and producing the milk is tiring; and so are women who lack strong intimate relationships, putting divorcees and single mothers in particular danger. Also at greater risk are those whose own mother died when they were young; for those whose mother is still alive, the risk is greater if they currently have a bad relationship with her or did so when small (and are insecure adults as a result). The sheer number of children is also a factor. Having three or more under fourteen, especially if one of them is under six, increases the risk: even if you have survived the firstborn, trying to cope with a second or third newborn offspring is nightmarish with little support. The increased risk of having more than one child to care for is neatly illustrated by the simple fact that significantly more mothers who have twins, rather than singletons, are depressed. All these factors, mostly predictable from before birth and many preventable if our society were differently organised, affect whether the mother becomes depressed. They also go a long way to explaining why English-speaking women are twice as likely as men to suffer depression and why this ratio is not found in societies which bend over backwards to support mothers, countries like Denmark. There, men are actually more likely than women to suffer depression.

Not surprisingly, given how much harder caring for infants is than being in the workplace for Virus-infected English-speakers, a major decision is at what point to return to work. Liz is very torn about this. She is a member of a mothers-and-babies group in her affluent Sydney suburb and has been amazed that only three out of twelve of them are thinking of returning soon. Despite the low status accorded to motherhood, the importance of professional roles to a young woman's self-esteem and the huge stresses of caring for a baby, a very high proportion of mothers would still prefer to care for their baby than do paid work and in many cases that is what they do, even in English-speaking nations. However, like most women of her generation around the world, Liz has been greatly deceived by the media about the true numbers of women with small children who work. When I asked her to guess what proportion of Australian under-twos are cared for by a mother who does any paid work, she hazarded '80 to 90 per cent', and was astonished to learn that it is only 30 per cent. (You can play the same game in England: what proportion of under-threes would you guess have a mother who does paid work? Contrary to what you may have read in the papers, it is only 57 per cent, the vast majority of it part-time – only 15 per cent of under-threes have a full-time working mother.) Liz is now in a quandary about when to have a second child and when to return to work. 'I'm really grappling with this. At three months I was thinking "Get me out of here!" I really wasn't enjoying it. I would do anything for my daughter but it wasn't a pleasure. But about a month ago my daughter turned into this cherub, divine. I was supposed to go back to work right now but I phoned them and said, "Actually, I'm not ready at all."'

The next part of our conversation seems to illustrate many of the competing tensions within mothers of small children, especially those who, like Liz, have introjected prize-hunting goals and motives for their careers from parents, compelled rather than choosing to pursue them, only to discover through having a child that there is more to life. I asked what would happen if she decided to put off going back to work altogether for six years, having a second child when her daughter is three.

> HER: I think I would go mad if I stayed at home for that time because I would be giving my child everything of myself, and I wouldn't be doing something 'for me': work, something pleasurable and fulfilling, subject to my child being happy. So when she's eighteen months I will go back to work because that's when my maternity leave runs out. But things could change. The last month has been extraordinary, seriously one of the most fulfilling things I've ever done.

I wake up in the morning and think, 'I'm going to be
spending the day with her' – and it's gorgeous.

ME: Does it feel like doing something 'for myself'
when you're doing that now?

HER: Um, no, it doesn't. But it's fulfilling to see her
advancement and to feel that I'm contributing to that
in some way.

ME: So why would meeting the needs of a corporation
be doing something 'for me', but it's not if you're
looking after your daughter, meeting her needs?

HER: Well, meeting her needs is much more important
to me than anything else. Actually, that's really
extraordinary, why is it that paid work is more 'for
me'? Perhaps it's because that work involves status, me
being independent and earning money and contributing to this household. I am not earning money now, my
maternity leave allowance has expired. It shouldn't be
like this, but I feel handicapped if I'm not earning. I've
been earning for years now, never had to think once,
'Can I buy this?', just bought it. Now that we're on one
income I can't just make that decision.

ME: Does that matter?

HER: Yeah, it does. It means I can't have something
when I want it. Though the reality is that if I do want

> something I just ask John [her husband] and he will
> buy it for me. We do have joint accounts but because
> I'm not actually contributing I feel I have to be
> cautious and I haven't had to be before.
>
> ME: You could easily rework this in your mind to say
> 'We've got plenty of money, no need to worry' …
>
> HER: … which is what John has been saying. But it's
> something mental, in here [taps her head]. Because
> I'm not contributing. I feel less worthy in a way.'

I found it fascinating that, when pressed, earning money in
order to be able to consume what she wanted was something
'for me'. It seemed a fine illustration of how deeply consumption is pickled into us, even very thoughtful people like Liz.
Here is a woman who adores being with her daughter and
meeting her needs, yet so profoundly has she confused wants
with needs that she seriously feels that being able to buy the
latest shoes is more 'for me' than meeting her daughter's
needs. It is true that caring for infants entails putting them
first, and most mothers point out that it requires relegating
your own needs to a very extreme extent, so that there is
barely a chance to wash your hair or even go to the toilet.
From that angle, it is very easy to see how a mother feels that
she wants something for herself. What makes less sense is the
idea that buying things she does not need will be more 'for
me'. It's great news for shoe manufacturers, much less so for
the mothers or their babies. That motherhood demands altruism is a fact, but in societies where the maternal role is viewed

positively, doing things for babies *is* doing things 'for me', more so than consumerism.

Liz is suffering a mild case of an extremely common cause of Affluenza amongst women, known as gender role strain. English-speaking women develop much of their identity through their job and come to equate their personal worth with how much they earn. Relying on a husband to provide money for a few years conflicts with that identity. At the same time, most of today's young women were actually raised by their mothers full-time and have imbibed the identity of mother as a suitable role too. When young, observing as well as listening to their full-time mothers, the mixed message was 'Do as I say, not as I do.' Even if their mother did work, whatever view you take of maternal instincts, it's undeniable that women bear the babies and can breastfeed, which often creates a greater intensity of feeling for babies, at least for a few months. Although the mothering role has no status, it's still one that is part of most women's idea of themselves, conflicting with their career identity, creating strain between these different roles. Into this equation must be added the difficulties men are having and compatibiility between partners.

By far the best study of the conditions under which role strain leads to depression in either sex identified four different kinds of marriage in a sample of 680 American couples.

● In the first type of couple, the wife does not have a job. She and her husband believe that her place is in the home, and she does all the housework and childcare. The wife was more likely to be depressed than the husband but less likely to be depressed than in the second type.

- The second type is the same as the first, except that the wife has a job, even though they both disapprove of her working. This is bad for both parties. The wife is more depressed than in any other type of couple, and *the husband is actually considerably more likely than the wife to be depressed* – the opposite of what is usual in marriages in the English-speaking world. In short, for both men and women, the worst scenario is where the woman works but neither of them would like her to.

- In the third type, the wife also has a job and both partners approve of it. The trouble is that the wife does all the home-making. Here, the man is contented but the wife is about as depressed as in the first type: whilst her husband approves of her job, she ends up having to run the home and feels that this is neither sensible nor fair.

- In the fourth type of marriage, both spouses approve of the wife's employment and share the running of the home. The wife is still considerably more prone to depression than the husband, but this is the least depressing for both sexes and the gap between them is the smallest.

This study suggests that role strain is extremely important in determining whether a mother or a father feels depressed and the size of the depression difference between the sexes. Many other studies have shown that, on the whole, employed wives are less depressed than unemployed ones, but the significance of this difference is not simply a matter of 'women like working and find home-making depressing'. The more tension there is about the woman's employment – from the woman as well as the man – the worse it is, and many further studies point to the importance of both partners' attitude to the principle of a mother working and of how much the husband helps out with childcare and housework if she does work.

Another important source of strain in English-speaking working mothers is the knowledge, however subliminal, that having unrelated people caring for their baby may not be good for it. The mother, who identifies with how the baby feels, is worried, but the career woman in her is saying, 'Come on, you need to get back to work.' Newspaper articles in English-speaking nations regularly report one-off studies suggesting that being a working mother is good or bad for babies. Depending on the parenting choices readers have made, these reports evoke twinges of guilt or triumph. Governments are very happy to spend millions emphatically denouncing the evils of smoking and drinking or promoting the importance of exercise and the immunisation of babies. But none have grasped the day-care nettle and made a systematic attempt to inform their population of nuances which emerge when you see the overall picture painted by the hundreds of scientific studies of this subject.

Alas, *not a single person* I met anywhere on my travels was aware that these studies prove beyond much doubt that for young children the time between six months and three years is highly formative in establishing patterns of relationships in later life. If a woman returns to work in that period of the child's life, the least-worst substitute carer needs to be someone who knows the child well, is responsive, looks after only the one child (if it is younger than two) and is the sole carer. The evidence is piling up that group day care before the age of three is not advisable – that one-on-one nannying is best. Otherwise the child runs a significant risk of becoming insecure in relationships, or aggressive or indiscriminately friendly (not forgetting, of course, that if the mother stays at home and gets depressed because she wishes she was at work, the child is even more at risk, a point to which I shall return).

Most mothers are largely unaware of this evidence and so cannot take it into account when considering going back to work, however concerned they are for the welfare of their child. When they do return to work, they may become aware that the new substitute care is not initially pleasing to the child, even if they ignore it. In Liz's case, for example, she was very surprised when I wondered whether even the one hour for which she leaves her daughter in a kindergarten *with complete strangers* when going to the gym might not be upsetting. On further reflection, she realised that it was. 'Now you mention it, she's normally so adoring of me, but the last few times I've left her in the gym, when I've returned to pick her up there's no direct eye contact with me, she turns her head when I go to kiss her. Are you saying that's her rejection of me, saying, "Don't leave me here for an hour?"' Of course, these brief separations are unlikely to cause long-term harm, but they might be a clue to what longer ones might result in, if the substitute care is unfamiliar or unresponsive.

My reading of Liz is that she is an exceptionally level-headed person in a society that gives her exceptionally misleading messages. There is tremendous pressure in corporate Sydney for her to downgrade her mothering role and to prioritise being a Marketing Character (something she is not – she does not treat herself or others as commodities), although her parents' high aspirations for her made her vulnerable to this. Her perfectionism is also stoked up by the competitive times she lives in, and her reaction to motherhood is an extremely common one in a generation of women who have been socialised to be Bridget Jones, not a mother. Fortunately, her parents were also very loving and she has enough sense of self to carve out something for herself from what they gave her. I suspect that she is on a journey from Virus values to the intrinsic. She is trying to work out what is best for her and her baby, with great honesty, not just putting her needs first, as parents are now encouraged to do by the barrage of media messages and structural pressures, such as having to earn in order to afford housing.

Whereas Sandra is being distressed by the Virus, depressed by her excess weight, I suspect that Liz will find a way to keep it at bay, by adopting some kind of compromise in which her husband does some childcare and works part-time. Indeed, it is very possible that men taking a much greater role in childcare will be the way out of this modern pickle. At present, in most couples all or nearly all of the role strain falls on the mother. It does not occur to the man that ensuring that the needs of their baby are met is every bit as much his business as hers. There is an urgent need for a redistribution of roles so that fathers feel the strain as much as mothers (in accord with Will Self's amusing short story 'The Quantity Theory of Insanity', in which the overall level of emotional problems within a population is always constant, so that if one group feel better, then another must feel worse). It may take some time for either men or governments (mostly one and the same in English-speaking societies) to recognise the huge importance of creating more flexible working, but eventually it is earnestly to be hoped that the husbands of Sandra and Liz will come to feel that who cares for their children is just as much an issue for them, including considering giving up full-time work while the child is small.

Unfortunately, not all of us had as good a childhood as Liz. Mothers who did not, and who find themselves in damaging, Affluenza-ridden environments, run a very high risk of making a horrible mess of their own, their children's and their partner's lives. The Virus is particularly poisonous for such mothers, and I met many examples on my travels. None illustrated the point so vividly as Debs, aged forty-one, a New Zealander whom I interviewed in Auckland.

Almost as soon as she had sat down, Debs flooded me with a torrent of words. She spoke with such rapidity that I could barely follow the thread. It was as if she was vomiting chunks of undigested emotions and thoughts over me, much of it toxic to her. 'I-grew-up-north-of-here, my-mother-was-having-a-raging-affair-although-none-of-us-knew-about-it-at-the-time, so-we- moved-down-to-Auckland. I-was-sixteen, very-upset-to-be-separated-from-my-friends-and-I-thought, "I-can-go-one-way-or-the-other," so-I-decided-to-do-well-and-became-this-immense-over-achiever, like-I-got-the-highest-scores-in-English-in-the-whole-of-New-Zealand.'

Continuing to speak at this velocity, she described an itinerant student career, with a changing of universities and cities halfway through her course, only to return to the first one after a term. After graduation her travels became international, and she ended up staying with relatives in Canada, from where her parents had emigrated when she was five.

Working in a pub there, she met Don, with whom she had an unplanned son, much to the horror of her parents. After the child was born they moved to Seattle. 'We wanted a bigger house – am-I-talking-too-fast? – and I took a year out to look after the baby, but I'm not the housewife type.' Over the last two years in Seattle she has built up a successful career as a care worker, and Don has been caring for their son, now aged three.

So far so good, you may think, yet the life she leads is not what she wants. 'My situation now is crap. We live in a bloody shack on the edge of the city, for Christ's sake. I've been very unhappy since January [it was now March], dissatisfied by our relationship for ages. This idea that "love is for ever" is bollocks. It's obvious we haven't got anything in common apart from my son and horses – he's a fantastic horseman, I've got three horses and that's all we do. So I've come over here for time out. I've been here for four days, and I'm thinking, "I want to leave him and come and live here, because the lifestyle is a lot healthier and easier, get a well-paid job." I've struggled for too long and I don't want to struggle any more. I left snowy Seattle and arrived here and thought, "Oh my God: the sun!" [She seemed to have forgotten that she had left Seattle in one season and arrived in New Zealand in another – she repeatedly conflated attributes of geographical place with the social and psychological.] The customs officers were so friendly: "Welcome home." People talk to you in the shops. [Only twenty minutes later she said, 'The people in Seattle are the friendliest I've met ever' – she frequently contradicted herself without noticing.] It's much more leisure-based here, I've been out every night whereas at home I've been out once in three years [quite forgetting that life without a child tends to lead to more nights out].'

A major obstruction to this latest in a long line of geographical moves by Debs is the legal rights of her son's father. 'The problem is that Don would be a bastard and fight it all the way. He's quite paranoid, so I'm going to have to literally pack up the bag, take the son and go when Don's not there, maybe to a refuge [given that she is planning to abduct their son, calling Don paranoid does not seem justifiable, at least in this particular]. It's not a case of being able to sit Don down and talk it through. I would be physically threatened. Well, okay, he's not violent, but he is menacing. Looking at it now, speaking to my friends, alcoholism is a huge issue, not gin on the Cornflakes, but occasionally he does go down the pub and there can be aggressive behaviour when he gets home. But I can't just get on a plane because I don't want it to be unresolved when I leave, I want to tie up the ends – he might come over here and chase me. Because we're unmarried I have sole responsibility for the child. He could argue that he has rights because he's looked after the child while I've been work-ing for the last two years. But I'm the mother, which goes in my favour, and his age and health are against him: heavy smoker, epileptic, heavy drinker. What am I going to do, stay in a bloody shack in Seattle with no parental support? Why would I work in bloody miserable Seattle when over here I could have a great life, maybe make some decent money?'

The words 'geographic fallacy' flashed into my mind – something rather like the pathetic fallacy, where a novelist employs descriptions of the weather as a method for convey-ing a character's feelings. If something sad has just happened, the author might make it rain and have the sad character notice the (tear)drops making tracks down a window. (Pop lyrics are also packed with the gag. When I was a child our parents went away for a weekend, and one of my sisters used to burst into tears every time she heard the words in a pop song, 'Listen to the rhythm of the falling rain, telling me just what a fool I've been.') Psychoanalysts would classify real-life pathetic fallacising as projection, the attribution of unwanted emotion to the weather. In much the same way, there is such a thing as the geographic fallacy, just as there is a geographic phallacy, in which people are liable to go berserk and have sex a lot with strangers when on holiday, as several studies – not to mention lurid TV documentaries – have shown. There is a powerful urge to believe that if you travel to a different location, you will feel different, but this is the fallacy – confusing attributes of the place with internal ones. It seemed clear that Debs has done this, from the time of her university travels and her flitting about in Seattle, to her present idealisation of New Zealand as the answer to all her problems and trashing of Seattle. She projected it as 'Shit. The weather is shit. It's tax, tax, tax if you work. The people are so unfriendly.' She transferred all the things she feels about herself onto Seattle: that it is shit (she feels she is), its weather is too (her negative inner climate, mood), it's highly taxed (she feels ripped off by life) and it's unfriendly (she feels antagonistic).

She was also projecting her problems onto her material circumstances, seeing her 'shack' as inadequate and complaining of lack of money, wanting highly paid work, showing signs of the Virus. She was deeply envious of her younger sister, who is living with a wealthy older man. 'I went to their house and he was like, "Here's a brand new Porsche you can borrow if you like," and coming from Seattle it was just, "Oh my God!'" However, she psychologised away her envy of this opulence by characterising her sister as emotionally disturbed and the man as having made his money from arms dealing. She seemed to be a classic example of someone who had pursued a career with intrinsic goals (a care worker) but with Virus motives. Now she wants to change the goals to Virus, money-making ones as well. The praise she received for doing Good Works was no longer sufficient to satisfy her motives. She had risen as high as she could in her chosen career, so for the time being there would be no immediate increase in power and status – praise or rewards – from that source.

I asked about her relationship with her parents, who divorced when Debs was in her teens following her father's affairs. 'I remember a lot of crèches. My mother's high-flying, big time, a career woman since she had us. But then I look at what she had to give to get there – and it was us.' Children with materialist parents are more likely to be materialists themselves. Such parents are also more likely to be cold and over-controlling, as her mother was (when she was around) and to divorce. All these things make children vulnerable to Affluenza. An insight into why Debs is not the housewife type came from a heartrending account of her son's birth. 'When that child was born I didn't even know how to pick him up – the midwife had to teach me. We young women are just not prepared for it at all. After the drama of the birth, everyone just buggered off, it was just me and a cleaner cleaning the blood off the walls. It was "Shit, what do I do now?" The cleaner ran me my bath and I forgot to take the baby with me at first. I know I said I've never been very close to her but I needed my mother, I wanted my mother. It was the loneliest I've ever felt in my life. I needed to be washed and loved but I just got on with it and I was fine. But I'd never get in a mess like that ever again – just gone through twelve hours of hell and no-one was there.'

I asked how her mother's preoccupation with work left her feeling when she was small, and whether that might not still be affecting her today. 'I do see some repetitive patterns. I work and work and work, and I look at my son and think, "Shit, that's what my mother did, I'm doing this to him." I just think childhood is the blueprint for everything in your life.' This last statement must have come from a purely intellectual understanding, for she showed few signs of having put it into practice.

Hoping to help her, I said, 'You talk very fast and have a good brain, moving through ideas so quickly that it enables you not to feel the emotions that go with what you are telling me. If you think about it too, not only do you rush from place to place when speaking, you have done so literally, in your life, geographically moving around New Zealand and then to Seattle and now back to New Zealand. You have been ducking and diving geographically, which is also what you do with your mind to keep emotions at bay. What you have to understand is that if you go on like that nothing will change inside you. You say that "This idea that 'love is for ever' is bollocks. In modern life we no longer should expect to only have one partner," but in another part of you, you know that isn't true for everyone, and if you make the connection to how your son is about to feel when he is suddenly permanently separated from his father, the person who has been primarily looking after him for the last two years, you may see what I mean. Hopefully your geographically peripatetic life will cease to be so, perhaps you will find a man you can stay with and perhaps your mind will become more settled as well.'

After a pause for thought, Debs replied, 'I am quite good at manipulating my thoughts, I hadn't thought of it like that. I don't normally suffer from depression but in January suddenly something went [clicks fingers] and I was suicidal. I was really, really low, which isn't like me. I thought, "My God, I've got to do something." What would happen if I stopped ducking and diving – a breakdown? I don't know.' I asked her what that would entail. 'I'm a "just get on with it" sort of person, quite practical. To break down for me would be to lose control. I hate the feeling of being powerless.' I said, 'When you were desperate and powerless as a toddler perhaps you "just got on with it" by playing with your toys or went to another room or into the garden – the start of your geographical manoeuvring – that's how psychological defences are built up.' 'Well,' she said, 'my parents were moving around a lot in childhood. Being upsticked as a five-year-old and taken halfway around the planet from Canada must have affected me.'

I wanted her to think about how her son might feel when she brings him here, about both the move and the loss of his father. 'Go back to before he didn't have words to describe it,' I prompted, 'think of what your son was like then.' Debs said, 'Actually, he's panicking [about] where I am because he thought I was going to work when I went out of the door, setting off for here, so he expected me to come back that evening. Now he's telling his father off, asking him where I am. It's worst in the mornings and night apparently, and he's telling Don off because daddy hasn't picked up mummy from work. So he knows I'm not there. Don says, "Do you want to speak to mummy?" when I phone up, and he just bursts into tears because he doesn't know where I am.' I wondered if he could be angry and rejecting her by refusing to talk. 'Yeah, that's true, he might be saying, "Fuck off, I'm not going to talk to you." I put him in kindergarten when he was one to give him a break and some interaction with other children. [These were not the true reasons: she had already told me it was because she was 'not the housewife type' and needed the daily 'buzz' of a workplace.] Before I picked him up from the crèche I used to watch him through the window, and he'd be fine watching the *Tweenies* or reading a story. But when he saw me he'd become absolutely screaming, throwing a tantrum and kicking and howling on the floor. Then he'd go "Grrrrr!" at me and be very naughty, a pain, piss around, wouldn't put his jacket on. He wasn't at all pleased to see me, not at all. I suppose that was, "Where the hell have you been for the last six hours, stupid bitch?" – happy as Larry until I was there, giving me the guilt trip for not being with him.' Calling it a manipulative guilt trip seemed her way of distancing herself from his true intention – to express rage at being separated from her too young and left with strangers (she told me that the carers kept changing).

Fortunately for her son, his father had soon taken over the care and they had given up the crèche. I asked again how her son was going to feel about being separated from Don, the person who has mainly cared for him over the last two years. 'That's going to be a huge problem. They're that close [she puts her fingers together]. He's going to lose a lot.' For a fraction of a moment she glimpsed his distress, but then, with equal rapidity, she rationalised it away. 'What do I do? International relationships! I would never go there again. None of it's an ideal situation but I've just got to do what I think is best for my son and for me, really.' It is strange how sophisticated is our capacity to directly contradict ourselves without noticing – it was abundantly clear that she is making the move from Seattle to avoid depression, not because it will be best for her son. It will be better for him if she is not depressed, but I fear that moving to New Zealand will not solve her problems in the long term, and anyway, there is certainly a case for saying that he will be better off staying with his father, who is clearly more of a housewife type than she is, binge-drinking, epileptic smoker though he may be.

When I raised the possibility that Debs might benefit from some therapy, it was clear that she was not really in a state to consider it. She had once been to a 'work counsellor' but managed to get little from him, reversing the roles. 'I quite enjoyed it, we were there for four hours and I ended up counselling him. I asked, "Are you a Pisces?" and he was, "How do you know?" and I said, "I'd hate it if you psycho-analysed me because you'd be in control." I don't like that.' Interestingly, however, she was able to engage with her son's problems. After our meeting I identified a child therapist who might be able to help and, who knows, perhaps by recognising that her son has a problem (a pathological fallacy?), she might be able to gain some insight into how her own sense of rejection by her mother is affecting her and him.

I found Debs' story disheartening. It is very unlikely that moving to the other side of the world is going to be much help in treating her considerable emotional problems, nor is leaving Don likely to do so. Not surprisingly, a recent study of 8,000 British mothers with a small child and a partner found that, when interviewed a year later, mothers who had split up were more likely to be depressed than those who were still with their partner. You might have thought that if a relationship was really shitty, then once out of it the mothers would have been happier. On the contrary, the study showed that however disharmonious and vile it was – up to and including wife-beating – the mothers felt no better on escaping. Indeed, being depressed can cause break-ups because if the mother was depressed during the relationship, separation was more likely: the depressed people were more prone to break-ups. This has been shown in many other studies.

Although some mothers become depressed because of incompatibility with their partner, there is no doubt that others, like Debs, will be unhappy whomever they are with. The Virus can be an important reason. The infected are more likely to have personality disorders, and such people do not fare well in relationships. In a sample of students, the Virus-infecteds' relationships were found to be shorter-lasting and more negative. In another sample, during the previous six months with their partner, the Virus-infected were more likely to have argued with, insulted and sworn at them, including pushing, grabbing, shoving and physically hurting. Blaming the collapse of the family and the fragmenting of communities on the decline of religion and louche morals is a favourite habit of the political Right. Virus values, driven by Selfish Capitalism, seem far more significant. It makes people like Debs much more likely to go in self- and other-damaging directions.

Here was a woman who had suffered considerable maltreatment as a baby and toddler, and was subsequently very upset by the divorce of her parents. Unable to cope with these feelings, Debs has availed herself of the modern opportunities to literally fly away from them (it is only in the last fifteen years that air travel has become affordable for most people in New Zealand). She is filled with the expectations of women of her generation for plentiful sex (she was horrified when I told her that in the average British relationship, after three years, sex happens two to three times a month) and for understanding from male partners; if these are not provided, she has the sense that it is right and normal for her to move on because 'love is not for ever'. With barely a glance over her shoulder, she is able to represent this self-interest as being in the interest of her son, even though she spoke extensively of the distress she felt when her parents divorced and is aware that her son is deeply attached to the man who is effectively his mother. Like many young English-speaking people of her generation, she is skilled in the art of Woody Allen-style psychologising, of using psychobabble to relocate her problems in her partner or her child. Finally, as the studies predict, she is increasingly inclined to pursue Virus goals to bolster her fragile self-esteem, just as her mother seems to have done, moving away from an intrinsic occupation which serves an important social purpose and towards one which will bring the money, status and power that she is so scared of lacking – again, just like her mother.

Of course, it must not be forgotten that female emancipation has led to very positive developments for Debs' generation, compared with their grandmothers'. They are properly educated and free to do everything that men are. But it is hard to believe that their freedom to repeat the same mistakes, over and over, is what Emily Pankhurst had in mind when she broke the chains to her kitchen sink and attached them to the railings of Westminster.

I saw the Virus having the same impact, to a greater or lesser degree, on mothers in all the English-speaking nations I visited. They felt obliged to return to work in order to pay the mortgage on a home that cannot be otherwise afforded; they experienced nagging anxieties about appearance following pregnancy and birth; they had the sense that only paid work is 'for me', whereas solely occupying the role of mother leaves 'me' powerless and worthless; and there was a tendency for insecure, disturbed mothers like Debs to cut and run if they hit a bad patch in their relationship, convinced that they deserved 'better' and 'more', be that money, love or attention. Interestingly, the same was not true in China, Russia and Denmark, although for different reasons in each case. In China, with its continued collectivism, role strain is only just beginning to rear its head. Grandmothers still take on the mothering role with gusto. Only a tiny minority of the very wealthiest, like Soo (the mother of the student at the Early MBA, described in the last chapter), hire a nanny or send their baby to a kindergarten. If the Chinese Government increases the extent to which the country is Selfish Capitalist, for example by privatising more of the economy (at present, two-thirds of Shanghainese are still employed by the State) and introducing more financial liberalisation, this is likely to change, and rapidly.

Although not a major worry at present, role strain will be a problem for future Russian mothers. The tradition there has always been that babies are the exclusive concern of mothers. This preceded Communism but was reinforced by it, with edicts dictating that women must hold themselves personally responsible should their child turn out a bad lot. One of the most revered Soviet authorities wrote that 'If you wish to give birth to a citizen and do so without parental love, then be so kind as to warn society you wish to play such an underhand trick. People brought up without parental love are often deformed people ...' Since horrifyingly large numbers of the menfolk were killed during the last century by wars, disease and totalitarian mass murder, it has long been accepted that men will play very little part; on top of that, divorce rates have been at a very high level for decades. In the post-Communist era women have been left holding the babies even more. Alongside the tradition of fathers being absent, whether through death, divorce or alcoholism, women are now also expected to work. So far this has not created strain because they still tend to have babies before the age of twenty-five (women older than this are categorised by maternity units as 'elderly') and do not yet define their worth through paid work. If and when that starts happening, the strains will begin to appear.

But by far the most interesting nation of those I surveyed was Denmark. If anything, its mothers derive their identity from paid work even more powerfully than those in English-speaking nations, and yet they suffer less role strain. Whereas in most developed nations there are usually two women for every depressed man, amongst Danes, some studies have found that more are male (13 per cent, versus 10 per cent female) and the only nationally representative study found no significant differences for severe depression. The same is true in other Scandinavian nations, like Finland and Norway. The most likely reason is that a good deal of the burden of domestic work and childcare is shared with male partners; and also, after eighteen months of age, three-quarters of Danish toddlers are cared for full-time in State nurseries. Indubitably, greater involvement of men in the home is a major vaccine against role strain and the Virus, as is a guilt-free handing-over of eighteen-month-olds for State care. However, for reasons I shall explain in some detail, day care for toddlers is not a vaccine, whereas a new role for men most certainly is.

The extent of the Danish male contribution to domestic life was itemised for me by Tøger Seidenfaden, the newspaper editor, using himself as illustration. He has been married for fifteen years, with three children and a wife who works full-time as a journalist on another paper. 'Nobody has cleaners in Denmark. Well, I say that, we do have a woman who comes in to clean once a week. But that's it, and it's unusual. We do everything else, the shopping, cooking, washing, the garden.' For some tasks they have fixed arrangements. 'I cook and shop for the food on Tuesdays and Wednesdays, my wife does it on Mondays and Thursdays and we do it collectively at weekends. I do the sandwiches for the children every morning, which is a real pain – we don't have school meals here so you have to make a special classic food package each day for them. I do a big shop for the basics on Saturday mornings.

Having said that, I suppose overall my wife still probably does 65 per cent of the domestic stuff and might like it if I did 10 per cent more [on average, Danish women do twice as much of the domestic work as the men]. She expends more energy on the basic upkeep and takes a much larger role in the logistics – getting the boy to his football, planning it, and so on. I play some part, but she's the manager and sometimes uses me as unpaid labour.' I have to rub my eyes and ears to believe what I am hearing. Anyone who knows how top British executives live would be doing the same.

Alongside this much greater male role in the home there is an almost totalitarian insistence that women work. A full-time mother in Denmark would have an even lower status, if that is imaginable, than one in an English-speaking society. Says Seidenfaden, 'There is a very strong sense that work defines your identity here, even more than in other societies. After her child is eighteen months old, a full-time mother would be a social disaster. She would be a pariah at dinner parties. The only example I know gets her identity from the fact that she is a countess, so she feels she has an identity beyond work, dating back to childhood. No-one gives her respect for being an aristocrat, but that gives her a sense that she does not have to prove herself. People think she's strange but she has enough confidence. It's a big weakness of the system that most people would not have enough security to do that. There is tremendously powerful agreement here about what is socially valued which is imposed on nearly everyone.' Three-quarters of Danish mothers of over-eighteen-month-olds work full-time and 95 per cent of those work more than twenty-five hours a week.

Underpinning the working mother's lack of role strain is a widespread refusal to even countenance the idea that eighteen months is too early for a toddler to be placed in group care. Unlike her sisters in English-speaking nations, the Danish mother reads virtually nothing in the national press about studies suggesting that it is not a good idea. The day-care tradition is very longstanding; in fact, until a few years ago, most infants were sent to nurseries full-time at six months of age. What is more, most mothers today witnessed their own mother doing the same: there was no 'Do as I say, not as I do.' In Denmark, not caring for your eighteen-month-old is just the way it is, what everyone does, just as handing your baby over to its grandmother is the done thing in China.

Like so many Danish practices, compelling men to do their bit in the home is admirably civilised, promoting well-being and helping to solve the problem of role strain. However, the powerful Danish work ethic seems less so, insofar as it parts parents from their toddlers and encourages the belief that only paid activities should be a source of status – even the current leader of the Tory party believes that there is a great deal more than work to having a fulfilling life. When I spent a week observing some toddlers in what is probably the best kindergarten in the world, I encountered both a worrying ignorance of the damage it may do and a good deal of self-deception about its true purpose.

I am put in touch with Jasper, the head of the kindergarten, who is helpfulness incarnate, innocent and open (but not naive). Proudly, he reveals that British MPs from all the political parties have visited his Copenhagen institution to learn about the system. Indeed, I have been told by a Danish academic that it is regarded as a model, nationally and internationally. If kindergarten care can work well, this is the place where it will. Unlike the Swedish kindergartens, Jasper explains, the Danish ones are relatively unstructured, with no attempt to teach cognitive skills. Apart from eating and a lunchtime nap, free play is the only activity. There is a strong emphasis on the emotional and social rather than the academic. In his institution, there is no division between the age groups under three, so that eighteen-month-olds are as likely to be in the group as children a year older. We agree that I'll spend five days observing a group. I shall have full access, able to interview the parents, observe the children in their homes and also quiz the pedagogues (as nursery teachers are known in Denmark).

From the moment that new parents and their child arrive, there is a specific pedagogue who is their contact. For the first week the mother or father is at the kindergarten all the time and the child only comes for a few hours. After a week or so, says Jasper, 'the child is ready to spend time on its own and start a new life together with us, waving goodbye to the mother every morning like the other children. It will have the pedagogue holding it when waving goodbye.' Crucial to a smooth progression, he believes, is the message the parent gives the child. 'A big part of our job is to make the parents feel good about it. The child will always be observing the mother to see if she likes the contact person, taking her lead as to whether they like her. We explain to the parents that it's important that you give your child easily to us, that if you can't let go of the child then it will take it much longer to adjust.' True, parental distress at the moment of leaving would evoke

anxiety in the child. But Jasper showed no sign that he understood what would really be bugging a toddler in that situation:
being separated from the main person who understands its
needs and upon whom it had relied until now for feeling safe.
Nor did he seem very sympathetic to the distress a parent
might feel about leaving their toddler with relative strangers.

I asked how the new toddlers react when the parent
leaves. 'They are always crying a little bit when the mother
says goodbye,' he said, 'but before she has even got out of the
outside door they are not crying. We tell the parent to call us
when they reach work and we will tell them how it is now,
and she can hear that it's quiet and comfortable, that their
child is starting to play with the others.' Pressed on this,
Jasper admitted that it was not always plain sailing. 'It can
take a very long time. Some will cry for a month or more
when the mother leaves.' His explanation suggested to me a
complete ignorance of the scientific evidence. 'Sometimes it is
just a game they are playing with their mother. Perhaps the
child thinks that its mother will be happy if it cries because
"That proves that I love her."' This 'cunning little blighters'
talk does not square with the evidence, confusing manipulative sophistication with emotional desperation. Calling it a
game seemed badly out of touch with what is really happening in these situations.

I asked Jasper if he was aware of attachment theory or
had heard of John Bowlby, its creator. He had not. Bowlby
was an English doctor and psychoanalyst who developed the
theory during the 1960s and 1970s. According to him, our
species evolved an instinct to form intense and specific attachments from around six months of age because it would have

been useful early in our evolution. There were many predators, and, just as it benefits monkeys living in the wild today, it would have paid to do your level best to stay close to mother once you were capable of crawling. If separated, you would let her know where you were through attachment behaviours such as crying out and seeking to physically connect with her by clinging.

Whether or not it is true that attachment is explained by our evolutionary past, it does seem clear that there is an instinct in toddlers to become attached. But that does not explain why about 40 per cent of children are insecure, rising to 50 per cent of adults. According to Bowlby, the difference between secure and insecure is determined by the kind of care you received between the ages of six months and three years, and over three thousand published empirical studies have broadly shown him to be correct. Emotional unresponsiveness or the physical absence of the carer at this age, or the combination of the two, create a state of fear that the carer will be emotionally unavailable. This anxiety endures into adulthood and is triggered by subsequent intimate attachments. Not having attachment needs met early in life leaves a person permanently jammed in attach mode, unable to relax and be confident that everything will be all right. Insecure adults fear being abandoned or rejected by intimates because that is what happened in early childhood. Having grown to expect intimates to behave in a certain way, they assume it will always be like this, and it becomes their internal working model of relationships.

The available evidence on the effects of non-maternal, substitute care before age three is highly controversial. The most reliable review concluded that 41 per cent of babies or toddlers (under three years old) cared for by someone other than their mother (or father) for more than twenty hours a week are insecure, whereas this is true of 26 per cent of children cared for exclusively by mothers. Further evidence has consistently revealed higher levels of aggression and hyperactivity in day-cared children, still evident at age seven. There are also studies suggesting that day-cared children are more likely to show 'indiscriminate friendliness', a lack of specificity in relating, which may impede later intimacy. In a recent British study of a large sample of children, Penelope Leach found that adverse outcomes at age five are commonest in the day-cared, then in children left with grandparents, then those left with minders, and rarest in those cared for exclusively by a parent. However, there are some very big buts about all this.

First and foremost, as a definitive review shows, if 41 per cent of toddlers with substitute care are insecure, that still leaves 59 per cent who are secure, which might go to show that it can work fine for the majority (although there could be all sorts of as yet unmeasured adverse outcomes). It is also apparent from a very rigorous American study of 1,000 children who have been monitored from birth that many factors are involved, not least the quality of the relationship of the child with its parents before and after entering day care. Finally, it cannot be stressed often enough that staying at home and caring for a child full-time directly causes depression in a significant proportion of mothers living in the role-strained, fractured mess of English-speaking societies. If that happens, the outcomes are considerably worse – half of children with such mothers will be insecure, putting them at greater risk of depression and aggression in later life.

Taken as a whole, this large edifice of evidence does have considerable implications for anyone who is providing day care, and it is remarkable that someone as senior and well-educated as Jasper has never even heard of what is easily the most influential corpus of developmental theory of the last fifty years. The research validating it is not only from English-speaking nations, it comes from Germany, Holland and Israel as well. It seems a bizarre omission from his training, but there is no doubting that attachment theory is Greek to Jasper, as his next comment revealed. Asked if it mattered what age the child comes to kindergarten, instead of what I expected (the later the better), he believed just the opposite. 'Of course, the older they are, the harder it is to get them to settle in. If they have been for a long time with the mother they feel safer with her.'

A common justification for day care is the idea that toddlers need other children to play with, even though it does not accord with the evidence. After initially offering this reason, Jasper admitted that under-threes do not really play together. Whereas they may appear to be playing, he admitted, if you looked more carefully you would see that they are simply sitting next to one another, not taking turns or joining together in a game. 'They may be talking but they are not really playing together. For most children it's not until about three that this happens properly.' Jasper's claim for the benefits of early day care was that 'it enables them to learn in a small way that other children have different personalities from them, that this child plays with sand in this way, that one does it in another, small things that lead them to realise that people are different. It's getting to know that if "I want to be in this group, I have to learn about the other children, that I have to wait until it's my turn." The earlier they take these small steps, the better.' This answer seemed to go to the heart of the matter. 'We play a very, very important part in socialising our citizens. We have a big responsibility for creating ones that help and support each other.'

He stressed that graduates of his kindergarten do not have the 'me, me, me' pushiness so common in America. 'They mirror the care they get. If I was to shout and scream at them or to be always only interested in myself, they would be like that. They look up to us. If we are not aggressive and talk quietly and calmly, they will be the same.' What about children who continue to be aggressive? 'We look behind it, ask what is happening. We talk amongst ourselves and with the parents to understand it: is there something wrong with us? Something with the family? We see aggression as a sign, "Help me, help me, I need some help," a way of standing out from the group to tell us something is wrong. Just saying, "Go and sit down and be quiet" would be quite wrong.'

My final issue was the motives of parents for leaving their children here before the age of three. 'The mothers will say they need to get out of the home to do something else as their first reason for sending the child to kindergarten,' Jasper said, 'but if you look deeper and give them a chance to reflect, you will see they also feel it's best for the child.' Pressed on this, he seemed unable to think of any real benefits for the children, only the society's need to create cooperation. Eventually he said, 'If you put a fast question you get a fast answer' –

perhaps implying that I was a bit of an aggressive English-speaking sexist trying to stigmatise working mothers.

In the event, there was a considerable gap between his account and what I observed over the next five days. The group to which I had been assigned consisted of six children nearing the age of three, and five others aged between nineteen and twenty-five months. All of the younger group had started kindergarten between three and twelve weeks earlier. I decided to concentrate on three of the children, paying particular attention to the times when their parents departed and reappeared. Studies testing Bowlby's theory have focused on these moments because they are the clearest indicators of the child's security in its relationship with its parents, and of the responsiveness and familiarity of the substitute carers.

The group leader was Martha, pregnant and in her thirties. The other pedagogue was Sara, who had joined the kindergarten only a week before (presumably that would have been quite distressing to the children for whom her predecessor was the main contact person). Nina was the helper, and a variety of students came and went in just the five days I was there. I concentrated my observations on Mike, Olga and Sylvia, visiting each of their homes as well.

Mike, aged eighteen months

The youngest in the group, Mike had been attending for three weeks. On the first day he howled for an hour if the pedagogue stopped holding him in her arms, a permanent frown on his face, very apprehensive, blank and empty. Gradually, he became more relaxed. By the second hour he was going down a slide and shovelling sand. He never once smiled, but his instinct to explore was operating and he had come out of his shell. The other children seemed of little interest to him, except when he found them menacing, which happened on several occasions. He cried when awoken from his lunchtime sleep but was quickly soothed by a pedagogue, sitting on her lap for a few minutes and then setting off to explore again. When his father arrived to take him home, Mike showed no excitement. Picked up, he was listless and made no eye contact. After only twenty seconds he wriggled until put down, wandering off, ignoring his father – pointedly, it seemed to me.

Each morning during the week there was a period of crying when Mike's father left, coupled with an expression-less, frozen face, mouth slightly open. When collected by his father he was unresponsive and floppy if picked up, uncom-municative and avoiding eye contact, and would soon want to wander away from him. However, in accord with Jasper's dicta, over the five days and with the end of his fourth week approaching, he protested for ever-shorter periods after being left. By the last morning, although he continued to howl whilst he could still see his father departing, within forty-five seconds he had ceased, and ten minutes later he was explor-ing the room. It was easy to believe that after a few more days he would no longer cry on being separated. He also seemed a bit more friendly to his father on being reunited with him on that last day, although still giving him a pretty cool reception.

An interesting question is what is happening in the child's mind as these changes occur. With some justification, Jasper would say that Mike is becom- ing accustomed to the arrange-ment, that it is a question of learning to feel safe. But that may not be all. He may also be learning that no-one can be relied upon and to suppress his emotions. Although not visibly distressed for most of the day, he wanders about in a rather aimless fashion and does not seem to be truly vitalised, really excited, by anything. It is as if he is simply surviving rather than enjoying himself. There were very few occasions on any of the days when I saw him actually interact with another human. The other children were largely in their own worlds, and the pedagogues simply did not have time to play games with Mike. On a rare occasion when one did, she kissed him, rocked him in her arms and held him out in front of her on her lap. He looked uninterested and turned his head away as she raised his arms and tried to engage his attention. She smiled and jiggled him, but there was no participation from him and she was soon distracted by another child's needs.

This lack of connection struck me most forcibly when I visited Mike at his home to interview his parents. He was a different boy. Whereas I was unable to get him to laugh when doing peek-a-boo at kindergarten, at his home he did so uproariously. Hiding behind his mother's legs, he would pop his head round, then pull it back, guffawing at the game. At other times, he ran about exuberantly (he never does so at the kindergarten), singing to himself, pointing out things of interest to his mother to share them. He was full of fun, and his facial expressions were much richer.

Mike's parents' perception of kindergarten and its importance was that "It's been pretty easy for him. He's still crying every morning when we go but he's pretty used to it now. The playground and the hallway are now familiar, and he knows most of the children around him. It's not hard for him at all.'

They were oblivious to the fact that he had still been crying after they left, believing it ended as soon as they were gone.

His mother started by saying that they sent him to kindergarten because 'it's good for him to have to relate to other kids, meeting others, respecting them, not just spoiled at home deciding everything'. However, this was flatly contradicted when we discussed whether children can relate to other children at eighteen months. 'They play alongside rather than with each other at this age, a lot by themselves. At eighteen months they pick something up, get bored and throw it down. It's not until two that it begins to be with others at all.' In which case, why does she not wait until he is at least two? 'It's because I have to, and want to, work. Anyway, he's very fine.' She had been raised on a farm and not gone to any sort of institution until she was five. She felt this had been good for her but that life in Denmark has moved on. 'Both the husband and the wife want to work, they don't want to stay at home all the time, they need some inputs, yeah. If someone wants to stay at home that's fine. I don't criticise them, it's good, positive, but it wouldn't suit me, my situation. I want to go out.' She could see only one problem with him going to kindergarten. 'Before he went there his life was less regimented, he slept and ate when it suited him. Now it has to be more according to what happens at the kindergarten, and that makes it a long day when they are so small. I think it would be quite wrong to send them before eighteen months.'

On the basis of this shallow dip of my toe in the water of Mike's life, it would be irresponsible of me to suggest that as an adult he will suffer distress as a result of attending kindergarten. There was no doubt that he was adapting to the arrangement, even over the short period in which I was observing him, and at home he still seemed full of beans, which suggested no lasting damage. However, whilst he may be crying less because he becomes habituated to his father leaving each day, he may also be learning to live without intimacy and on a flat emotional plain.

When I described all this to a friend who looks after her two-year-old son full-time, she made an interesting point. Because her son has spent most of his waking hours in her company, she understands and responds to all but the most obscure things he says. For instance, he recently demanded a blue-wrapped muesli bar, but when he opened it he asked, 'Where's the fruity?' She had recently given him some fruit sweets also in a blue-coated wrapper and he had concluded, reasonably enough, that all blue sweety products are fruity ones. Only my friend would have realised what her son was on about and been able to explain that not all blue-wrapped purchases contain the same contents, and indeed that one should not use colour as the sole criterion for inferring what lies within. Although it is definitely an advantage to learn not to make mistakes of this logical type, the benefits of being so well understood are not only intellectual. The feeling of being understood is closely allied to feeling loved. By contrast, from now on, for 37 hours a week, Mike will be surrounded by adults who are too busy, and do not know him well enough, to comprehend him in this individual manner. Will that not diminish his capacity for intimacy?

During the interview with Mike's parents, his father had been positive about kindergarten, but that had not been the case on my second day there, when he arrived to find Mike's face bloodied by another eighteen-month-old, Olga. After the lunchtime nap she had followed him along the passage out of the bathroom, knocked him down from behind and scratched or bitten his cheek (I could not tell which from where I was standing). Although Mike had howled for a short time afterwards, he did not seem particularly put out by the incident (not nearly as upset as by his father leaving him) but there was quite a kerfuffle. 'I don't know why, but she keeps biting and scratching everyone,' said one of the pedagogues. 'It may be that she's been the little one before starting here so she wants the attention. She does it with other children, especially if they are on our lap. It's just a shame it happens so often to Mike. I think they are going to talk to the parents.' When Mike's father arrived he waved his arms around a lot and made his feelings known (in Danish) to the pedagogue. Then he had a good moan to me. 'It's happened three times now. Jasper's tried to explain but I don't understand. I feel that my kid is lonely because I am not here. Why has this happened three times with nobody taking care? The problem is that the grown-ups are supposed to be here to work, not to talk with their colleagues but to take care of the kids. I accept that they work hard and they can't be all the time with one kid. But I feel my kid is lonely and no-one cares.' Nervously, he added, 'Of course, I do not blame.' I asked the group's pedagogue leader about it. 'We always talk to the parents,' she said, 'tell them what happened and that we are aware of the problem. Sometimes they do it because they want attention from adults, the hugs and protection that the other child is getting.' By the time I interviewed Mike's parents at home, a good deal of talking to them had taken place and his father was pacified

– or, depending on how you view it, brainwashed into ignoring his instinct that his son was suffering.

Olga, aged nineteen months

Mike's assailant, Olga, started at kindergarten in June, with a break for holiday in the month of July, making seven weeks in all so far. She did not cry when her parents dropped her off in the mornings. However, when they came to pick her up she never seemed pleased to see them, largely ignoring their friendly gestures, carrying on as if they were not there, not especially eager to leave and avoiding eye contact. I witnessed three other aggressive acts by her, apart from the scratching of Mike, two of them involving him. She seemed to get less time on the laps of the pedagogues than the other youngsters did. I was unable to make out whether this was a deliberate policy (perhaps to teach her that bad behaviour is not rewarded) or because there were always other children perceived as being in greater need. She seemed to find it hard to play on her own, hanging around at the edge of other children's activities and occasionally disrupting them. She made odd faces at them, seemed angry and disconnected, and unlike Mike, she was no different when she was at home.

One clue to the cause of Olga's aggressiveness was that her mother had found the first six months very difficult, perhaps suffering mild depression. Another was that her older brother definitely bullies her. But it should also be pointed out that the strongest evidence of ill-effects of kindergarten care is that, compared with children reared at home, its alumni are more likely to be aggressive. Their anger at being separated from their parents is redirected at other children. I asked if Olga had been aggressive before she started kindergarten. Her mother said, 'She didn't do it before she went. She's never been that aggressive before. It might be that she's frustrated because there are a lot of children there, a lot of noise, a lot of input – it's hard to cope with at nineteen months. I think that's the reason. When there are ten kids in one room you have to wait your turn, and she is not used to having to do that at home, so she gets confused and aggressive.'

At first she rationalised that she sends Olga to kindergarten because her daughter needs 'challenges', but eventually she said that it was because she could not get on with finishing her degree, which she is doing from home. Her husband had taken paternity leave and been the 'mother' for five months from when Olga was seven months old. Although they did not actually say so, I got the impression they had not been getting on too well with each other. They live in a very small flat and have been short of money.

The combination of her mother's possible depression, witnessing parental disharmony, and bullying from her brother would have been likely to make Olga aggressive. Going to kindergarten on top of all that may have been the last straw, but it could be argued she is better off there than at home. Full-time mothering could depress her mother even more – she struck me as still mildly depressed – in a system where she would be a pariah, which would make the relationship between the parents even worse (couples with one depressed partner are at greater risk of splitting up). The social pressure at the kindergarten not to be aggressive may be the lesser of the evils. She might grow into a rather fragile adult, but the outcome might be even worse if she were to stay at home until she was three. This is a good illustration of the dangers of the crude formulation 'mother best, everything else worse'.

Sylvia, aged twenty-one months

Jasper held up Sylvia's parents as models of how to leave a child at the kindergarten. 'They are very relaxed about it, making it much easier for us to settle her in. Their reactions tell her that "We are happy you are here, this is a good place for you," and she picks that up. The child relaxes if the parents do. The length of time it takes the child to settle depends on how supportive the parents are of the idea of kindergarten.' In fact, Sylvia did not illustrate this at all.

After eight weeks at the kindergarten she was still inconsolable on the three days a week she was there, needing to be on the lap of one of the pedagogues for much of the time to stop her crying, and even then looking glum and blank. On the first day she was unable to explore at all, immediately putting out her arms to be picked up if attempts were made to get her to sit in the sandpit or to interest her in a tricycle. The pedagogues' lack of success in comforting Sylvia rammed home how tough the job is, because they still had to cater to the other children. A dummy was put in her mouth, which made me realise an oddity about the smaller children: not one of them has a special object, like our daughter's Bear-Bear, to fall back on in times of crisis, a sign of how un-child-centred the care truly is. We do not dare go anywhere without B-B, and wake up screaming at the thought of what would happen if B-B was lost. Interestingly, cross-cultural research shows that B-Bs (known technically as 'transitional objects') are by no means found everywhere: their use depends very much on what society you are in.

Sylvia had a marked preference for the group's leader, a pregnant and very busy woman who could not hold her all day, so she had to be farmed out to less familiar figures, with whom she would often continue crying until passed back to the leader. Another strategy was to put her in her pram, with a harness to prevent her from climbing out. Perhaps its familiarity was reassuring, but it rarely worked for more than a few minutes.

Unlike the other children, none of whom showed pleasure at seeing a parent, when Sylvia's mother arrived she smiled and ran towards her, arms outstretched. But the message was not 'Hello Mum, how are you?', it was 'I'm a toddler, get me out of here!' On the second and third days she was also absolutely delighted to see her mother, letting out a little cry of excitement and running across for an embrace. She seemed like a different child altogether, pointing things out to her mother, suddenly confident and able to explore her surroundings. She played a little game of hide-and-seek with her mother, and when they left she was smiling and waved goodbye.

Sylvia's mother was tremendously enthusiastic about the experience of having looked after her child full-time. 'This has been the best one and a half years of my life, it was just so nice looking after Sylvia. I'm not very pleased to be back at work.' So why go back? 'I have to earn a bit of money. If I did not I would lose my job.' But could she not get another one? 'Well, yes, in my profession it would be easy, that's true' (she works in a health care centre as a sort of social worker). Does she really, really need the money? 'We could afford it if

I wanted to stay at home, but going back to work is just what everybody does here.'

Regarding Sylvia's well-being at kindergarten, she said, 'It was difficult at first, she was very sad. I am glad we did not start when she was younger. She's a very happy girl normally, so I did not expect it would be a problem. Sylvia is very close to me, we have spent a lot of time together, and my husband adores her. Now she has changed her contact pedagogue, who is a little bit more expressive, and I think it's going better. She's very happy to be here, but I am pleased she stayed at home for so long.'

Her pedagogue's account was intriguingly different from this. 'It's been quite difficult for Sylvia, it's been almost a month and she's still quite upset.' I pointed out that this was actually Sylvia's eighth week, and she said, 'Oh yes, that's right. She needs to spend more time with us so she can feel more secure. At the moment, if we leave the room or attend to another kid even for a short period she does not like it. She's been with her mum all the time before this, so it could be difficult because she's very attached to her.' That having a strong relationship with your mother makes you less able to cope with day care does not seem a particularly good advertisement for it. 'We thought she'd be all right after a week or so but it's now – what, her eighth? – yes, that's right.' That the contact pedagogue didn't know that one of her children had been there for eight rather than four weeks suggests that she did not know that child terribly well.

By the end of my time at the kindergarten I was unconvinced of its merits. For Olga, it would be better if she had a nanny since she is already showing signs of feeling deprived, and the last thing she needs is group care. Group care might benefit Danish society in making its citizens cooperative and compliant before they can even talk, but at what cost to their individuality and emotional security? Even in this virtually ideal setting, the best pedagogue in the world cannot be attuned very well to the unique experience of each child if they have three others to worry about (recall my friend's comment about knowing the meaning of her son's 'fruity'). Anyone who has spent even a few days caring for a toddler full-time (as I have) will tell you that really meeting their needs is extremely exacting. The prospect of trying to meet the needs of several at the same time gives me the heebie-jeebies. Since the youngest ones take up such a lot of attention, I wondered how much adult interaction the older children in the group were getting. On top of that, there is a fair amount of coming and going of the pedagogues as they take holidays, get pregnant, and so forth, which must be unsettling; and the contact system seems pretty loose, at best – I did not see much evidence of specific attachments of children to particular adults. I suppose the constant pressure to be cooperative throughout the education system creates more altruistic, courteous adults and douses the aggression that is found in kindergarten-cared children in other countries. But I would doubt that their intellectual development is well served by this system because there is so little opportunity for adults to respond to their unique communications and experiences.

You might argue that the different responses of the children I observed are explicable by genetically inherited temperament, but reviews of the relevant studies do not support that idea. Whether measured shortly after birth or a few weeks later, traits (like active or passive, calm or irritable) do not correlate with how children are one year or two years or five years later. What is more, studies which have deliberately selected the most difficult babies at birth and then followed them prove that maternal care is critical for how they develop, not genes.

The only one of Jasper's claims to be borne out by what I had witnessed was that the longer a child spent at the kindergarten, the less overt distress it showed on being parted from its parents. Almost without exception, parents say that the major reason for going back to work before the child is three is money. The next commonest reason is that the child needs the stimulation of other children. Only after quite a few teeth have been extracted do they admit that the core reason is that *they* are the ones seeking greater stimulation, not their offspring. Perhaps most disturbing of all, Sylvia was the only child who seemed to be securely attached enough to her mother to be genuinely pleased by being reunited with her. When I think of how joyful and playful Sylvia became when back with her mother, it makes me sad that this will probably be gradually suppressed as she becomes used to the relative impersonality of life at kindergarten.

Having said all that, the Danish day-care system does have to be understood in the context of the wider society. For at least seventy years, Danish society has been a curious mixture of, on the one hand permissive attitudes, encouraging self-expression in areas like sex and free speech, and on the other, harsh conformity. This conformity is epitomised by the Jante Code, created in the 1930s as Ten Commandments for Danish life, by the Danish-Norwegian novelist Aksel Sandemose. The code obliges you not to think of yourself as good, smart, better, knowing more or being more important than others, or having anything to teach them. You must not think you are a somebody, will ever be anybody or that anyone will ever give a damn about you. You must never get above yourself, or believe you are superior to the mass; everyone is equal, and cleverness or intelligence do not make you a better person.

Tøger Seidenfaden was able to illustrate this to me. 'Bragging is really not approved. Even if people admire you or you are proud of what you have achieved, you must be very low-key. One of my most disastrous remarks was when I was interviewed by another paper and asked if it was necessary to be a visible, well-known public figure to be the editor of this one. After about the eighth time of asking me this question in different ways I made the mistake of replying that it was probably fair to say that I was, to a degree, a well-known person – which I was, because of my previous job – and at the time it seemed an innocuous aside. But when that came out in print it was a complete disaster. For several months afterwards many complete strangers on the street would point at me and laugh out loud – "Ah, there's the well-known person," humiliating me completely because this was the most horrible breach of decorum imaginable in our society.'

Seidenfaden believes that there is an astonishing level of social conformity, one so strong that it would not be wrong to use the words 'totalitarian' and 'tyrannical'. For example, there is the weirdly total conformity in waiting to cross the road when the light is red, even when there is no traffic.

Seidenfaden gave an amusing example. 'During the Oil Crisis in 1973, no cars were permitted to drive at all on Sundays to save petrol, yet on those days pedestrians still would not cross the road until the red man turned green. I was fifteen at the time, and because I had spent quite a bit of my youth in Paris, where they wander off the pavements as if there are no cars at all, it seemed utterly absurd to me. I would go up to people and say, "There is not a single car driving today anywhere in the whole of Denmark, they've been banned. Cross the street!" But still they wouldn't.'

Seidenfaden agreed when I speculated that this extreme conformity is linked to the early age at which children are placed in day care. 'Ensuring that everyone is similar for the group to be harmonious is crucial. I agree that in a perfect system not so many children would go to kindergartens. My wife and I did not at all like the idea of sending our children when they were six months, which was the age they were supposed to be sent at the time. We hired a young woman to come during the eight hours we were at work, until our children were two. Even sending them then is probably not ideal, and I find the idea of six months much too young: they are not able to have social interactions and they pick up a lot of illness. Even though it's three children to one pedagogue, and even though it's cosy and warm with lots of toys, I don't much like it, which is why we tried to cheat – perhaps not enough,' he added ruefully.

Unfortunately, there is no scientific evidence whatsoever on the emotional consequences of day care in Denmark or anywhere else in Scandinavia. It appears that there has been a total refusal on the part of their scientific establishment to investigate it, or else, on the part of their government to fund research proposals to do so. Talking to academics there, I encountered widespread ignorance of the international studies indicating that day care for young children might diminish individuality or be distressing, and no desire to hear what it might be. Seidenfaden possibly went to the heart of the matter when he told me that 'Every time the day-care problem is brought up as a debate, the critics say, "What can we do? We will not accept the undermining of gender equality which would follow from longer maternal leave. It's not acceptable."' But most interesting of all were his perceptions of how Danish women regard the care of small children. 'I just think that the reason it's stabilised in the way it has here is because women don't actually want to do it that much. The truth is that it's pretty boring looking after babies. Of course women have a maternal instinct, stronger than my paternal one, but it's not so strong that it's still fun to stay at home after eighteen months and take care of the fucking baby all the time. Status is through work. I have discussed it with some women who were frank enough to say that after the first six to twelve months it gets very boring. The trouble is that it only gets really interesting when the children get close to talking.' How sad, then, that mothers there, like Sylvia's, feel compelled by social pressure to miss out on the huge intrinsic pleasures that can come from caring for small children just at the age (eighteen months) when many find them becoming their most enchanting.

I have great admiration for most aspects of the Danish social system, but it would seem that in their addiction to work as a source of status and the consequent consignment of toddlers to day care, they are making a mistake. The former is not a vaccine against the Virus and the latter can be harmful. It is probably reducing the capacity of their children to take advantage of the tremendous opportunities to express individuality which their educational and subsequent system offers. It may also explain why so many Danes seem rather bland. As we shall see when we come to the last vaccine, the prescription for a fulfilling life must include vitality and play-fulness. Denmark is not the place to go in search of tips on how to foster these qualities.

My conclusion is that throughout the English-speaking world the Virus is contaminating the enjoyment of mother-hood during the child's early years, particularly by fostering role strain. In China and Russia it has not yet done so, although there is a high likelihood that it will. In Denmark they have developed a method for protecting against role strain, but its human price is too high for us to pay. Unfortunately, the British Government seems oblivious to this. Its SureStart scheme for low-income mothers has been turned into little more than day-care provision, and there are frequent promises (luckily, so far, largely broken) to make it universally available for two-year-olds. There is a simple way to demonstrate the hypocrisy of SureStart.

To the best of my knowledge, day care is used by few, if any, of the children of Labour's many working mother MPs, or of the many male Labour MPs whose spouses work full-time. They are gung-ho about low-income parents' children having day care, but when it comes to their own offspring, only a nanny will do. Day care in Britain entails paying largely untrained women badly to look after children usually far from satisfactorily. If the New Labour leaders put their personal lives into practice and set up a national nannying system with good rates of pay, at least they would be consistent. But where would that lead us? There would need to be several million women (for most nannies are female) being paid to work full-time at looking after the children of other women, so that those other women could go out to work (some of them as nannies – imagine that: leaving your infant to be cared by someone else so that you can be paid to nanny another woman's). Apart from the enormous cost of such a scheme, it would raise a fundamental question which hardly anyone seems willing to ask: if, like Soo (the Chinese mother described in the last chapter) and many New Labour leaders, you are hardly ever going to see your children when they are small, why have them?

The truth about modern parenthood almost everywhere is that it is infected by the notion that the only worthwhile activities are paid ones. Well, so be it. At least follow through the logic of that toxic message: pay parents to care for their children until they are three or, if neither parent wants to do it, then pay one person properly to be a substitute.

Vaccines

1. If you possibly can, divide the care of small children between yourself and your partner

I feel sure that in the not too distant future men breaking off from their careers to care part-time for their small children will be as taken for granted as mothers going back to work already is today. Until that happy day, parents must duck and weave their way through the career thickets as best they can, but if it is at all possible, sharing the care of under-threes between you does seem to be the best solution. Of course, there will be some couples in which the woman is completely unsuited to caring for small children and others in which the man is, and a few where both are. But my suspicion is that in most cases both could do it and the relationship would thereby greatly benefit: instead of the woman feeling put-upon and downgraded, the sharing could reduce her risk of depression, and it may eliminate role strain for both parties.

2. Try to find a nanny, rather than using a kindergarten, in choosing substitute care

If substitutes are unavoidable, the message from research is clear: under three, a child is best off with one person, the same one every day and one who is responsive. That might seem prohibitively expensive, perhaps cancelling out the amount that can be made from working. If it's a case of 'stay at home and go mad or go to work and stay sane', then going to work is what you must do, even if it is not economic. As long as the substitute meets the right criteria, that will be far better for your child than being cared for by someone who is depressed.

3. Enjoy being a mother

Whatever you choose, whether working or not, see if you can find a way to enjoy being a mother rather than being ground down by it. The great problem is the lack of status it attracts and our having been brainwashed into believing that only paid work is admirable. Unfortunately, it will be rare that anyone other than your partner will give you the credit you deserve. But in its absence, remember this: however much you were raised to be a prize-hunter, intrinsic pleasure is far better for your emotional well-being. It may not seem so very often, but the authenticity, vivacity and playfulness of small children is hugely rewarding, a much greater boon than any number of promotions or pay rises. If you have a baby and are at the end of your tether, it's also worth recalling that it usually gets better. As several of the mothers described in this chapter pointed out, once they had survived the turbulence of the early months they found themselves doing something far more enriching than anything else in their life to date. It's tragic how many mothers, worn down by the stress of early care and the shocking contrast to their life before mother-hood, go back to work when their child is just about to become a ray of sunshine.

4. Do not deceive yourself about the reasons you are returning to work

Do you really need the money that would come from return-ing to work? Can you not live in a cheaper house or cut down on your outgoings? How much is this idea of more money Virus-driven wanting, rather than authentic needing? If you still feel that you must go back to work, for whatever reason, and the economic gain will be small or non-existent after you have paid for substitute care, do not lie to yourself about your motives. By all means tell others that you need the money, if that is what will keep them quiet, but it will do you no good to pretend to yourself that this is the reason. Much better to take the financial hit of good substitute nanny care and not beat yourself up if you acknowledge that small babies are not for you – that really is best for the child, as well as for you. It is particularly unhelpful to fall back on the line that you are doing it because your toddler needs the stimulation of other children, or even more absurd, requires early learning (nothing is as effective at achieving this as having a responsive one-on-one carer who encourages free play, not acquisition of skills). Toddlers need neither, and these are no justification for day care or minders with more than one small child in their care.

Chapter 10

Be Authentic (Not Sincere), Vivacious (Not Hyperactive) and Playful (Not Game-playing)

The vaccines I have described so far have been primarily concerned with Being, in general, as an alternative to Having. Less attention has been paid to what kind of Being is desirable.

Where I went on my travels, only the most blinkered of mind tourists would not have noticed that, regardless of culture, class or gender, certain kinds of Being emerged as more desirable than others. The three characteristics which the most contented, emotionally mature people I met seemed to have in common were authenticity, vivacity and playfulness. These are somewhat different from the faith, hope and charity urged upon us by the Bible, but the more a person possessed these characteristics, the less likely they were to be afflicted by either the Virus or emotional distress. Whilst very few manifested all three, and whilst their distribution varied from society to society, in the 240 people I interviewed, a full house was a guarantee of immunity.

In common parlance, 'authenticity' means being real rather than false. 'Vivacity' is feeling vitalised, fascinated and excited by life, living in the here and now. 'Playfulness' is being able to take what is going on inside and around you, and to use your imagination to transform it into something amusing and beyond what it seems, best exemplified by children's play. All three are closely linked to intrinsic values: authenticity is more likely where basic needs (rather than confected wants) are being met; vivacity comes from having identified with, rather than emptily introjected, parental ideas; and playfulness flows, with complete absorption, so that time seems to fly (rather than drag). Virus values impede authenticity, vivacity and playfulness and often replace them with, respectively, sincerity, hyperactivity and game-playing.

Authenticity versus sincerity

Authenticity is best understood in terms of its contrast with 'sincerity' (see Lionel Trilling's book *Sincerity and Authenticity*), a word whose meaning has changed over time. In England, until the sixteenth century it meant being sound or pure or whole. By the mid-seventeenth century it had changed to mean the absence of a gap between the face you present to others and what you really feel, as suggested in Shakespeare's dictum 'to thine own self be true' (Polonius' advice to Hamlet). As Trilling puts it, a pact was proposed between me and my self, and of that self with others, in which there shall be no subterfuges: I shall be loyal to this self and honest about it with others. Subsequently, during the nineteenth and the early twentieth century, sincerity developed its modern meaning. To honesty and openness was added intense passion about one's convictions.

In our Oprah Winfrey world, as long as you feel that your sexual infidelity or paedophilia or invasion of Iraq is true to yourself, as well as publicly proclaiming it, your sincerity is accepted if you are believed to have acted on the basis of powerful emotions. I mention Iraq because the crowning English example of sincerity is Tony Blair. All the people I have met who have known him personally have attested to this. Although he is notorious for leaving one person with the conviction that he is wholly committed to their view, and only minutes later leaving a second equally convinced of his belief in the rectitude of exactly the opposite, I have met no-one who doubts that he sincerely means what he says, however self-contradictory, because of his passion. Perhaps his all too manifest sincerity is part of why he appeals so much to the American public, by whom this modern form of sincerity is so prized. However, even if he is sincere, that is no guarantee that he is authentic.

Authenticity is being real: as actual, hard, durable and densely weighty as stone. Like art historians authenticating pieces for auctioneers, the authentic individual labours to distinguish the true original from the false, searching for the impenetrable and the autonomous in human existence. Someone who is grieving for a loved one or has been moved by a mountain dawn to write a poem may be sincere in doing so, or they may be authentic. The distinction depends on whether the feelings are governed by considerations wider than 'I feel it strongly, I express it, therefore it is true.' To be sincere, one must be seen by others to express grief or feel passion for the mountain dawn, but this is not essential to authenticity. Authenticity requires wider, often moral frames of reference, be they personal experience or national history, or the natural world. In seeking it out, writers have often turned to nature – sunsets, storm-tossed seas, flora and fauna. But clues may also be found in the commonplaces of every-day life, epiphanies of the extraordinary gleaned from overheard utterances on the bus or carrying out ordinary domestic tasks, the unsophisticated and unpretentious: children, uneducated simpletons, the oppressed and the poor. The authentic go back to basics, seeking something that is true in all times and places, not subject to fashion, making the natural and the unfashionable good places to look. The consequent Being is often at odds with received, habitual convention. But the authentic do not have to speak out in order to be defined as such, whereas sincerity always entails plain-speaking, even if that requires telling the offensive truth to those who do not want to hear it.

The contemporary colloquial use of 'authenticity' often merges it with the concept of sincerity, and this is illustrated by how art and artists have evolved. Where once the artist's job was to please through beauty and enrich through truth, now it is to instruct us in our inauthenticity and to urge us to overcome it. During the last century, the wheels-within-wheels relativity of moral and scientific strivings turned with increasing frequency, culminating in post-modernism, which sees everything as a narrative which can never represent larger or absolute truths. 'Serious' novelists grew increasingly reluctant to shackle themselves by the convention of chronological storytelling to give pleasure. Only the artist's sincerity mattered. Sincere autobiography, having started in the eighteenth century, evolved into the 'more information than we need' modern celebrity striptease.

Meanwhile, art itself became often unpleasant or disturbing, so that shitting on a canvas or writing down horrible thoughts would suffice, if intended sincerely. The twentieth-century viewer or reader, having had these horrors communicated to them, would in turn osmotically become more authentic, yet even this came to be not enough. The very act of seeking authenticity, either as artist or art admirer, was now inauthentic (Trilling is drily dismissive of this notion that serious art is diluting of self: 'surely on this ground or nowhere a man can set up the smithy in which to forge his autonomous selfhood?'). Even relationships with other people were declared inauthentic as sources of authenticity – because second-hand – ruling out Jane Austen's notion of 'intelligent love', in which knowledge of right conduct was given and received in order to improve character. The past ceased to be the sanction of authority or an aide to understanding how to forge one's destiny: only the here and now mattered. Our commonplace, hackneyed, everyday thoughts or deeds, once so prized as clues to authenticity, were now depicted as empty, shameful evidence of petit bourgeois existences.

In the terms of this book, modern sincerity is liable to be associated with Virus goals and motives, because it is so closely tied to how others view us, whereas traditional authenticity accompanies the intrinsic. Everywhere on my travels I encountered the coincidence of modern sincerity with the Virus, but it was in New York that the association seemed clearest of all. A radical estrangement from (authentic) truth seems to plague American mass culture.

I happened to be in New York on 11 September 2004, which also coincided with the final stages of the presidential campaign that preceded George W. Bush's re-election. At the one-block gap in the lower jaw of west Manhattan where the World Trade Center once stood (histrionically and inauthentically renamed 'ground zero' – what does that mean?), the final plans for replacing the late lamented twin towers are still unagreed. Beside the half-built and pretentiously labelled Freedom Tower, I listen to the politicians mawkishly milking the dead. 'It has been said', intones Mayor Bloomberg, portentously reading from the script prepared by his spin doctor, 'that a child who loses its parents is an orphan.' Err, yes, that is the word people use for such a child. 'A man who loses his wife is a widower,' he goes on, 'a woman who loses her husband is a widow, but there is no word for a parent who loses their child because no words can describe the grief they feel.'

At the end of his oration, a procession of bereaved relatives come to the podium to share their grief, interrupted only by brief silences to commemorate the exact moments on the morning when the two planes hit the towers and, later, when the towers collapsed. A father plays his violin with a racked, agonised expression on his face, the sad sound of his slightly off-key instrument playing our heartstrings, Bush's spinmeisters doubtless weeping with joy at the thought of the extra votes this performance will bring them. A mother provides a miserable but dignified summary of the grief her family feels. Bush appears on a huge television screen, standing with his wife at the White House, looking solemn.

There seems to be almost no part of private life which will not be made public in America if there is financial or political profit to be made. Sincerity is big business and a source of votes. Observing the mourners, you have to wonder whether it is really helpful for them to share their grief quite so publicly and to have it reactivated each year in this way. If one of them were my patient, I would not be very happy about their participation because they must be aware of the cameras and millions watching, of having to act a part rather than to stay with what they are truly feeling. Of course their sorrow is real, and that is what makes it such 'good television' in a land where authentic feeling is so hard to spot amongst the commercially driven, confected emotion that marketing and machiavellianism require.

In the field of American reality TV, competition is hot for the most grotesque example of such exploitation, but surely the grossest is a series called *The Bachelor*. A handsome, wealthy young man (heir to a vineyard – why would he need to be part of this charade?) declares his commitment to picking a wife from a bevy of sixteen attractive (but not beautiful) potential brides. After snogging a fair few of them, over the months they are whittled down to three. Going on dates with them at a hotel, he has sex (using the words 'made love') with each (the camera decorously withdrawing after we have witnessed the initial fore-play in their bedroom – but why stop there?). After he has sampled all the goods, one is returned to sender and the remaining two are introduced to his family. Both women claim to have fallen in love with him, and with great plausibility he claims abiding affection for them, as he has done for many of the departed competitors (his plausibility is terrifying, perhaps assisted by clever coaching from the production staff). Finally, he chooses his bride.

His sincerity in talking to each woman is chilling, as is his courtesy and charm in explaining his attraction to them. When he dismisses the losers in the 'game' (except that this is not a game – he is actually going to get engaged to the winner) he does his best to spare their feelings – 'you are a beautiful person', 'you are an outgoing, loving woman', 'you've got a great sense of humour'. The trouble is that this sincerity cannot be authentic because however earnest, it is always also a performance for the cameras. He is making the most personal of decisions, yet he has allowed it to become a commodity, an experience to be manipulated, packaged and sold worldwide (I actually saw this series whilst in Copenhagen).

In discussing differences between the English and Americans, Lionel Trilling points to the legacy of social position, of class. In eighteenth- and nineteenth-century England, knowing your place and sticking to it were taken as signs of authenticity. Characters in novels who achieved upward mobility were subjected to close scrutiny for signs of amoral chancing. Trilling cites Henry James's account of Americans as 'thinly composed' and contrasts this with the impermeability, solidity of composition, the thick, indubitable 'thereness' of the English character. Whereas the Americans are held to have severed the chains of the monarchically founded class system, freeing themselves to strive for transcendence without limit, the English acceptance of societal bounds is held to increase authenticity. According to Trilling, the English person's supposed obedient service in the performance of everyday tasks also confers authenticity. One wonders whether Trilling, who was writing in 1970, would still take this view of the (Americanised) English character.

Having endured as much as I can of The 9/11 Show, I make my way to a Greenwich Village café to meet Gus, the thirty-five-year-old features editor of a lifestyle magazine. Short, slight and bearded, he speaks in rapid bursts, often not choosing his words very well – emitting a splurge of ideas and high-anxiety thoughts. He paints a picture of his social circle as domestically contented and professionally fulfilled, but with himself as a troubled figure. Raised in a small town in Virginia, south of Washington, his middle-class parents (both nurses) divorced when he was small, and his mother got remarried to a working-class plumber, from whom she also divorced. Gus believes that, having been imbued with middle-class values and aspirations, he was out of place in the low-income suburbs and schools of his youth. 'I was smarter than my friends but was separated from them by dint of what I was interested in – doing my homework, what I was reading. It was bad to be smart there, people made fun of you for that. I was a nerd before nerds had been invented' (he made frequent attempts at aphorisms like this which did not have quite the cleverness which I felt he imagined they possessed).

Things picked up when he was sixteen and got in with a middle-class set. 'They were from private schools, which was the first time I had met someone like me, great and liberating. It was much the same the first time I walked into my magazine office. I looked at the journalists at their computers and thought, "This is what I should be doing, with people like this."' Life took an even better turn when Gus gained entry to the only university to which he applied, one largely populated by very rich kids. 'That was the most important four years of my life, I had a wonderful time.' However, his enjoyment was marred by feelings of guilt and the slights of class. His mother had to make very considerable sacrifices to help support him. Although he developed lifelong friendships with children of the super-rich, there was no escaping the differences in background. 'At a school [i.e. university] like that, some of the kids have to work in the canteen scrubbing pots and doing a steady job, and some don't. When working in the admissions department to earn money, I pulled my file because I was terrified I had only been accepted to fulfil some "single parent" quota. I felt it was a liability to have my origins and frankly, there was guilt. I knew that my mother was giving up all that she could in order for me to be educated, a big thing to do. But it was the right decision. It gave me everything I have in my life, my job and my friends.' It also gave him his wife.

Having spent a few years after university back in his hometown, Gus headed for the Big Apple, reconnecting with his rich friends from university days, through whom he met his wealthy wife, and worked his way into magazines. Unfortunately his marriage into money has not helped to salve his lifelong sense of being socially in the wrong place. 'We come from really different situations. She went to a privileged college and was coddled by her parents. In some ways I'm better equipped to deal with the real world than she is.' His father-in-law is a working-class, self-made businessman, and he paid for their house in Brooklyn. Ironically, he has more of a bond to his parents-in-law. 'Her parents love me and I love them because we come from similar backgrounds.

We actually have more in common than their daughter does. In a way I feel superior to her and most of my rich friends.'

Throughout our meeting, Gus frequently spoke of feeling superior or inferior to others. He has kept in touch with two of his friends from his hometown and goes to visit them regularly, worrying about the welfare of the ones he no longer sees, one of whom has disappeared and he has tried to trace. He puts this preoccupation down to guilt, but I wondered whether there was not also a secret enjoyment and reassurance at their adversity, from which he has escaped. Gus was keen on having his motivations analysed and, apparently inevitable in this city, had undergone therapy. Unfortunately, this had proved no more satisfactory than his marriage. Whilst repeatedly claiming to have been greatly helped – 'I got an amazing amount out of it' – he also is very critical of, and feels superior to, his analyst. 'Sometimes I'd feel above her, that "I get what this is, you don't." Also, I'm the kind of guy who wants to understand the process and would say to her, "So, what are you thinking?" She would reply, "Well, why do you ask that?" I'd be, "No, but you do this for a living, there must be some sort of criteria that you have, what do you talk about when with your therapist friends?" I wanted to know what category I was in, but she made me feel that was prevarication. It was true to some extent: I realise I was holding back some things. But I wouldn't go back, at some point you have to deal with your own shit.'

This unsatisfactory experience of thereapy leaves Gus prone to earnest psychologising, but without great insight. For example, he feels he was just getting to know his biological father when he died, and has developed some unpersuasive-sounding theories about how he was really like him and not like his mother. A lot of his ideas sound like the right sort of thing to say, but it is as if he is parroting a clever orthodoxy rather than truly speaking from experience. He philosophised about his guitar jam sessions with hometown friends: 'I always say of the recordings we make, "It's not the fact that we did it so badly which matters, it's the laughter when we finish the song."' Whilst I am sure that there is a part of him that genuinely feels this, I wonder if there is not another, much more competitive, slighted side which is more concerned with appearance and status. Of his friends from his hometown, he says that 'At least half of them are not in a good place at all. They don't know themselves, can't get out of the cycle of drinking, pot, drugs, maybe working in super-markets and being married to crazy people. Every day they wake up and are not happy but can't do anything about that. Only a couple of my friends from that era rose above [supe-riority again] that, they're the ones I'm still close to. The others I check up on and worry about but they're not with me on a day to day basis.'

I have a suspicion that Gus may have projected the failed, inadequate, trapped parts of himself, which he still experi-ences very strongly, onto these friends. 'I have always had an undercurrent of worry, sadness and fear. I have worried every day of my life about money. I still do. I fear that I'm bad for not saving as much as I should, even though we don't have to worry about that really. Actually, the most depressed times have been when I have not had much work. I saw other people not as good as me and wondered, "Why is that guy working when I'm not?"'

Although he presents himself as fulfilled by his work and part of a satisfied social group, I fear that Gus is still massively insecure and needs to prove to himself that he is superior to these wealthy friends. He sees himself as emotionally literate and putting well-being and relationships first, but when it comes to the idea of being a father he is less than enthusiastic. 'My wife's looking to have babies now, but I don't feel a pull towards it. I see my friends having kids and realise it would be nice for mine to be friends with theirs, but also I am a selfish only child and I don't quite feel I've fulfilled my career potential enough yet. *You* have a life where you write books and do what you like. I want that.' He voraciously compares himself with everyone, not just me – a key symptom of the Virus.

Gus's sense of social dislocation runs deep. At school he feels out of place because he has middle-class values in a working-class setting. Hanging out with privately educated friends at sixteen, he feels more at home. Choosing a rich-kids university, he makes rich-kid friends and although he has a 'wonderful time', he feels out of place again because his mother must scrimp and save to support him. Returning to his hometown, instead of building up a business and making himself rich as a way of closing the disparity between his perceived status and reality, which is what some socially displaced people do (in a British study, this was one of the predictors of who becomes a top entrepreneur; George Davis, the founder of the Next fashion retail chain, is an example), he heads off to New York to join his rich-kid chums again. By accident or design (whilst it may not have been a conscious case of bounty-hunting, one cannot imagine him choosing a penniless wife), he marries into money and becomes a rich kid himself, which induces discomfort and guilt about the contrast with his hometown friends (and mother) and bringing him closer to his working-class parents-in-law than his wife.

Whilst Gus may be sincere, he does not strike me as authentic. For sure, this is partly due to his difficult childhood, but it is exacerbated by the money- and status-dominated culture in which he exists. He seems a prime example of Henry James's 'thinly composed' American, an increasingly common species in England. They search for the real but are distracted by the lure of prizes, ironically ones often linked to the social class structure from which America was originally so eager to break. Gus finds himself in a culture in which he is supposed, on the one hand, to achieve his individuality and his personal truth without any reference to the social order, to find the real him, a spirit which is supposed to be beyond any social constraint or ultimate truth. On the other hand, America today is as status-obsessed a society as any ritualised European court from earlier centuries.

Trilling painstakingly traced this curious evolution of American unreality. The seeking of authenticity within the boundaries established by life, death and society is still evident in the young male characters of English and French novels in the nineteenth century and the early twentieth. They seek happiness through the pursuit of worldly objectives, hoping, according to Trilling, 'to enter the fair courts of life; how one conducted oneself in that enterprise was what morality was about'. It was not until the second half of the twentieth century that fictional characters' aspirations for a successful life became widely regarded as embarrassing, so that Herzog, the Saul Bellow character who attempts this, was derided by critics for doing so. Much more popular today are Arthur Miller's despairing Willy Loman in *Death of a Salesman*, Martin Amis's ludicrously greedy John Self (in *Money*) and the characters in Tom Wolfe's *Bonfire of the Vanities*. In terms of Gus, there is a bewildering tension between two opposing cultural forces. America infects him with Virus preoccupations for money and status, while at the same time the youth and therapy culture is directing him to pursue a personal, unique odyssey in search of his true self, whether through the intro-verted despair of Lou Reed and Leonard Cohen, or the hedonism of rap music and The Beach Boys.

A marked contrast to Gus was Lizzie, a twenty-seven-year-old New Zealander who has also had to overcome adversity, but has done so in a much less Virus-infected soci-ety. She seemed to be much more the real authentic deal, and on top of that was both vivacious and playful. On the phone, her bouncy, modern patois could be that of any thrusting young London TV producer or journalist. She was the only New Zealander I met who talked in this way. However, as I listen to her speaking in person, I realise that I have done her a disservice in comparing her to the average savvy media Brit. True, she uses language to amuse and charm and flirt her way past your scepticism and to win your attention and admira-tion. And she is very clever. But she is also authentic, vivacious and playful.

After studying communications at university, she carved out a meteoric media career, first in TV and then as the manager for leading New Zealand rock bands, and also doing a weekly column in a leading newspaper in the *Sex and the City* mould. Recently she wrote two plays of a social-realist bent which ran successfully in Auckland, and serious film companies have taken options on two of her film scripts. Such prodigious (premature, in my dad's terms) achieving is often accompanied by a cocky, brattish, false personality, using success to compensate for feelings of low self-esteem and powerlessness. Indeed, Lizzie felt this applied to her. Her parents divorced when she was small. 'I do love my mother,' she says, 'but we never really got on. I was definitely a child who was overachieving from a young age to deal with feeling unloved.' So far, so Affluenza. But what seems to have cured her, at least as it would first appear, is that since the age of eighteen she has suffered life-threatening diseases.

First there was the cancer which she refused to tell her parents about and which was thankfully destroyed by chemotherapy and surgery. Then there was the heart attack when she was given a drug to which she was allergic. There were the several times during her frequent hospital admissions when she witnessed people die in beds near her. 'I just seem to have this body which works totally against me,' she tells me. 'Now I've got a bleeding disorder which is like haemophilia and means I end up with lots of scarring and bleeds that put me in agony. From time to time they have to put pipes in my back to drain the blood and clots, when they press against my pelvis. They had to open me up and my bowels were in a dreadful state. The disease is such that I could die at any moment of the day or night. It's quite painful, and I could have a lifetime of morphine, but I think it's better without.'

In all she has endured twenty-five surgical interventions over the last nine years, yet she is in no doubt that her physical illness is what has saved her from an endless quest for glittering prizes and a life of continual dissatisfaction. 'When I got sick, I looked at my career and thought, "This is bollocks, what's this for?" If you have an illness like that which is potentially life-ending, it can be life-changing. The only positive is to learn that you can't take anything with you and you have to teach yourself to concentrate on what is really important.' Which is? 'To realise what a little speck you are, that you are so alone on this planet. Sometimes I'm a bit like a dog that gets hit by a car – you just want to crawl away and be on your own. But you are also forced to re-evaluate what matters. I was one of those people that's so scared of fucking up, that thing of "You've had the chances your mother never had, the education, the freedom, the travel, the opportunities, what if I pick the wrong person, the wrong job?" But I could drop dead at any minute, and I think, "I have my family, I have my friends, God knows they're a complicated lot, but thank goodness that's what's there."' Here is someone who has managed to turn the lead of their distress into the gold of true insight, not the fool's gold of mere success.

The best literary account of the threat of death causing a re-evaluation of life is Tolstoy's work of genius, 'The Death of Ivan Ilyich'. In this short story, Ilyich is a distinguished member of the ruling elite, in the judiciary, when he is struck by a fatal illness. This spurs him to take a good look at himself. He comes to grasp the aridity of his relationships with everyone and decides to seek something more authentic. This might seem to imply that a powerful vaccine would be to develop a life-threatening illness. However, Lizzie is a bit more optimistic than that. I asked what Polonius-like advice she could offer a fifteen-year-old girl today that would help her to evade the pitfalls that had made Lizzie so distressed. 'Women my age have been so warned off from babies, the messaging is all wrong. I resent having been told that motherhood is something you should think about at the other end after everything else is sorted out. When you are young and single you think, "I don't want children", but I've got this sneaking suspicion we should listen to all the advice the older women give when they say, "Relationships and marriage can crumble to dogs but don't let the example of our marital fuck-ups put you off what is going to be the best thing you will ever do, I promise." When I look at my friends I am appalled by how unhappy they seem to be. The only thing that seems to make them happy is when I see them with their children. Put my usually miserable friend William in a room with his little girls, put my muddled pal Jimmy – who basically hates his wife – with his son going for a walk, they come alive. For all her madness, if you put my mother with her three children around the table, it's like you've plugged her into an electrical circuit.'

Perhaps Lizzie's attitude is coloured by the fact that after her many operations she might never be able to reproduce. But she is passionate in her conviction that young women have been badly misled. 'What the hell have we as women been taught over the last ten to fifteen years? At secondary school we were force-fed this 'girls can do anything' slogan. Everybody said that getting married and having kids means you're a bit of a failure, yet everything would suggest that the further away we go from that, the more miserable we become. I've got four friends who always wanted kids, and having done so, they love it. Everybody else, we're just these weird people. So I would say to fifteen-year-old girls, "Forget this idea that you can have babies when you're thirty-five, have babies when you're younger than that." Babies are hard, tireless, thankless, but they enable women to focus on what matters.' This return to the importance of children as models for adult authenticity is a classic illustration of the use of simplicity to establish something more fundamental than here-and-now sincerity.

She is equally scathing about the materialist dream that is promised to young New Zealanders, especially those living in Auckland. Along with a host of writers, from Rousseau to Tolstoy to Orwell, Lizzie praises the authenticity of the uneducated, the rural and the poor. 'When I travel out of the city I think everybody does seem more happy. So much of their life is agricultural, with people working in relation to the land. Self-determination makes people happy, not traffic jams and parking tickets. You're not actually earning much money living here because the prices you are paying for accommodation are like London and New York, relatively speaking. [This is true, in terms of the ratio of incomes to property prices.] But if you go up north, people are really poor, God they're poor, but they're community-based. Here, in the city, you don't even see your good friends who are twenty minutes away. I have such a stupid life that I can't get a dog because it would be alone all day. But I would go, "Oh my God, I love you!" every morning if I had one. The quality of life is incomparably worse here than in smaller cities or the country.'

Lizzie has abandoned all prize-hunting in favour of the intrinsic. She never complains about her medical problems and instead blooms with enthusiasm for her various projects. I witnessed several occasions where, variously, her mother, separated father, brother and boyfriend were present, and she was always lively, amusing and playful, but not attention-seeking. When I spoke separately with these intimates, they all said how considerate she had been in helping them to deal with all manner of problems. Sceptics may scoff at her claims about the redeeming features of children and accuse her of idealising poverty-stricken agricultural life, as Tolstoy and Orwell did. But, the merit of such scepticism notwithstanding, I would counter that at least she lives in a much healthier social environment than Gus's New York.

The vast majority of the New Zealanders I met were honest, decent and had no side. Almost without exception, they would bend over backwards to help out if you were having problems. For example, whilst I was touring the country with my wife and our daughter, the camper van's loo outlet refused to cooperate during a stay at a campsite in the remotest reaches of the South Island. Despite suffering from multiple sclerosis, the husband of the camp manager fought his way through wind and rain after a hard day working as a town surveyor to sort it out. I would have loved to give him some money for his trouble, but it was obvious from his demeanour that he would have been most embarrassed and pained by any such offer. This was not just a matter of rural palliness. In Auckland, by far the nation's largest city (a quarter of the 4 million New Zealanders live there), whether it was shopkeepers, mums with their toddlers or pub-goers, all were friendly and did their best to help if there was a problem. Most surprising of all to a Briton, even representatives of multinational companies put themselves out to get you sorted. My international datacard, for instance, did not work on my computer. A quiet, unassuming young man in the relevant shop spent many hours trying to sort it out with no sign at all that he was hoping for anything in return other than the satisfaction of having done his job well.

The all-pervasive New Zealander concern with authenticity at the cost of pretentiousness must have something to do with the fact that the vast majority of the original settlers came out of choice, in the mid-nineteenth century. Whereas a large slice of the original white Australian population (including a relative on my mother's side) were forcibly deported there from Britain as convicts, New Zealanders chose their new life down under. Nearly all the early settlers were British, a link that continues (one-fifth of New Zealand citizens were not born there, and of these, one-third were born in Britain). Some were enticed by offers of golden opportunities to farm their way to wealth; others felt that nineteenth-century Britain's rigid class system offered little chance of progression. On arrival, contrary to the rosy picture painted by the false prospectuses sold them in Britain, they found virtually no infrastructure. It may have been, and still is, one of the most beautiful countries in the world (as is apparent from the *Lord of the Rings* films), but railways, roads, houses, everything had to be built from scratch. A long, thin strip of land divided by a small channel of sea into the two Islands, its landmass is about the same as that of Britain. But geographically and temporally, it is about as far as it is possible to be from Britain – their winter is our summer, their night is our day. As true pioneers, the first white New Zealanders overcame tremendous obstacles to create a functional society, very different from that of their motherland. There was no room for hierarchy or airs and graces in the struggle to create farms and build towns.

Thirty-two-year-old Terence is the most striking illustration I can give of the continued endurance of New Zealand's concern with authenticity – a deep distaste for pretension and a disdain for chamaeleonism. A mutual acquaintance described him to me as precisely the kind of man women here go for, a 'humble doer'; British women might call him 'sex on a stick'. His shoulder-length blond hair, slender waist, well proportioned muscular legs visible beneath his shorts, sleepy eyes and measured, deep voice would all surely make him very attractive to women (though men are notoriously bad at judging this; whereas women always seem to know if another of their sex is sexy, I am not alone in often being amazed when a woman says 'he's really attractive' about a male friend). Not that I fancied him or anything, just that he has a certain something, which may be part of why he is a cult TV figure in New Zealand. I have known or interviewed many British media people, and many live up to the popular idea of the 'slimy reptile'. Not Terence. Seated in a relaxed posture on the sofa of my hotel room, he looks great, but in his psychology and values he is as unlike Paula Yates or Jools Holland or their more modern British equivalents, Ant and Dec, as a fish is to time.

Terence is best known for his work as a presenter of an almost non-existent phenomenon, a New Zealand TV satire show. One of its main gags was to unsettle famous celebrities who pass through from time to time. In place of the usual 'we think your country is beautiful and we love your people' interview, Terence did his best to disorientate them. The American rock star Marilyn Manson has a reputation for saying and doing outrageous and disgusting things. Terence obtained a picture of the schoolboy Manson with short hair, looking very conventional, had it printed on a tee shirt and claimed that it was a bestselling New Zealand garment. Manson was completely floored by the idea that his former self could be the reason for his fame. But the show did not stop at taking the piss out of overseas celebs, it also satirised their own people. 'In the South Island you get some pretty hick-like places. We went down to a little one called Gore and claimed for it the title of "Gay Capital of New Zealand". The next day the headline in the local paper was GORE REELS AT GAY QUIP. The mayor was furious and said, "If those people come down here again we're going to take to them with sticks and smash them out of the town." Homophobia is still very common in much of New Zealand.'

This is the kind of stuff you expect to hear from a satirist, but I was in for a big surprise when I put it to him that the people I had met in his country had nearly all been truly down-to-earth practical people; decent, open and ethical; not especially motivated by the pursuit of power, status and wealth; not interested in appearances or being either cool or uncool; and not cynical but healthily sceptical. He agreed wholeheartedly and offered what was, coming from the mouth of a satirist, an astonishing observation: 'It really would be bad to knock that, because those are things that we are quite proud of. How could mocking that be good?' I had no difficulty in imagining Ian Hislop or Rory Bremner's answer to that, but Terence went still further, speaking with some earnestness. 'I would not want to contribute to a subculture of cynicism about traditional New Zealand virtues, personally. Simple people are easy targets, and we're not really a bunch of complicated people.'

When we turned to how fame works here, he provided more insights into the national culture. 'For me, fame is not something major, nor do I get stopped in the street. People look at you for longer and obviously recognise you, but it's not the done thing to stop you. If they have drunk a lot they do sometimes come up and say things to me, but we're really quite shy.' 'So they do get nasty?' I asked. 'No, never. They tell you about things they like that you've done. I've never been had a go at. If I'd done things that were bad I suppose they might say something.'

I asked Terence whether his fame affected the way women related to him, and he said that in small towns he did attract their attention, perhaps because they rarely saw someone from a TV programme in real life. But this was not the case in Auckland, also illustrative of the national character. 'We're quite standoffish, don't want to embarrass ourselves, quite considerate, prepared to put ourselves in other people's shoes.' 'Could it be', I wondered, 'that New Zealand women actually realise that just because you've been on TV it doesn't mean it would be fun to sleep with you, or that you'd be very nice?' 'Yes,' I think that's true, a strong chance that it's so.' But surely, if he was in a pub, being famous would improve his chances of pulling, even in Auckland? 'I'm not the sort to go up to someone and say, "How are you going, can I buy you a drink?", which is similar to most New

Zealand males. It's not seen as being a good thing by men, and New Zealand women don't like it either. A guy who walks into a bar, behaving like The Man, spinning it up large and saying to women, "How're you doing, love, you're looking great" – that's not on, not the way. Well, some girls might like it, but most would find that quite tragic.' 'By that reasoning,' I said, 'you're only going to meet someone to sleep with if you're introduced to them.' 'Yes, that's why it's quite hard. And particularly because the girls I would think of as nice for me would never come up and say anything to me, ever, so I don't actually meet a lot of people. Luckily I've had the same girlfriend for a long time, but if it wasn't for that I'd be in a lot of trouble. I find it very hard to meet people now.'

British readers might imagine that when Terence talks of doing 'things that were bad' he means acting foolishly. But it gradually dawned on me that he was talking about 'bad' as in 'you've been a bad person', moral good and bad. It helped to explain another mystery of New Zealand life: the largely non-existent tabloid press. I had been told that the magazines that do run kiss-and-tell stories did not have large enough circulations to pay more than about £800 to the teller. Whilst some stars do *Hello*-like spreads for about £2,800 a shot, women looking to sell their 'I shagged an All-Black rugger star' memoirs simply could not attract enough cash to make it worth their while. Another theory is that the country is dominated by a tiny elite who quickly suppress any stories about them, something Terence (who is from an old family, very well connected) confirmed as true. But it seems that neither of these reasons is as important as the New Zealand character.

'There'd be real stigma attached to selling your story here. For example, there was a New Zealand girl who slept with Robbie Williams and sold her story. People just wouldn't like her, we're very simple, humble people ... oh dear, this is sounding like "we're such simple people" – but we really are, we don't like gloating, we don't like kiss and tell. In a small country people are very worried about what other people know about them because sooner or later you will meet someone who knows you, almost wherever you go. If you are the person who is known for having sold the story of having slept with a pop star, it's going to mean you lose friends and you would have to weigh that up before doing it.'

This absence of a celebrity culture would lead one to suspect that the Affluenza Virus is not widespread. However, Terence had little doubt that there's plenty of depression in privileged Aucklanders. 'Amongst my friends I would say there isn't one who hasn't suffered at some point. People are not particularly proud of it so they don't discuss their mood, which only tends to make it worse. The most successful are often the most at risk. As a child you're told, "Work hard now, get a good job and it'll be fine," so you do, and you get there, and you think, "Is that it, is there no more?" A lot of it is too high expectations of what success will bring. I know any number of examples from well-to-do families. Like my friend who has had a Number One single in New Zealand, made TV that's won awards, he's made radio, produces other people's music, a very sharp guy, but he's depressed. He's motivated by insecurity, has to prove himself by hard work. Or another guy, he's just had his first child, works in advertising, about to get married, everything seems to be going well for him. Yet he's not happy with himself: he's dissatisfied because having achieved the goals he set himself, he realises that it's just not that great. So he wants more in the hope that that will be better, but I don't think he'll ever be satisfied.'

And Terence? 'I certainly do get down, less and less now, but it was quite bad after two or three years of doing TV – I was really not that happy at all. I think I've got no excuse to be unhappy with myself: I've got everything that I want, I've got all these friends. But that almost makes it worse in a way: there's a lot of people worse off than me. The worst thing is not knowing why you're unhappy, what the fuck is wrong with me. Then I realised that the more I thought about my unhappiness the more unhappy I got. At some point I'd have to just get on with it. Now if I start going down that road, I know I've got to stop and go and do something I like because one thing leads to another, and you end up down here, and it takes quite a long time to get back up.'

In theory, New Zealanders being so tough with themselves raised an interesting possibility. Very moralistic people are much more at risk of irrationally thinking themselves bad. It is also hard for them to experience pleasure if they are constantly feeling guilty at 'indulging' their desires, sexual or otherwise. Such punitive consciences could cause depression. However, I soon realised that this was unlikely to be the cause of modern New Zealand depression. Any propensity towards over-zealous moralising would have been even stronger back in the fifties and sixties. Whilst there is no hard evidence either way, it seems extremely likely that New Zealand then was as near to a social paradise as you can get. The statistics show that half a century ago New Zealanders did not work especially hard and led comfortable, well-organised lives, with strong communities and very little sense of dissatisfaction.

If Auckland's gilded youth are miserable, Affluenza seems a far more plausible diagnosis than punitive consciences, and Terence seemed to agree. 'The key is to readjust expectations to realistic levels and work out if you really are the kind of person who will take pleasure in your job and your status. If you're one of those, then by all means go for it and work as hard as you like, but if you take pleasure in more simple sorts of things, then all that other stuff is not going to help.' He specifically identified conspicuous consumerism as the main problem. 'In Auckland twenty years ago there was wealth, but an unwritten rule that it was not the done thing to show it off with cars and houses, or talking yourself up. Now you see a lot of flash cars here, although most are actually borrowed. It's that theory, "if you've got it, show it", which is an American thing. I suppose if I'm really honest with myself, I have it a bit. One part of me wants to live in a humble way and another thinks it would be quite nice to have a nice car, a nice house. But underneath it all there's that thing that I'm very proud of: you still hear about people who are very, very wealthy who you never guessed were, which is the most wonderful thing. But it's slowly dying out. It's tragic.'

The New Zealanders are the most individualistic nation on earth, even more so than the Americans. Like many Americans, New Zealanders' cultural roots lie in nonconformist sects, such as Calvinism and Quakerism. These sects reflect the institutionalisation of belief and its most ostentatious manifestations, like huge churches and cathedrals or the 'smells and bells' of Catholicism. But I suspect that the New

Zealand individualism takes a much more genuine form than that confected in America, where the unpretentious puritanism has been colonised by positive psychology in order to further conspicuous consumption.

Towards the end of our time together, Terence and I became quite mournful, a bit like two old buffers sipping our postprandial brandies in the leather chairs of our London club, both raised as we were in the elites of our respective societies. However much we might regard ourselves as having questioned our backgrounds, we could not help bemoaning the creeping effects of the commercialisation and coarsening of modern life. Of course, we were aware of the contradiction between this moan and the egalitarian liberal consensus that everyone should have an equal chance to acquire wealth, status and power. But being so privileged, we knew better than anyone that achieving these does not increase well-being. We were like the central character in Giuseppe Lampedusa's *The Leopard*, a novel about a Sicilian aristocrat witnessing the collapse of an aesthetically advanced, traditional social order. Forced to sell his estate to a brash peasant who has made good, the Leopard dies despairing of the present and hopeless about the future of his beloved country as new money replaces the old.

Had Lionel Trilling been present at our meeting, he might have sympathised with our lamentations. He argued that, in the eighteenth century, 'plebeian democracy' destroyed Shakespeare's noble goals of order, peace, honour and beauty, trashing them and society in the name of the achievement of personal integrity and individualism. He highlights a number of literary characters from the 1760s and 1770s who illustrate the growth of the ideal of a self divorced from the social order and from history. There is Rousseau's Noble Savage, an innocent uncorrupted by the artifices of modernity and social pressures; Diderot's Rameau, who lays bare the insincerity and inauthenticity of convention; and Goethe's Werther, a sort of eighteenth-century Lou Reed or Morrissey, who refuses to be part of society, insisting on clothing himself only in one costume, the dark blue coat, yellow waistcoat and boots in which he dies by his own hand, insisting that this fate is the sole means to avoid false selves and remain true to his only one. In the nineteenth century, individualism became even more prized and insecurity concomitantly increased, so that, 'through the nineteenth century there runs the thread of anxiety that man may not be a man, that his relation to the world may cease to be a human one'. Long before Erich Fromm, Matthew Arnold was writing that 'culture is not a having but a being and a becoming', and Oscar Wilde that 'the true perfection of man lies not in what man has but what man is', in accord with Karl Marx's 'the less you *are* ... the more you *have*'. Allied to the Having/Being dichotomy was a fear that machines were dehumanising us. Subsequently, with the likes of Hegel, Nietzsche, Sartre, Foucault and their successors, came the logical intellectual conclusions: nihilism and postmodernist relativism.

Trilling comments, as Terence or I might have done, that 'this breaking up of everything ... is anything but a happy activity'. He summarises his view of modern life as characterised by 'the ever more powerful existence of the *public*, that human entity which is defined by its urban habitat, its multitudinousness, and its ready accessibility to opinion. The individual who lives in this new circumstance is subject to constant influence, the literal *in-flowing*, of the mental processes of others, which, in the degree that they stimulate or enlarge his consciousness, make it less his own.' It is easy to see the truth of this observation if you contrast what influences you with what influenced the average rural English citizen in the fifteenth century. Country-dwellers only ever met a few hundred people in their whole life, many of them related by blood or marriage, and rarely travelled more than a few tens of miles from their birthplace. Their knowledge of the wider world or the people therein was minimal. By contrast, the modern child is exposed via the mass media, books and teachers to a huge diversity of influences. Through the media you come to feel that you 'know' a vast number of people whom you have never met. It occasionally horrifies me that large chunks of my brain are devoted to storing so many details of so many people who are far removed from my actual social and professional circles, from soccer players to politicians to thinkers. Whilst some pleasures and benefits accrue from this, it seems inevitable that it will entail a dilution of my self, and that being exposed to so many alternatives to what I am will increase my uncertainty of who that is and should be. As Trilling puts it, the modern person 'finds it ever more difficult to know what his own self is and what being true to it consists in ... knows how to live only in the opinion of others, and it is, so to speak, from their judgement alone that he draws the sentiment of his being'. This seems a good description of Gus in his New York predicament, required by modern culture to be both a seeker of personal integrity, independent of his social context, while at the same time worrying himself sick about accumulating markers of status (jobs, money) relative to his peers.

Trilling's formal social-science analysis of the causes of the difficulties experienced by people such as Gus combines elements of Freud with Emile Durkheim and Marx. Durkheim's monograph *The Division of Labour in Society* demonstrated how the shift from traditional rural society to the urban, specialised form we take for granted today creates anomie (rootless emptiness). Marx showed how becoming a unit of labour that can be bought and sold by employers fosters 'alienation'. Freud left us not so much in permanent conflict with society as with ourselves, in a terminal state of tension between life and death instincts. An Affluenza analysis accepts most of this but updates it in the light of changes in the last thirty-five years: the further diminution of authenticity in English-speaking nations caused by globalisation, free-market economics and Americanised mass media. A simple example is my feelings about watching Chelsea Football Club's team.

From the age of six, at the beginning of the sixties, I lived in Chelsea and was taken by my father to watch many of the team's home games, standing at the front of the terraces with the other small boys in the Shed stand. My dad, incidentally, had little interest in football but found plenty to interest him in what he believed was unconscious letting-off of steam by the mainly working-class spectators; he was amazed at their anger towards referees and the ebullience of the chanting. This continued throughout my teens. At the risk of sounding like an advertisement for Hovis bread, I never witnessed any hooliganism, the swaying and roaring of the crowd conferred a profound sense of being part of something collective, and the eating of absolutely disgusting half-time hamburgers reinforced a tribal bonding. Whilst I daresay hardly any of the team actually hailed from Chelsea – although all were British, as were the managers – I felt it represented where I lived. Being a supporter was part of my identity.

Today's Chelsea – the place as well as the team – has been transformed by Selfish Capitalism and the mass media. Great swathes of the property in the area have been bought up by foreigners and corporations, very few of the innumerable clothes shops are owned by British companies, and the coffee shops and restaurants are awash with rich foreigners. As for the team, Roman Abramovich, its owner, was enabled by globalisation and free-market economics to remove his huge financial stake in Russian natural resources from its country of origin and convert it into international ready cash. With it he bought Chelsea FC and installed a Portuguese manager who, at astronomical expense, set about assembling a largely foreign team of players. Although it may be some time before this becomes anything like a commercially viable enterprise, Rupert Murdoch is the reason it could do so. By buying the TV rights to Premiership games, he massively increased the value of British football.

The authenticity once conferred upon me by supporting Chelsea has been greatly diluted. I no longer have any feeling that I am backing a team of players who were born in my country and represent my area. Although I do confess to a slight initial excitement at the team becoming a winning one, this has rapidly disappeared. So enormous has been the investment in the team that they hardly ever lose. Unless they play outstandingly, it gives me little pleasure when they win because winning seems inevitable. There is no escaping the knowledge that, had the market offered Abramovich a better opportunity, a different club would sit at the top of the league table. This sense of ennui is increased by the fact that I can watch all their games on television and by the feeling that there is no point in going to watch live. Following Mrs Thatcher's insistence on all-seater stadiums to get rid of hooliganism, the atmosphere at the ground is now somewhere between cold and lukewarm. It may seem a long intellectual leap from Gus's New York inauthenticity to my feeling about Chelsea FC, but both are signs of post-Trilling dilution. Someone from Gus's background in 1970 would have been much less at risk of Affluenza – and that year just happens to be the last truly significant one for Chelsea supporters, the year 'we' beat Leeds in the FA Cup Final replay. Chelsea winning that cup now would mean very little to me or my identity.

Some readers might have drawn the conclusion from the last few pages that I am advocating a return to rural, settled living, to a rigid class system and to traditional gender roles. Others, particularly modern women from low-income backgrounds, might have got the impression of three privileged men (Terence, Trilling and I) longing to return to a patriarchal order. Those are not my views at all, but I shall leave it until Chapter 12 to explain this.

Terence also highlighted another crucial respect in which the Virus erodes authenticity: the blurring of professional with personal. 'Especially when I was appearing a lot on television, I got muddled about what was work and what was play. You constantly find yourself being friends with people who are also vital to your career, and there is a risk you lose track of whether the friendship is essentially instrumental – a way of advancing your aspirations – or actually about intimacy and having fun with someone, including your love-life. You try not to think about those things because you despise people like that and rail against them, but they still bug me.' Virus infection increases the risk of seeing others as pawns. The Virus-infected agree with statements such as 'If a friend can't help me to get ahead in life, I usually end the friendship.' In the workplace, the worst infected are cynical, distrustful, self-centred and manipulative. They avoid telling people why they have done something, unless it is to their advantage, and perceive others as lazy and deceptive – anyone who completely trusts them is seen as asking for trouble – and feel that lying is acceptable, and chamaeleonism (which is neither sincere nor authentic) is desirable. Such cold-hearted exploitation in the workplace inevitably trickles into personal relationships, resulting in unhappy love-lives and fickle friendships, skin-deep. This lack of intimacy creates loneliness, but worst of all it removes a critical frame of reference for seeking authenticity (Jane Austen's 'intelligent love'). Since 40 per cent of Britons now meet their spouse through work, the grey area between home and work is becoming ever greyer.

Cyril, the Australian millionaire mentioned in Chapter 6, illustrated these problems from both sides of the authenticity fence. For a while he had been a billionaire, and that had corrupted all his relationships. He was surprised to find that, on becoming so rich, he was instantly invited to join The Club, and he started hanging out with other billionaires. 'I was working ridiculous hours, charging around the world on a white horse. It was very strange: wherever I went, the other very rich folk all invited me round. I would go to their islands or sit about in incredibly elite hotels and restaurants, as if we were part of some very special brotherhood.' He began to attend The Club's charity dos, but 'my wife was increasingly unhappy: the richer we became, the unhappier she was. She felt all the charity stuff was terribly false, whereas I was dazzled by it.' When there was a sudden change in world markets which slashed his billion down to a matter of millions, his wife breathed a sigh of relief, but Cyril was bruised. 'I was distressed by the loss. I simply had started to believe all the rubbish that was written about me in the press, to imagine that my membership of The Club really did confer an important difference.' Sure enough, within a very short time of the collapse of his empire, he was voted out. So-called friends suddenly ceased to return his calls; he was no longer invited to the charity dos. As his wife began to feel better, he managed to avoid deep depression but his attitude to friend-ship changed. 'I had begun to muddle up real friendship with relationships that were purely dictated by work or my wealth. If anything, now, it has made me probably too suspicious of people.' All his relationships had been perverted, even with casual acquaintances. On one occasion, when he took his clothes to the dry cleaners, the man there started plugging him in detail about how much money was left. It was not that the man feared Cyril would be unable to pay the bill, it was that he had a voyeuristic desire to find out whether he was down to his last twenty million, rather than his last forty.

These reflections on friendship may be an indicator of the

Americanisation of Sydney. Studies of American patterns of life between 1974 and 1992 found a decrease in visits to neighbours and to parents, and an increase in visits to friends and of the number of friends that people said they had. However, these friendships seemed to lack the intimacy of family relationships. They often had manipulative, instrumental elements, with friends and lovers frequently doubling as colleagues. Close intimates amongst these friendships were few. In America, authentic concern with others' feelings, and moral principles governing the relationships, are less common in friendships than in family relationships, compared with other countries. In Asian nations and amongst mainland Europeans there is a tendency to have fewer friends but greater intimacy with them. The development of American patterns in Australia would be in accord with Cyril's experience of manipulative, status-based, materialistic friendships.

On my travels, authenticity seemed most evident – and least confused with sincerity – in New Zealand, Denmark and Russia. New York and Australia were bursting with sincerity but the very concept of authenticity seemed alien, except as a device for manipulation. In Singapore and China it was harder to evaluate what was happening because the cultures actively encourage Face and are strongly informed by the dangers of losing it. There was also the legacy of totalitarian politics in those nations, which must have ingrained the habit of caution in making private thoughts public. Allowing for these factors, my impression was that the Singaporeans are, to a large extent, cowered into not contemplating their inner lives and that the issue of authenticity therefore simply does not arise.

As described in Chapter 3, although for different reasons (e.g. Confucianism), the Chinese seem similarly reluctant to intro-spect, except for pragmatic purposes of improving their performance through self-criticism. It seemed to me unlikely that many Chinese are concerned to audit their sincerity with the ferocity we now take for granted, although some contem-porary Chinese fiction does so. Several of the Shanghai Gals who had experienced Western education showed signs of searching for clues from nature, history, and so forth, against which to evaluate authenticity; one of them was so appalled by the modern world that she was reluctant to bring a child into it. However, that these Gals also lambasted their peers' lack of concern with authenticity is a strong indication of its widespread unimportance there. The same cannot be said of vivacity, with which they were brimming.

Vivacity versus hyperactivity

Vivacity is feeling alive, being able to savour the here and now, having an active, buoyant mind. Despite their apparent lack of concern with authenticity and widespread infection with the Virus, the Chinese seemed the most vivacious of all. Vivacity is not to be confused with hyperactivity, compulsive Doing, nor with flirty extroversion. In women, vivaciousness is often used to connote a lively sexual persona, a bouncy 'hello boys' vitality, but this is not what I mean. I am referring to an inter-nal state rather than how others perceive you. Infused with excitement at their new freedoms, the Chinese were buzzing with ideas about their world and their nation's place in the wider one, although their cultural pragmatism kept them firmly anchored in the here and now. By contrast, the

Singaporeans seemed the least vivacious, although I did meet one who was hyperactive, which could be conflated with it.

Cherry is a slim woman of Malaysian origin in her late thirties who in her early twenties converted to Roman Catholicism. Rather incongruously, her hair is dyed blonde. She was garrulous and laughed a lot in cackling, hysterical sten-gun bursts which she sprayed at me regardless of whether what she had said was intended to be humorous. Her emotional palate seemed restricted to the positive, whether she was talking about dark or light matters. There were no shades of emotional difference, nothing in how she spoke that reflected her true feelings or the subject matter. She was quick-witted, clever and moderately skilled at manipulation, a Marketing Character in many (although not all) respects. (A psychiatrist might want to debate whether she was suffering from subclinical bipolar disorder or adult hyperactivity; I would say that she had developed a manic psychological defence against having true feelings.)

In the early 1990s, Cherry was working as an estate agent when she was headhunted by a man who was investing in the Sydney property market. In effect, she won the lottery. Perhaps spotting the commercial potential of her mania at their first meeting, her new boss suggested that she become his marketing manager, and off they went to Australia. As it turned out, he had shown considerable foresight, and within a couple of years the company was thriving and worth millions. Since the boss had partly motivated her with share options when he sold the company, she was still able to return to Singapore with quite a few million. Now she lives a frenetic life, travelling a great deal, shopping, having numerous affairs, a very busy bee who says, 'I must stay active. I go mad if I have to sit still. I get bored very easily.'

Her religious beliefs seemed to have arisen as a way of coping with a period of despair she went through in her late teens. At first it was well-nigh impossible to get her to explain what the difficulties had been because she seemed to conflate them with the world economic crisis of that time. 'In 1990 I was introduced into the Roman Catholic church, baptised by the Pope in Rome, actually. I have always believed that God led me there. Certain things happened in my life at that time. Asia was still recovering from a very bad economic crisis.' This did not seem to be a very personal event, but eventually she explained that 'my dad and my mum were having a lot of problems. My father was having affairs, very big problems, and He [God, not her father] showed me the way.' Perhaps because of the distress she felt about her parents' troubles, she is very emphatic that she will never marry or have children, but instead has affairs with married men. I could not make out how she squares encouraging husbands to cheat on their wives with her zealous religious convictions, because every time I drew her attention to any contradiction in her thinking it was greeted with a splurge of words and hails of inappropriate laughter.

She was visibly concerned to tailor her views to what she felt the listener wanted to hear. For example, she explained the 'inevitable' triumph of free-market capitalism through a biblically supported version of the selfish gene theory (one which would have given its passionately atheist author, Richard Dawkins, a seizure). 'It's hot-wired into us to want better things by God. Remember Adam and Eve? They've got everything in the garden and yet they want the tree. We will always want to fight to be better. If I was a caveman I would want a better cave than the man with the cave next door. Look at the animals you see on the BBC natural world programmes: there is always the Alpha male, everyone aspires to that position. It's ingrained in us to want to be better. I have never met a parent who wanted their child to be stupider. You're ingrained to grow, like your body is.' However, after I had questioned some of these ideas she changed her tune, perhaps realising that this customer needed a different sales pitch. 'Now I am rich I have choices: do I take the train, a taxi or do I buy a car and always want a better one? So I thought, "What's the point in buying a car, I can take taxis." Then it's "Louis Vuitton, or normal clothes?" Having the best iPod is not enough because a better one comes along. God always wanted us to know Him but we all chase for material goods, so that's it: materialism doesn't satisfy the soul, the spirit, who you really are. We can't reconcile this tension between materialism and the spirit until the day that God comes back.' Her marketing tendencies extended to the way she presented her life to herself. When treating herself as the customer, she would misrepresent whatever she was trying to sell according to what she needed to hear. By this method, she was able to persuade herself that she was happy.

Because she was so busily manipulative, I could not work out whether Cherry is distressed, but I would guess so. For most of his working life, my dad had eight patients for fifty minutes of psychoanalysis each a day, five days a week. They were not discharged until he felt they were well enough to go it alone. He used to say that the sign that a person who had come to him for a consultation needed treatment was that he found himself feeling bored (and that he knew that they were better when they were boring no longer). By that criterion, this woman would have been a suitable case for treatment. Indeed, when a person says they are often bored, or if you find them boring, these are not bad as rule-of-thumb guides to distinguishing the vivacious from the hyperactive person.

In this connection, Erich Fromm made some interesting observations about the Virus-infected which are directly applicable to Cherry. 'If one asks these people … whether they feel unhappy and bored they answer, "Not at all, we're completely happy. We go on trips, we drink, we eat, we buy more and more for ourselves. You aren't bored doing that!" … in fact, the anxious, bored alienated person compensates for his anxiety [and depression] by a compulsive consumption.' Fromm takes this further, suggesting that the Virus actually promotes 'emotional necrophilia' – a tendency to feast on the deadness of others and a lifeless culture. Modern machines save time, but for the modern man, argues Fromm, 'after he has saved time, then he does not know what to do with it. Then he is embarrassed and tries to kill this saved time in a respectable way. To a large extent our entertainment industry, our parties and leisure activities are nothing but an attempt to do away with the boredom of waiting in a respectable manner … necrophilia … is the state of being attracted to that which is dead.' People who live to Have become emotionally necrophile, the exact opposite of the vivacious, who savour emotional life.

As it happens, although Singapore might be described as a city of the living dead, it was there that I met a rare example of someone with the full house of authenticity, vivacity and playfulness. Shiv is a delightful and energetic fifty-three-year-old multi-millionaire Liverpool supporter and proprietor of his own Singapore soccer team. Amazingly for an entrepreneur, he is neither a raving narcissist nor a tyrant. Raised in India, he was the son of an inventive farmer who sold chickens and eggs to the British army. 'Father was always experimenting, trying out different breeds so his flock produced a higher egg yield. One time his whole flock was wiped out by disease. The way he built that up again showed me how to deal with things – just start again, don't moan, work hard.' His dad was successful enough to pay for both his son and daughter to go to university in Britain, and Shiv sounded as though he'd had a cracking good time at Liverpool studying law. Afterwards, he spent another seven years working in British firms, where he met his wife, a Singaporean. They moved back home, and he managed to persuade a colleague to back a company which he set up to provide law courses. 'Here, net worth is very important – and I didn't have any. I said to myself, "Either you stay in this firm or you set up a business and be richer." I had no money in my pocket.' There followed the toughest time of his life. For several years he teetered on the brink of bankruptcy, working seven days a week. Unimpressed by his lack of instant success, his wife left him. 'The family pressures were too strong. In a different environment it could have worked. Her family were pressurising her, saying "There's no money in this man" – they were well off – "Why are you with this hopeless man?"'

Whereas Cherry went on smiling and letting out inappropriate, inauthentic cackles of forced laughter while she was talking about her bad times, Shiv appeared to be authentically upset at having to recall this. He looked down into his beer, his face creased with pain. 'That was the lowest part of my life. I remember those days, several months when I could not think how I could put it back together, talking with her to try and make it work. They [his wife's family] sent messages to my home town in India saying I was no good, but my family stuck up for me. Ten minutes in the mosque each morning was crucial. You need that, that's what saw me through.' Shiv used religion as a solace in difficult times, as did Cherry, but the difference was that he did not employ it as a magical device to solve his problems. There were no spells cast to get his wife to come back: it was about dealing with the feelings of depression which, also unlike Cherry, he was visibly able to acknowledge.

His wife's family must be kicking themselves today because Shiv is now the owner of a huge international company. Like virtually every entrepreneur I have interviewed, he claims that wealth is not important. 'I always put my wages up in proportion to my employees. It's not about money.' In his case, I think this is true. He remarried and has adopted children of whom he speaks with real affection, able to describe details of their lives that suggest to me that he is actively involved in their upbringing. He does not seem to be motivated by conspicuous consumption. His clothing looks like that of any middle-class Liverpool supporter, while his car is a bog-standard Toyota. Rather than the Virus-infected person's concern with having money to seem important or to buy things to indicate status, he spoke with passion of trying to create offices where the employees can have a good time, and he seems genuinely excited by the education and training which his business purveys. He loves making educational presentations himself and believes that he is helping people by providing them with the chance to learn professions. He is not a managerial control freak, having trained up others to do many of the key executive roles and truly delegating power to them. But the most convincing indicator that money is not his lodestar was his enjoyment of helping the Muslim community in Singapore.

'After my divorce,' Shiv told me, 'I realised I knew hardly anyone here, had not connected with my people. So I made a point of doing community work. I was a founding member of an organisation that helps Muslims here. That, to me, was very rewarding, it helped me. You earn money, you give it back, but you've got to contribute time as well as money.' Although he has set himself the goal of owning a billion-dollar company, he does not seem obsessed by it. He works only forty to fifty hours a week and intends to start cutting down, passing the management over to younger people and spending more time on his community work. In short, he seemed a clear-cut case of a millionaire with some Virus goals (like becoming a billionaire) originally activated by survival materialism, but intrinsic motives, such as helping his community. His comment on Affluenza in Singapore was simple and to the point. 'In the village where I came from, our basic needs were lower. We survived on one dollar for a month if necessary. When the economy develops, the people's aspirations get higher, even at the lowest level. There's TV, keeping up with the Jameses [er, Joneses], but in my father's day the aspirations were much lower. Here, today, you feel deprived if you do not have air conditioning.'

He kept coming back to the example of his father in explaining how he had managed to achieve so much, and I found myself coming back to mine. Ultimately, as my dad would have said, proof that this man was not bullshitting me with a load of blarney about people being more important than money and so forth, was that he was just not boring. I came away from our meeting feeling really stimulated, cheerful and optimistic.

This was true of the handful of other people I met around the world who held the full house of desirable Being (authenticity, vivacity, playfulness). What they also nearly all had in common was that they had suffered pretty severe adversities. Whether it was Chet, the vibrant New York taxi driver wrestling with emigration and diabetes (described in Chapter 1), Ross, the New Zealander whose wife had gone off with his best friend (Chapter 4), Lizzie, the New Zealander with life-threatening illnesses, or Shiv – all had been driven by extreme circumstances to re-evaluate their lives and develop more intrinsic values. The only exception was Tøger Seidenfaden, the Danish newspaper editor. Of course, for every person who responds to adversity in this way, I would guess that there are ten thousand who succumb to lifelong subsequent bitterness and despair. Nonetheless, they do prove that it can be done (I shall return to this in the next chapter).

On my mind tour, despite the authenticity of the Danes and the New Zealanders, vivacity did not seem much in evidence amongst them. In Singapore, Australia and New York, hyperactivity usually impersonated vivacity. The Russians also lacked vivacity, although not giving much evidence of hyperactivity either. Perhaps they have been ground down by their recent political and economic history, but perhaps it is also because of a distinctly melancholic note sounding throughout their cultural history, a melancholia that seemed to predispose them to a passive acceptance of destiny.

During the Soviet era it was essential to develop a very sharp demarcation between behaviour and experience, between thought and action. Only by presenting oneself as a good Party worker and showing considerable commitment to rapidly shifting socio-political goals could one stay alive, physically. Obviously the same was true in (now vivacious) China, but it is important to stress that the Russian tradition of outward adherence to official reality and keeping one's personal life to oneself, and of ineffectual paralysis, goes back much further than the Soviets. Pushkin's Eugene Onegin and Lermontov's Petchorin (from *A Hero of Our Time*) are prime examples of the powerless 'lost personality' who frequents nineteenth-century Russian literature. As with Tolstoy (Ivan Ilyich) and Dostoevsky (*The Idiot*), these characters experienced profound thoughts, tremendously intense passions and ideals, yet are utterly passive. Often, they cannot convert their thoughts or their will into effective action, unable to carry out their well-meaning spiritual or social intentions, paralysed by depression or over-complexity. These considerations may also help to explain the preoccupation with authenticity that I encountered in the Russians, but a big surprise was the tremendous playfulness that ran alongside it, more so than in any of the other nations, apart perhaps from England.

Playfulness versus game-playing

To a considerable extent, playfulness is what makes life worth living. In English-speaking workplaces, there has been a strong tendency to prohibit it or to exploit it through faux 'fun', like that satirised in Ricky Gervais's *The Office*. The modern office also provides abundant opportunity for charlatans, charmers, machiavels and Marketing Characters to employ playfulness as a method for self-advancement. Such game-playing perverts a fundamental human need, but fortunately, this perversion is not global.

Everywhere you go in Moscow you encounter a humorous undercurrent, often coloured by a black dye. During the Soviet era the populace would cheer themselves up with jokes about the grotesque actions of their leaders, and today the people still gain considerable amusement from the outrages perpetrated in their name by President Putin. They talk about them with a long-suffering, dry sarcasm.

Serena is a woman in her fifties who, although a direct descendant of the Romanovs, the Russian former royal family, is still a passionate believer in Communism. She is certainly earnest, severe and venomous in her criticisms of modern Russia, but for much of the time she spoke in a humorous, playful way. She railed against the impact of the financial 'shock therapy' in the early 1990s ('Shock therapy? Shock murder, more like!') but with a rueful smile never far from her lips. 'How many times did we suffer an economic depression under the Soviets after 1953? None at all. We had calamities before that, but during my life there had been none. Then, in the 1990s, we lived through the equivalent of the United States' Great Depression – twice. All the savings of the whole nation were wiped out overnight, twice. You try going home now, going to bed and waking up to find you have no money whatsoever. Try to imagine that.' With bleak chuckles, she told me about the privatised electricity supply: 'On the news only yesterday there was a report that a whole city had been disconnected and their sewers now don't work, so doctors have to distribute pills against typhoid. How can they do that? Where's our government?' You could not help being reminded of Michael Moore: 'Dude, where's my country?'

Of course, Americans also have a strong tradition of jokes about their ruling elite, nowadays whizzed around by email. All too often, the telling of these jokes is done competitively, with the hidden objective that the cleverness of the joke will raise the status of the sender. In the case of Michael Moore, for example, his narcissism is legendary amongst friends of mine who were involved in his British TV series. Although the funniest situation comedies are often now American, there is rarely anything more significant to them than the exploitation of our enjoyment of humour to make the producers, authors and actors rich and famous (*The Simpsons* being the honourable satirical exception). In Russia, the point of the sardonic bleakness is not 'look how clever I am', so much as 'what a bunch of shits we have running our country'.

Although various attempts have been made to elevate playfulness in the pecking order of Western Culture's desirable character traits, none have been successful. Writing at the end of the eighteenth century, the poet Schiller stressed its importance as an antidote to the earnestness of duty and destiny, and went as far as to offer it up as man's truest being:

'Man only plays when he is in the fullest sense of the word a human being, and he is only fully a human being when he plays.' Unfortunately, he has gone unheeded.

The best way to understand the value of playfulness to adults is by examining its purpose amongst children. In their fantasy play, they use imagination to convert the seemingly mundane into the magical, enthralling and amusing. For example, yesterday our daughter corralled four teddies into a game as pupils, with her and me as the teachers. Two teddies were singled out as having been naughty and deserving a smacking (corporal punishment, I hasten to add, has played no part in her nurture, so I don't know where this idea comes from). These miscreants have devised the idea of putting books down their trousers to prevent pain. However, our daughter has spotted their ruse. They are now to be subjected to a fantastical 'smacking machine'. Using sticks, she makes circular movements on the wall to start the machine, then smacks (more like batters to death) the naughty children with a coal spade. I let out shrill squeals of pain on their behalf to indicate that this is getting a bit bloodthirsty, but she says, 'Don't worry, it's only pretend, dada,' speaking as if I must be very thick to have failed to grasp this basic point. The game is repeated, as necessary, until our daughter decides that it's time to set fire to the bears. She rubs the sticks together 'like how fire was in olden days', gets me to imitate her, then we poke the bears with the burning sticks, setting fire to them. Again I shriek on their behalf, again our daughter reassures me that it's only pretend, repeating this several times as if to reassure herself as well as me. Now she employs magic to set the sticks alight, banging a drumstick on a plastic toy and casting a spell with the words 'abracadabra-fire-comes-*now*'. More burning ensues, more reassurance from her that it's only pretend, and finally it's time for bed.

Perhaps I shall pay a heavy price for regaling you with this story. When our adult daughter comes up in court charged with arson and torture, you will be able to testify against me for having encouraged her. However, the likely consequences or meaning of this play are a matter of debate, for, as our daughter was at some pains to point out, she was only pretending. Some psychoanalysts interpret such play as a method for exorcising anxieties and forbidden impulses, of enacting them harmlessly, and to my mind there is little doubt that it can serve this purpose. For example, when our daughter was aged two years and eight months, my wife, heavily pregnant with our son, went off for a hard-earned ten-day residential yoga retreat. At that age, her mother's disappearance was not too great a problem for our daughter, but she used a fantasy to express the degree of annoyance she did feel about it. On the second morning after my wife had left, we set off to visit my sister, and as we passed over a speed-bump she began talking about a hole in the road and the need for me to call Mr Builder to repair it – 'You call Mr Builder on your teffone.' Having got Mr Builder to the hole, she said, 'Mama's in the gweat big hole and she's covered in mud. What happens now?' I suggested that Mr B would get her out, but that particular plot development was disallowed, so that mama was left there in a 'serves her jolly well right' sort of way. The story of the gweat big hole was returned to again and again over the next few days. Thankfully, as her anger towards mama decreased, mama was allowed to be rescued.

Indeed, it was our daughter, rather than Mr Builder, who eventually came to the rescue. (Subsequently it was Bear-Bear who was in the hole; for much of that time, Bear-Bear was her baby rather than her solace, being cradled and put in a toy pushchair. She was very aware of her forthcoming sibling, wanting to watch the episode of Pingu the penguin in which his younger sister is born out of an egg, over and over again.) You do not have to be Sigmund Freud to see that our daughter's chucking of her mama into the hole was a way of expressing rage towards her, and there can be little doubt that some portion of the fantasies children enjoy are serving a similar sort of purpose.

Some psychoanalysts take this further, connecting children's play with art and artists. The adult artist's working life is portrayed as an attempt to deal with anxiety or suppressed wishes, and the resultant art as technically indistinguishable from neurotic symptoms. Just as some people develop a fear of cars or an obsession with dirt, an artist may deal with the underlying feelings that these symptoms symbolise by painting pictures of cars or of clean rooms. Although this theory is not completely unfounded, it does leave a great deal out. The English psychoanalyst Donald Winnicott (along with Schiller) regarded both art and play primarily as sources of joy in our lives, a way of Being with its own justification, more than a container for anxieties, and distinct from dreams and neurotic symptoms. In this view, an adult may infuse their work or leisure time with playfulness simply in order to make it fun, not just for catharsis. Winnicott's non-cathartic play has no goals beyond this: it is designed neither to achieve any practical end nor to express suppressed conflict. Rather, it is a temporary exit from normal reality into the world of imagination, with all the freedom that brings from social convention and the laws of physics and chemistry, a place where pigs can fly. I can enter a transitional mental space, expressing both myself and what is out there, a place that is neither me nor not-me, where I am neither seeking to impose myself on the world nor aping its dictates.

A primitive, childish example of playfulness is the full-throated laughter that comes from our daughter if I subvert an expectation. When I sing 'Twinkle, Twinkle Little Star', she finds it hilarious if I begin the next verse 'Baa-Baa Black Sheep'. Obviously, children and most artists are cut a great deal more imaginative slack than adults with conventional occupations, but it is only a matter of degree. Playfulness is possible in the execution of all social roles, be they professional or otherwise. Putting on funny voices, making odd facial expressions and gestures, or using strange ideas or forms of words – all of these can and are employed in playfulness in even the most serious of contexts, including during births, weddings and funerals. Whether cathartic or not, what distinguishes this as play, as opposed to manipulation or game-playing or being charming or entertaining to further your interests, is that it has no self-aggrandizing goal, nor is it an attempt to control the outside world. This distinction is subtle. If you imitate another person's dialect or eccentric use of language when talking about them to a mutual friend, it may seem playful to a stranger who happens to overhear it. But without knowing the precise details of your motives it would be impossible to tell, because motive is all. In the Marketing Society, politicians and business people frequently impersonate both playfulness and authenticity in order to convince. Exploitation of play is rife, whether in advertising products, closing deals, seducing sexual partners or marketing one's self. Disentangling the real from the false can be difficult, and is made ever more so by the immense complexity of modern culture and its history.

In Britain at the end of the nineteenth century, there was a wave of revulsion by some artists and thinkers in response to the moral and social earnestness of Victorian society. Oscar Wilde was the greatest exponent of pretence, both as an antidote to being 'proper' and as a paradoxical route to authenticity. 'The first duty in life is to be as artificial as possible. What the second duty is no one has yet discovered,' he famously wrote. Even more explicitly, he penned the epigram 'Man is least himself when he talks in his own person. Give him a mask and he will tell you the truth.' With reference to art, he wrote that 'all bad poetry springs from genuine feeling'. This amusing love of not taking anything too seriously became a lynchpin of upper-class English culture, enshrined in the characters of P.G. Wodehouse and more contemporaneously evident in the life and work of Stephen Fry. Fry has commented that 'Oscar Wilde teaches one to take the serious things in life trivially and the trivial things seriously. That's ultimately my attitude.' During a TV interview in 1988 he told me that 'A fiction is the best way to be true' and, at least at that time, he rarely if ever stopped assuming personae, paradoxically feeling most real when pretending to be someone else. That may have been what lay behind his confession to me that his greatest fear is 'being found out – most men live in fear of a nameless "being found out"'.

In fact, most men feel nothing of the sort. There is a world of difference between our daughter acting the role of Peppa the Pig and Fry's kind of imposture. Whereas it is true that all of us probably sometimes feel more real through fictions of one sort or another, that is not our main source of authenticity. I can recall shedding tears at the end of the film *Casablanca*, because I had recently broken up with a girlfriend and was upset at the thought of a relationship ending. The fiction briefly gave me access to my true feelings, but that is not the same as living most of my life as if I am someone else. The actual relationship with the real girlfriend lasted rather longer than the film and my subsequent tears. Through social roles, certainly, as well as through consuming or creating art, we can play and achieve authenticity, but we can be manipulative, deadened and deadening in these roles as well. Having sat through dozens of best man's and bridegroom's speeches, I have noted the authentic ingenuity of play in some, and the inauthentic emptiness of over-contrived, uncomfortably self-referential artifice in others.

The second-hand living that afflicted Stephen Fry is fuelled, particularly in America and England, by an addiction to irony: saying one thing when another is meant in order to establish a disconnection between the speaker and his listener, or between the speaker and that which is being spoken about, or even between the speaker and himself. This particular species of second-hand living is not restricted to a highly educated elite of the literary-minded: it is found widely in the upper echelons of British society, such as merchant banks or commercial law firms, where irony is used as a method for putting people down in office politics or as a device for being charming during financial negotiations rather than to achieve entertaining or artistic ends. Unfortunately, it is not only the elites who suffer second-hand living: less complex forms are widespread.

Studies show that the mental state we enter whilst watching TV is a passive, floating, vicarious consciousness. The emotional and sometimes visible animation of a person attending live theatre or ballet or opera, or when watching a deeply moving film, or when reading a great novel, are very rarely present. Occasionally television does achieve this effect in viewers. During exceptional sporting events, such as the 2005 Ashes cricket matches, it can happen. It can too at high points in soap operas, as in the programme with the highest-ever TV audience in Britain, the powerful episode of *EastEnders* in which Den announced that he was leaving Angie, and she trumped him by claiming to have cancer. The doublethink-named reality TV shows (which are nothing of the kind because they are heavily edited: even when broadcast live there is a lot of editing in choice of camera shots and actual censorship of what the participants say) very occasionally achieve the same, such as Nasty Nick's exposure as a machiavel in the first series of *Big Brother*. But for the vast majority of the time, watching TV is a form of dead, second-hand living.

Increasingly, to save money, broadcasters are exploiting the greater availability of cheap video cameras to bring together our lumpen need for low-grade TV with our desire to record our lives rather than simply live them. Viewer-as-programme-material is found not just on shows compiled from clips of 'hilarious' misfortunes (increasingly contrived to get them onto the small screen) – dogs falling into swimming pools and dads banging their heads on sharp edges – there is also greater use of it in documentaries, with contributors asked to keep video diaries of their experiences. As we find ourselves scrabbling to switch on the digital camera or mobile phone in time to catch our child's first steps, the authentic experience is increasingly supplanted by the need to make a record of it. Worst of all, the activities we record are increasingly modified by us and our children to correspond to a desired end. Never mind 'say cheese', our children are becoming alert at ever younger ages to the need to perform for the camera. The urge to use home footage to gain fifteen seconds of fame on TV is rampant amongst young people in England and America, millions of whom have now prepared brief videos of themselves to send to TV companies as applications for a shot at fame in a reality TV show.

Significant numbers dream of being famous, of having others fantasising about them. In England, 16 per cent of sixteen- to nineteen-year-olds truly believe that they will become famous, and 11 per cent would abandon their education for a stab at fame on a reality TV show, even though the victors of such contests seldom remain in the public eye. Young people's fascination with the famous has mushroomed. A substantial number of English and American studies in the last five years suggest that about three-quarters of young people report having had a strong attraction to a celebrity at some stage in their life. In itself, this is a form of virtual relationship, of second-hand living, a fantasy relationship with a stranger. For 7 per cent of eighteen- to forty- seven-year-olds, the relationship becomes obsessive and worshipful. People with such attachments to celebrities are also prone to emotional distress.

Adolescents with weak attachment to parents, or who are exceptionally reliant on peers for their sense of status and well-being, are at greater risk of becoming obsessive.

Conclusion

Rousseau's Noble Savage never existed in reality, but we are a very great distance from that less idealised marker of authenticity, the baby we started life as. Our son, fourteen months old as I write, has no capacity for artifice and cunning, but that will not last long. By the time our daughter was thirty-three months old she already had a great many tricks up her sleeve for duping her indulgent and soft-headed father. One evening, offered the prospect of a bath with the inducement that she could pour the bubble mixture in, she appeared very enthusiastic. But when the time came, since we were playing a very important game of 'swimming' in the sitting room, she refused to go. After the fourth attempt at persuasion, I reminded her that she could put the bubbles in herself. She paused and then said, 'I don't want no bubbles,' having worked out that I was attempting a bribe.

Developing the skill of misrepresenting yourself to others, up to and including bare-faced lies, has surely occurred every-where and at all times. Nor is this problem of falsehood a new one. 'Born Originals, how comes it to pass that we die Copies?' wrote the poet Edward Young two and a half centuries ago, and it is a truism to assert that we have to develop façades for dealing with one another, ways to sepa-rate our true thoughts and feelings from what we say and do. Nonetheless, these gaps are now greater and exist for a higher proportion of us and to a greater extent than at any previous time in history. They were widened after the sixteenth century in England by urbanisation, industrialisation, individualism and social isolation, and further extended by technology, especially after 1945. But since the late 1970s, in the English-speaking world, Selfish Capitalism and the Virus have stretched the gaps into canyons.

Vaccines

1. Don't wait for a disaster before getting real

There is all too great a risk that the unreality in which most of us live for too much of the time may become visible to us only when we know we don't have much longer to live. A good start, therefore, is to picture that very situation: imagine that you have a fatal illness and are reviewing your life from that standpoint. As the saying goes, 'No-one lies on their deathbed cursing the fact that they did not spend more time at work.' Much more likely is that, if you do this mental exercise, and if you are a parent, you will wish that you had spent more time with your children when they were small. In seeking greater authenticity, the clichés come true: less materially prosperous people, the sick, the disenfranchised all have things to teach us, but less miserably, so does the commonplace. There are people and sights to savour everywhere, so seek the humour and drama in the lives of the people around you, on buses and trains. If your appreciation of nature is blunted, do something about it, and likewise if your enjoyment of the arts needs enhancing. Our material affluence and the social contrivances adopted to achieve it must be resisted in favour of real needs and authentic Being.

2. Scale down your interest in people you have never met

Regular readers of *Hello* magazine should ask themselves seriously how much of a laugh it really is – and so should regular newspaper readers. Even the 'quality' papers devote a great many column inches to people who simply do not matter to you and yours. Do you really need to read one? If you do, could you not restrict yourself to a weekly digest of the news? With television, use modern technology to be very judicious about what you watch – record, don't graze live. It does not matter what book you read: reading rather than watching the box before you go to sleep nearly always leaves you feeling more satisfied when you turn out the light.

3. Develop habits that prevent hyperactivity

People today sleep for an average of two hours less than our forebears and pay a heavy price. You need to be highly organised about getting a good night's kip, like a pilot preparing for touchdown. Get the row with the spouse out of the way over supper, resist the urge to chase up that business colleague on the phone, hunker down in bed with a good book well before you switch off the light, and make sure you get the full eight hours, at least. Yoga, transcendental meditation, exercise, masturbation, it does not matter what – the important thing is to find some activity that relaxes your body.

4. Be honest with yourself about your dealings with others

If Jane Austen were alive today, who knows, she might have published a bestselling pop psychology book entitled *Intelligent Love*. Ultimately, you only need a few intimates, people to whom you can tell the truth about yourself and who will listen if you are concerned about them. It would do no harm to sit down with a piece of paper and list the people you would regard as close friends (for most men, this will be a short list). A good criterion would be whether they would be supportive if you were having a major crisis. Most important of all, try dividing them into close friends, friend-professional connection, professional. An alarming number will fall into the middle category. You need to be more honest with yourself about how emotionally close you really are to these people, or whether you just use them or are used by them in your career.

5. Play with small children

No other single activity is more likely to induce authenticity – theirs rubs off on you – but also, it increases your playfulness. We are shackled by worries, many connected with money. We are bogged down in rage, boredom, exhaustion and falsehood. Playing with children is the perfect antidote. If you are childless, or yours have grown up, play with those of friends or relatives or join a parenting support organisation, like Home-Start, who will put you in touch with an unlimited supply of parents desperate for someone to entertain their children. When you are with adults, if you stop seeing them as fellow consumer durables, you will find that a space opens up. Fill it with play.

Part Three
Wakey Wakey!

Warning for readers of Part Three

Those of a delicate disposition and with a refined sensibility may find some parts of what follows shocking, because now the gloves come off. Having attempted so far to adopt a position of relative impartiality (except when presenting the vaccines at the end of each chapter), in Part Three I allow myself to tell you what I really think. I make no apology if I come across as a particularly bigoted and offensive taxi driver, for that is what we are like when we reveal our true convictions. So here is a blunt, unsparing statement of what needs to change, personally for you and politically for all of us.

Chapter 11

Personal Implications:
Prepare to Feel Better

Some time ago, my wife and I were agonising over whether to increase our mortgage in order to build an extension. There were many other changes we wanted to make to the inside of the house, having done virtually nothing to it since moving in. One day, pretty much out of the blue, the answer came to my wife: do nothing. We had a house that was easily large enough for our needs. Whilst some of it was seriously run down (grotty-looking kitchen, dreary carpets), the truth was that we should be bloody glad to have a house at all. There were all sorts of things we wanted to do, but we *needed* to do none of them, apart from installing a new boiler (a real need, in the sense that we need hot water and heating during the winter).

This is not a bad metaphor for what has gone wrong. Nearly all of us want bigger and better. Not just houses, breast implants and penis extensions, better cars and tellies –

you name it, you probably want it bigger or better. In 'More Bigger Snacks Now', a mime show performed by the Complicite theatre company in the late 1980s, three men are in a sitting room. One of them gets out a pack of cigarettes and offers them round. The man searches for a light, unsuccessfully, and the others join the hunt. They become frenzied, turning the place upside down. At last a matchbox is found ... but it's empty. The frenzy is rejoined until another box is tracked down and, with exaggerated glee, they finally settle down for a smoke. Before long another hunger develops amongst them, and similar frustrations of consumption are played out, satirising our insatiable desire for ever better, ever more, provoked by one another.

An important personal implication of this book is that, whenever you are thinking of spending money, small amount or large, ask yourself 'Do I need this – or do I *want* it?' As a rule of thumb, this works equally well for housing extensions, hair extensions or buying a packet of Maltesers, although, of course, the distinction between needs and wants is not black and white. In the matter of Maltesers, one that arises more frequently in my case than I would care to admit, a strict application of the rule would require asking myself, 'Do I actually need the nutritional and calorific intake of this product?' Put like that, on the vast majority of occasions the honest answer will be 'No'. The one-quarter of British children and one-fifth of our adults who are clinically obese most definitely do not need it, and in fact most of us are lugging around rather more flesh than is necessary: we live in one of the parts of the globe where excess food killing us is the problem, not the lack of it. However, posing the question in that coldly analytical form does not do justice to the complexities of the predicament. The grey appears when you get to thinking, 'No, of course I don't need the choccies to avoid starvation, but I've been looking after my fractious toddler for four hours/working all day/just had a row with a friend, and I do need something to cheer me up, however transiently.' The cold rationalist will retort that you would do much better to remove the cause of your cheer-lessness by altering the structure of your life or having therapy. But that isn't much help as your hand hovers over the confec-tionery in the garage shop before you pay for the petrol and return to the screaming nipper in the car.

Further illumination of the murk of our deliberations comes from Avner Offer, author of *The Challenge of Affluence*. He makes a persuasive case for the idea that we have become increasingly myopic about the consequences of our decisions, imprudent and less able to delay gratification. Rather than saving the money for the extension, we are more likely to borrow it. Rather than putting the Maltesers off, we expand our waistline. Rather than cope with the bad patches that most marriages usually go through, we jack it in and start again with someone new. This analysis provides a possi-ble indication of how to bring the grey area between needs and wants into sharper, black and white contrast. If you have asked yourself whether you really need something, and no clear answer emerges, try asking, 'How will this affect me if it becomes a pattern, and in the long term?' But this is still pretty idealistic and hair-shirted. For further nuances you have to dig deeper than that, down to your core values.

Some readers might have thought that the word 'success-ful' in this book's subtitle implied that it was going to offer

tips on how to get more money, possessions, desirable appearances and fame – the conventional indicators. I suppose that,
since you are still reading, you will not have been too disappointed to learn that by 'success' I meant something entirely
different. In my last book I exhorted readers to scrutinise their
early years and to use that knowledge to live more fully. In this
one, my exhortation is to examine how your society is affecting you and use that knowledge to the same end.

Beyond replacing wants with needs and short-term with
long-term, most fundamentally of all you need to replace
prize-hunting with intrinsic values, thus challenging the
status quo – something that usually feels uncomfortable. This
does not mean that you have to give up your job and become
a potter (apologies to anyone who already has), but it does
call for some important adjustments to your priorities. As I
mentioned in the Prologue, when searching for vaccines I
always bore in mind the lawyer who told me that, 'My goal
is to keep earning for thirty years, educate the kids, pay for
my daughter's wedding and then die.' The most significant
implication of this book for personal well-being is that you
need to closely scrutinise your motives and goals and, as
described in Chapter 4, shift from Virus to intrinsic wherever
possible. Easily said, but not so easily done. What actual
practical steps can you take to achieve this? Here, I offer two.

Step one: Sort out your childhood

Whether you are emotionally distressed or not (as ascertained
by the questionnaire at the start of the book), you may need
help from a professional. Just because you are not actually
chewing the carpet does not mean that you can do it all on

your own. As you will have gathered by now, we are not equally vulnerable to the Virus, and a crucial factor is how we were nurtured in early life. I estimate that, at most, only a quarter of us probably had the kind of childhood that immunises against Affluenza. The rest of us probably need help to free ourselves from the damaging values and maltreatment that most parents unwittingly impose on their children.

Talking about this to intimates and reading relevant books may do the trick on their own. But they can only take you so far. If you decide that you also need the more independent help of a therapist, the first problem is to decide which kind. You can safely rule out anyone who calls themselves a cognitive behavioural therapist because they are specifically instructed during training to discourage investigation of childhood experience. You can also rule out most people who are trained as psychiatrists – they are doctors who have done further training, primarily in the administration of drugs. Whilst increasingly many psychiatrists are now qualifying to do talking cures, they usually train in cognitive methods. This leaves what are known as 'psychodynamic psychotherapists' (see the notes at the end of the book for a list of organisations who train people in this tradition), a catch-all term that by no means indicates that they are what you are looking for. This kind of therapy entails a huge commitment of time and money, so before going down that road there are two less arduous alternatives to consider.

In the last few years I have become aware of the Hoffman process, and in making referrals I have come to favour it over the alternatives. It is the most systematic method I know for properly exploring the role of childhood as well as offering a motorway back from the past. In so doing, it will reduce your vulnerability to the Virus. Whilst many of the techniques it employs are not in themselves original, the specific combination used is original, as is the fact that therapy is conducted as an eight-day residential course. Four studies suggest that it works for the commonest ailments, such as anxiety and depression (see www.hoffmaninstitute.co.uk). I have not been through the process myself, but I do know many who have, and for some of them the experience has been far more productive than years of other therapies.

Because the Hoffman process entails cutting yourself off completely from the outside world and placing yourself at the mercy of complete strangers for over a week, it rightly provokes suspicion and scepticism. However, I can assert with absolute confidence that this is not some dodgy cult – there's no donating 10 per cent of your entire wealth to a Rolls Royce-driving Maharishi. During the first half of the course, the layers of scar tissue created by past experiences are stripped away in sessions with individual therapists and in groups of other 'students' (usually about twenty per course). Methods include visualisation, where you are asked to picture past experiences and relive them, and externalising of emotions – shouting, punching cushions, letting off steam. Students are asked to produce written accounts of their childhoods.

In the second half of the course, forgiveness of parents is encouraged by methods such as holding imaginary conversations with them. The spiritual dimension is also vital at this point. This is nothing to do with conventional religion or any hocus pocus, just reconnection with a level of existence which we all have but which modern life distances us from. The group relationships are also very important. Revealing oneself to others and hearing their stories is cathartic but also, after the course, enduring mutual support is provided through regular get-togethers, telephone and email.

The Hoffman has only been going for ten years in this country, its originator having been (inevitably) an American, Bob Hoffman. A lively self-help account of the process is *You Can Change Your Life* by Tim Laurence, the director of the British Hoffman Institute. At £1,930 the process is not cheap, but then neither is psychoanalysis or cognitive behavioural therapy, and they usually take longer than eight days.

If you cannot afford this help or it does not appeal, my next suggestion is what is known as cognitive analytic therapy (CAT). It begins with four sessions looking at how your parents cared for you that culminate in the therapist writing you a letter summarizing what you have told them. The remaining twelve sessions use this understanding to focus on a particular problem that you have chosen to tackle. I suspect that almost anyone, however well-adjusted, would benefit from this when it is done well, which, inevitably, is not always. You can find out whether there is a cognitive analytic therapist near you from the CAT website (www.acat.me.uk).

If, having tried either of these, you do not feel much wiser about your childhood, then the only remaining alternative is a psychodynamic therapist. Finding a good one is far from easy. Ideally, they would have treated an intimate of yours with similar sorts of problems and history to you, someone you are sure is better when you consider what they were like before and after. Unfortunately, this is very rarely going to happen, so you have to use word of mouth from friends and relatives, or simply take pot luck from the list of potential ones offered by training organisations.

I would recommend going to see three different therapists before signing up, and I would also suggest seeing someone of the same gender as you. Above all, in each case you should ask them this question: 'To what extent will the therapy entail asking me about my childhood and finding out ways in which my past is continuing to poison my present?' If they reply, 'That's an interesting question, I wonder why it concerns you?' or some such drivel, it's unlikely that they are appropriate. You need someone who says, 'Yes, that will be a big part of the treatment.' In particular, if they fob you off with 'We will investigate how your past is affecting you through the way you relate to me,' say, 'But what about help with directly recalling what went on in my childhood?' If they say something neutral at that point it probably means that they have no intention of exploring this much, if at all.

In making these recommendations, I would not want you to think that I reject either pills or cognitive behavioural therapy altogether – they can be useful as short-term expedients for reducing distress – but I do reject them as means of finding out about your childhood. For more detailed information about methods for dealing with distress, my earlier book *Britain on the Couch* has chapters devoted to pills and to therapy. This advice was developed in my last book, *They F*** You Up*.

Having got your childhood out of the way (not that we ever do that completely), the next step is to navigate the choppy waters of modern society.

Step two: Reject much of the status quo

English-speaking nations are designed to maximise the profits of a tiny minority of very rich people, not the citizens' well-being or, for that matter, the survival of the planet. This is crazy, and Erich Fromm was absolutely right to say that being well-adjusted to the status quo is a prescription for distress. As people get older, they tend to work this out for themselves, to a greater or lesser degree, but even then a lot of us remain considerably deceived.

It's time to get really personal in following through the practical implications. The broad generalisations with which I began this chapter apply to all; I have divided the rest of it, speaking separately to people who are parents or believe they may become one, and those who believe they will always be childless. Although Selfish Capitalism affects all of us, there are significant differences in the implications for these two categories.

Parents or potential parents

Many of the implications of how to disentangle yourself from this mess are the same for both genders. However, there are also important respects in which men and women have been differently screwed up by the system. I now offer each gender a no-holds-barred account of how to extricate yourself. In doing so, I realise that on occasions I am probably telling you more about my prejudices than what is best, but I can only give it my best shot. I have absolute faith, dear reader, that you will be quite capable of telling me to bog off in your mind when what I am suggesting sounds to you like sexist or patronising drivel.

FOR WOMEN (men should turn to page 452)

I contend that many of you have been hoodwinked by Selfish Capitalism into believing that (male) prize-hunting has something to do with female emancipation. Fair enough: if you are someone who gains intrinsic satisfaction from working long hours and being highly competitive, then go for it. But this road leads to emotional well-being in very few cases. For most, the solutions are different.

1. *Educashun* Many women now under thirty were unprecedentedly pressurised to do well at school. Too many mothers are doing the same to their daughters today. Women need to review what their education was for and what its impact has been on their capacity to identify intrinsic interests. Exam fever entails people-pleasing, and that drains away creativity. You need to face the fact that you may have left school feeling a failure. If you got poor results, you left feeling a thicko; if you did well, you probably still left feeling you should have done better. This has undermined your self-esteem and focused you on Virus prize-hunting in your subsequent career or made you feel that, just because other women are rising high in many professions, you are a lesser person. *If you can grasp the fact that modern education is largely about creating good little consumers and producers, and boxing us up ready to be sold to future employers, you can start to feel better about yourself and begin to think about what actually interests you.*

2. *Career* Having been packaged and labelled by the education system, the majority of women find themselves doing low-paid, part-time work (although women who have bought this book are less likely to fall into that category). Those who made it to university and into professional or managerial jobs are probably still reeling at the extent to which the workplace operates through networking and office politics rather than merit. Finding work that satisfies you rather than merely enabling employers to get richer is not easy. If you have chosen a vocational profession, such as teaching or medicine, it can be frustrating and entail incredibly long hours. If you are in financial services or some other high-paid support career, such as law or consultancy, the hours are even worse and your daily tasks so uncongenial that you are constantly struggling to decide whether the salary is worth the grief. The solution is to ask yourself 'What, actually, do I enjoy doing?' – and just do it. That need not mean switching to another career. *The key is to examine what it is about your work that you find truly interesting, and put that before pay and promotion in seeking positions*. You may find that you earn more by this approach, although that is not its purpose.

3. Motherhood Nothing about the modern female upbringing will have prepared you for the massive shock to the system when your first baby comes along. Many women in their teens and twenties simply never consider that one day they will probably become a mother. No-one explained what it is like to have a baby depend completely upon you, twenty-four hours a day. No-one told you to look long and hard at potential partners in assessing the kind of emotional and childcare support they might provide, and to have serious talks with them about it before embarking on reproduction. Above all, no-one warned you how addicted you had become to consumption and the status that comes with a job, however lowly, compared with your positional non-existence in the role of mother. Taken together, these things mean you will struggle with motherhood. The most fundamental thing you can do is hook up with other mothers with children of the same age. Having a good moan to them is great, so is the relief from loneliness. However, there are, of course, alternatives to caring for your baby full-time.

The first is to return to work full-time. If you are of the view that how babies turn out is largely due to their genes, so long as their basic material needs are met, or you simply find that you and babies do not go together, then this might well be the course you need to take. It does not make you a bad person or mean there is something wrong with you. Also, if you do head back to work, do not assume that it will be for ever. Plenty of women find babies impossible but adore caring for toddlers or small children, so keep an open mind about whether you might give up or cut down on work in a few years' time. In choosing substitute care (assuming that your man or none of your relatives are up for it), if you possibly can, avoid day care and take the financial hit entailed in hiring a one-on-one nanny – not a child-minder with several other kids to look after. Take care to find someone who is going to stick it out until the child is three, perhaps drawing up a contract to this effect, and do not sack her/him unless they are grossly unresponsive to the child or irresponsible. I realise how hard this is to arrange, and that you may already have older children – in which case this advice is irrelevant, and may just be making you feel guilty or angry. But for those who still have babies, and want to go back to work, a consistent, responsive nanny is the best investment you will ever make, even if it means that you are barely earning more than you are paying out. Bear in mind that your child will not be a baby for ever.

The second solution is part-time work. Perhaps you rub along okay with babies, but sometimes find them dull or just too demanding. Some work will enable you to get time away from the relentless domestic drudgery and have some adult contact. The lack of time for yourself is a terrible drain on identity, and the absence of status of the role of motherhood is disgraceful. Having even a few mornings a week to do something else may be essential if you are to be much use to your kids when you do look after them. It helps to be honest with yourself (but not necessarily with anyone else) about why you are doing this work. Rather than pretending that it is for the child's good – 'they need to learn to play with other children', 'it's good for their mental development', and so forth – admit that it is for yourself, and only in that indirect way good for the child. But if you are this sort of woman, and many are, *it will be good for the kids in the longer term if it helps you stay sane during this most insanity-provoking (as well as joyful) period in your life*, so feel no guilt.

However you decide to tackle motherhood, the great thing is not to give a toss what other people think and say. It's fine to read advice in books like this one, because you can easily ignore what you disagree with. If people start glazing over in the pub or at a dinner party when you tell them you are a full-time mother, then let them have it, both barrels. If full-time mothers tell you you're being neglectful or selfish because you work, tell them it's none of their business. The same applies if you are a full-time mother and feel put down by one who works. A measure of sisterhood is lacking at the moment in this area because working mothers feel that their choice is questioned by full-time mothers, and vice versa. The truth is that if a mother works when she has a baby, it does not make her a bad person, and if another chooses to care for her baby full-time, she should be shown the respect she deserves.

4. *Gender role strain* Selfish Capitalism has discouraged you from investing time in any unpaid activity. Yet you still have strong impulses to cooperate with others, to give gifts without any guarantee of anything in return, to make homes (without necessarily having to extend them). The pressure to put work before everything is phenomenal, creating role strain, since most women also want, as the saying goes, to 'get a life'. The trite notion of a work/life balance is really Selfish Capitalism's pretence that it actually cares about your well-being. It doesn't. In fact, it prefers you to be a wreck because then you will consume more, to compensate for your feelings of worthlessness, in turn requiring you to work ever harder to pay off the credit card and mortgage. The solution to role strain is to reject the prevailing obsession with educational and career performance, and consumer goods, as the foundation of your identity. Once you stop seeing your self-worth largely in terms of your career, you will automatically start investing more in friends, family, partners and children, and you will start seeking out activities, both at work and at play, which actually interest you rather than making a tiny minority of fat cats even fatter.

5. *Not all men are bastards* True, some men are, but so are just as many women. You need to understand that you live at a moment in history when the sexes have never got on worse, and set out to beat the trend. This gender rancour has economic foundations. Because the vast majority of male incomes have stagnated since the 1970s, and because our consumer 'needs' have risen dramatically since then, dual-income households have increased. That has driven up the standard of what is regarded as necessary, such as a prestigious house or car, or just an iPod, because dual-earning households are wealthier. With more women in the workforce than men, men are more fed up, especially when the children come along. But that's nothing compared to how pissed off working women are. On top of coping with increasingly pressurised and insecure working environments, they end up doing the lion's share of the housework and feeling more responsible for the kids. If the man expresses his fury at your busyness and preoccupation with work and kids rather than him by pushing off with a newer model, your rage is incandescent. You swallowed the story that he would love you for who you are, not what you look like, and now he has gone off with some bimbo in her early twenties, a betrayal on every level. What a swizz!

The solution goes like this. Having gone through Step One (above), you will know that your relationship with your family, but especially your dad, affects the type of man you are attracted to. If your dad was a bastard it makes you more likely to chase after bastards – but you know about this now, so hopefully you will be able to seek out decent men. You have your teens and early twenties to sort all this out, but because of the cruel gender inequity of the biological clock, if you want children you are going to have to start to get real from around the age of twenty-five. As well as emerging from the shadow of your family history, you will need to stop letting Virus values influence your choice. If you are getting real, as your twenties become your thirties, you will probably be admitting to yourself that what you are after is a reliable man to mate with, not just for reproduction, but someone who will actually be a real help. It really, truly does not matter how rich, possessioned-up, good-looking or famous he is. What you need is a partner who fits with your mothering game-plan. Ideally, if you are someone who is never going to enjoy babies very much and is always going to want to be a winner in *The Apprentice*, then you will need to find a maternal man who is longing (though he may not yet know it) to be a mother. If you are not like that, then you want someone who is going to happily contribute to the washing-up, shopping, cooking and nappy-changing. Sure, you also need him to be someone you desire, but the further you get beyond thirty, the harder it will be to meet this part of the job spec. Part of your getting real is accepting that sex is not everything once children come along. If you end up with a man who does not ring your bell five times a night, then it is not the end of the bloody world.

Many readers will already have made their beds and be lying in them with someone they feel is less than perfect. The key is provided by the study I described on p. 322. Reread that page now. For well-being in relationships with children, you and your partner need to be singing from the same hymn sheet. Given that most of us are not, there is a lot to be gained from renegotiating the deal with him, possibly by going to see a relationship counsellor. The alternative is to start with someone new, but this is a precarious decision to make, full of pitfalls.

6. *Divorce* – The other study you need to consider is described on p. 336. It was the one showing that women who divorce or separate are often more depressed after doing so, even if they were with a truly vile man or if they were depressed beforehand. The rise in broken relationships is little short of disastrous in most cases, for all concerned. Of course, if you have not gone through Step One and really are married to a complete shit, you probably do need to get out – and this is now possible, financially and without stigma. But be very, very wary of accepting your own appraisal of your man's shittiness or of the idea that someone else will be any better. If you are depressed, you may not realise that you are. Depressed people are paranoid and much more liable to misconstrue other people. Before ditching the father of your children, be sure to see a therapist and check out what you are bringing to the feast.

On top of that, remember that we live in a crazy society. The notions that we are not designed to stay with the same person for life and that there is always someone or something more attractive just around the corner serve Selfish Capitalism very well (there are economic advantages to the system of having large segments of the population unhappy and spending money on setting up a second home because of separation), but they are not true in the vast majority of cases. It may sound harsh, but getting real requires growing up, and growing up means accepting that your life is always going to be a great deal less than perfect.

7. *Appreciate beauty, not appearances* As we saw in Chapter 5, you are targeted by powerful forces to worry about your weight, prettiness and fashion sense. A concern with inherent beauty is an equally potent countervailing vaccine. To generalise this beyond physical appearance may strike some readers as patronising middle-class claptrap. But studies have shown unambiguously that people who like looking at flowers and sunsets, or find beauty in music or other arts, are less likely to be Virus-infected and more likely to seek out the intrinsic. Writing as someone who records all episodes of *The Bill*, I am not immune to 'low' culture. You may still dismiss me as a highfalutin, patriarchal tosser, but when I implore you to seek out the beautiful in life, whatever you may regard that as, you ignore me at your peril.

FOR MEN

In 2005 the *Observer* devoted an issue of its magazine to an alleged 'crisis of masculinity'. Needless to say, it offered barely a scrap of scientific evidence that any such crisis actually exists, and indeed, I contend that it is a myth. By and large, in all English-speaking nations, women are at far greater risk of emotional distress than men. Bridget Jones may have big problems, but her brother Brian is relatively chipper.

If you believe that There Is No Alternative to being traditionally male, then Selfish Capitalism has hoodwinked you. You are more likely to be a New Man than your dad was, but only in a few, largely cosmetic respects. The ostensible cause of your lack of development lies in simple economics. Since the 1970s the income of the great majority of men in English-speaking nations has stagnated. Even if you are amongst the 1 per cent of Britons who earn more than £100,000 a year, Selfish Capitalism has done a brilliant job of persuading you that you do not have enough money. Your substance abuse (much commoner in men than women), violence, personality disorder or more rarely, depression and anxiety, have been heavily exacerbated by this.

1. *Educashun* The door of the prison that incarcerates the lawyer who told me of his miserable life goals slammed shut when he was around the age of eight. By then he had become convinced that only through exceptional exam performance could he achieve Virus goals, which he had already taken for granted. His subsequent years of education taught him that the world is not a particularly nice place, that as well as being hyper-competitive in every part of his life, it was essential that he develop a certain cunning, deviousness and charm if he were to be popular – something which he could see was also very important for success. Of course, as we saw in Chapter 8, in believing this he was exceptional. Most teenage boys do not take exam results or school performance anything like as seriously as girls do, although they are rarely so blasé in other aspects of their life, such as on the sports field, in front of their PlayStation or in the matter of masturbation. The problem is that the education system still contrives, as it does with your sisters, to spit you out feeling a failure and largely clueless as to your true intrinsic interests. The solution is to realise just how humiliated you felt back then (which is true for many of the highest achievers) and to squeeze out the poison still remaining. You must also recognise how far you have been distanced from the passions that vitalised your early years, and rediscover that vitality and playfulness.

2. *Career* In most cases, you never much doubted that one day you were going to have to be a breadwinner. As a child, your mum probably did not work and your dad did. Some of you may have been very single-minded about preparing yourself for this task, but most probably gave it little or no thought during your teens and early twenties. After the 1970s, some very big changes took place. Within a decade there were as many women undergraduates as men, and jobs requiring bulging muscles largely disappeared, to be replaced by gender-neutral jobs in the service industries. By the end of the nineties, it was very likely that you had experienced having a woman as your boss. Meanwhile, for the vast majority, your income had ceased to grow, in real terms. The winner-takes-all system of remuneration had emerged, with a tiny minority getting vast sums. Jobs became less secure, hours became longer and more antisocial. The competition was ever tougher as bright young women joined you in nervously waiting outside the interview rooms, filling in the tests of your personality and aptitudes.

At the same time, the measure of a man was increasingly coming to be what they earned and possessed, and in recent years their proximity to celebrity. Appearances were now extremely important to women, and by no means did you object to the return of the miniskirt and the much greater preparedness of women to sleep with you at ever-younger ages (despite the AIDS crisis). However, you were feeling some of that pressure yourself, taking much more interest in your clothes, grooming and weight than had previous generations. Although you could see that you would most likely end up marrying a woman who professionally was doing just as well as you, your basic assumption that you would need to be the breadwinner when the nippers came along remained unchanged. Half of you were not mistaken, for that is the proportion of mothers with under-threes who, even today, do no paid work.

These changes seemed to leave very little alternative to working ever longer hours and competing ever more fiercely. That left virtually no room for discovering, let alone pursuing, what actually interested you. So much of your time was taken up working (contrary to the fantasies of the fifties and sixties, in which it was foretold that we would live in a leisure society) that there was little left over to consider such things – and anyway, the moment you escaped from the office, the more likely you became to reach for the booze or drugs, to medicate your feeling of frustration, emptiness and boredom.

The solution is to think hard about what you really enjoy. The chances are that you have not done this, truly, for a very long time. The starting point is the bits of your current job, however minuscule, that do actually hold your attention, keep you absorbed, fascinate you. Once identified, you can seek positions with more of those bits, even if it means less money or status. The alternative is a complete change of career, but this may not be necessary. It is quite possible that if you pursue what really interests you in your current line of work, you will actually earn more, although that should not be your reason for making the change.

3. Fatherhood – or should that be motherhood? For men as well as women, this is where the shit really hits the fan. Before fatherhood, you can exit a relationship (whether married or not) without too much damage, but after it the penalties are of a completely different order. Nothing in your life up until now comes anywhere near the disruption caused by the arrival of your first baby. The loss of sleep is bad enough, but what about the loss of your partner to the baby, the virtual end of your sex life and the breathtaking bateyness of your even more sleep-deprived partner? No wonder you hit the bottle or spend more time at work or start taking a keener interest in that secretary in accounts who has been giving you the eye.

To you as the breadwinner, this looks an incredibly bad deal. Your partner never ceases bending your ear about your failure to contribute enough to the cooking, shopping and housework, yet you have worked a fifty-hour week on very little sleep and even less sex. Everyone keeps saying how cute the baby is, and maybe sometimes you agree, but by and large it just seems like a machine for eating, shitting and screaming which shows a minimal interest in you and takes up every last jot of your partner's attention. What a swizz!

The solution to this situation is not to get into it. I don't mean never shack up and have babies, I mean get real, well before it happens: go in with eyes wide open and only when you are truly ready. Getting real is growing up, putting away the childish things of your protracted adolescence – the booze, the drugs, all that lad stuff. Only when you are ready to do that will you be ready to make the commitment to babies. Fatherhood does not mean that you will never have another drink, but it should mean that you get very few indeed for the first few months, the first year even. Another part of getting real is rethinking what you are looking for in a woman. The modern media have created utterly absurd notions of what matters. Nubility and bare flesh are not remotely the basis on which to make babies.

If you have been through Step One, you will know that your family history, especially your relationship with your mother, profoundly affects what sort of women attract you. Now that you know that, you do not have to be a slave to it. Even more important, you have to challenge your Virus values in this department. Forget about what she looks like, concentrate on whether you and she are going to see eye to eye on the baby thing. By definition, your partner needs to be someone you want to have sex with, otherwise there will be no babies, but you really have got to accept that she does not have to be a Babe, that after she's had the babe she will look less like one, and that sex will probably take a back seat for a few years. You also need to think very carefully about whether a potential partner is going to fit with your life plan, and you must talk that through exhaustively before committing to anything – go back to p. 226 to read about the relevant study.

If you are someone who wants the traditional deal, in which the little woman stays at home and looks after it while you win the bread, then make damn sure that's how she sees it too. Likewise, if you hope to be more involved than that, be sure she sees it that way. If she is likely to want to do some work before the child is aged three, be sure you are barking up the same tree when it comes to who is going to substitute for her. You have probably never given this much or even any thought, but it's your responsibility too. If she is proposing to dump the nipper in a nursery at the age of three months, you should make yourself aware of the damage this could do. You should also be fully committed to taking the financial hit that the alternative to a nursery will deliver – a nanny.

Most radical of all, take a long, hard look at your life and ask yourself whether you would actually like to do some or all of the mothering. You might even be better suited to it if your partner is someone for whom the cut and thrust of the workplace is preferable to baby care. It would be a huge step for you to do it full-time, even if it is the right one. Or, are you sure there isn't a way to organise things so that you share the care, splitting the working week? The key point is that, if you want your ankle-biter to turn out clever, lively and full of beans, the most effective way is for one or both of you to look after it until age three. If you agree to a plan in which your under-three is cared for by a succession of young, not very educated women, whether in day care or in nannying, do not be surprised if that child turns out not to be the sharpest knife in the drawer or the most emotionally seaworthy ship on the sea.

For a significant number of readers, all this is more or less ancient history. Nonetheless, it is not irrelevant because it may help you to make sense of your troubled teenager, providing some clues to what they might need if you are to repair the damage. Although there is no point in dwelling excessively on the past, you may find it a basis for reconnecting with your partner.

4. Gender rancour and divorce If you have sorted out your childhood, there's a good chance that you are amongst the 60 per cent of people who do not divorce or separate. However, in our imprudent, myopic society there is still a very strong pressure to jack in relationships if they are less than perfect. The notion that all relationships go through extremely bad patches seems to have been forgotten. Being a man, you are likely to find nubility beguiling, and once the baby shit has hit the fan you will be particularly vulnerable to the fallacy that it would all be so different if you were with someone else or that you can get away with the odd fling. You may be feeling that you work your arse off during the week and get nothing back at the weekend, not even the odd game of golf or a football match. You may also have come to the conclusion that your partner is not the woman you shacked up with, has become an over-emotional, nagging cow with a large repertoire of unpleasant and tellingly vicious criticisms of what you are like, that you have made a terrible mistake.

My advice is to think more than twice before accepting such an analysis of your partner. The price of divorce goes far beyond the value of half your house (see p. 226). If you proceed with it, you are much more likely to die younger, or to become even more distressed and to divorce again if you remarry, never mind the carnage for your children. I am not saying that true and insoluble incompatibility never happens, and there are plenty of women around who are almost unliveable with. If you really are in either of these situations, then fair enough, you may have to leave. But long before you do that you need to have checked and double-checked that you and modern myopia are not part of the problem. If you have reached the point where you have decided to leave, then before you do it, go and talk it over with a therapist. You may find that many of your negative feelings about your partner are actually misperceptions based on your own problems, or that this is just a grisly stage which needs to be survived in the hope of something better between you. It goes against the British grain, but try to be open to the idea of going to see a relationship counsellor in order to make that happen.

Part of getting real and growing up is realising that a measure of stoicism is essential in life. You may splutter that you do not need me to tell you this, that you already half-live your way through a fifty-hour, gruelling working week and have been putting off pleasures since you were tiny, on the grounds that your reward will come later. But that was the point I was making in the 'Career' section above. Hopefully, if you realign your working life to provide greater intrinsic satisfaction and make it less central to your identity, then when you get home you will feel less deprived and less need to behave like the baby whose screams greet you, both reaching for the bottle. You may imagine that nothing could be as hellish as your present relationship, but most people who think that are wrong. Beware of having that affair: do not deceive yourself that it will be different next time. If, after following all the steps I have suggested, there really is no alternative to leaving your partner and children, then prepare for a very tough time.

5. *Friends and intimacy* 'Intimacy? Yuck!' you may be thinking. But the truth is that, unless you are pretty unusual, you probably have much less intimacy in your life than is good for you. Whereas women seem to have an almost unlimited capacity to yack away with their friends about their most private moments, men prefer to stick to the football or to office or national politics. Nothing wrong with a bit of that, but you also need to have people you can open your heart to, and who can do the same with you. The reason you may not have any such confidant, or only one or two, is likely to be the Virus, combined with your Big Boys Don't Cry upbringing. The Virus encourages you to regard other people as pawns and with suspicion. Whereas women often keep a few friends dating way back to childhood, men often have friendships based on work, exclusively so if they are Marketing Characters.

The solution is to make a list of all the people you consider to be a friend and divide them into work-related and purely social. You may find that there is hardly anyone in the latter category, and you may also find that not one is a woman. Whilst it is possible to be an intimate friend of someone with whom you work, it is tricky. Your best bet is someone where there is no financial link at all. Contrary to the *When Harry Met Sally* bollocks, that might be a woman. Once you have got real and grown up, you should be perfectly capable of pouring your heart out to a woman without having to rip her knickers off or fall in love with her. Once you are no longer looking at people in terms of what you can get out of them and what they may be trying to get out of you, intimacy becomes a whole lot easier.

6. Big houses, boys' toys and flash holidays As we saw in Chapter 6, by far the greatest financial cross that you bear is most probably your home. On a personal level, this is the single most powerful hold that Selfish Capitalism has over you. If you are young, and especially if you went to university, you already have substantial debts even before you embark on the largest one of all, the mortgage. It's what nails you into the workforce, and it seems very hard to imagine a way to pull those nails out. If you change job or stop chasing the higher-paid but less intrinsic career opportunities, you run the risk of not being able to afford your mortgage repayments or not being able to move up the property ladder.

All this you have long accepted, so you take the view, 'in for a penny, in for a pound'. Sod it, since there is no escape, you might as well also upgrade the car, buy the new golf clubs and spend the three grand on the holiday in Barbados. But it does not have to be that way. If you make the shift to intrinsic values, suddenly you will be spending a lot less money. Above all, once you have those values, a lot of the housing needs that you thought you had are exposed as mere wants. Instead of moving up the ladder, you stay put; instead of enlarging your perfectly good residence, you get on with enjoying it. As your spending decreases, you are finally at liberty to start paying off the mortgage. The more you pay off, the greater your freedom to put the intrinsic ahead of money, at work and at play.

Step two (rejecting much of the status quo) for childless people

If you are gay or lesbian and intend never to have children, if you are heterosexual and have chosen not to, or if you are childless for some other reason, then you have already rejected the status quo or been forced outside it (if you cannot

have children for biological reasons). Like all previous societies, ours is predicated on parenthood, and if you are not
and never will be a parent, for whatever reason, you are by
definition outside the norm, albeit part of a substantial
minority. The proportion of women who get past the age of
forty without having reproduced is now one-fifth. Whilst
some of them will go on to have children, and medical science
continues to make it possible for women to do so at ever later
ages (a sixty-three-year-old recently gave birth to a child),
when you add in gay men or heterosexual males who do not
reproduce (e.g. because they are sexually inactive), around
one-fifth of all British adults today will never have children.

Whatever your circumstances, if you are in this category
I strongly recommend that you go out and buy a copy of
Anthony Storr's superb book *Solitude*. It provides telling
evidence that we have become fixated upon relationships as
the only source of pleasure and solace in life, and instead
shows that solitude is a state with much to recommend it.
Not that I am assuming that merely because you are childless
you are lonely or lack relationships – in fact the opposite may
be the case: children, at least in the early years, eat heavily
into time spent with friends or relatives. But Storr is the most
benign and powerful advocate I have encountered for the
notion that there is an alternative to family life.

FOR CHILDLESS WOMEN

About 3 per cent of women were born incapable of reproduction or were made so by a misfortune, such as a car
accident or exposure to poisons in the environment. About
half of childless fifty-year-old women have chosen to be, with

the remainder having not attempted pregnancy until relatively late in life and, as a result, found themselves unable to. Thankfully, whatever the reasons for your childlessness, the stigma that used to attach to this state is considerably less than it used to be. However, as with everything else, Selfish Capitalism looks upon your circumstance as not a problem but an opportunity.

Virus values may seem very attractive if you are feeling lonely or ostracised. Since work is the major source of identity for everyone, for some childless women it becomes everything. Indeed, the very high rates of childlessness amongst the most educated suggest that prize-hunting can supplant reproduction altogether. Increasingly, the upper reaches of business, politics and the civil service are likely to contain significant numbers of such women. For them, it is particularly important to seek out the intrinsic, and there are plenty of examples in public life of distinguished childless women, from Florence Nightingale to Shirley Williams to Ann Widdecombe, who have pursued extremely worthwhile lives without, as far as I know, being distressed. However, the key to such women may be that they had intrinsic motives, and although they became famous they had intrinsic goals as well. Their lives may have been woven around their careers, but they may have avoided the pitfalls of the Marketing Character, having authentic friendships and making tremendous contributions to their communities. Whether a high achiever or not, if you are a childless woman it is even more imperative for you to involve yourself in other people's lives and to find interests which absorb you and give you flow – losing track of time, totally wrapped up – whether at work or at play.

FOR CHILDLESS MEN

The proportion of men who never become a father is considerably less than that of women. In the definitive survey of the sex life of 19,000 Britons, who filled out a booklet-size questionnaire in the privacy of their home, 1.5 per cent of men between forty-five and fifty-nine said that they had never had any sexual experience at all. At some point, the vast majority of men do impregnate a woman.

Perhaps the largest group who will never do so are exclusively gay men, but they are also rarer than you might suppose. In the survey, 3.6 per cent of men said they had had some form of homosexual genital contact or a homosexual partner. This is actually a rather higher proportion than that found in other studies. Only 0.5 per cent of the men in the survey said they had only ever felt attracted to their own sex, but 5.5 per cent said they had felt homosexual attraction at some point in their life; so bisexuality is a much commoner variant of homosexuality than exclusive same-sex attraction.

Although I know of no studies of the values of gay men, I would not be surprised if they are less afflicted by the Virus than heterosexual ones. Although homophobia is decreasing in younger generations, it still exists, helping to marginalise gays from the status quo. A significant proportion of gay men plug into the gay culture, which in some respects is a counterculture. Whilst the media makes much of the 'pink pound', the greater disposable income of gay men may derive largely from the absence of the costs of children, and possibly from there being a larger proportion of them from high-income families, so that they tend to find better-paid jobs. Those bisexual or exclusively gay men who remain childless are less easily nailed to the hedonic treadmill. It's easier for them to scrap a job that has no intrinsic interest and decide to travel the world for a year or to retrain in something that does appeal.

Nonetheless, gay men are at greater risk of loneliness and distress, and part of the reason can be adherence to Virus values. As with childless women, there is a temptation to become completely taken over by Virus prize-hunting. This may be combined with rampant hedonism in their spare time, but the kind of hedonism that does not bring long-term well-being. It is therefore of particular importance if you are a gay man to find work that has intrinsic flow and is absorbing, and to get involved in the lives of others, the community, whether through charity work, friends or a vocational career.

'So, Guv, we're at the end of this bit of your journey and I can only hope you feel we've reached the right destination. Just before you pop off, there are one or two things I want to tell you about Politics today. You see, I had that Tony Blair in the back of my cab ...'

Chapter 12

Political Implications:
The Unselfish Capitalist Manifesto

If my dad's mother wanted to be reincarnated as a public lavatory attendant and his idea was to be a middle-aged Frenchwoman, mine is to be a Third World taxi driver, running one of those battered old Mercedes, picking up tourists and regaling them with my views on the world. Metaphorically speaking, I have had several of those New Labour sorts in the back of my cab, and before I hop onto the electoral stump and present my manifesto, I intend to share with you some of what they told me and my conclusions about them.

So, guv, there I was, sat on a train (my taxi is very portable) in an empty carriage, returning from a conference in the North of England, when a very powerful New Labour woman embarked, one with whom I have a passing acquaintance. She is about as quick-witted as it's possible to be. If she

were to take an IQ test the paper would probably sponta-
neously combust; yet she is also beguiling and unassuming in
her manner, famously charming company, a brilliant ques-
tioner and a careful listener. Rose, as I shall call her, is one of
the (rapidly diminishing) handful of stars in the New Labour
galaxy that Tony Blair trusts completely, one of his oldest
friends. As she bustled down the carriage she spotted me, and
settled in a seat across the aisle. A large briefcase containing
Matters of State weighed down her minder, but those affairs
must have been especially tedious because she decided to
engage me in conversation. We spent a fascinating three
hours shooting the breeze about the state of the nation in
general, and her career in particular.

In best taxi driver mode, I argued that where it had all
gone wrong was that 'people today', or at least, the top two-
thirds of earners, did not realise how lucky they were to be so
affluent and relatively healthy, that they did not value what
they had got. Everyone seemed to be obsessed with having a
better job or a better house or a better personality or a better
sex life. As tends to be the case with taxi drivers, the evils of
Young People Today figured prominently in my exegesis,
with their yearning for prestigious clothes labels, hi-tech
equipment and expensive holidays. Above all, I moaned, they
seemed fixated upon being famous regardless of whether they
had any talent or were prepared to work hard.

Rose agreed and gave an illustration of this last point. She
had been ferrying two nine-year-old girls to a party and asked
them what they wanted to be when they were older.
'Famous,' said one. 'Famous for what?' asked Rose. 'Err,
umm, I don't know,' came the reply, 'being an actress or a TV

presenter, something like that.' This is consistent with a 2004 survey of English under-tens. Asked to name 'the best things in the world', they put 'being famous' first (followed by 'my family', 'football' and 'holidays'). Although she was worried by this obsession with celebrity and our increasing levels of emotional distress, Rose commented, 'But is it really the role of government to influence how happy citizens are? I'm not sure it is.' It would seem that she was unaware of the BBC's nationally representative poll which found that four-fifths of us agree with the statement 'A government's prime objective should be to achieve the greatest happiness of the people, not the greatest wealth.'

The subject turned to her career. She had done exceptionally well at school and university ('I'm afraid I was one of those people who adored exams') before proceeding in the orderly direction that such people do, towards a remunerative career. Unusually for a businesswoman, Rose was a member of the Labour Party, and before that had been keen on radical politics ('at university we vied with each other to join more extreme branches of obscure neo-Marxist splinter groups'), and shortly after Blair's accession to the leadership he arranged for her to be interviewed for selection as a candidate for a safe seat in Parliament. The selection meeting must have been the first test she had ever failed. Unfortunately, as she put it, 'I had got too big for my own boots, become arrogant', so she told the assembled comrades that she would not be going to live in the constituency because it was too far from London. She did not get the candidacy.

The odd thing was that, ten years later and despite huge success in politics as a key figure in New Labour, this reverse was still poisoning her sense of fulfilment. Because she could now never be the second female prime minister, none of her formidable political achievements seemed to satisfy her. Here is a woman who has witnessed at first hand what happens at the heart of power and has also directly determined many major legislative decisions, through the posts conferred on her by Blair. At the same time she has indirectly influenced most of the important steps he has taken, through being one of the tiny number of people he consults when taking a big step. Despite this, just like the little girl she had described, her aspirations far outstripped what reality could supply. I pleaded with her to forget about what might have been. She should be thrilled with what she had achieved and delighted to have been lucky enough to sit at the top table of British political life. Alas, I fear that she was not convinced.

Strangest of all, she was very worried about money. In her senior government post she receives what most people would regard as a substantial wedge (remember: only 1 per cent of the population earn more than £100,000 a year) and her husband makes an even better living. But what with the school fees and the desire for a larger London home to go with their sizeable country one, there were constant 'cash-flow problems'. She felt resentful that she had sacrificed her business career for public service, although stressing that she would not have it any other way.

Unfortunately, it has become increasingly clear that most of Blair's inner circle have a similar avariciousness. Whilst there are some senior figures who are not afflicted, money beats very strongly in the heart of New Labour and they have made no secret of the fact. Not long before the 1997 election

I remember being rather startled when Peter Mandelson, then an MP, told me that 'we are seriously relaxed about people becoming very, very rich'. In 2004 some interesting details emerged about just how much this applies to Tony Blair himself. It was the week after the Party conference, in September, when, following an operation for a heart tremor and yet more rumours of a split with Gordon Brown, he announced both that he would step down from the leadership at the end of the next parliament and that he had purchased a home in fashionable Bayswater for £3.6 million. The mortgage is said to cost the Blairs £22,000 a month, although lenders must have queued up to supply it since Tony Blair is expected to earn at least £10 million from lecturing in America – where they worship him – when he finally does decide to step down from political life, and that's before he starts accruing company directorships.

Currently the prime minister earns £183,932 a year, not a lot of which can get spent because most of what he does is covered by the taxpayer, or in the case of his holidays, by staying at homes of 'friends' like Sir Cliff Richard and Silvio Berlusconi. Cherie Blair earns about £200,000 a year as a QC. In 2002 they bought two flats in Bristol for £270,000 apiece, and she recently received £100,000 for writing an anodyne book about prime ministers' wives, for which she embarked on a US promotional tour at an alleged £30,000 a talk. The Blairs were said to be much miffed by the fact that the Islington home they sold in 1997 for £615,000 (a not untidy profit of £240,000 since its purchase five years before) when they moved into 10 Downing Street went for £1.6 million in 2005.

I suspect that Mandelson would not regard all this income as amounting to 'very, very rich', but most people would. Such sums of money and property transactions may be indicative of Virus values. For half of what they paid for their new Bayswater home, and much more within their means, they could have bought an enormous home not too far from the centre of London, but perhaps that would not have satisfied their social aspirations.

Famously, property fever injured Mandelson himself. Failure to declare a loan when he applied for a mortgage caused his first resignation from the Cabinet. I got to know him a bit in 1996 when I interviewed him in some depth for a BBC series (during the interview he famously shed a tear when he recalled the death of his father). This was at the time he was looking for a home, and I happened to know of a relatively modest flat that was on sale near where I lived, which he went to view. His budget was then in proportion to his salary, but soon afterwards he received that infamous loan from Geoffrey Robinson, the Labour magnate, and in true Affluenza style he proceeded to buy a house in Notting Hill that was way beyond his means (in its style there were shades of the one-bedroom, five-storey home of Sam, the millionaire New Yorker). Mandelson's second, politically fatal resignation followed allegations that he abused his official position to influence the citizenship application of a rich Indian businessman, one of a coterie of very wealthy men with whom the New Labour inner circle seem to spend a surprising amount of time rubbing shoulders.

The same fate befell one of Blair's closest political allies, David Blunkett, a man whose credentials as a socialist had been forged on Sheffield City Council when fighting Mrs Thatcher in the eighties. He misused his political power to help a rich person, in this case his girlfriend, with a residence visa application for her nanny. Soon after these events, we gawped, slack-jawed with amazement, at the Tessa Jowell/David Mills farrago. Jowell is a Cabinet minister, another of Blair's closest and most trusted allies. Mills is a millionaire lawyer, an expert in finding ways for the super-rich to avoid contributing their fair share of taxes (in one year, Mills paid virtually no taxes himself). Leaving aside the legal rights and wrongs of this saga, Jowell was asking us to believe she had no idea that her husband had received a 'gift' (later reclassified by the taxman as income) of £350,000, which Italian prosecutors allege was a payoff to Mills for giving false testimony on behalf of his client, Silvio Berlusconi. Blair has been a house guest of Berlusconi, a surprising 'friend' for a Labour leader. Jowell also expects us to believe that she signed several re-mortgage applications – forms which require the applicant to declare any outstanding loans – without realising that she might be providing false information about the gift/income. Her story is that the sudden arrival of £350,000 in the household finances was not worthy of a mention over the breakfast table.

Perhaps that is true, but, like Blunkett, Jowell appears to be a perfect example of someone who started out with intrinsic goals but for whom those goals subsequently shifted. She was a psychiatric social worker and charity administrator who served as a Labour councillor, but after she became an MP, in 1992, she seems to have embraced Blairite, Virus politics with zeal. In the mid-nineties, a friend described her as 'seething with New Labour enthusiasm and ideals ... brilliantly on-message'. Her appearance became increasingly Virus-driven – expensive togs, lots of slap – and she fitted very comfortably into the millionaire circles in which her husband moved.

Letting Virus motives dictate aspects of personal relationships is something that the New Labour machine has required on occasions. It has been claimed with some authority that when Robin Cook was revealed to be having an extra-marital affair with the woman he later married, the party insisted he ditch his former wife if he wished to save his career. This Marketing attitude to personal relationships is normal for someone with the Virus: both friends and lovers are dispensable if they obstruct successful Marketing, because relationships with them are founded not on authenticity but on expedience.

Numerous New Labour poodles to be found in all sections of the press felt free to speculate on Jowell's misfortunes. A smug example is Andrew Rawnsley, of the *Observer* and Radio 4's *Westminster* programme. For nearly a decade he has been slanting his political commentaries to suit the Blairite agenda. But about that loan, he wrote that 'it is simply incredible that Ms Jowell could be so blithely unaware of what her husband was doing'. What is more, as the winds of political change blew towards Gordon Brown, Rawnsley went on to dish the dirt on the Blairs. 'After the umpteenth ugly headline about Blair and money, I once asked one of the Prime Minister's closest advisers why he and his wife had such reckless disregard for what it did for their reputation. "They spend too much time with very rich people" was the blunt reply. Because they work hard and carry so many responsibilities, ministers argue themselves into believing that they deserve a similar level of lifestyle to the mega-rich.' Nouveau-riche Labour ...

I am not suggesting that the Labour Party, or even all those who have been close to its Nouveau core, is populated entirely by Marketing Characters. I have met (and know a good deal about) several key advisers to Blair whom I am certain have wholly intrinsic values. As the wheels rapidly come off his project, with the 'peerages for honours' (huge 'loans' from businessmen in return for honours) the latest in what will doubtless be a long line of shocking revelations about his perfidy in the time until he leaves Downing Street, and beyond, even his sincerity is coming to be doubted, even by respected columnists as opposed to naked ideologues. One of the most outspoken is Matthew Parris, widely felt to be someone with integrity, an ex-MP under Mrs Thatcher whose homosexuality became public and who resigned from politics to become a truth-seeking press missile. 'I believe Tony Blair is an out-and-out rascal, terminally untrustworthy and close to being unhinged,' he wrote in *The Times* in March 2006. 'I said from the start that there was something wrong in his head, and each passing year convinces me more strongly that this man is a pathological confidence-trickster. To the extent that he ever believes what he says, he is delusional. To the extent that he does not, he is an actor whose first invention – himself – has been his only interesting role. Books could be written on which of Mr Blair's assertions were ever wholly sincere, which of his claimed philosophies are genuine and how far he temporarily persuades himself that each passing passion is real ... Suffice it to say that I used to believe that, at the moment of saying anything, our Prime Minister probably thought that what he said was true – that there was no secret, internal wink. Today I have lost confidence even in that.' I suspect that in terms of the Virus, most of Blair's inner circle will, like their leader, emerge as prime specimens of inauthenticity, hyperactivity and game-playing – Marketing Characters.

In the autumn of 2006, evidence of the kind of distress you would expect to follow from such Affluenza has emerged from some of Nouveau Labour's main players. David Blunkett diagnosed himself as having been 'clinically depressed' during the period leading up to his resignation as Home Secretary. Spinmeister-in-chief Alastair Campbell declared that during his time at Number 10 Downing Street he'd had periods when he knew he was depressed. Although it was not explicitly reported in newspapers at this time, I have it on good authority that the daughter of one of the families at the heart of the party made a suicide attempt. And Stephen Fry, very much a supporter of Blair and his doings, took up two hours of prime BBC2 television time explaining how he came to the conclusion that he suffers from bipolar disorder and is at a loss to know what to do about it (take the pills and lose his creativity, or push on and hope for the best?). In none of these cases was there any discussion at all of the considerable body of evidence that vulnerability to the distress usually has its origins in childhood. But even more striking – if unsurprising – is the fact that none of these people showed any sign of recognising that their Virus values may have been crucial causes of their problems, let alone that the politics they purveyed may have contributed considerably to distress amongst the wider population.

But enough of this tittle-tattle. We might have been able to forgive the inner circle for being like this if their policies had immunised us against Affluenza. Although their apologists in the media are at pains to try to persuade us otherwise, the truth is that neither the political nor the personal chambers in their hearts were ever going to pump out the blood of the intrinsic values that we so desperately need. Again, I have first-hand evidence of this.

Since 2003 I have been a member of the Happiness Forum, a small group of boffins convened by Professor Richard Layard at the London School of Economics. Our deliberations would probably seem laughable to a disinterested observer, as we squabble over the true definition of pleasure-seeking or the nature of nurture. But our discussions are not purely academic, for Layard is closely linked to Nouveau Labour, and in 2005 we had an opportunity to present our conclusions at a seminar held in a government department. There were many top civil servants present, most notably Tim, a highly influential Permanent Secretary.

Whilst not as architecturally splendiferous as the Foreign Office, which has baronial staircases and many magnificent paintings on the walls, the edifice where the seminar was held is on the same scale as the British Museum. I felt a little over-awed as I navigated my way through the extremely tight security into a smallish room crammed with forty-five people. First up for our team was a psychologist who works at the heart of government but is also a member of the Forum. In the past, he had been involved in a substantial analysis of the role that government might play in promoting well-being, which the politicians received with a resounding silence.

Today he started with a graph showing that, throughout the developed world (except Denmark and Italy), whilst our real incomes have increased substantially since 1950, the proportion of people who say they are happy or very happy has not changed. He ran through the many factors that contribute to happiness, and summarised the evidence with the (anon) dictum, 'If you want to be happy for a few hours, get drunk; if you want to be happy for a few years, get married; if you want to be happy for life, get a garden,' adding, 'and indeed, there is evidence that regular gardeners are happier.' Next up was a university psychologist. She presented evidence that about half of happiness is traceable to a basic set point, a sort of thermostat-controlled state to which each of us return almost whatever happens. You win the lottery, and happiness temporarily goes up, but before long it returns to the usual level; you get a parking ticket, and it drops, but only for a bit. Whilst this baseline was supposed by many to be set by genes, she suggested that it was also heavily influenced by early childhood. Apart from our individual set points, about 10 per cent of our happiness level is due to current circumstances and the remaining 40 per cent to our active choices, volition. This suggested that there was plenty of room for government to help citizens to be happier. Coming in at number three for our team, Layard played a stylish innings. He summarised the key toxic elements as the social pollution created by large wage disparities and the addictiveness of consumption. These drive the hedonic treadmill on which most of us live, constantly seeking higher incomes, feeling ill-rewarded for our work compared with the fat cats and needing ever more money to pay for our shopaholia.

It fell to Tim, the thin, shaven-headed, tall Permanent Secretary, to provide the civil service response. His opening observation was that well-being is an 'incredibly important subject', and he stressed that we must avoid the trap of economists demonising social scientists, and vice versa. However, he immediately (and not without justification) proceeded to cast doubt on the reliability of surveys of mere happiness. Apparently, the commonest comment that civil servants make to their ministers is, 'We don't know,' and he urged greater rigour in measurement. He would find it easier to trust studies of actual behaviour than of what people say about what they do (a fair point – just asking people how happy they are on a five-point scale from 'very happy' to 'very unhappy' is superficial). A list of government actions that had addressed well-being followed, including the attempt to reduce child poverty and the SureStart programme (which offers help to low-income parents but has, since Tim's talk, been shown not to have worked – perhaps because, unfortunately, it has been largely turned into a giant scheme for getting mothers of babies back to work by providing day care). He joked that at least civil servants could not be accused of being solely motivated by the pursuit of money in their careers, a point that Layard and I subsequently agreed was a bit disingenuous since they can, and increasingly do, scurry off to make big money as directors of companies after their time in public service. But his choice of his final point may have been indicative of his true view of our preoccupations.

The government department that attracts most applicants is the one that deals with International Overseas Development (IOD), and he had ended up in his present one only because the IOD turned him down. He believed that reducing sickness and poverty in the developing world was the most important task facing us, and that the IOD attracts so many civil servants because it is an area in which they feel they can make 'a huge difference'. I may be wrong, but I am fairly sure he was suggesting that government cannot expect to make much difference to our well-being, and that we should stop sitting around gazing at our navels and concentrate on some people with real problems that we can really do something about.

It was time for questions, and by good fortune the chairwoman gave me the first chance. 'I take your point about the limits of surveys of well-being,' I said, addressing Tim, 'but no-one has yet mentioned the evidence I do trust, namely that an American today is between three and ten times more likely to suffer a major depression compared with one in 1950, and that there seems little serious doubt about rising violence, addictions and other signs of ill-being since then. You have sat here today and seen all this evidence that increasing our wealth has made no difference to our national happiness, and that once people have their basic material needs met, increasing individual wealth makes no difference either. So my question is, if well-being is as "incredibly important" as you say, why not just forget altogether about trying to encourage the population to earn more by working harder and forget about economic growth altogether?'

A thin smile appeared on Tim's lips as the laughter died away. 'The answer to that is enormously complicated,' he began, sighing as if I were a tiresome four-year-old who had asked what God is. He agreed that emotional distress had increased and said that our population's concern with spending is excessive and concerned him. However, just like Rose, he doubted whether these were the government's business. 'That's about values, and trying to intervene in them makes me uneasy' (as if his masters' pursuit of privatising economics is value-free). Who was to define what are good or bad values? A lot of people enjoy gambling, and so the government are presenting a Bill that makes this easier to do. Perhaps it was not for him to say that people should not gamble. People defined for themselves what their needs and their wants were, he went on, 'or, in my jargon, the fixed utility value of goods and services. It's tricky for governments to lead on what that utility value should be. If people say they want to gamble, I am not sure it would be easy for government to persuade them to actually do what would be good for them – to fulfil their needs rather than wants.' This was downright disingenuous. Tim knows better than most that it is the government that controls how much we gamble. Indeed, in April 2006 a study was published revealing that gambling has increased sevenfold since the government deregulation of it in 2001, with £50 billion a year now gambled by Britons. (In a radio interview, the inevitable 'representative of the industry' stressed the new jobs and inward investment this expansion has brought with it, and that the soon to be opened super-casinos will bring.) Tim also knows that one of the choices we make as voters is to bestow power on our rulers to control our behaviour. He and his colleagues use exhortation, through the media, to persuade us to do things like saving more of our income and voluntary work. They use legislation to provide day care and schools to strongly encourage our children to behave in certain ways. And if that fails, they use the power we have given them to coerce us not to do bad things, such as speeding, taking illegal drugs or – until now – gambling and boozing as much as we want, when and where we choose.

Tim's comment on the final part of my question was that if economic growth were no longer the goal, unemployment would increase and there would be less funding for projects such as ending child poverty, and people would be *un*happier. This seemed to me to sum up the extent to which he is trapped in the Selfish Capitalist model, one that seems to be taken for granted by the vast majority of British politicians.

Thatcherism was a grim imitation of American Market Liberalism, and in the key respects Blairism is a perpetuation of Thatcherism. Whichever of these records are played, the tune is essentially the same, and the result is Affluenza. So, guv, what's the answer? What political formula would be a true vaccine against Affluenza?

Our ideals

If we are to answer this question, we must start by examining what has happened to our core political ideals. Soon after his accession to the leadership of the Conservative Party, David Cameron announced the setting-up of six commissions to enable it to rethink Tory policies from scratch. I was asked to join the commission dealing with quality of life, and they enjoined me to start with a completely blank piece of paper, to think as radically as I chose. But I find it very hard to believe that they will be inclined towards any of the solutions I regard as necessary. Of course, it is possible that Cameron will turn out to be Blatcher in reverse. Perhaps his followers will go along with his left-wing pronouncements on the assumption that he is only making them to get elected, only to find, after three terms of office, that he really meant it, and was a closet Aneurin Bevan. It seems pretty unlikely, but then so did the collapse of the Soviet Union and 9/11, or indeed that Blair would be Thatcher in almost all but name.

Let's look at the four basic, closely related, defining political ideals of modern social organisation which my travels call into question, at least in their present form: meritocracy, egalitarianism, female emancipation and democracy itself. I want to examine them not because I doubt their desirability, but because I fear they have been hijacked by Selfish Capitalism.

None of the societies I visited has achieved anything remotely resembling true meritocracy. In Russia you can use nepotism to have your children's exam grades changed, and we are hardly in a position to scoff at such kinship-based advancement. In all the English-speaking nations, family background rather than ability is by far the strongest predictor of who will go to the best universities and get the best jobs. Even in the sainted Denmark, the education system ultimately functions as a means for the elite to reproduce itself. Widening the focus, systems everywhere are seen to favour their elites, with bad things much more likely to happen to the poor. Conviction for committing a crime, for instance, is still far more determined by background than by malfeasance. In Britain, the judicial system continues to be heavily weighted towards detecting, prosecuting and incarcerating the poor, not the rich – little different at heart from Tolstoy's brilliant denunciation of the system in late nineteenth-century Tsarist Russia.

Shocking proof of this class disparity, if it were needed, came recently in the findings of a study by the Financial Services Authority. Analysing patterns of share-dealing, it found that one-third of takeovers are preceded by insider dealing, and that the same is true in one-quarter of cases of dealings in a company before the annual results are announced. Whilst there have finally been a handful of convictions for these crimes by the affluent, they remain largely uninvestigated or prosecuted, and even if a conviction is achieved, the sentence is often no more than an easily affordable (by the rich perpetrators) fine. (For many years there was not a single such conviction – I recall making this point to Jack Straw at the time of Jeffrey Archer's venture into Anglia TV's shares, and seeing him exchange a smile with his private secretary; unable to have a go at nobbling Archer for insider dealing, it emerged a few days later that they had managed to nail him for perjury.) The real punishment for the rich and famous is disgrace, but that is hardly fair compared with what is meted out to the poor. In education, punishment, access to health and transport or other basic requirements, merit is rarely as important as who you are in determining what you get.

Those things aside, the meritocratic ideal urgently requires a rethink. It is as though Michael Young's 1958 satire *The Rise of the Meritocracy* had never been. Even if a government were able to break the link between family background and success, it is very doubtful that this would in itself improve our well-being. As long as our values are focused on us being material winners while we continue to call the disadvantaged losers, a true meritocracy will only leave the less successful with no place to hide. This applies as much to the elite as to the rest of us. As I have tried to show throughout this book, regardless of how much money or status is attained, for the Virus-infected there is nearly always a pervasive awareness of someone with more. Even the minuscule minority who are number one in their domain are not spared – there is the ever-present fear of being knocked off their perch. Indeed, a study of people from ten different nations who had moved up a notch from their parents found no increase in their well-being, compared with their lowly progenitors. Having discussed these issues with several Nouveau Labour luminaries, I know that these matters have not been thought through by the present administration at all, either by the Brownite or by the Blairite faction. We have to think again about what we regard as meritorious before going any further.

Closely linked to meritoriousness is the ideal of egalitarianism. In much of the world, instead of a more level playing field, things have got worse. The gap between rich and poor nations has grown, as has the gap between classes in the English-speaking world. The talk may be of ending poverty, nationally and internationally; the walk is very different. Again, there is no sign of any deep thinking. The assumption is that we must impose Selfish Capitalism on the world and from this will flow economic growth. The reality is that, even if it were achieved, it would merely spread the Virus. Even more fundamentally than that, infected or not, within the foreseeable future of this American Dream being realised, vast numbers of people would start dying from the knock-on effects of accelerated Global Warming. Suppose that Africa and South America, as well as India and China, geared up their economies to provide their people with the material standards we now take for granted amongst the top two-thirds of earners in the developed world: two-car families, central heating (or air-conditioning), a PC needing to be replaced every few years, a mobile phone for every family member. Just on its own, the energy required to produce the billions of such goods would melt the polar ice caps in double-quick time.

As with meritocracy, egalitarianism as it is presently construed cannot be unthinkingly pursued any further. As long as we are infected with the idea that it applies solely to our material and social status, it is disastrous; equality of opportunity is all very well, but we might as well forget it if it doesn't go beyond the material. In political circles, the key players seem as unaware of this as hyperactive hamsters.

You will by now be well aware that I am less than enamoured with how the ideal of female emancipation has been implemented. Making more than a third of the most privileged fifteen-year-old girls emotionally distressed, making women all around the world dissatisfied with their appearance, converting a potential hard-working, able female workforce into high-achieving bullies in corporate suits. None of these is what Emily Pankhurst or Germaine Greer had in mind, any more than the despising of unpaid women (or men) who care for their relatives, old or young. Again, a complete rethink is required; again, there is no sign of mental life in this respect amongst our rulers. We know what it was that we hoped to emancipate women from, but we have allowed Selfish Capitalism to dictate what replaces it, to create new chains which bind them in ways that are every bit as damaging and constricting, in some respects even more so.

And what of the most fundamental ideal of all, democracy, the one Bush and Blair invoked as their excuse for invading (liberating) Iraq after their lies about weapons of mass destruction were exposed? Surely, this dream of popular self-rule cannot be questioned? A recent scholarly book by Cambridge political theorist John Dunn dares to do so. Pointing out that the concept of democracy originated in Greece as a value rather than a form of governance, he shows how it was regarded with disgust for two thousand years afterwards, resuscitated by the American and French Revolutions, but only achieving its present acceptance as the basis for a particular form of governance (rather than referring solely to the value that was its original meaning) after the Second World War. Whereas the original ideal was of self-government, Dunn demonstrates that what we really mean by the word today is conceding governance to our rulers, on the assumption that we can get rid of them if they do not do our bidding.

In some of its earlier incarnations, democracy meant the rule of all, by the poor majority for the poor majority. But it has come to mean an unsavoury and unequal rule of all by a rich minority, for a rich minority. It was discovered in the eighteenth and nineteenth centuries that extending the franchise to all or many citizens in genuinely free votes usually resulted in the overthrow of those who introduced the wheeze. This made politicians under- standably nervous, but they persevered. In the heat of the battles against Hitler and then the Soviet Union, Western governments managed to forge a version of democracy which sustained the illusion of control of destiny by the populations of the Western world. Unfortunately, serious thought and debate about what this actually entailed, the gulf between the ideal and the reality, disappeared completely as the twentieth century wore on. The inevitable fact that majority rule entailed coercion of dissident minorities was ignored as a problem. In this coun-try, for example, it has been possible for the three-quarters of the population who don't smoke to force the one-quarter who do smoke to do it only in private, and for the majority who do not like fox hunting to ban the minority who enjoy it. Indeed, if true democracy existed, say by internet voting by a 100 per cent netted electorate through referenda on all important matters, there could follow a great many outcomes which are thought undesirable by the educated elite, from the elevation of Richard Branson to President of Britain to homo-phobic legislation. To a certain extent, the rule of the lowest common denominator is already being applied through tele-vision, with far more British young people voting in the annual *Big Brother* series than in general elections. The educated elite would be no happier with true adherence to democratic values than with the present façade.

In the late twentieth century, writes Dunn, American democracy 'was presented and welcomed as a well-estab-lished recipe both for nurturing the order of egoism and combining its flourishing with some real protection for the civil rights of most of the population. It threatened relatively few and held out modest hopes to a great many.' With no sound of political axes grinding, Dunn points to the irony that Bush invoked democracy as his justification for terror (remember 'shock and awe'?) and tyranny in fighting terrorist and tyrannical regimes. What had once been acceptable tyranny (Saddam when he was a bulwark against Iran) was now unacceptable (Saddam sitting on the second largest oil puddle in the world, refusing to dance to American tunes). In pointing up the many other rich ironies of what is done in the name of democracy, Dunn asserts that the age of democracy has actually entailed a far greater control of citizens by governments: 'The world in which we all now live is governed more extensively and more intimately than it has ever been before.' Democracy in English-speaking nations today has come to mean the handing over of a vast number of decisions and powers to rulers in return for the freedom to pursue egotistical, hedonistic consumer choices (as Herbert Marcuse predicted it would, back in the 1960s).

An important if implicit part of this pact is the acceptance that true meritocracy, equality and female emancipation are sacrificed on the altar of materialism. Modern democratic society, according to Dunn, 'is a disenchanted and demoralised world, all too well adjusted to lives organised around the struggle to maximise personal income ... If this is the triumph of democracy, it is a triumph which very many will always find disappointing ... Over the two centuries in which it has come to triumph, some have seen it simply as an impostor, bearer of a name which it has stolen, and instrument for the rule of the people by something unmistakably different. No one anywhere nowadays can plausibly see it as rule by the people.' At best, the case for our democratic system is that it is the least worst.

By the end of the Labour Government of 1945, the four ideals were accepted by the Tories as unquestioningly as free market economics is a Labour given today. All the ideals have been rock-solid vote-winners: what majority of Western electorates would not want to be able to advance through merit rather than class, to have equality of opportunity and to liberate women from their traditional role? As time passed, both ruling parties subtly perverted the use of these words to refer to Virus values, rather than their true meanings. Insidiously, meritocracy became a method for educating the workforce and selecting the most promising managers of an economy increasingly geared to making the rich richer and consumers carry on consuming. Opportunity became a mantra for becoming rich, for the material aspiration of everyone to better themselves, so that consumption would flourish. Female emancipation became a cracking good stunt for increasing the size and quality of the workforce and enabling employers to smash the unions in an economy with gender-neutral jobs. Democracy became the right to vote for people who would make you richer and better able to pleasure yourself. All these changes were invariably served up with lavish helpings of the word 'freedom', which must have set George Orwell turning in his grave, muttering 'remember doublethink, remember doublethink'.

The problem was not with the four ideals but with what was done in their name. If they had been implemented to increase our emotional well-being, rather than the wealth of a tiny minority, they would have taken very different forms.

The Unselfish Capitalist manifesto: some modest and immodest proposals

If the present lot have been useless and the other lot are hardly likely to be any better, what's the answer? Resisting the temptation to preface my reply with, 'Well, it's like everything, really' – that time-honoured device of London cabbies before launching into a tedious tirade – I shall try to keep it short. I am not a politician or a social administrator, and it is all too easy for social scientists to shoot their mouths off about what men and women of action should be doing, when, if truth be told, I am the first to admit that many of us would be hard-pressed to organise a piss-up in the proverbial. I have discussed with various Nouveau Labour figures the problem of getting even the simplest policy implemented, and I do appreciate that it is extremely hard.

One of the most worrying things that Rose told me (the frustrated politician with whom I began this chapter) was how arbitrary are the processes of decision-making, how subject to the vagaries of group and individual psychology. 'The strangest single thing I have noticed since being in government is how random it is. You can have a very small group of like-minded people at a meeting to make a final decision about which of several options we should proceed with. The one that finally gets chosen depends on all sorts of essentially emotional factors: one of the key players can be in a bad mood, personality clashes can push people into alliances that having nothing to do with the merits of the policies, sheer exhaustion might mean one person swings in favour of the line of least resistance, or worst of all, political expedience wins out. Deciding policy is terrifyingly at the

mercy of human vagaries.' Alas, having sat on a few commit-
tees myself, I am sure she is right, so when I propose specific
changes, I am all too aware that it's much easier to be an
armchair policy-maker than to actually get things done.

Let me also make it clear that I do not subscribe to any of
the existing party political creeds. My sole excursion into this
realm was a lacklustre membership of the Labour Party for a
couple of years at the start of the eighties. I am not against
capitalism, which in itself does not cause Affluenza. It is possible to have a system which accepts the principles that define
capitalism – commercial profit, private property and prices in
markets as signals for the allocation of resources – without
causing the Virus. Some versions of Socialism also accept these
principles. Only Communism, which mendacious or ignorant
Conservatives conflate with socialism, does not.

So, guv, Unselfish Capitalism has as its primary goal the
meeting of our basic needs: for emotional attachments,
community, effectiveness and autonomy, to which I would add
beauty, authenticity, vivacity and playfulness. The evidence is
now overwhelming that, as well as having self-interested
tendencies, we also have powerful urges to cooperate, to
further the interests of others and to play fair – that genes are
at least as unselfish as they are selfish, if you want to put it
that way. The crucial determinants of which of these traits
predominates in a population are upbringing and society.

By far the most important step any government would
need to take would be to directly challenge Virus values,
through active exhortation and watertight legislation to
pressurise us to place less importance on money, possessions, appearances and fame, almost the opposite of what

our present and recent governments have done. The slogan of any Unselfish Capitalist would be 'Meet your needs, not your wants; Be, don't Have; cooperate as well as compete.' But how might that be achieved in practice? I have only two suggestions to make which are practicable, given both the present political climate and the high proportion of the electorate who are blinded by the Virus from seeing the necessity of more radical changes.

The first is that parents should be given the option of one of them being paid the national average wage while they give up work to care for any children under the age of three. This could be paid to one parent to do so full-time or divided between the parents, if they wish to split the care. If neither is prepared to do the caring, then no payment should be made, unless there were exceptional circumstances, such as illness in both parents, in which case it could be paid to a relative or nanny. I shall leave it to others to squabble over the funding of such a plan. I am not a pacifist but it could be done, for example, by assigning about two-thirds of the £30 billion currently spent each year on defence – most of which is actually used for offence, under our present leader; the Ministry of Offence also own 1 per cent of the British land-mass, another clue as to where the money could be found. My point is that we need to restore the status of caring for children, and in a society where only paid work is valued, paying parents to care for their own youngsters is the best way to achieve that. I am not talking about Child Tax Credits, I mean that the sum of £20,000 a year – or whatever the current average wage – should be paid. Obviously, that money should not be paid to families who are rich, for example the 1 per cent of people who earn more than £100,000 a year or who have large capital assets.

I place proper remuneration for parenthood at the heart of my proposed changes because it would break the logjam currently afflicting dual-income households trapped in an upward spiral of consumption. It would no longer be possible for men, or women, to say that they were returning to work 'because we need the money'. The benefits to children would be enormous, and the pressure for men to start pushing the pram more often would be greatly increased. This latter is the single most important change which I believe could transform us for the better, individually and nationally.

My second proposal is the obvious one: that the richest in our society must be divested of a significant portion of their wealth, and the amount that senior managers are paid must be regulated so that they do not earn more than five times the national average. I leave it to others to work out how to enforce this, but some obvious candidates would be taxation primarily based on the value of homes, replacement of current inheritance tax with one that does not provide a blatant loophole (no tax paid if money passed on seven years before death) and much tighter policing of tax havens.

As for other ideas, if I'm going to play the game of Fantasy Political Policies then here are some examples of the sort of things that might help, albeit that many will feel that they have as much chance of becoming reality as I have of discovering a cure for cancer. Some readers will like some of the ideas and others will hate them, but almost everyone will think, 'You must be joking, it'll never happen.' But a large part of my intention in proposing them is to show just how far we are from ordering our society in a way that will maximise well-being. My ideas may sound like the ravings of a Panglossian optimist, but consider this: why might they never come into being? My answer is that Selfish Capitalism has locked us into a mindset which despairs of much good ever coming from any radical changes promoted by government. Yet stranger things have happened: who would have predicted that Britain would change to the extent that it did under Mrs Thatcher? Who foresaw the end of the Soviet Union? Who predicted that Blair would be the keenest British warmonger since 1945? If those things happened, so can what I'm about to suggest.

1. Unselfish Capitalist democracy

If we return to the original meaning of 'democracy', a citizenry engaging in self-government, then we will have a model of governance that will allow us to meet our true needs. Some steps for achieving this would be:

- *Referenda on all major national decisions, with sub-referenda to define which issues are to be decided by referenda.* This is already done in California and the Swiss Cantons, and although some of the results have been disastrous, at least the citizens are themselves directly responsible for all decisions, good and bad.

- *Forcing government to make nearly all information available to any citizen.* As John Dunn puts it, 'The more governments control what their fellow citizens know, the less they can claim the authority of those citizens for how they rule.'

- *Making ownership of all British mass media possible only for people born in Britain.* Whilst this provides no guarantee of making the media more truly reflective of the citizens' wishes, at least it rules out the possibility of people with no stake whatever in our national well-being milking us for all they can get (and in the case of Rupert Murdoch, paying minimal tax to boot), regardless of the damage done by the values they purvey. In Adolf James's utopia, no television channel would be permitted to broadcast more than one American-originated programme a day.

- *Active intervention by government to force international corporations to prove their commitment to national priorities.* As part of this move, legislation would be introduced specifically to restrict the operation of American corporations in this country, with strong laws against damaging American fast-food chains whose products are deemed likely to cause harm to mental or physical health. It might sound bonkers, but remember that a quarter of our population is clinically obese, with fast food making a major contribution. Remember also that the more Americanised a culture, the more consumerist it is.

2. Unselfish Capitalist meritocracy

What should be meritorious is that which increases the likelihood of fulfilling our basic needs. This requires us to look afresh at what is really 'merited' at almost every level of our society, following the underlying principle that public good is placed higher than personal gain.

Beginning at the top, we need *a system which selects leaders who are emotionally mature*. At present, the system is strongly biased in favour of the workaholic, the chamaeleon, the machiavellian, the Marketing Character and sufferers from certain personality disorders. Creating working patterns like those in Denmark, based on men participating fully in the home, and creating a work culture in which long hours are not rewarded, either culturally or financially, will go some way towards achieving this goal. Another idea might be that, following their election, all Members of Parliament would have to spend two weeks caring full-time for a two-year-old. This would need to be strictly enforced, with direct monitoring by an independent authority to check that they really do it. Only then will our leaders (female as well as male – the sort of women who become MPs are often also the kind of people who find the dependence of babies intolerably demanding) grasp the difficulty of this work, and also its huge importance.

If a criterion of real merit were applied, the people who do the shitty jobs would be paid more than the ones doing the exciting, stimulating ones. As any adolescent politically minded fule knos by the age of fifteen, the logic of the present working system is to pay the least to the people who do the jobs that no-one wants (cleaning, teaching in violent inner-city schools) and the most to those who are often doing their dream one. The idea that merchant bankers have to be paid millions on the basis of merit and shortage of suitable candidates is nonsense. Most leaders would be doing the job they do, or a similar one, working just as hard, regardless of the money. They do it because they have to, are hyperactively needing the feeling of control or status.

Following the Danish lead, *education must be much less focused on exam results and divorced from the needs of industry. Its primary goal must be the short- and long-term well-being of pupils.* Whilst it may be inevitable that ruling elites will have a strong tendency to reproduce themselves, we could be doing a great deal more than we do to undermine this. For instance, we might insist that only 7 per cent of students in a university can have been educated at a private school (7 per cent is the proportion of children at a private school). The measure of a good education should be an emotionally literate adult who is capable of fulfilling themself, rather than one with high exam grades.

If you think these ideas are from La-La Land, look at some of the things the government currently merits as requiring money. At present, as discussed above, the Ministry of Defence owns 1 per cent of the British landmass and receives over £30 billion a year. Some of its property is amongst the most valuable real estate in the world, such as the various barracks sprinkled around Knightsbridge and Westminster. Is this really necessary for our defence, or is it more concerned with offensive military actions? How much do we really need to spend on our defence – who is going to invade us, given that we have nuclear weapons? The government seems all too happy to consider privatising our health and education services, and to flog off school playing fields, but somehow it never seems to notice that it could also *sell off most of the MOD land and slash its budget, and only meet defensive needs.* That would free up an awful lot of money for much more meritorious goals.

3. Unselfish Capitalist equality

We can't help comparing ourselves with our neighbours, but what if the social pressures were no longer to regard material equality (money, possessions, appearances, fame) as highly merited? Again, this is not far-fetched, as the Danes prove.

A total ban should be introduced on the use of exceptionally attractive models in all forms of advertisement, closely policed by the Advertising Standards Authority.

Housing property should cease to be a means of defining status. Inconceivable though it may seem for any political party to consider, suppose for a moment that the government were to value all properties in the country and then knock a nought off – a house formerly worth £500,000 would be revalued at £50,000. Great care would be taken to enforce the law, so that no properties changed hands at the old values through hidden measures, like tax havens. Only the government-determined price could be paid, and it would stay at that level in perpetuity, regardless of inflation and rising earnings. If there was more than one potential buyer for a property, a computer would choose at random. On its own, that would help to reduce the number of foreign citizens who own property here, at present a major cause of price inflation, but just to be on the safe side, foreign nationals would be forbidden from owning property. Suppose also that the government were to use some of the monies gained from cutting the MOD budget and selling off its land to nationalise estate agency. Instead of the pointless replication of estate agents' premises on every high street (these could be converted into badly needed accommodation), each town could have a government estate agent's office, with a national website displaying details (including video footage, shot according to strict rules) of all the properties for sale everywhere in the country. Apart from the massive savings for buyers and sellers that would ensue, it would also remove the inflationary effect of the estate agent's profession.

Also from the MOD windfall, public services could be improved, so that *the much longed-for (by Old Labour voters) withering of private schools and medicine* would finally come about. In some cases, services that are currently paid for could be offered free, such as public transport within cities.

4. Unselfish Capitalist female emancipation

There are still areas in which women do not have the same equality of opportunity as men, and that does require attention, but more important would be a return to the questions that exercised feminists before the movement was hijacked by Selfish Capitalism: what can women teach men, and how would men and women differ if there were true equality of opportunity?

First and foremost, as described above, *apart from the very richest, all parents would be provided with the option of taking paid leave, at the national average wage, whilst they have a child under the age of three. The money could also be paid to a close relative to do the job*. This would be as open to fathers as to mothers. Again, the MOD windfall could help to fund it (doubtless there are other government activities, unmerited by the new values, which could be curtailed to pay for it), and it would not be paid to people in the 1 per cent of the population who earn over £100,000 a year.

Flexible working would be a right for all parents with a child under three, making it much commoner for fathers and mothers to share childcare.

Considerable resources would be devoted in schools to preparing children for parenthood, with particular attention paid to stimulating interest in it in boys, and discouraging girls from defining themselves through exam results, especially in the early teens. Sod citizenship, this is much more important.

It is with some fascination that I await the response of the Conservative Party to this manifesto. In the meantime, at the next election, I exhort you to place your cross in the Unselfish Capitalism Party box, or if it does not yet exist, in the box of the party that most closely approximates to it.

Epilogue

Preposterous though the contention 'All you need is love' may be, it is not the one that most sums up the extent to which our intellectual vision had become blurred in the sixties. That honour goes to the final words on the Beatles' album *Abbey Road*: 'And, in the end, the love you take is equal to the love you make.' Beyond wanting something to rhyme with 'take' and get the album out of the way during a period of extreme internal warfare, it is hard to imagine what impelled the mop-topped ones to produce such gibberish. Perhaps they supposed that we would infer from it, somehow, that 'the love you express is equal to the love you receive', which is what they actually seemed to think, judging from their other work and public utterances. Whatever. The point is that, although the giving and receiving of love is – and presumably always will be – the foundation of everything most valuable in human life, it is a big mistake to believe that love is all you need, because all of us also contain a good deal of hate.

Whilst in New Zealand I came across a book of jokes about Australians, illustrating the ubiquity of hatred. Here are a few examples:

Bruce's mates thought he deserved to get into the *Guinness Book of Records* for completing a sixteen-piece jigsaw in just three hours: on the box it said '3–4 years'.

An Englishman wanted to be an Irishman, so he went to the doctor and asked if there was an operation he could have. 'I just remove half your brain,' came the reply. The following day the Englishman awoke in the hospital to a look of horror on the doctor's face. 'I'm frightfully sorry,' said the doc, 'but your whole brain was removed.' The patient replies, 'That's all right, mate. Chuck us a Fosters!'

The great Aussie game-hunter was stalking the jungles of Africa when he stumbled across a beautiful woman lying provocatively on her back in a clearing.

'Wow!' he said. 'Are you game?'

With a seductive smile she replied, 'Why, yes, I am.'

So he shot her.

An Aussie and his Sheila were sitting on the sofa. He was watching TV, she reading her horoscope. Suddenly she turned to him and slapped his face. 'That', she shouted, 'is for next week!'

That the New Zealanders cordially loathe the Aussies is nothing special. Hatred is everywhere. I was reminded of the human capacity for cruelty when I was in Moscow. To someone of my vintage, it's still incredible that one can hang out by the walls of the Kremlin at all. During most of my adult life it stood for what James Bond or George Smiley were trying to outwit. That I'm able to amble past the KGB's Lubyanka headquarters and not be decapitated by Oddjob's metal bowler hat or jabbed in the leg by Olga Kleb's poisoned shoe-dagger seems unimaginable. Now, one can sit at a café in Red Square and be served freshly pressed orange juice by ostentatiously gay waiters at the famous Gum apartment store. Practically in the Kremlin, stores stocking Dior, Hugo Boss, Kenzo and all the other labels compete for your attention just across the way from Lenin's last resting place, where he is probably turning cartwheels in his grave at the changes. There's talk of putting him in a proper coffin in the earth as a symbol of the absolute demise of his ideology, but for now his remains are in a basement beneath a dark green square of marble by the Kremlin wall. In a tiny room of maybe three by six metres, you shuffle around his body under the scrutiny of scarily heavily armed soldiers, surrounded by sombre black marble. Still clad in his matching black suit (he was The Boss but not in Boss), Lenin's expression is ... well, dead, or just possibly sleeping. This man started out with some very high ideals, sincerely felt, but his dream became a nightmare of oppression and mass murder. As anyone familiar with Simon Sebag-Montefiore's biography of Stalin will know, you needed a great deal more than love to survive under the Soviet leadership.

Arguably, the single most radical finding in this book is that, just as Lenin started out with some very estimable intentions, our most cherished ideals – of democracy, meritocracy, equality and female emancipation – have been hijacked and perverted by Selfish Capitalism. In particular, these ideals have been used to seduce low- and middle-income citizens, and especially women, into believing that Virus values are all, that adopting them will bring well-being and that their acquisition is open to everyone. Having succeeded in this perversion, Selfish Capitalism is now attempting the same with developing nations.

To counteract this we need to restate our ideals and be clear that the idea that anyone can do anything is malevolent nonsense, and that, anyway, even if on psychological grounds it were not disastrous, ecologically it is. The solution is not, of course, a return to pre-Neolithic hunter-gathering social forms, nor is it the re-establishment of cloying social orders which deny opportunities to the poor and to women. Rather, it is to create societies which redefine what the meritorious opportunities actually are, and emphasise our cooperative, authentic and playful tendencies – societies in which citizens devote much less of their time and effort to being superior to one another.

I do not despair of this happening. On a purely personal level, at the end of 2001 and the start of 2002 I had two experiences of life and death in quick succession which encouraged me to believe that the future is not necessarily bleak: my mother died, and I became a father for the first time. Both these experiences have helped me to stay alive.

In the summer of 2001 my mother complained of pains

in her back. Since she was aged eighty-five, no-one worried too much about this, but as October approached it became clear that she was not a well woman. Admitted to hospital on a Sunday, she was dead from cancer a week later. What was so enlivening was the precise manner of her last few hours.

On her last Sunday the pain became a lot worse during the afternoon. My mother had always been emphatic that, were she to contract a terminal illness which was painful or impairing her mental faculties, she wanted to be helped to die as soon as possible. I put this to the doctor, and with characteristic humour my mother told him, 'I really don't mind if you kill me.' A few minutes later, in the company of my sisters, she was given an injection.

Having witnessed a friend nearly die within two minutes of taking a heroin overdose, I had always assumed that death would follow almost immediately. Instead, her face became very calm, and although her eyes were closed she could still understand what we were saying, nodding in answer to questions and even smiling occasionally. After about half an hour, she pulled herself upright. She opened her eyes and looked at each of us with an unmistakable volition, pausing as she saw each face. When my turn came, I smiled and gave her a wave – 'Hello mum.' She smiled back. Her eyes closed, and about twenty minutes later she stopped breathing.

Her final goodbye look and smile, a deliberate act of farewell, was a triumph of self-assertion in the face of vast quantities of morphine and severe difficulty in breathing. Who knows what she was feeling or thinking at the moment she looked at me, but it was an extraordinary display of human will asserting itself in the most adverse of circumstances.

That memory was with me when, just three months later, our daughter was born. Here was another speechless, powerless being, but one going in the opposite direction from my mother, towards rather than away from physical and social existence. About an hour after our daughter's birth, I was holding her and staring into her eyes, and she was staring inquisitively back.

These basic, simple experiences of seeing and being seen by my mother and then my daughter renewed my joy in life. It may be a cliché, but death and birth coming so close together force one to get on with living.

As the months passed by, I experienced the usual awe at each increase in our daughter's capacity to communicate intimately. One morning, when she was about six months old, she made some strange snorting noises through her nose, smiling and chuckling. My wife pointed out that she was humorously imitating a particular part of my morning yoga routine which she had now witnessed numerous times.

Not long afterwards, my daughter illustrated a telling joke on consumerism which I had heard my mother often make: that babies usually find the wrapping paper of the presents they are given more interesting than the shiny or noisy or furry objects inside. My mother always delighted in this as a triumph of the intrinsic over the socially prescribed, commercially motivated function of the product. In the same way, she felt that much formal education was a destructive imposition that curtailed self-expression and vivacity. The same can be said of much paid employment, and of consumerism. We are constantly pressurised to believe that our possessions are outdated and that new ones will increase our enjoyment, yet a moment's thought reveals that this is rarely true. When I used to play tennis with my wooden Dunlop Maxply or drive golf balls from the tee with an old-fashioned wooden club, if I hit a shot cleanly it gave me as much satisfaction as when I do so today with much more technically advanced modern equipment. Likewise, we are encouraged to believe that talented sports people are in some way more fortunate than us. Yet again, when I think back to the two goals I scored in a match in 1972, I am sure that the thrill I felt then was every bit as great as any that David Beckham has now when he curls in a free-kick. What matters is not how sophisticated the equipment is but how you use it, just as scoring a goal is not necessarily more satisfying in front of 600 million television viewers than it is in the park on a Sunday morning with no spectators.

This book prescribes less worry about the audience, and forgetting the idea that more, bigger, technologically advanced snacks, supplied immediately, means better. Instead it offers a reconnection with what really matters and learning to value what you have already got – emotionally, socially and materially. The death of my mother and birth of my daughter provide strong clues to the escape routes from the hamster's wheel: volition, humour and playfulness.

Eliot's 'The Love Song of J. Alfred Prufrock' was one of the readings we chose for our wedding. It ends with these lines:

> *We have lingered in the chambers of the sea*
> *By sea-girls wreathed with seaweed red and brown*
> *Till human voices wake us, and we drown.*

With these words, Eliot is warning us of the dangers of dozing through life in a fantasy world, and if woken, of being drowned in banal reality. My final thought, then, is that it does not have to be that way. If, individually and collectively, we grasp that there is more to life than 'more bigger snacks now', then that authentic, vivacious and playful experience is all you need.

Appendix 1

Emotional Distress and Inequality in the WHO Study

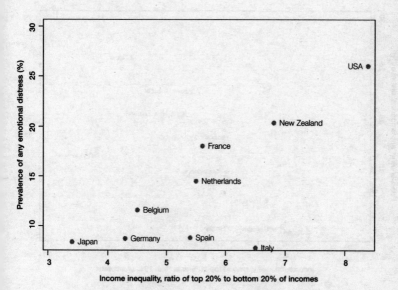

*Twelve-month prevalence of emotional distress
(depression, anxiety, substance abuse, impulsivity)
and inequality in developed nations.*

Sources Emotional distress prevalences: for New Zealand, Oakley-Browne et al. (2006); for all other nations, Demyttenaere et al. (2004). Income inequality ratios are from UNDP (2003).

Appendix 2

Emotional Distress and Inequality:
Selfish vs Unselfish Capitalist Nations

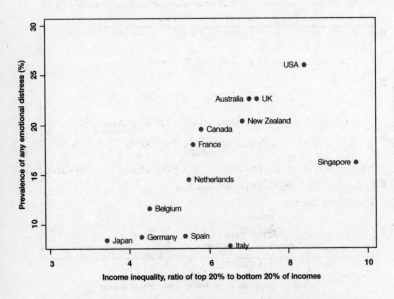

*Inequality of income and prevalence of emotional distress
in English-speaking nations, Western Europe and Japan.*

Notes

1. The mean prevalences of emotional distress for the six English-speaking nations combined is 21.6%. The mean for the other nations, mainland Western Europe plus Japan, is 11.5%.

2. There is a strong and statistically significant linear Pearson correlation between the prevalence of any emotional distress and income inequality (see the table on the next page).

3. Prevalences in the USA, France, the Netherlands, Belgium, Japan, Germany, Spain and Italy are for 12 months and are taken from Demyttenaere et al. (2004).

4. Prevalence in the UK is for 12 months, and taken from ONS (2000, p. 32).

5. Four-week prevalence of emotional distress in Australia is from ABS (2003, p. 4).

6. Prevalence for 12 months in Canada is from ICPE (2000).

7. Prevalence for Singapore (only depression and anxiety measured) is for 12 months and is taken from Fones et al. (1998).

8. Prevalence for 12 months in New Zealand is from Oakley-Browne et al. (2006).

9. Income inequality ratios are from UNDP (2003).

Correlations for emotional distress and inequality in different developed nations.

Association between income inequality and prevalence of emotional distress	Correlation	P-value
8 countries with WHO data	0.73	0.04*
7 countries with WHO data, excluding USA	0.24	0.6
9 countries with WHO, New Zealand added	0.76	0.02*
8 countries with WHO data, NZ in, USA out	0.52	0.19

12 countries (WHO + UK, Canada, Singapore, Australia)	0.63	0.03*
11 countries as row above, excluding USA	0.63	0.09
13 countries (WHO + English-speaking + New Zealand)	0.63	0.02*
12 countries as row above, excluding USA	0.55	0.06
12 countries (excluding Singapore as a less developed country)	0.79	0.002*
4 English-speaking countries (USA, UK, Australia, Canada)	0.996	0.003*
5 English-speaking countries (as row above, + New Zealand)	0.96	0.01*
4 English-speaking countries (as row above, excluding USA)	0.86	0.14

p-values less than 0.05 indicate a statistically significant association, indicated by *

Appendix 3

Emotional Distress in the Fifteen Nations of the WHO Study

Cross-national prevalence of emotional distress (depression, anxiety, substance abuse and impulsivity-aggression) (Demyttenaere et al. 2004).

Nation	Percentage of population having suffered any form of emotional distress in previous 12 months
USA	26.4
New Zealand	20.7
Ukraine	20.5
France	18.4
Colombia	17.8
Lebanon	16.9
Netherlands	14.9
Mexico	12.2
Belgium	12.0

Spain	9.2
Germany	9.1
China (Beijing)	9.1
Japan	8.8
Italy	8.2
Nigeria	4.7
China (Shanghai)	4.3

Notes

Prologue

xvi **I pointed out that a twenty-five-year-old American**: see James (1998, appendix 1).

xvii **By the standards of the fifties**: Twenge (2000).

xvii **In the case of British people**: For Britons, 1 in 6 is often cited as the proportion, but this is mistaken. Close scrutiny of the two large studies of nationally representative samples of Britons reveals the true figure of 23%, buried on page 32 in '2.6 Co-occurrence of disorders', ONS (2000).

xvii **and there is strong evidence**: Andrews et al. (2005), Lewinsohn et al. (2004).

xvii **There are strong reasons for supposing**: For example, people who refer themselves for help are very likely to be technically suffering from a mental illness (Brown et al. 2005); there is little doubt that older people in surveys are less likely to recall having been depressed when younger, because of the length of time since the episode and possibly because they are less infected by psychobabble, but this is unlikely to wholly explain the much higher prevalences found in younger age groups (Patten 2003, Wells et al. 2004). The most sophisticated exploration of the mental health of the American population has been made by Corey Keyes (e.g. Keyes 2005). He finds that only 17% can be classified unambiguously as 'completely mentally healthy'.

xvii **What is more, a considerable body of evidence**: James (2007).

xvii **many American authors**: most notably Frank (1999), Schor (1999), Lane (2000), Puttnam (2000) and Schwartz (2004).

xvii **and, more recently, British**: e.g. Layard (2005), Martin (2005).

xvii **nearly all of them concentrating on happiness**: e.g. Layard (2005), Martin (2005). However, the main impetus for this outbreak of happiness was provided by two Americans, Seligman (1991) and Diener et al. (2000). The great problem with surveys of happiness, life satisfaction or well-being is that they are paper-thin, based on asking (albeit often huge) samples of people variants of the simple question, 'Are you very happy, happy, OK, unhappy, very unhappy?' This leaves enormous room for differences in how different nations interpret the word 'happiness'. As will become clear in Chapter 3, whereas Americans live in a culture where they are strongly encouraged to depict themselves as happy, the opposite is true in most of the Far East. Attempts to 'prove' that happiness surveys are solidly founded (e.g. Layard 2005, p. 17) because studies of patterns of brainwaves correlate with answers do not address this problem – they are restricted to American samples (e.g. Davidson et al. 2000). Even if it is a fact that there is more electrical activity on the left side of the brain when people say they are feeling happy, in itself that tells us nothing about whether they really are. Studies of 'repressors' (Myers 2000) – who make up 15% of the population – show that they will claim to be happy when they are not.

An even greater problem with happiness surveys is that their results do not correlate at all with the results of cross-national studies of 'mental illness'. These latter studies ask many more questions and dig much deeper to explore a person's mental state. Whatever else one may say about psychiatrists, for instance, they are good at measuring depression. Decades of research have established fourteen criteria for deciding whether a person is depressed, including empirical, measurable problems such as erratic sleep patterns. If you attempt to correlate the fifteen countries in the most reliable cross-national study of mental health (see Appendix 3) with the findings of surveys of happiness, life satisfaction and well-being in those countries (where available), you will find no relationship. For example, America is by some margin the most mentally ill nation in the WHO study, but in happiness surveys it is nowhere near the unhappiest, the least satisfied or the nation with the greatest ill-being. Equally telling, studies of well-being (e.g. Blanchflower et al. 1999) claim that well-being is increasingly good among young people, yet studies of mental illness demonstrate the opposite (Robins et al. 1992, Rutter et al. 1995, European Commission 2004), showing as they do very measurable things such as rising suicide and substance abuse.

For these reasons, as demonstrated in Chapter 3, I am inclined to view the results of cross-national studies of happiness as merely reflecting differences in national cultures and ways of talking about contentment, not as true reflections of the quality of emotional life or mental health of the different nations. Economists find happiness studies attractive as a basis for discussion because they provide very convenient statistics based on large samples which can be correlated with all manner of social and economic data. But the work of Diener and similarly minded Britons (e.g. Gardner et al. 2001, Huppert et al. 2005) has little or nothing to tell us about true cross-national differences in emotional distress.

xviii **First, in a developed nation**: Pickett et al. (2006).

xix   **The kind of care we receive**: James (2003a, 2003b).

xix   **Likewise, being of low social class**: for further details see James (2007).

xx   **Like many before me**: e.g. Laing (1967), Szasz (1984), Smail (2005).

Chapter 1: New York

8   **an in-depth study of New York stockbrokers**: Cass et al. (2000); there is also considerable evidence that many successful people in business have high rates of depression and anxiety (e.g. Korman et al. 1981) and of personality disorder (e.g. Board et al. 2005).

11   **In a report on burnout**: Berger (2000).

12   **Studies from fourteen countries**: Kasser (2002).

13   **Erich Fromm, an American psychologist**: Fromm (1976, 2002).

14   **Face-to-face or telephone selling**: Offer (2006, p. 94).

14   **advertising has accounted for over 2 per cent**: Offer (2006, p. 122 and figure 6.3, p. 123).

14   **Studies show that they regard themselves**: Saunders et al. (2000), Saunders (2001).

16   **He quotes an executive**: Packard (1956, p. 23).

16   **David Ogilvy, a British advertising executive**: cited by Packard (1956, p. 25).

16   **One ad executive had this to say**: cited by Packard (1956, pp. 24–5).

16   **Fifty years later**: Kasser (2002, p. 91).

16   **in the words of a contemporary executive**: cited by Kasser (2002, p. 91).

17   **Mainland European nations have long spent**: Offer (2006, p. 123).

17   **and they are less materialistic**: Ger (1996).

17   **a steady rise in the proportion of people**: information obtainable from <www.cultdyn.co.uk>, accessed 9 Oct. 2006.

17   **Indeed, there is now overwhelming evidence**: Kleinman et al. (1997), James (2007).

18   **children raised in poor homes**: Kasser (2002, p. 33).

18   **Likewise, women are more materialistic**: Kasser et al. (1999).

18   **the problem comes when**: For a seminal analysis of how the Keeping-Up-With-The-Joneses that locks us into these wants is fostered, see Hirsch (1977).

20   **much to the consternation of social scientists**: Smith et al. (2003).

20   **One study, of 860 young American adults**: Perkins (1991).

20   **Compared with non-believers**: Ryan et al. (1993).

23   **A large body of scientific evidence**: summarised in Kasser (2002) and James (2007).

30   **a notion cooked up by psychiatrists**: e.g. Rolf et al. (1990).

31   **Studies of resilience nearly always turn up such a person**: Rolf et al. (1990); however, it must be acknowledged that one study (Caspi et al. 2003) has come up with good evidence that genes may create resilience against developing depression as a consequence of childhood maltreatment. Whilst full replication of this study has not yet been done (though see Wilhelm et al. (2006) for a near miss), were it to be done it would be strong support for the 'bit of both' nature and nurture explanation for depression.

32   **people who undergo therapy often become more secure**: Fonagy et al. (1995).

35   **Strongly materialistic people are often using money**: Kasser et al. (1995), Cohen et al. (1996), Assor et al. (2004).

35   **Another important factor is parental divorce and separation**: Rindfleisch et al. (1997).

41   **Americans watch 50 per cent more TV**: Nationmaster, 'Television viewing by country', <www.nationmaster.com/graph-T/med_tel_vie>, accessed 12 Sept. 2006.

41   **and two and a half times as many films**: Nationmaster, 'Cinema attendance (per capita) by country', <www.nationmaster.com/red/graph-T/med_cin_att_cap& int=-1>, accessed 12 Sept. 2006.

43   **Depressed people make a greater number**: James (2003a, pp. 59–63).

44   **A tendency towards upward social comparison**: Richins (1991, 1992), Saunders (2001).

44   **Many studies have demonstrated the cumulative effects**: James (1998, pp. 96–110), Sigman (2005), James (2007).

45   **A clever proof of this was a study**: Satoshi et al. (2000).

45   **An analysis of twenty-five different studies**: Groesz et al. (2002).

45   **A particularly telling study was done in Fiji**: Becker et al. (2002).

45   **A key American researcher**: cited by Sigman (2005, p. 157).

46   **A study of 10,000 Chinese**: Ma et al. (2002).

46   **Researchers who followed**: Johnson et al. (2002); see also James (1995), Anderson et al. (2003).

46   **Even increases in shoplifting and theft**: Hennigan et al. (1982).

Chapter 2: Global Infection

50   **Consider the spread of Starbucks**: Distribution of Starbucks outlets (supplied to me directly by the company in 2004): America and Canada: 6,228 (1 per 53,000 people); New Zealand: 36 (1 per 28,000 in Auckland); Australia: 49 (1 per 7,300 in Sydney); Singapore: 35 (1 per 114,000); UK: 415 (1 per 145,000); Shanghai: 47 (1 per 425,000); Russia: 0; Denmark: 0.

50   **Take the amount spent in different nations**: The data on which this is calculated are from Nationmaster, 'US exports of records, tapes, and disks by country', <www.nationmaster.com/graph-T/eco_tra_wit_us_us_exp_of_rec_tap_and_dis>; and 'US exports of sports apparel and gear by country', <www.nationmaster.com/graph-T/eco_tra_wit_us_us_exp_of_spo_app_and_gea>, both accessed 12 Sept. 2006. For GDP differences in national wealth, see 'The World in 2005', <www.economist.com/theworldin/index.cfm?d=2005&Go=GO>, accessed 12 Sept. 2006.

50   **The most comprehensive study of globalisation**: Dholakia et al. (2004); see also ILO (2004).

51   **In the first, over one-third**: Diener et al. (1985).

51   **The second study found no difference**: Brickman et al. (1978).

52   **Almost a quarter of Britons**: ONS (2000, p. 32).

52   **and another quarter are on the verge**: Lewinsohn et al. (2004), Andrews et al. (2005).

52   **Two-thirds of Britons believe**: Hamilton (2003).

52   **Men with this latter income were recently**: MHF Men's Mental Health Forum, <www.menshealthforum.org.uk/userpage1.cfm?item_id=84>, accessed 12 Sept. 2006.

59   **Over a fifth of Australians are now emotionally distressed**: ABS (2003).

59   **according to studies of two nationally representative samples**: ABS (2003, p. 4).

59   **Two-thirds of Aussies now say**: For all the statistics in this paragraph, see Hamilton (2002).

65   **It so happens that the first studies**: Saunders et al. (2000).

66   **A subsequent study showed**: Saunders (2001).

66   **As one observer puts it**: Belk, cited by Saunders et al. (2001, p. 194).

67   **In many commentators' views**: e.g. Whybrow (2005).

73   **children who watch TV for two hours a day**: See Sigman (2005, pp. 14–16, 26–8, 190–94) for abundant evidence of the causal role of television viewing in ADHD.

79   **other Selfish Capitalist developments since the 1990s**: Hamilton et al. (2005).

79   **the proportion of Australians who believe that emotional distress**: Jorm et al. (2005).

79   **other studies show that people who believe that genes**: Read et al. (2004).

80   **They are also more likely to hold Conservative political beliefs**: Keller (2005).

80   **to regard childhood nurture as largely unimportant**: Bugenthal et al. (1989, 2004).

80   **This makes them less likely to support**: Murray (1984, 2000).

80   **just like their sisters in the rest of the English-speaking**: European Commission (2004, pp. 34–8), Jenkins et al. (1997), Weissman et al. (1977).

80   **they are much more likely to suffer**: ABS (2003, p. 7). The proportions of 18–24-year-old Australian women suffering very high levels of psychological distress went from 2.1 to 5.4%, of 25–34-year-olds from 2.8 to 4.6%, of 35–44-year-olds from 2.4 to 4.2%, and overall, for all women, from 2.4 to 4.4%. There were similar rises for women in prevalences of moderate and high levels of psychological distress. See also James (1998, appendix 1) and James (2007) for evidence of rises in distress in the developed world.

83   **Rates of distress amongst Australian women**: ABS (2003, p. 7).

86   **there have been four sizeable ones**: Jose et al. (1998), Pakriev et al. (1998), Averina et al. (2005), Bobak et al. (2006).

86   **The most recent was of over 900**: Bobak et al. (2006).

86   **One survey, done in 1990**: Shiller et al. (1991).

86   **Caroline Humphrey, an anthropologist**: Humphrey (1995).

87   **A recent survey of attitudes**: Rose (2005).

88   **Russian cinema attendances**: Nationmaster, 'Cinema attendance (per capita) by country', <www.nationmaster.com/red/graph-T/med_cin_att_cap&int=-1>, accessed 12 Sept. 2006.

92   **Russia's sky-high divorce rate**: Nationmaster, 'Divorce rate by country', <www.nationmaster. com/graph-T/peo_div_rat>, accessed 12 Sept. 2006.

97   **In Singapore, shopping is the favourite**: Ho et al. (1995).

97   **When Singapore became independent**: Murray et al. (1996).

98   **Singapore is twenty-four times richer**: Peebles et al. (2002).

98   **The Singapore government website**: <www.gov.sg>, accessed 22 May 2004.

98   **the findings of a representative nationwide study**: Fones et al. (1998).

102 **Until they are married**: Quah (2003).

102 **By all accounts, in the fifties and sixties**: Bassett (1998).

102 **In just six years they laid waste**: Kelsey (2002).

103 **New Zealand is the most trans-nationalised country**: UNCTAD (2000).

103 **Surveys show that they want much stricter**: Perry et al. (1999).

103 **despite the huge increase in inequality**: Kelsey (2002).

104 **The results of a huge nationwide survey**: Oakley Browne et al. (2006).

104 **distress has spread, especially in urban areas**: Oakley Browne et al. (2006, table 2.3).

108 **they have virtually abolished poverty**: Larsen (2003).

108 **a staggering 80 per cent of convicted criminals**: Singleton et al. (1998).

108 **In the developed world, only Finland**: Nationmaster, 'Prisoners per capita by country', <www.nationmaster.com/graph/cri_pri_per_cap>, accessed 12 Sept. 2006.

108 **In common with their Scandinavian neighbours**: Dahlberg et al. (1999).
109 **their economy is extremely successful**: 'The World in 2005', <www.econo-mist.com/index.cfm?d =2005&Go=GO>, accessed 12 Sept. 2006.
109 **but not prohibitively high**: <www.statbank.dk>, accessed 3 July 2004.
109 **a survey of rates of major depression**: Olsen et al. (2004).
109 **When rates of psychiatric disturbance**: Bilenberg et al. (2005).
109 **that age group in the developed nations**: Rutter et al. (1995).
110 **When happiness or life satisfaction is rated**: Diener (2000).
110 **Studies comparing Denmark**: Khanna et al. (2001).

Chapter 3: Have Positive Volition (Not 'Think Positive')

118 **culture of complaint in which everyone**: Hughes (1993).
120 **Shanghai has the lowest prevalence**: Demyttenaere et al. (2004).
121 **there were 'Four Big Pieces'**: Beijing Youth Daily (2004, p. 85).
121 **in the last six years, 400 have been built**: Jonathan Watts, 'China's new consumers get a taste for luxury goods', *Guardian*, 18 June 2005 (<http://business.guardian.co.uk/story/ 0,,1509454,00. html>, accessed 12 Sept. 2006); the other statistics and quotes in this paragraph are also from this source.
125 **about 15 per cent of people in Britain**: Myers (2000).
126 **It goes back to 1980, when an American**: Kleinman (1986, 1988).
128 **more recent, thorough studies**: Simon et al. (2002), Parker et al. (2005).
128 **It is true that when depressed**: Parker et al. (2001).
128 **Until 1980, under Mao**: Bond (1995).
128 **Somatisation, a condition in which**: Tsai et al. (2004).
129 **There is a potent tradition of quiescence**: Xu (1987).
129 **It does not find high levels of optimism … nor of happiness and life satisfaction**: For optimism see Lee et al. (1997); for happiness and life satis-faction see Spencer-Rodgers et al. (2004).
129 **These demonstrate a self-critical, modest**: Heine et al. (1999).
130 **an optimistic bubble of positive illusions**: Taylor et al. (1994), Dunning et al. (2004).
130 **Some American researchers have gone so far**: Mezulis et al. (2004).
130 **In one study, repressors accounted**: Myers et al. (2000).
130 **artificial boosting of self-esteem**: Heine et al. (1999, p. 778).
130 **indeed, there is currently talk of fostering**: London School of Economics and Political Science, 'LSE Depression Report urges choice of psychological therapy for all' (<www.lse.ac.uk/collections/pressAndInformationOffice/ newsAndEvents/archives/2006/LSEDepressionReport.htm>, accessed 19 Oct. 2006).
131 **when Americans are asked about their self-esteem**: Heine et al. (1999), Ryan et al. (2003).
131 **When asked to rate their 'interpersonal sensitivity'**: Myers (1987).
131 **In contrast, the average Chinese person**: For assertions in this paragraph and the next, see Heine et al. (1999).
132 **One study presented Chinese and American**: Li (2004).
133 **Underpinning Confucianism are three primary tenets**: Peng et al. (1999), Spencer-Rodgers et al. (2004).
133 **Another vital difference is that the very concept**: Kitayama et al. (1997).
134 **On the other hand, when the Chinese**: See Heine et al. (1999) for this and the next two paragraphs.

136 **disastrously so, in the case of some violent men**: Bushman et al. (1998).
137 **Children from high-income homes**: Erikson et al. (1992).
137 **since 1970 there has been no increase**: Bynner et al. (2001), Ferri et al. (2003, chapter 2), Buxton et al. (2005).
139 **guilt and failure are common themes**: Heine et al. (1999).
145 **In a study comparing levels of concordance**: Sheldon et al. (2004a).
150 **Five necessary and sufficient conditions**: Olson et al. (1986).

Chapter 4: Replace Virus Motives (with Intrinsic Ones)

164 **The opposite of Virus motivation**: Deci et al. (2000).
164 **The studies prove that, overall**: Kasser et al. (1993), Kasser (2002).
165 **for the studies also show that people**: Carver et al. (1998), Srivastava et al. (2001), Malka et al. (2003), Sheldon et al. (2004b).
165 **has been characterised as 'flow'**: Csikszentmihalyi (1997).
166 **This has been proved many times**: Deci et al. (1999).
167 **For example, students were given three-dimensional cubes**: Deci (1971).
167 **In the context of work**: Gagné et al. (2005).
167 **The virus even penetrates the dreams**: Kasser et al. (2001b).
168 **their self-consciousness, triggered**: Schroeder et al. (1995).
168 **People with such high levels of self-consciousness**: Gibbons (1990).
168 **The infected tend to watch a lot of TV**: Sirgy et al. (1998), Csikszentmihalyi (1999).
168 **They work longer hours and amass more debt**: Schor (1992, 1999).
169 **When asked to name their most important possession**: Richins (1994).
169 **Virus-infected business students and entrepreneurs**: Srivastava et al. (2001).
169 **studies of people with this aholia shed light**: Faber et al. (1988, 1992).
169 **a low value on the self-expression and autonomy**: Khanna et al. (2001).
171 **One study of the issue, which had the subtitle**: Carver et al. (1998).
171 **Other studies have shown that pursuing money**: Srivastava et al. (2001), Malka et al. (2003), Sheldon et al. (2004b).
171 **A recent study bears this out**: Van Boven et al. (2003).
180 **Nonetheless, the overall message from the research**: Sheldon et al. (2004b).

Chapter 5: Be Beautiful (Not Attractive)

183 **Valuing beauty is a defining feature**: Kasser (2002).
189 **Sixty per cent of doctors were women**: Einhorn (1993).
189 **In 1970, 49 per cent of adult women worked full-time**: Bronfenbrenner (1968, p. 116).
190 **Russian mothers have always been expected**: Bronfenbrenner (1970).
190 **Today, amongst forty-five- to sixty-five-year-olds**: Marmot (2004).
190 **capitalism has ushered in very substantial gender inequalities**: Einhorn (1993), Mroz et al. (2004).
190 **A study carried out in 1999**: Ryan et al. (1999).
191 **Subsequent studies support Ryan's conclusions**: e.g. Stetsenko et al. (2000), Chirkov et al. (2001), Ryan et al. (2005).
191 **On average, an English-speaking girl**: e.g. Moffitt et al. (1992); see James (2003a, footnote 119, p. 323) for further references.

191 **Girls who are not close to their fathers**: Ellis et al. (1999).

191 **Coming at it from a different angle**: James (1998, pp. 201–3).

192 **Russian women are especially lacking in 'self-actualisation'**: Ryan et al. (1999).

192 **results from a survey of sixty-one sixteen-year-old schoolgirls**: O.W. James, unpublished data (2004).

193 **When you consider that Americans**: Nationmaster, 'Cinema attendance (per capita) by country', <www.nationmaster.com/red/graph-T/med_cin_att_cap&int =-1>, accessed 12 Sept. 2006.

196 **Evolutionary psychologists, nearly all of them male and American**: Buss (1989).

198 **One survey has shown that in the matter of sexual jealousy**: Buss (2000). However, for evidence that the gender difference disappears when, instead of being asked about a hypothetical infidelity (on which Buss's research is based – 'how would you react if…'), they are asked after an actual infidelity; see Harris (2002).

198 **Another (of fifty-two nations)**: Schmitt (2003); see also Schmitt (2005).

198 **Most important of all was a thirty-seven-nation**: Buss (1989).

198 **Two re-analyses of the thirty-seven-nation study**: Eagly et al. (1999), Kasser et al. (1999).

198 **Most recently of all, an analysis**: Shibley Hyde (2005).

202 **which just happens to knit neatly**: James (2007).

Chapter 6: Consume What You Need (Not What Advertisers Want You to Want)

211 **executives in the Selfish Capitalist nations**: Piketty et al. (2006, figure 3).

212 **a period (1997–2001) in which young Aussie women's rates**: ABS (2003, p. 7).

223 **This is borne out by the evidence**: Tiffen et al. (2004, table 4.25).

224 **the housing boom that now echoes**: Hamilton et al. (2005, pp. 20–25).

225 **In America between the 1950s and 1970s**: For the evidence in this paragraph see Offer (2006, pp. 282–5).

230 **in 2002 it was 20 per cent**: UNECE (2002).

231 **A study comparing trends in advertisements**: Tse et al. (1989); for more recent evidence see Wong et al. (1998).

231 **Avner Offer's book *The Challenge of Affluence***: For evidence in succeeding paragraphs regarding advertising, see Offer (2006, pp. 103–37).

235 **In 2005, Copenhagen was the city**: Ashley Seager, 'Experts chart a steady path for house prices', *Guardian*, 17 Dec. 2005.

Chapter 7: Meet Your Children's Needs (Not Those of Little Adults)

240 **The Shanghainese have one-quarter of the emotional distress**: For Singapore, see Fones et al. (1998); for Shanghai see Appendix 3.

240 **70 per cent of Singaporeans are of Chinese genetic stock**: <www.gov.sg>, accessed 27 May 2004.

240 **studies of Chinese emigrants to English-speaking nations**: Takeuchi et al. (1998) and Parker et al. (2001, 2005); for rates in Taiwan, a Chinese-descended population with a market economy, see Hwu et al. (1989) and Cheng (1989); for recent evidence of similar prevalences of mental illness

amongst Taiwanese elderly people and elderly British people, see Chong et al. (2001).

245 **Parents do it in two main ways**: For a brief review of the two ways, see Assor et al. (2004, pp. 49–55).

246 **It was, in fact, my own father**: James (1960).

247 **Introjection of parental wishes**: Crocker et al. (2002, 2003a, 2003b).

247 **Controlling parenting puts children at a high risk of both anxiety and depression**: For a review of the evidence on anxiety, see Chorpita et al. (1998); for depression see Blatt et al. (1992); a recent large cross-national study is Barber et al. (2005); for cross-national evidence of maladjustment resulting from lack of parental acceptance, see Khaleque et al. (2005).

247 **Depressed people can be divided into two main types**: James (2003a, pp. 58–68).

248 **Dozens of studies show that this often results**: For reviews see Blatt et al. (1992), Barber et al. (2005), Khaleque et al. (2005).

248 **an intriguing study of 109 adoptees**: Parker (1982); see also James (2003a, chapter 1).

248 **evidence that distinct patterns of child-rearing**: Blatt et al. (1992), James (2003a, pp. 58–68).

248 **at least one in ten of all British children**: NSPCC (2001).

248 **the materialist prospect of glittering prizes**: For further elaboration and evidence see Kasser (2002, pp. 30–32) and James (2003a, pp. 58–68).

248 **a carefully constructed study of the impact of controlling parents**: Barber et al. (2005).

249 **Supportive nurture has a completely different outcome**: Assor et al. (2004); see also Grolnick et al. (1989).

250 **On top of this, the kind of parents**: Kasser et al. (1995), Cohen et al. (1996), Williams et al. (2000), Kasser (2002).

250 **studies of what is called the authoritarian personality**: Stone et al. (1992); see also Jost et al. (2003).

250 **the sort of regime found in Bush's White House**: Frum (2003).

251 **If the results of a 1994 study are to be believed**: Wah (1994, p. 182).

252 **Another important trend amongst Singaporean youth**: Tin et al. (1994).

253 **In a study of eighteen- to nineteen-year-olds**: Choo et al. (1994, p. 216).

253 **where Singapore is very different**: Tan (1994).

253 **As one researcher put it**: Ball et al. (1994, p. 53).

254 **Singapore is as individualistic as America**: Oyserman et al. (2002).

254 **China is still strongly collectivist**: Oyserman et al. (2002).

254 **China has not jettisoned Communism**: Starr (2001).

254 **At least some of the younger generation of city-dwellers**: Fuligni et al. (2004).

254 **veering, albeit gradually, in the direction of individualism**: Schaefer et al. (2004).

254 **There is four times as much depression**: For Singapore, see Fones et al. (1998); for Shanghai see Demyttenaere et al. (2004).

255 **In 1975, 90 per cent of women under forty-five**: Women of China (1987).

256 **scientific studies of Chinese parenting**: Chen et al. (2000), Xu et al. (2005), Liu et al. (2005), Wu et al. (2005), Sorkhabi et al. (2005).

257 **Studies comparing Chinese with American**: Chiu et al. (1992), Greenberger et al. (1996), Wu et al. (2002).

257 **There is a much greater desire amongst Chinese teens**: Fuligni et al. (1999).

257 **Indeed, in one study, Chinese teenagers**: Fuligni et al. (2004).

258 **many studies show that Chinese only children**: Tao (1998).

258 **In Western homes, such upbringing**: Chiu et al. (1992), Greenberger et al. (1996), Ablard et al. (1997), Elliot et al. (2004).

258 **research suggests that Confucian parenting often is**: Chao (2001).

259 **Studies show that introjection occurs only**: Assor et al. (2004).

Chapter 8: Educate Your Children (Don't Brainwash Them)

266 **a study published in 2003**: West et al. (2003).

266 **In 1987 there was virtually no difference ... but by 1999**: JCGQ (2000).

267 **In fact, English fifteen-year-olds**: Currie et al. (2000).

268 **create a markedly greater tendency amongst girls**: Petersen et al. (1991), Cyranowski et al. (2000).

268 **They become far more law-abiding**: James (1998).

268 **it seems to be harder for girls to avoid worrying**: Alpert-Gillis et al. (1989).

269 **an outbreak of perfectionism amongst high-income daughters**: James (2003a, p. 63).

269 **The perfectionist feels that her best**: Blatt (1995), James (2003a, pp. 64–7).

269 **several studies have found an association**: Drake et al. (1984), Isohanni et al. (1999), Davidson et al. (1999).

269 **the most able schizophrenics are four times**: Alaräisänen et al. (2006).

269 **Since schizophrenia can be caused**: James (2003a).

270 **British fathers now do one-third of childcare**: Fisher et al. (1999).

271 **what studies there have been of this issue**: Frost et al. (1991), Blatt (1995, p. 1011), Ablard et al. (1997), Elliot et al. (2004).

271 **girls from fee-paying schools are more at risk**: Mann et al. (1983), Walkerdine et al. (1989).

271 **high-income girls are even more likely than others**: Dornbusch et al. (1984), Wolfe et al. (1996), Lucey (1996), Levine (2006).

271 **In a sample of women at an Oxford University college**: Sell et al. (1998).

271 **Perfectionism, academic success and eating disorders**: Blatt (1995).

272 **Between 1979 and 2000, the proportion of the UK workforce**: Offer (2006, p. 256).

273 **Since 1998 the number of people in Britain**: Bunting (2004, p. 9).

275 **research undertaken by the Cambridge Student Counselling Service**: Surtees et al. (2000).

277 **One study related the average ability level**: Marsh et al. (1984).

277 **Another study found that high achievers**: Pettigrew (1967).

277 **What is critical is perceived social status and power**: James (1998, chapter 2).

279 **American children suffer the same problems**: Luthar et al. (1999, 2002).

279 **A particularly telling study of university students**: Crocker et al. (2003a).

279 **As previous studies had found**: e.g. Deci et al. (1999), Crocker et al. (2003b).

279 **The study concluded that**: Crocker et al. (2003a, p. 709).

279 **in a sample of 14,000 Americans**: Snibbe et al. (2005).

282 For thirteen centuries prior to this one, literati competed: Luo (1996).
282 However, since 1978, with the expansion of the university system: Watkins et al. (1996), Luo (1996).
285 Fantasising or using imagination: Chen et al. (2000).
285 Studies comparing Chinese with American children: Wu et al. (2002), Chiu et al. (1992), Greenberger et al. (1996).
285 in other Asian societies, notably Japan and Singapore: For Japan see Hashimoto (2004); for Singapore see Biggs et al. (1996).
290 A large study comparing twelve- and thirteen-year-olds: Osborn (2001); see also Currie et al. (2000).
290 The official rhetoric is that education is for creating: Jensen et al. (1992), Kryger et al. (1998).
295 A recent study of American children: Lillard et al. (2006).
296 'Throughout the developed world, politicians: Wolf (2002, p. 53).
297 That Denmark has lower rates of depression: Olsen et al. (2004).
298 there has been remarkably little progress for the poor: Hauser et al. (2000).
298 some studies suggest that a woman is far likelier: Goldthorpe (1987); the best account of this is by Hakim (2000, pp. 160, 216), where she concludes (p. 216) that 'Overall, the less qualified a woman is, the more likely she is to use the marriage market to acquire a husband with better qualifications, higher earning power and better career prospects.'
298 About one-third of the American population: Hauser et al. (2000).
298 In England, there has been no increase: Bynner et al. (2000, 2001).
298 As long ago as 1995: BSA (1997).
299 This point was made nearly fifty years ago: Young (1958).

Chapter 9: Enjoy Motherhood
(Not Desperate Housewifery/Househusbandry)

307 Their education and income have improved: Offer (2006, p. 245).
307 a twenty-five-year-old woman today is at least three times: James (1998, pp. 344–5).
307 women are twice as likely to be depressed as men: Weissman et al. (1977, 1993), James (1998, pp. 176–89).
308 In 1970, UK fathers with an under-five: Fisher et al. (1999).
308 But the vast majority of domestic work is still done by women: Offer (2006, p. 319).
308 it is still very rare for men to give up paid work: Kodz (2003), O'Brien (2005).
308 Even more than women, men must prove: Ruxton (2004).
310 in recent years cosmetic surgery in Australia: A 50% rise between 1995 and 1999, see Hamilton et al. (2005, pp. 127–8).
311 fortunes are being made by food manufacturers: Offer (2006, pp. 138–69), Critser (2003).
311 Just as the governments of New Zealand: Kelsey (2002).
312 to buy properties in expensive areas, just to keep up with the Joneses: Offer (2006, pp. 282–6).
313 The vast majority of women have very low pay: Hakim (1996, chapter 3; 2000, chapter 3).

315 **10 to 15 per cent develop a full-blown**: Nicolson (1998).

316 **A survey of a thousand British mothers**: *Mother and Baby Magazine* (2002).

316 **Most people imagine that post-natal depression**: For references for this paragraph and the next, see James (2003a, pp. 211–20).

318 **astonished to learn that it is only 30 per cent**: ABS (2003).

318 **You can play the same game in England**: *Labour Market Trends* (2000, p. 10).

322 **known as gender role strain**: James (1998, pp. 178–83).

322 **a sample of 680 American couples**: Mirowsky et al. (1989, pp. 87–90).

323 **Many other studies have shown**: e.g. Schwartz (1991, footnotes 9–18).

324 **many further studies point to the importance**: James (1998, pp. 185–91).

324 **these studies prove beyond much doubt**: James (2003a, chapter 4).

324 **The evidence is piling up**: For a popular summary, see Biddulph (2006, pp. 56–76).

326 **in most couples all or nearly all of the role strain**: Offer (2006, chapter 14).

330 **when on holiday, as several studies**: e.g. Bellis et al. (2000).

336 **a recent study of 8,000 British mothers**: O'Connor et al. (2005).

336 **This has been shown in many other studies**: James (1998, pp. 173–6).

336 **Although some mothers become depressed**: James (1998, pp. 173–6).

336 **The infected are more likely to have personality disorders**: Cohen et al. (1996).

336 **the Virus-infecteds' relationships were found to be shorter-lasting**: Kasser et al. (2001a).

336 **In another sample, during the previous six months**: Sheldon et al. (2001).

338 **two-thirds of Shanghainese are still employed by the State**: Yatsko (2003).

339 **One of the most revered Soviet authorities**: cited by Bronfenbrenner (1970, p. 3).

339 **Since horrifyingly large numbers of the menfolk**: Marmot (2004).

339 **divorce rates have been at a very high level for decades**: Buckley (1997).

339 **women are now also expected to work**: Ashwin et al. (2002).

340 **some studies have found that more are male**: Christensen (2001, p. 10).

340 **the only nationally representative study**: Olsen et al. (2004).

340 **The same is true in other Scandinavian nations**: Lehtinen et al. (2003).

340 **after eighteen months of age, three-quarters**: *Statistical Yearbook* (2004, p. 4) <www.statbank.dk>.

341 **on average, Danish women do twice as much**: Christofferson (2002).

341 **Three-quarters of Danish mothers**: *Statistical Yearbook* (2004, p. 4) <www.statbank.dk>.

342 **Like so many Danish practices, compelling men**: Christofferson (2002).

344 **Bowlby was an English doctor and psychoanalyst**: See James (2003a, chapter 4) for an explication of attachment theory and evidence for the assertions made in the following paragraphs.

346 **In a recent British study of a large sample**: Lucy Ward, 'Free nursery scheme could be bad for young children, says study', *Guardian*, 4 Oct. 2005 (<http://education.guardian.co.uk/earlyyears/story/0,,1584530,00.html>, accessed 8 Oct. 2006).

347 **even though it does not accord with the evidence**: e.g. Thompson (1993), Rolfe et al. (2002).

357 **Interestingly, cross-cultural research shows**: Gulerce (1991).

360 **I did not see much evidence of specific attachments**: In this connection, it is interesting to note a recent meta-analysis (Ahnert et al. 2006) of 2,867 nine-month-olds in various kinds of substitute care. It found that 42% of them were securely attached to the substitute, compared with 60.2% who were securely attached to their mother and 66.2% securely attached to their father.

360 **reviews of the relevant studies do not support that idea**: e.g. Vaughan et al. (1999).

361 **studies which have deliberately selected**: e.g. Van Den Boom (1994).

Chapter 10: Be Authentic (Not Sincere), Vivacious (Not Hyperactive) and Playful (Not Game-playing)

372 **As Trilling puts it**: Trilling (1971, p. 3); in this chapter I draw heavily on Trilling for the historical development of the meaning of the words and the illustration thereof through art and artists.

375 **Trilling is drily dismissive**: Trilling (1971, p. 67).

375 **Jane Austen's notion of 'intelligent love'**: Trilling (1971, p. 82).

378 **Trilling points to the legacy**: Trilling (1971, p. 115).

378 **Trilling cites Henry James's account of Americans**: Trilling (1971, pp. 113–14).

383 **in a British study, this was one of the predictors**: Jennings et al. (1994).

384 **America today is as status-obsessed a society**: Frank (1999).

384 **Trilling painstakingly traced**: Trilling (1971, pp. 113–14).

391 **the vast majority of the original settlers**: White (2003).

391 **one-fifth of New Zealand citizens were not born there**: SNZ (2002).

397 **Very moralistic people are much more at risk**: James (2003a, pp. 103–12).

397 **The statistics show that half a century ago**: White (2003).

398 **New Zealanders are the most individualistic**: Oyserman et al. (2002).

399 **He argued that, in the eighteenth century**: Trilling (1971, p. 40; developed p. 61).

399 **He highlights a number of literary characters**: Trilling (1971, pp. 24–33).

400 **'through the nineteenth century there runs the thread**: Trilling (1971, p. 124).

400 **Matthew Arnold was writing that**: Arnold, Wilde and Marx cited by Trilling (1971, pp. 124–5).

400 **Trilling comments, as Terence or I might have done**: Trilling (1971, p. 43).

400 **He summarises his view of modern life**: Trilling (1971, p. 61).

401 **the modern person 'finds it ever more difficult**: Trilling (1971, p. 61).

402 **Marx showed how becoming a unit of labour**: For a rare example of a book by him that is both readable and brief, see Marx (1964).

402 **Freud left us not so much in permanent conflict**: Freud (1961).

403 **Today's Chelsea**: Glanvill (2005).

405 **Virus infection increases the risk**: Khanna et al. (2001).

405 **They avoid telling people why they have done something**: McHoskey (1999).

405 **trickles into personal relationships**: McHoskey (1999), Kasser (2002, chapter 6).

405 **Since 40 per cent of Britons**: Hakim (2000).

407 **Studies of American patterns of life**: Reis (1990), Puttnam (2000).

407 **In America, authentic concern**: Khanna et al. (2001).

412 **Erich Fromm made some interesting observations**: Fromm (1995, p. 69).

412 **argues Fromm, 'after he has saved time**: Fromm (1995, pp. 80, 82).

417 **During the Soviet era it was essential**: Humphrey (1995).

419 **Although various attempts have been made**: By far the most influential was by Winnicott (1972).

419 **Writing at the end of the eighteenth century, the poet Schiller**: Trilling (1971, p. 121).

420 **In their fantasy play, they use imagination**: Winnicott (1972).

421 **Some psychoanalysts interpret such play**: Most notably Freud (1965) and Klein (1932).

422 **Some psychoanalysts take this further**: For the definitive critique of this position see Storr (1972); see also James (2003a, chapter 6).

424 **In Britain at the end of the nineteenth century**: Trilling (1971, pp. 118–20).

424 **the life and work of Stephen Fry**: James (2003a, pp. 62–3).

424 **During a TV interview in 1988**: *Room 113*, Channel 4 Television.

426 **Studies show that the mental state**: Sigman (2005, chapter 3).

427 **In England, 16 per cent**: LSC (2006).

427 **A substantial number of English and American studies**: English, see e.g. Maltby et al. (2004); American, see e.g. Boon et al. (2001).

427 **For 7 per cent of eighteen- to forty-seven-year-olds**: Maltby et al. (2004).

427 **People with such attachments to celebrities**: Maltby et al. (2006).

428 **Adolescents with weak attachment to parents**: Giles et al. (2004).

428 **'Born Originals, how comes it to pass**: cited by Trilling (1971, p. 93).

Chapter 11: Personal Implications: Prepare to Feel Better

436 **The one-quarter of British children**: Offer (2006, p. 142).

439 **This leaves what are known as 'psychodynamic psychotherapists'**: Any clinician who has been trained by a training institution which is a member of the British Psychoanalytic Council should have the minimum knowledge, although that is far from being a guarantee of their excellence. Their website, <www.bcp.org.uk>, includes a list of therapists which will enable you, if nothing else, to find a practitioner who lives near you. Other training organisations that are not members of the BCP but which I know to be reliable are the Women's Therapy Centre, the Institute of Group Analysis, the Tavistock Centre for Couple Therapy, the Centre for Attachment-Based Psychoanalytic Psychotherapy, and Regent's College. If you encounter someone who calls themselves a counsellor, ensure that they have been trained by an organisation which belongs to the British Association of Counselling, although counsellors encompass a huge variety of different approaches.

440 **Four studies suggest that it works**: summarised at <www.hoffmaninsti-tute.co.uk/articles/ results.htm>, accessed 8 Oct. 2006.

459 **60 per cent of people who do not divorce or separate**: data download-able from <www.statistics. gov.uk/STATBASE/ssdataset.asp?vlnk=6150>, accessed 8 Oct. 2006.

463 **The proportion of women who get past the age of forty**: McAllister et al. (1998).

463 **About 3 per cent of women**: Bewley et al. (2005).

463 **About half of childless fifty-year-old women**: McAllister et al. (1998).

465 **In the definitive survey of the sex life**: Wellings et al. (1994).

465 **higher proportion than that found in other studies**: reviewed in Wellings et al. (1994).

466 **gay men are at greater risk of loneliness and distress**: Fergusson et al. (1999, 2005), Meyer (2003).

Chapter 12: Political Implications: The Unselfish Capitalist Manifesto

469 **consistent with a 2004 survey**: Anushka Asthana, 'I want to be Beyoncé (or Thierry Henry)', *Observer*, 19 Dec. 2004 (<http://education.guardian.co.uk/schools/story/0,,1377052,00.html>, accessed 12 Sept. 2006).

469 **the BBC's nationally representative poll**: *The Happiness Formula*, BBC2 series, May 2006 (<www.bbc.co.uk/pressoffice/pressreleases/stories/2006/05_may/03/happiness.shtml>, accessed 12 Sept. 2006).

470 **only 1 per cent of the population earn more than £100,000**: Polly Toynbee, 'The Byers plan deliberately ignores obscene inequality', *Guardian*, 22 August 2006 (<www.guardian.co.uk/ Columnists/Column/0,,1855483,00.html>, accessed 12 Sept. 2006).

472 **interviewed him in some depth for a BBC series**: *The Chair* (1997), BBC2.

473 **a friend described her as 'seething**: The Insight Team, 'Mills wanted to use wife's name to deflect Revenue', *Sunday Times*, 5 March 2006.

474 **about that loan, he wrote that 'it is simply incredible**: Andrew Rawnsley, 'Tessa Jowell's sudden marital split won't stop the questions', *Observer*, 5 March 2006 (<http://observer.guardian.co.uk/columnists/story/0,,1724007,00.html>, accessed 12 Sept. 2006).

475 **he wrote in *The Times* in March 2006**: Matthew Parris, 'No more excuses. Just hand in your homework and go, Prime Minister', *The Times*, 18 March 2006 (<www.timesonline.co.uk/article/0,,1065-2091566,00.html>, accessed 12 Sept. 2006).

476 **David Blunkett diagnosed himself**: Marie Woolf, '"I really thought I was going mad" – Blunkett', *Independent on Sunday*, 8 Oct. 2006.

476 **Spinmeister-in-chief Alastair Campbell**: Sophie Goodchild, 'Exclusive: Campbell on the couch', *Independent on Sunday*, 8 Oct. 2006.

476 **Stephen Fry, very much a supporter of Blair**: Stephen Fry: The secret life of the manic depressive, BBC2, 12 and 19 Sept. 2006.

476 **vulnerability to the distress usually has its origins in childhood**: James (2003a).

479 **been shown not to have worked**: Rutter (2006).

484 **a study by the Financial Services Authority**: Patrick Hosking, 'Shares soar but cheats prosper', *Sunday Times*, 18 March 2006.

485 **a study of people from ten different nations**: Marshall et al. (1999).

487 **A recent scholarly book**: Dunn (2005).

489 **Modern democratic society, according to Dunn**: Dunn (2005, p. 184).

493 **the £30 billion currently spent each year**: Ministry of Defence, *MOD Annual Report and Accounts 2004–05*, <www.mod.uk/DefenceInternet/ AboutDefence/CorporatePublications/AnnualReports/MODAnnualReport s0405/ModAnnualReportAndAccounts200405.htm>, accessed 12 Sept. 2006.

493 **1 per cent of the British landmass**: or 240,000 hectares (Defence Estates Website, 'About the estate', <www.defence-estates.mod.uk/about_estate/ index.htm>, accessed 12 Sept. 2006).

Bibliography

Ablard, K.E. et al., 1997, 'Parents' achievement goals and perfectionism in their academically talented children', *J of Youth and Adolescence*, 26, 651–67.

ABS (Australian Bureau of Statistics), 2003, 'K10 ranges to approximate levels of psychological distress', in *Use of the Kessler Psychological Distress Scale in ABS Health Surveys*, Section 3.1, catalogue no. 4817.0.55.001, Canberra: Australian Bureau of Statistics (<www.abs.gov.au/ausstats/abs@.nsf/Lookup/B9ADE45 ED60E0A1CCA256D2D0000A288>).

Ahnert, L. et al., 2006, 'Security of children's relationships with nonparental care providers: A meta-analysis', *Child Development*, 74, 664–79.

Alaräisänen, A. et al., 2006, 'Good school performance is a risk factor of suicide in psychoses: A 35-year follow up of the Northern Finland 1966 Birth Cohort', *Acta Psychiatrica Scandinavica*, 114, 357–62.

Alpert-Gillis, L.J. et al., 1989, 'Gender and sex-role influences on children's self-esteem', *J of Personality*, 57, 97–114.

Anderson, C.A. et al., 2003, 'The influence of media violence on youth', *Psychological Science in the Public Interest*, 4(3), 81–110.

Andrews, G. et al., 2005, 'Lifetime risk of depression: Restricted to a minority or waiting for most?', *British J of Psychiatry*, 187, 495–6.

Ashwin, S., 2002, '"A woman is everything": The reproduction of Soviet ideals of womanhood in post-communist Russia', in A. Rainnie et al. (eds), *Work, Employment and Transition: Restructuring livelihoods in post-communist Eastern Europe*, London: Routledge, pp. 56–70.

Assor, A. et al., 2004, 'The emotional costs of parents' conditional regard: A self-determination theory analysis', *J of Personality*, 72(1), 47–88.

Averina, M. et al., 2005, 'Social and lifestyle determinants of depression, anxiety, sleeping disorders and self-evaluated quality of life in Russia: A population-based study in Arkhangelsk', *Social Psychiatry and Psychiatric Epidemiology*, 40, 511–18.

Ball, J. et al., 1994, 'Risk-taking behaviours among teenagers', in Cheong et al. (1994), pp. 43–59.

Barber, B.K. et al., 2005, *Parental Support, Psychological Control and Behavioral*

Control: Assessing relevance across time, culture and method, Monographs of the Society for Research in Child Development, vol. 70, no. 4, Oxford: Blackwell.

Bassett, M., 1998, *The State in New Zealand 1840–1984: Socialism without doctrines?*, Auckland University Press.

Becker, A.E. et al., 2002, 'Eating behaviour and attitudes following prolonged exposure to television among ethnic Fijian adolescent girls', *British J of Psychiatry*, 180, 509–14.

Beijing Youth Daily & Youth Humanities and Social Science Research Center of the Chinese Academy of Social Sciences, 2004, *Modernization in China: The effect on its people and economic development*, Beijing: Foreign Languages Press.

Bellis, M.A. et al., 2000, 'Ibiza uncovered: Changes in substance use and sexual behaviour amongst young people visiting an international night-life resort', *International J of Drug Policy*, 11, 235–44.

Berger, B., 2000, 'Prisoners of liberation: A psychoanalytic perspective on disenchantment and burnout among career women lawyers', *J of Clinical Psychology*, 56(5), 665–73.

Bewley, S. et al., 2005, 'Which career first?', *British Medical J*, 331, 588–9.

Biddulph, S., 2006, *Raising Babies*, London: HarperThorson.

Biggs, B.J. et al., 1996, 'Western misperceptions of the Confucian-heritage learning culture', in D.A. Watkins (1996), pp. 45–67.

Bilenberg, N. et al., 2005, 'The prevalence of child-psychiatric disorders among 8–9-year-old children in Danish mainstream schools', *Acta Psychiatrica Scandinavica*, 111(1), 59–67.

Blanchflower, D. et al., 1999, 'The rising well-being of the young', NBER Conference Paper, University of Warwick.

Blatt, S.J., 1995, 'The destructiveness of perfectionism', *American Psychologist*, 50, 1003–20.

Blatt, S.J. et al., 1992, 'Parent-child interaction in the etiology of dependent and self-critical depression', *Clinical Psychology Review*, 12, 47–91.

Board, B.J. et al., 2005, 'Disordered personalities at work', *Psychology, Crime and Law*, 11, 17–32.

Bobak, M. et al., 2006, 'Depressive symptoms in urban population samples in Russia, Poland and the Czech Republic', *British J of Psychiatry*, 188, 359–65.

Bond, M.H., 1995, *Beyond the Chinese Face: Insights from psychology*, Oxford University Press.

Boon, S.D. et al., 2001, 'Admirer-celebrity relationships among young adults: Explaining perceptions of celebrity influence on identity', *Human Communication Research*, 27, 432–65.

Brickman, P. et al., 1978, 'Lottery winners and accident victims: Is happiness relative?', *J of Personality and Social Psychology*, 36(8), 917–27.

Bronfenbrenner, U., 1968, 'The changing Soviet family', in D.R. Brown (ed.), *The Role and Status of Women in the Soviet Union*, New York: Teachers College Press, pp. 98–124.

Bronfenbrenner, U., 1970, *Two Worlds of Childhood*, New York: Sage.

Brown, J.S.L. et al., 2005, 'Are self-referrers just the worried well?', *Social Psychiatry and Psychiatric Epidemiology*, 40, 396–401.

BSA (Basic Skills Agency), 1997, *International Numeracy Survey: A comparison of the basic numeracy skills of adults 16-60 in seven countries*, London: The Basic Skills Agency.

Buckley, M., 1997, *Post-Soviet Women: From the Baltic to Central Asia*, Cambridge University Press.

Bugenthal, D.B. et al., 1989, 'Perceived control over caregiver outcomes: Implications for child abuse', *Developmental Psychology*, 24(4), 532–9.

Bugenthal, D.B. et al., 2004, 'Predicting infant maltreatment in low-income families: The interactive effects of maternal attributions and child status at birth', *Developmental Psychology*, 40(2), 234–43.

Bunting, M., 2004, *Willing Slaves*, London: HarperCollins.

Bushman, J. et al., 1998, 'Threatened egotism, narcissism, self-esteem and direct and displaced aggression: Does self-love or self-hate lead to violence?', *J of Personality and Social Psychology*, 75(1), 219–29.

Buss, D.M., 1989, 'Sex differences in human mate preferences: Evolutionary hypotheses tested in 37 cultures', *Behavioral and Brain Sciences*, 12, 1–49.

Buss, D.M., 2000, *The Dangerous Passion*, London: Bloomsbury.

Buxton, J. et al., 2005, 'The long shadow of childhood: Associations between parental social class and own social class, educational attainment and timing of first birth; results from the ONS longitudinal study', *Population Trends*, 121, 17–26.

Bynner, J. et al., 2000, *Equality Mapping*, London: Smith Institute.

Bynner, J. et al., 2001, *Obstacles and Opportunities on the Route to Adulthood*, London: Smith Institute.

Carver, C.S. et al., 1998, 'The American dream revisited: Is it what you want or why you want it that matters?', *Psychological Science*, 9, 289–92.

Caspi, A. et al., 2003, 'Influence of life stress on depression: Moderation by a polymorphism in the 5-HTT gene', *Science*, 301, 386–9.

Cass, A.M. et al., 2000, 'Casualties of Wall Street: An assessment of the Walking Wounded', paper presented to the American Psychological Association Convention, Washington, DC.

Chao, R.K., 2001, 'Extending research on the consequences of parenting style for Chinese Americans and European Americans', *Child Development*, 72, 1832–43.

Chen, X. et al., 2000, 'Parental warmth, control and indulgence and their relations to adjustment in Chinese children: A longitudinal study', *J of Family Psychology*, 14, 401–19.

Cheng, T.A., 1989, 'Symptomatology of minor psychiatric morbidity: A crosscultural comparison', *Psychological Medicine*, 19, 697–708.

Cheong, A.C.S. et al. (eds), 1994, *Growing up in Singapore: Research perspectives among adolescents*, Singapore: Prentice Hall.

Chirkov, V. et al., 2001, 'Differentiating autonomy from individualism and independence: A self-determination theory perspective on internalization of cultural orientations and well-being', *J of Personality and Social Psychology*, 84, 97–110.

Chiu, M.L. et al., 1992, 'The influence of immigration on parental behavior and adolescent distress in Chinese families residing in two Western nations', *J of Research on Adolescence*, 2(3), 205–39.

Chong, M.-Y. et al., 2001, 'Community study of depression in old age in Taiwan', *British J of Psychiatry*, 178, 29–35.

Choo, A.S. et al., 1994, 'Psychological disorders in adolescence', in Cheong et al. (1994), pp. 215–29.

Chorpita, B.F. et al., 1998, 'The development of anxiety: The role of control in the early environment', *Psychological Bulletin*, 124, 3–21.

Christensen, E., 2001, 'Difficult children: A serious sign of children at risk', Working Paper, Danish National Institute of Social Research, Copenhagen.

Christofferson, M.N., 2002, 'Trends in fatherhood patterns, children, youth and families', Working Paper 15, Danish National Institute of Social Research, Copenhagen.

Cohen, P. et al., 1996, *Life Values and Adolescent Mental Health*, New Jersey: Erlbaum.

Critser, G., 2003, *Fat Land: How Americans became the fattest people in the world*, New York: Houghton Mifflin.

Crocker, J. et al., 2002, 'Hopes dashed and dreams fulfilled: Contingencies of self-worth admissions to graduate school', *Personality and Social Psychology Bulletin*, 28, 1275–86.

Crocker, J. et al., 2003a, 'Levels of self-esteem and contingencies of self-worth: Unique effects on academic, social and financial problems in college students', *Personality and Social Psychology Bulletin*, 29, 701–12.

Crocker, J. et al., 2003b, 'When grades determine self-worth: Consequences for contingent self-worth, for male and female engineering and psychology majors', *J of Personality and Social Psychology*, 85, 507–16.

Csikszentmihalyi, M., 1997, *Finding Flow*, New York: Basic Books.

Csikszentmihalyi, M., 1999, 'If we are so rich, why aren't we happier?', *American Psychologist*, 54, 821–7.

Currie, C. et al., 2000, *Health and Health Behaviour Among Young People*, Copenhagen: WHO Regional Office for Europe.

Cyranowski, J. et al., 2000, 'Adolescent onset of the gender difference in lifetime rates of major depression', *Archives of General Psychiatry*, 57, 21–7.

Dahlberg, G. et al., 1999, *Beyond Quality in Early Childhood Education and Care: Postmodern perspectives*, London: Routledge.

Davidson, M. et al., 1999, 'Behavioral and intellectual markers for schizophrenia in apparently healthy male adolescents', *American J of Psychiatry*, 156, 1328–35.

Davidson, R. et al., 2000, 'Emotion, plasticity, context, and regulation: Perspectives from affective neuroscience', *Psychological Bulletin*, 126, 890–909.

Deci, E.L., 1971, 'Effects of externally mediated rewards on intrinsic motivation', *J of Personality and Social Psychology*, 18, 105–15.

Deci, E.L. et al., 1999, 'A meta-analytic review of experiments examining the effects of extrinsic rewards on intrinsic motivation', *Psychological Bulletin*, 125, 627–88.

Deci, E.L. et al., 2000, 'The "what" and "why" of goal pursuits: Human needs and the self-determination of behavior', *Psychological Inquiry*, 11(4), 227–68.

Demyttenaere, K. et al., 2004, 'Prevalence, severity, and unmet need for treatment of mental disorders in the World Health Organization World Mental Health Surveys', *Journal of the American Medical Association*, 291, 2581–90.

Dholakia, U.M. et al., 2004, 'How social influence affects consumption trends in emerging markets: An empirical investigation of the consumption convergence hypothesis', *Psychology and Marketing*, 21(10), 775–97.

Diener, E., 2000, 'Subjective well-being: The science of happiness and a proposal for a national index', *American Psychologist*, 55(1), 34–43.

Diener, E. et al., 1985, 'Happiness of the very wealthy', *Social Indicators Research*, 16, 263–74.

Diener, E. et al., 2000a, *Culture and Well-Being*, Cambridge, MA: MIT Press.

Dornbusch, S.M. et al., 1984, 'Sexual maturation, social class, and the desire to be thin among adolescent females', *Developmental Pediatrics*, 5, 308–14.

Drake, R.E. et al., 1984, 'Suicide among schizophrenics. Who is at risk?', *J of Nervous Mental Disease*, 172, 613–17.

Dunn, J., 2005, *Setting the People Free: The story of democracy*, London: Atlantic.

Dunning, D. et al., 2004, 'Flawed self-assessment: Implications for health, education, and the workplace', *Psychological Science in the Public Interest*, 5(3), 69–106.

Eagly, A.H. et al., 1999, 'The origins of sex differences in human behavior: Evolved dispositions versus social roles', *American Psychologist*, 54, 408–23.

Einhorn, B., 1993, *Cinderella Goes to Market*, New York: Verso.

Elliot, A.J. et al., 2004, 'The intergenerational transmission of fear of failure', *Personality and Social Psychology Bulletin*, 30, 957–71.

Ellis, B.J. et al., 1999, 'Quality of early family relationships and individual differences in the timing of pubertal maturation in girls: A longitudinal test of an evolutionary model', *J of Personality and Social Psychology*, 77, 387–401.

Erikson, R. et al., 1992, *The Constant Flux: A study of class mobility in industrial societies*, Oxford University Press.

European Commission, 2004, *The State of Mental Health in the European Union*, (n.p.) European Commission.

Faber, R.J. et al., 1988, 'Compulsive consumption and credit abuse', *J of Consumer Policy*, 11, 97–109.

Faber, R.J. et al., 1992, 'A clinical screener for compulsive buying', *J of Consumer Research*, 19, 459–69.

Fergusson, D.M. et al., 1999, 'Is sexual orientation related to mental health problems and suicidality in young people?', *Archives of General Psychiatry*, 56, 876–80.

Fergusson, D.M. et al., 2005, 'Sexual orientation and mental health in a birth cohort of young adults', *Psychological Medicine*, 35, 971–81.

Ferri, E. et al., 2003, *Changing Britain, Changing Lives*, London: Institute of Education.

Fisher, K. et al., 1999, *British Fathers and Children*, London: Institute for Economic and Social Research.

Fonagy, P. et al., 1995, 'Attachment, the reflective self, and borderline states', in S. Goldberg et al. (eds), *Attachment Theory: Social, developmental, and clinical perspectives*, New Jersey: Analytic Press, pp. 233–78.

Fones, C.S.L. et al., 1998, 'Studying the mental health of a nation: A preliminary report on a population survey in Singapore', *Singapore Medical Journal*, 39(6), 251–5.

Frank, R., 1999, *Luxury Fever*, New York: Free Press.

Freud, A., 1965, *Normality and Pathology in Childhood*, London: Hogarth.

Freud, S., 1961, *Civilization and Its Discontents*, vol. 21 of *The Complete Psychological Works of Sigmund Freud*, standard edn, London: Hogarth Press.

Fromm, E., 1976, *To Have or To Be?*, London: Abacus.

Fromm, E., 1995, *The Essential Fromm: Life between having and being*, London: Constable.

Fromm, E., 2002, *The Sane Society*, 2nd edn, London: Routledge Classics (1st edn: Routledge, 1955).

Frost, R.O. et al., 1991, 'The development of perfectionism: A study of daughters and their parents', *Cognitive Therapy and Research*, 15, 469–89.

Frum, D., 2003, *The Right Man*, New York: Random House.

Fuligni, A.J. et al., 1999, 'Attitudes toward family obligations among American adolescents, from Asian, Latin American, and European backgrounds', *Child Development*, 70, 1030–44.

Fuligni, A.J. et al., 2004, 'Attitudes toward family obligation among adolescents in contemporary urban and rural China', *Child Development*, 74, 180–92.

Gagné, M. et al., 2005, 'Self-determination theory and work motivation', *J of Organizational Behavior*, 26, 331–62.

Gardner, J. et al., 2001, 'Does money buy happiness? A longitudinal study using data on windfalls', University of Warwick, March.

Ger, G. et al., 1996, 'Cross-cultural differences in materialism', *J of Economic Psychology*, 17, 55–77.

Gibbons, F.X., 1990, 'Self-attention and behavior', in M.P. Zanna (ed.), *Advances in Experimental Psychology*, San Diego: Academic Press, pp. 239–303.

Giles, D.C. et al., 2004, 'The role of media figures in adolescent development: Relations between autonomy, attachment, and interest in celebrities', *Personality and Individual Differences*, 36, 813–22.

Glanvill, R., 2005, *Chelsea FC: The official biography*, London: Headline.

Goldthorpe, J.H., 1987, *Social Mobility and Class Structure in Modern Britain*, Oxford: Clarendon Press.

Greenberger, E. et al., 1996, 'Perceived family relationships and depressed mood in early and late adolescence: A comparison of European and Asian Americans', *Developmental Psychology*, 32, 707–16.

Groesz, L.M. et al., 2002, 'The effect of experimental presentation of thin media images on body satisfaction: A meta-analytic review', *International J of Eating Disorders*, 31, 1–16.

Grolnick, W.S. et al., 1989, 'Parental styles associated with children's self-regulation and competence in school', *J of Educational Psychology*, 81, 143–61.

Gulerce, A., 1991, 'Transitional objects: A reconsideration of the phenomenon', *J of Social Behavior and Personality*, Special Issue, 6, 187–208.

Hakim, C., 1996, *Key Issues in Women's Work*, London: Athlone.

Hakim, C., 2000, *Work–Lifestyle Choices in the 21st Century: Preference Theory*, Oxford University Press.

Hamilton, C., 2002, 'Overconsumption in Australia: The rise of the middle-class battler', Discussion paper no. 49, The Australia Institute, Canberra (available from <www.tai.org.au/Publications_Files/ Publications.htm>).

Hamilton, C., 2003, 'Overconsumption in Britain: A culture of middle-class complaint?', Discussion paper no. 57, The Australia Institute, Canberra (available from <www.tai.org.au/Publications_Files/ Publications.htm>).

Hamilton, C. et al., 2005, *Affluenza*, Sydney: Allen & Unwin.

Harris, C.R., 2002, 'Sexual and romantic jealousy in heterosexual and homosexual adults', *Psychological Science*, 13, 7–12.

Hashimoto, A., 2004, 'Power to the imagination', *Asia Program Special Report*, 121, 9–12.

Hauser, R. et al., 2000, 'Occupation status, education and social mobility in the meritocracy', in K. Arrow et al. (eds), *Meritocracy and Economic Inequality*, Cambridge, MA: Princeton University Press, pp. 179–229.

Heine, S.J. et al., 1999, 'Is there a universal need for positive self-regard?', *Psychological Review*, 106(4), 766–94.

Hennigan, K.M. et al., 1982, 'Impact of the introduction of television on crime in the United States: Empirical findings and theoretical implications', *J of Personality and Social Psychology*, 42, 461–77.

Hirsch, F., 1977, *Social Limits to Growth*, London: Routledge.

Ho, K.C. et al., 1995, 'Cultural, social and leisure activities in Singapore', Census of Population 1990 Monograph No 3, Singapore: Department of Statistics.

Hughes, R., 1993, *Culture of Complaint*, London: Harvill.

Humphrey, C., 1995, 'Creating a culture of disillusionment: Consumption in Moscow, a chronicle of changing times', in D. Miller (ed.), *Worlds Apart: Modernity though the prism of the local*, London: Routledge, pp. 43–68.

Huppert, F.A. et al., 2005, *The Science of Well-Being*, Oxford University Press.

Hwu, H.-G. et al., 1989, 'Prevalence of psychiatric disorders in Taiwan defined by the Chinese Diagnostic Interview Schedule', *Acta Psychiatrica Scandinavica*, 79(2), 136–47.

ICPE (International Consortium in Psychiatric Epidemiology), 2000, 'Cross-national comparisons of the prevalences and correlates of mental disorders', *Bulletin of the World Health Organization*, 78(4), 413–26.

ILO (International Labour Office), 2004, *Economic Security for a Better World*, Geneva: International Labour Office.

Isohanni, I. et al., 1999, 'Can excellent school performance be a precursor of schizophrenia? A 28-year follow-up in the Northern Finland 1966 Birth Cohort', *Acta Psychiatrica Scandinavica*, 100(1), 17–26.

James, H.M., 1960, 'Premature ego development: Some observations on disturbances during the first three months of life', *International J of Psychoanalysis*, 41, 288–94.

James, O.W., 1995, *Juvenile Violence in a Winner-Loser Culture: Socio-economic and familial origins of the rise of violence against the person*, London: Free Association Books.

James, O.W., 1998, *Britain on the Couch*, London: Arrow.

James, O.W., 2003a, *They F*** You up: How to survive family life*, London: Bloomsbury.

James, O.W., 2003b, 'They muck you up: Developmental psychopathology as a basis for politics', *Psychologist*, 16, 296–7.

James, O.W., 2007, *Selfish Capitalist Origins of Emotional Distress*, in preparation.

JCGQ (Joint Council for General Qualifications), 2000, *GCSE by Subject*, London: Joint Council for General Qualifications.

Jenkins, R. et al., 1997, 'The national psychiatric morbidity surveys of Great Britain: Initial findings from the household survey', *Psychological Medicine*, 27, 775–89.

Jennings, R. et al., 1994, *Business Elites: The psychology of entrepreneurs and intrapreneurs*, London: Routledge.

Jensen, B. et al., 1992, *The Danish Folkeskole: Visions and consequences*, Copenhagen: Danish Council for Educational Development in the Folkeskole.

Johnson, T.N. et al., 2002, 'Television viewing and aggressive behavior during adolescence and adulthood', *Science*, 295, 2468–71.

Jorm, A.F. et al., 2005, 'Public beliefs about causes and risk factors for mental disorders', *Social Psychiatry and Psychiatric Epidemiology*, 40, 764–7.

Jose, P.E. et al., 1998, 'Stress and coping among Russian and American early adolescents', *Developmental Psychology*, 34(4), 757–69.

Jost, J.T. et al., 2003, 'Political conservatism as motivated cognition', *Psychological Bulletin*, 129, 339–75.

Kasser, T., 2002, *The High Price of Materialism*, London: MIT Press.

Kasser, T. et al., 1993, 'A dark side of the American dream: Correlates of financial success as a central life aspiration', *J of Personality and Social Psychology*, 65, 410–22.

Kasser, T. et al., 1995, 'The relations of maternal and social environments to late adolescents' materialistic and prosocial values', *Developmental Psychology*, 31, 907–14.

Kasser, T. et al., 1999, 'Reproductive freedom, educational equality, and females' preference for resource-acquisition characteristics in mates', *Psychological Science*, 10(4), 374–7.

Kasser, T. et al., 2001a, 'Be careful of what you wish for: Optimal functioning and the relative attainment of intrinsic and extrinsic goals', in P. Schmuck et al. (eds), *Life Goals and Well-Being: Towards a positive psychology of human striving*, Göttingen: Hogrefe & Huber, pp. 116–31.

Kasser, T. et al., 2001b, 'The dreams of people high and low in materialism', *J of Economic Psychology*, 22, 693–719.

Kasser, T. et al., 2002, 'Early family experiences and adult values: A 26-year, prospective longitudinal study', *Personality and Social Psychology Bulletin*, 28, 826–35.

Keller, J., 2005, 'In genes we trust: The biological component of psychological essentialism and its relationship to mechanisms of motivated social cognition', *J of Personality and Social Psychology*, 88, 686–702.

Kelsey, J., 2002, *At the Crossroads*, Wellington: Bridget Williams Books.

Keyes, C.L.M., 2005, 'Mental illness and/or mental health? Investigating axioms of the complete state model of health', *J of Consulting and Clinical Psychology*, 73, 539–48.

Khaleque, A. et al., 2005, 'Perceived parental acceptance-rejection and psychological adjustment: A meta-analysis of cross-cultural and intracultural studies', *J of Marriage and the Family*, 64(1), 54–64.

Khanna, S. et al., 2001, 'Materialism, objectification and alienation from a cross-cultural perspective', unpublished study, cited in Kasser (2002).

Kitayama, S. et al., 1997, 'Individual and collective processes in the construction of self: Self-enhancement in the United States and self-criticism in Japan', *J of Personality and Social Psychology*, 72(6), 1245–67.

Klein, M., 1932, *The Psychoanalysis of Children*, London: Hogarth.

Kleinman, A., 1986, *Social Origins of Distress and Disease: Depression, neurasthenia and pain in modern China*, New Haven: Yale University Press.

Kleinman, A., 1988, *Rethinking Psychiatry: From cultural category to personal experience*, New York: Free Press.

Kleinman, A. et al., 1997, 'Psychiatry's global challenge: An evolving crisis in the developing world signals the need for a better understanding of the links between culture and mental disorders', *Scientific American*, 276(3), 86–9.

Kodz, J., 2003, *Working Long Hours: A review of the evidence*, Employment Relations Research series no. 16, London: Department of Trade & Industry.

Korman, A.K. et al., 1981, 'Career success and personal failure: Alienation in professionals and managers', *Academy of Management J*, 24, 342–60.

Kryger, N. et al., 1998, 'The Danish class teacher: A mediator between the pastoral and the academic', in P. Lang et al. (eds), *Affective Education: A comparative view*, London: Cassell, pp. 126–31.

Labour Market Trends, 2000, 'Labour market spotlight', January, p. 108.

Laing, R.D., 1967, *The Politics of Experience and The Bird of Paradise*, London: Penguin.

Lane, R., 2000, *The Loss of Happiness in Market Democracies*, London: Yale University Press.

Larsen, J.E., 2003, 'Social inclusion and exclusion in Denmark 1976 to 2000', Social Policy Research Centre, UNSW and the Department of Sociology, University of Copenhagen, paper prepared for the Australian Social Policy Conference on 'Social Inclusion', University of New South Wales, 9–11 July 2003.

Layard, R., 2005, *Happiness: Lessons from a new science*, London: Allen & Unwin.

Lee, Y.-T. et al., 1997, 'Are Americans more optimistic than the Chinese?', *Personality and Social Psychology*, 23(1), 32–40.

Lehtinen, V. et al., 2003, 'Urban-rural differences in the occurrence of female depressive disorder in Europe: Evidence from the ODIN study', *Social Psychiatry and Psychiatric Epidemiology*, 38, 283–9.

Levine, M., 2006, *The Price of Privilege*, New York: Random House.

Lewinsohn, P.M. et al., 2004, 'The prevalence and co-morbidity of subthreshold psychiatric conditions', *Psychological Medicine*, 34, 613–22.

Li, J., 2004, 'Learning as a task or a virtue: US and Chinese preschoolers explain learning', *Developmental Psychology*, 40(4), 595–605.

Lillard, A. et al., 2006, 'The early years: Evaluating Montessori education', *Science*, 313, 1893–4.

Liu, M. et al., 2005, 'Autonomy- vs. connectedness-oriented parenting behaviours in Chinese and Canadian mothers', *International J of Behavioral Development*, 29, 489–95.

LSC (Learning and Skills Council), 2006, 'Kids seeking reality TV fame instead of exam passes', press release, Learning and Skills Council, London.

Lucey, H., 1996, 'Transitions to womanhood: Constructions of success and failure for middle and working class young women', paper presented at conference on 'British Youth Research: the New Agenda', Glasgow, 26–28 January.

Luo, G., 1996, *Chinese Traditional Social and Moral Ideas and Rules*, Beijing: University of Chinese People Press.

Luthar, S.S. et al., 1999, 'Contextual factors in substance abuse: A study of suburban and inner-city adolescents', *Development and Psychopathology*, 11, 845–67.

Luthar, S.S. et al., 2002, 'Privileged but pressured? A study of affluent youth', *Child Development*, 73, 1593–610.

Ma, G.S. et al., 2002, 'Effect of television viewing on pediatric obesity', *Biomedical Environmental Science*, 15, 291–7.

McAllister, F. et al., 1998, *A Study of Childlessness in Britain*, York: Joseph Rowntree Foundation.

McHoskey, J.W., 1999, 'Machiavellianism, intrinsic versus extrinsic goals, and social interest: A self-determination theory analysis', *Motivation and Emotion*, 23, 267–83.

Malka, A. et al., 2003, 'Intrinsic and extrinsic work orientations as moderators of the effect of annual income on subjective well-being: A longitudinal study', *Personality and Social Psychology Bulletin*, 29, 737–46.

Maltby, J. et al., 2004, 'Personality and coping: A context for examining celebrity worship and mental health', *British J of Psychology*, 95, 1–19.

Maltby, J. et al., 2006, 'Extreme celebrity worship, fantasy proneness and dissociation: Developing the measurement and understanding of celebrity worship within a clinical personality context', *Personality and Individual Differences*, 40, 273–83.

Mann, A.H. et al., 1983, 'Screening for abnormal eating attitudes and psychiatric morbidity in an unselected population of 15-year-old schoolgirls', *Psychological Medicine*, 13, 573–80.

Marmot, M., 2004, *Status Syndrome*, London: Bloomsbury.

Marsh, H.W. et al., 1984, 'Determinants of students' self-concept: Is it better to be a relatively large fish in a small pond even if you don't learn to swim as well?', *J of Personality and Social Psychology*, 47, 213–31.

Marshall, G. et al., 1999, 'Social mobility and personal satisfaction: Evidence from ten different countries', *British J of Sociology*, 50, 28–48.

Martin, P., 2005, *Making Happy People*, London: Fourth Estate.

Marx, K., 1964, *Pre-Capitalist Economic Formations*, London: Lawrence & Wishart.

Meyer, I.H., 2003, 'Prejudice, social stress, and mental health in lesbian, gay, and bisexual populations: Conceptual issues and research evidence', *Psychological Bulletin*, 129, 674–97.

Mezulis, A.H. et al., 2004, 'Is there a universal positivity bias in attributions? A meta-analytic review of individual, developmental, and cultural differences in the self-serving attributional bias', *Psychological Bulletin*, 130(5), 711–47.

Mirowsky, J. et al., 1989, *Social Causes of Psychological Distress*, New York: Aldine de Gruyter.

Moffitt, T.E. et al., 1992, 'Childhood experience and onset of menarche', *Child Development*, 63, 47–58.

Mother and Baby Magazine, 2002, 'Mother and baby sleep survey', April.

Mroz, T. et al. (eds), 2004, *Monitoring Economic Conditions in the Russian Federation*, The Russia Longitudinal Monitoring Survey 1992–2003, Chapel Hill, Carolina: University of Carolina.

Murray, C., 1984, *Losing Ground: American social policy 1950–80*, New York: Basic Books.

Murray, C., 2000, 'Genetics of the right', *Prospect*, April.

Murray, G.E. et al., 1996, *Singapore: The global city-state*, London: Palgrave.

Myers, D., 1987, *Social Psychology*, New York: McGraw-Hill.

Myers, L.B., 2000, 'Deceiving others or deceiving themselves?', *Psychologist*, 12(8), 400–403.

Myers, L.B. et al., 2000, 'How optimistic are repressors? The relationship between repressive coping, controllability, self-esteem and comparative optimism for health-related events', *Psychology and Health*, 15, 667–88.

Nicolson, P., 1998, *Post-natal Depression: Psychology, science and the transition to motherhood*, London: Routledge.

NSPCC (National Society for the Prevention of Cruelty to Children), 2001, *Child Maltreatment in the United Kingdom*, London: National Society for the Prevention of Cruelty to Children.

Oakley Browne, M.A. et al. (eds), 2006, *Te Rau Hinengaro: The New Zealand Mental Health Survey*, Wellington: Ministry of Health (downloadable free of charge at <www.moh.govt.nz/moh.nsf/ pagesmh/5223/$File/mental-health-survey.pdf>).

O'Brien, M., 2005, *Shared Caring: Bringing fathers into the frame*, London: Equal Opportunities Commission.

O'Connor, T.G. et al., 2005, 'Factors moderating change in depressive symptoms in women following separation: Findings from a community study in England', *Psychological Medicine*, 35, 715–24.

Offer, A., 2006, *The Challenge of Affluence*, Oxford University Press.

Olsen, L.R. et al., 2004, 'Prevalence of major depression and stress indicators in the Danish general population', *Acta Psychiatrica Scandinavica*, 109, 96–103.

Olson, J.M. et al., 1986, 'Resentment about deprivational entitlement and hopefulness as mediators of the effects of qualifications', in J.M. Olson et al. (eds), *Relative Deprivation and Social Comparison*, The Ontario Symposium, vol. 4, New Jersey: Erlbaum, pp. 57–78.

ONS (Office of National Statistics), 2000, *Psychiatric Morbidity Among Adults Living in Private Households, 2000*, London: Office of National Statistics.

Osborn, M., 2001, 'Constants and contexts in pupil experience of learning and schooling: Comparing learners in England, France and Denmark', *Comparative Education*, 37, 267–78.

Oyserman, D. et al., 2002, 'Rethinking individualism and collectivism: Evaluation of theoretical assumptions and meta-analyses', *Psychological Bulletin*, 128, 3–72.

Packard, V., 1956, *The Hidden Persuaders*, London: Pelican.

Pakriev, S. et al., 1998, 'Prevalence of mood disorders in the rural population of Udmurtia', *Acta Psychiatrica Scandinavica*, 97, 169–74.

Parker, G., 1982, 'Parental representations and affective symptoms: Examination for an hereditary link', *British J of Medical Psychology*, 55, 57–61.

Parker, G. et al., 2001, 'Depression in the planet's largest ethnic group: the Chinese', *American J of Psychiatry*, 158(6), 857–64.

Parker, G. et al., 2005, 'Depression in the Chinese: the impact of acculturation', *Psychological Medicine*, 35, 1475–83.

Patten, S.B., 2003, 'Recall bias and major depression lifetime prevalence', *Social Psychiatry and Psychiatric Epidemiology*, 38, 290–96.

Peebles, G. et al., 2002, *Economic Growth and Development in Singapore*, Cheltenham: Edward Elgar.

Peng, K. et al., 1999, 'Culture, dialectics and reasoning about contradiction', *American Psychologist*, 54, 741–54.

Perkins, H.W., 1991, 'Religious commitment, yuppie values, and well-being in post-collegiate life', *Review of Religious Research*, 32(3), 244–51.

Perry, P. et al., 1999, *New Zealand Politics at the Turn of the Millennium*, Auckland: Alpha Publications.

Petersen, A. et al., 1991, 'Adolescent depression: Why more girls?', *J of Youth and Adolescence*, 20, 247–71.

Pettigrew, T.F., 1967, 'Social evaluation theory: Convergences and applications', in D. Levine (ed.), 1967, *Nebraska Symposium on Motivation*, vol. 15, Lincoln: University of Nebraska Press.

Pickett, K. et al., 2006, 'Income inequality and the prevalence of mental illness: A preliminary international analysis', *J of Epidemiology and Community Mental Health*, 60, 646–7.

Piketty, T. et al., 2006, 'The evolution of top incomes: A historical and international perspective', NBER Working Paper 11955 (available from <www.nber.org/papers/w11955>).

Puttnam, R.D., 2000, *Bowling Alone: The collapse and revival of American community*, New York: Simon & Schuster.

Quah, S.R., 2003, *Home and Kin: Families in Asia*, Singapore: Eastern Universities Press.

Read J. et al., 2004, 'Public opinion: Bad things happen and can drive you crazy', in J. Read et al. (eds), *Models of Madness*, London: Routledge, pp. 133–46.

Reis, H.T., 1990, 'The role of intimacy in interpersonal relations', *J of Social and Clinical Psychology*, 9, 15–30.

Richins, M.L., 1991, 'Social comparison and the idealized images of advertising', *J of Consumer Research*, 18, 71–83.

Richins, M.L., 1992, 'Media images, materialism, and what ought to be: The role of social comparison', in F. Rudmin et al. (eds), *Meaning, Measure, and Morality of Materialism*, Provo, UT: Association for Consumer Research, pp. 202–6.

Richins, M.L., 1994, 'Special possessions and the expression of material values', *J of Consumer Research*, 21, 522–33.

Rindfleisch, A. et al., 1997, 'Family structure, materialism and compulsive consumption', *J of Consumer Research*, 23, 312–24.

Robins, L.N. et al., 1992, *Psychiatric Disorders in America*, New York: Free Press.

Rolf, J. et al., 1990, *Risk and Protective Factors in the Development of Psychopathology*, Cambridge University Press.

Rolfe, S. et al., 2002, 'Quality in infant care: Observations on joint attention', *Australian Research in Early Childhood Education*, 9(1), 86–96.

Rose, R., 2005, *Evidence of Dissatisfaction*, New Russia Barometer XIV, SSP 402, Aberdeen: CSPP Publications.

Rutter, M., 2006, 'Is Sure Start an effective preventive intervention?', *Child and Adolescent Mental Health*, 11, 135–41.

Rutter, M. et al., 1995, *Psychosocial Disorders in Young People*, London: Wiley.

Ruxton, S., 2004, *Gender, Equality and Men*, London: Oxfam.

Ryan, R.M. et al., 1993, 'Two types of religious internalization and their relations to religious orientation and mental health', *J of Personality and Social Psychology*, 65(3), 586–96.

Ryan, R.M. et al., 1999, 'The American dream in Russia: Extrinsic aspirations and well-being in two cultures', *Personality and Social Psychology Bulletin*, 25, 1509–24.

Ryan, R.M et al., 2003, 'Why we don't need self-esteem: On fundamental needs, contingent love, and mindfulness', *Psychological Inquiry*, 14(1), 71–82.

Ryan, R.M. et al., 2005, 'On the interpersonal regulation of emotions: Emotional reliance across gender, relationship, and cultures', *Personal Relationships*, 12, 145–63.

Satoshi, K. et al., 2000, 'Teaching may be hazardous to your marriage', *Evolution and Human Behavior*, 21, 185–90.

Saunders, S., 2001, 'Fromm's marketing character and Rokeach values', *Social Behavior and Personality*, 29(2), 191–5.

Saunders, S. et al., 2000, 'The construction and validation of a consumer orientation questionnaire (SCOI) designed to measure Fromm's (1955) "Marketing Character" in Australia', *Social Behavior and Personality*, 28(3), 219–40.

Schaefer, A.D. et al., 2004, 'A cross-cultural exploration of materialism in adolescents', *International J of Consumer Studies*, 28, 399–411.

Schmitt, D.P., 2003, 'Universal sex differences in the desire for sexual variety: Tests from 52 nations, 6 continents, and 13 islands', *J of Personality and Social Psychology*, 85, 85–104.

Schmitt, D.P., 2005, 'Sociosexuality from Argentina to Zimbabwe: A 48-nation study of sex, culture, and strategies of human mating', *Behavioral and Brain Sciences*, 28, 247–311.

Schor, J., 1992, *The Overworked American*, New York: Basic Books.

Schor, J., 1999, *The Overspent American: Why we want what we don't need*, New York: HarperCollins.

Schroeder, J.E. et al., 1995, 'Psychological correlates of the materialism construct', *J of Social Behavior and Personality*, 10, 243–53.

Schwartz, B., 2004, *The Paradox of Choice: Why more is less*, New York: HarperCollins.

Schwartz, S., 1991, 'Women and depression: A Durkheimian perspective', *Social Science and Medicine*, 32, 127–40.

Seligman, M.E.P., 1991, *Learned Optimism*, New York: Knopf.

Sell, L. et al., 1998, 'Perceptions of college life, emotional well-being and patterns of drug and alcohol use among Oxford undergraduates', *Oxford Review of Education*, 24, 235–43.

Sheldon, K.M. et al., 2001, 'Extrinsic value orientation and dating violence', cited in Kasser (2002).

Sheldon, K.M. et al., 2004a, 'Self-concordance and subjective well-being in four cultures', *J of Cross-Cultural Psychology*, 35(2), 209–23.

Sheldon, K.M. et al., 2004b, 'The independent effects of goal contents and motives on well-being: It's both what you pursue and why you pursue it', *Personality and Social Psychology Bulletin*, 30, 475–86.

Shibley Hyde, J., 2005, 'The gender similarity hypothesis', *American Psychologist*, 60, 581–92.

Shiller, R.J. et al., 1991, 'Popular attitudes toward free markets: The Soviet Union and the United States compared', *American Economic Review*, 81(3), 385–400.

Sigman, A., 2005, *Remotely Controlled: How television is damaging our lives and what we can do about it*, London: Vermilion.

Simon, G.E. et al., 2002, 'Understanding cross-national differences in depression prevalence', *Psychological Medicine*, 32, 585–94.

Sirgy, M.J. et al., 1998, 'Does television viewership play a role in the perception of quality of life?', *J of Advertising*, 27, 125–42.

Smail, D., 2005, *Power, Interest and Psychology: Elements of a social materialist understanding of distress*, Ross-on-Wye: PCCS Books.

Smith, T.B. et al., 2003, 'Religiousness and depression: Evidence for a main effect and the moderating influence of stressful life events', *Psychological Bulletin*, 129(4), 614–36.

Snibbe, A.C. et al., 2005, 'You can't always get what you want: Educational attainment, agency, and choice', *J of Personality and Social Psychology*, 88, 703–20.

SNZ (Statistics New Zealand), 2002, *People Born Overseas* (2001 Census), Wellington: Statistics New Zealand/Te Tari Tatau (also at <www.stats.govt.nz/census/2001-census-statistics/2001-born-overseas/default>).

Sorkhabi, N. et al., 2005, 'Applicability of Baumrind's parent typology to collective cultures: Analysis of cultural explanations of parent socialization effects', *International J of Behavioral Development*, 29, 552–63.

Spencer-Rodgers, J. et al., 2004, 'Dialectical self-esteem and East-West differences in psychological well-being', *Personality and Social Psychology Bulletin*, 30(11), 1416–32.

Srivastava, A. et al., 2001, 'Money and subjective well-being: It's not the money, it's the motives', *J of Personality and Social Psychology*, 80, 959–71.

Starr, J.B., 2001, *Understanding China*, London: Profile.

Statistical Yearbook, 2004, Copenhagen: Danmark Statisbank.

Stetsenko, A. et al., 2000, 'Gender effects in children's beliefs about school performance: A cross-cultural study', *Child Development*, 71, 517–27.

Stone, W.F. et al., 1992, *Strength and Weakness: The authoritarian personality today*, London: Springer-Verlag.

Storr, A., 1972, *The Dynamics of Creation*, London: Penguin.

Surtees, P.G. et al., 2000, 'Student mental health, use of services and academic attainment', Report to the Review Committee of the University of Cambridge Counselling Service.

Szasz, T.S., 1984, *The Myth of Mental Illness: Foundations of a theory of personal conduct* (rev. edn), New York: Harper & Row.

Takeuchi, D.T. et al., 1998, 'Lifetime and twelve-month prevalence rates of major depressive episodes and dysthymia among Chinese Americans in Los Angeles', *American J of Psychiatry*, 155, 1407–14.

Tan, E., 1994, 'At odds with society: The problem of juvenile delinquency', in Cheong et al. (1994), pp. 203–14.

Tao, K.-T., 1998, 'An overview of only child family mental health in China', *Psychiatry and Clinical Neuroscience*, 52, S206–S211.

Taylor, S.E. et al., 1994, 'Positive illusions and well-being revisited: Separating fact from fiction', *Psychological Bulletin*, 116(1), 21–7.

Thompson, R.A., 1993, 'Socioemotional development: enduring issues and new challenges', *Developmental Review*, 13, 372–402.

Tiffen, R. et al., 2004, *How Australia Compares*, Cambridge University Press.

Tin, G.K.L. et al., 1994, 'Loneliness among adolescents', in Cheong et al. (1994), pp. 189–202.

Trilling, L., 1971, *Sincerity and Authenticity*, Oxford University Press.

Tsai, J.L. et al., 2004, 'Somatic and social: Chinese Americans talk about emotion', *Personality and Social Psychology Bulletin*, 30(9), 1226–38.

Tse, D.K. et al., 1989, 'Becoming a consumer society: A longitudinal and cross-cultural content analysis of print ads from Hong Kong, People's Republic of China, and Taiwan', *J of Consumer Research*, 15, 457–72.

Twenge, J.M., 2000, 'The age of anxiety? Birth cohort change in anxiety and neuroticism', *J of Personality and Social Psychology*, 79, 1007–21.

UNCTAD (United Nations Conference on Trade and Development), 2000, *World Investment Report*, New York: United Nations.

UNDP (United Nations Development Programme), 2003, *Human Development Report 2003. Millennium development goals: a compact among nations to end human poverty*, New York: Oxford University Press.

UNECE (United Nations Economic Commission for Europe), 2002, *Towards a Knowledge-Based Economy: Russian Federation*, New York: United Nations.

Van Boven, L. et al., 2003, 'To do or to have? That is the question', *J of Personality and Social Psychology*, 85, 1193–202.

Van Den Boom, D., 1994, 'The influence of temperament and mothering on attachment and exploration: An experimental manipulation of sensitive responsiveness among lower-class mothers with irritable infants', *Child Development*, 65, 1457–77.

Vaughan, B.E. et al., 1999, 'Attachment and temperament', in J. Cassidy, et al. (eds), *Handbook of Attachment: Theory, Research, and Clinical Applications*, New York: Guilford, pp. 198–225.

Wah, E.L.H., 1994, 'What Singapore adolescents think of themselves', in Cheong et al. (1994), pp. 177–88.

Walkerdine, V. et al., 1989, *Democracy in the Kitchen: Regulating mothers and socializing daughters*, London: Virago.

Watkins, D.A. et al. (eds), 1996, *The Chinese Learner: Cultural, psychological and contextual influences*, Hong Kong: Comparative Education Research Centre; and Camberwell, Victoria: Australian Council for Educational Research.

Weissman, M.M. et al., 1977, 'Sex differences and the epidemiology of depression', *Archives of General Psychiatry*, 34, 98–111.

Weissman, M.M. et al., 1993, 'Sex differences in rates of depression: Cross-national perspectives', *J of Affective Disorders*, 29, 77–84.

Wellings, K. et al., 1994, *Sexual Behaviour in Britain*, London: Penguin.

Wells, J.E. et al., 2004, 'How accurate is recall of key symptoms of depression? A comparison of recall and longitudinal reports', *Psychological Medicine*, 34, 1001–11.

West, P. et al., 2003, 'Fifteen, female and stressed: Changing patterns of psychological distress over time', *J of Child Psychology and Psychiatry*, 44(3), 399–411.

White, M., 2003, *The Penguin History of New Zealand*, London: Penguin.

Whybrow, P.C., 2005, *American Mania: Why more is not enough*, New York: Norton.

Wilhelm, K. et al., 2006, 'Life events, first depression onset and the serotonin transporter gene', *British J of Psychiatry*, 188, 210–15.

Williams, G.C. et al., 2000, 'Extrinsic life goals and health risk in adolescents', *J of Applied Social Psychology*, 30, 1756–71.

Winnicott, D.W., 1972, *Playing and Reality*, London: Penguin.

Wolf, A., 2002, *Does Education Matter? Myths about education and economic growth*, London: Penguin.

Wolfe, J.L. et al., 1996, 'The poverty of privilege: Therapy with women of the "upper classes"', *Women and Therapy*, 18, 597–611.

Women of China, 1987, *New Trends in Chinese Marriage and the Family*, Beijing: Women of China.

Wong, N.Y. et al., 1998, 'Personal taste and family face: Luxury consumption in Confucian and Western societies', *Psychology and Marketing*, 15, 423–41.

Wu, C. et al., 2005, 'Intergenerational cultural conflicts in norms of parental warmth among Chinese American immigrants', *International J of Behavioral Development*, 29, 516–23.

Wu, P. et al., 2002, 'Similarities and differences in mothers' parenting of preschoolers in China and the United States', *International J of Behavioral Development*, 26, 481–91.

Xu, J.M., 1987, 'Some issues in the diagnosis of depression in China', *Canadian J of Psychiatry*, 32, 368–70.

Xu, Y. et al., 2005, 'Mainland Chinese parenting styles and parent-child interaction', *International J of Behavioral Development*, 29, 524–31.

Yatsko, P., 2003, *New Shanghai*, London: Wiley.

Young, M., 1958, *The Rise of the Meritocracy*, London: Penguin.

Acknowledgements

First and foremost, I thank my wife, Clare. The impetus for a globe-trot came from her. She held the familial fort whilst I was away for months on end and subsequently forbore the emotional absences that inevitably resulted when I was writing this book at home. That it took a year longer to complete than originally intended resulted in a relative impecuniousness: a rich irony, given the book's subject-matter. But the resulting conversations and support from her only served to make it a better book. Clare has greatly added to my understanding by helping me to acknowledge my own materialistic elements. She has also ploughed through the various incarnations the book has suffered, mixing encouragement with important suggestions for amendments. Thank you also to my sister-in-law Anna-Louise Garner for all the support she has provided to our family during my three years of travelling, and to my parents-in-law William and Penny Garner for theirs.

The turning point in the book's literary fortunes came in December of 2005, when Jemima Biddulph provided her verdict on the manuscript so far: incoherent, sometimes sexist, often ethnocentric and frequently self-obsessed – and that was before she got to the bad things. Despite having a small child and a full-time job as the head of an English department in a secondary school, she found the time to propose the structure which the book now has and tactfully guided me towards a less congealed and bombastic content. Since she played the same role for my last book, I am hugely in her debt and of the view that publishers everywhere should be beating a path to her door to do the same for other authors.

Crucial to this book's genesis was Harry Cummins. In autumn 2003 he persuaded the British Council to back the book and provide me with both accommodation and contacts in all the countries I visited. Without this logistical support, the book would have been a practical impossibility: thank you, Harry, and thank you, the British Council.

My nephew, Jack Mosse, enlivened my time in Australia, Singapore, Shanghai, Moscow and Copenhagen by accompanying me. Whilst I did not make very good company (nearly always either writing or interviewing), it was a great pleasure to have him along, keeping me out of trouble. Thanks also to his mother Lucy, and my other sisters, Jessica and Mary, for ploughing their way through the early drafts and doing much to make up for the absence of my mother.

At Vermilion, thank you to Amanda Hemmings for commissioning the book, and subsequently to Clare Hulton for making it her own, contributing to the restructuring and providing excellent advice on how to make it work for a general readership. Thanks, too, to the copy-editor, John Woodruff, who has chiselled away at every last detail. As ever, I am indebted to Gillon Aitken for his loyal patience and good advice. Thanks also to Robin Eccles at Macfinders who got my computer set up before I set off and then fielded despairing calls from all over the world with total equanimity.

At a late stage in the proceedings, Avner Offer not only published a book which has greatly influenced the content of this one, but he was kind enough to offer extremely helpful advice on the theories and evidence herein. Thanks also for assistance, encouragement and clarifications from Tim Kasser, on whose work I draw heavily, and to various clarifications and communications with his colleagues, Richard Ryan and Ken Sheldon. For other academic assistance of various kinds, thanks to Howard Meltzer, Lynn Myers, Paul Gilbert, Richard Wilkinson and Kate Pickett.

For reasons of confidentiality, I cannot thank by name any of the 240 people I interviewed in the eight different nations I visited. I am wholly in their debt for giving up their time and offering me the stories of their lives.

Many other people helped me in all sorts of ways, especially the following:

New Zealand – From the British Council, Jodie Molloy went far beyond the call of duty in Auckland. In Dunedin, Roberta Highton provided invaluable assistance. Joe Cavanagh was the engineer who patiently sorted out my IT.

Australia – Thank you to my sister-in-law Emma Garner for looking after us in Sydney and for her interesting insights into the Aussie psyche. At the British Council, particular thanks to Elizabeth Ramsey in Sydney. From the world of publishing, thanks to Debbie McInnes and Andrew Hawkins for their help whilst I was there. For a fascinating insight into the Australian mind and a very pleasant weekend, thanks to my relatives Sam and Mary Jacobs in Adelaide, and to their son Peter for his subsequent practical help. Thanks also for the insights and entertainment provided by Stan and Margaret Gold in Melbourne. Shaun Saunders and Richard Eckersley both considerably advanced my understanding of the academic issues relating to Australia. Thanks also to Jenny Garber.

Singapore – At the British Council, thanks to Martin Hope. Many thanks to Anne and Abbas Nakhoda for their assistance and hospitality. Thanks also to Constance Singham.

Shanghai – At the British Council, thanks to Jim Hollington for looking after me so well and to Christina Chen and Penny Tang there. Thanks to Frances Great for putting me in touch with Adrey Low, to whom further thanks. Above all, thanks to Arthur Jones and his beautiful wife, whose assistance and company made all the difference to my time in Shanghai.

Moscow – I would have got nowhere without the help of many people from the close-knit sorority at the British Council there, including Melissa Cook, Anna Tarasova, Maria Kroupnik and Elena Kharitonova. For accommodation I can recommend The Apartment Service, <www.flatlink.ru>. Most of all, thanks to Polly Boikoi for being such an able and willing fixer and helper.

Copenhagen – Many thanks to Michael Sørensen-Jones and Brid Coneely at the British Council. Particular thanks for their assistance to Vibeka Sperling and Tøger Seidenfaden at the *Politikien* newspaper, and to Igor Malakhov for putting me in touch with them.

New York – I am greatly indebted to Henry and Leslie Astor for accommodating me and my cigarette smoke, and for providing tremendously useful help. Many thanks too, to Hugo Guinness for his extensive help and very enjoyable hospitality; also to Eamon Roche for lending me his flat. It was not only a great pleasure to see a good deal of Andrew Tyndall and Bruno Pajacowski again, but I am tremendously grateful to them and their fellow housemates for providing me with accommodation. Thanks to Lucy Leicester Thackera for her help, and to Chet Cutick.

Britain – Judy Douglas-Boyd went to tremendous lengths to offer me help, and I am only sorry that I was unable to make greater use of it. Thanks also to Simon Skelding for his friendly hospitality and accommodation, and to Sally Markowska.

Finally, I thank the Young Foundation for permission to reproduce passages from Michael Young's book *The Rise of the Meritocracy*.

Index